Family Abuse: Consequences, Theories, and Responses

D1372773

Family Abuse: Consequences, Theories, and Responses

Sylvia I. Mignon

University of Massachusetts, Boston

Calvin J. Larson

University of Massachusetts, Boston

William M. Holmes

University of Massachusetts, Boston

Allyn and Bacon

Boston ■ London ■ Toronto ■ Sydney ■ Tokyo ■ Singapore

Editor-in-Chief, Social Sciences: *Karen Hanson*
Series Editor: *Jennifer Jacobson*
Editorial Assistant: *Tom Jefferies*
Marketing Manager: *Judeth Hall*
Composition and Prepress Buyer: *Linda Cox*
Manufacturing Buyer: *Joanne Sweeney*
Cover Administrator: *Kristina Mose-Libon*
Production Administrator: *Deborah Brown*
Editorial-Production Service: *Susan McNally*
Electronic Composition: *Galley Graphics*

Library of Congress Cataloging-in-Publication Data

Mignon, Sylvia I.
   Family abuse : consequences, theories, and responses / Sylvia I. Mignon, Calvin J.
Larson, William M. Holmes.
     p. cm.
   Includes bibliographical references and index.
   ISBN 0–205–29569–X
     1. Family violence. 2. Family violence—Psychological aspects. 3. Deviant behavior. I.
Larson, Calvin J. II. Holmes, William M. (William Michael), 1946– III. Title.
HV6626.M53 2001
362.82′92–dc21

                                               2001022489

Printed in the United States of America

10 9 8 7 6 5 4 3 2 1   06 05 04 03 02 01

For Mom, Dad, Anna, and Cameron
SIM

For Edith Mary
CJL

For Lenore and Pat
WMH

CONTENTS

PART III

5 Physical Abuse, Sexual Abuse, and Deviancy: Theoretical Interpretations   108

PREFACE

Although behavioral and social scientists have long expressed interest in the behavioral effects of family abuse, the bulk of research on family abuse has been developed during the past three decades. Factors that spurred the effort to document the extent of family abuse include the recognition of child abuse as a significant social problem since the 1960s, the rise in the 1970s of the feminist movement and its concern with abusive male behavior such as wife battering, the prevalence of juvenile crime and violence, and widespread concern with the alleged decline in family values. The evidence indicates that family abuse is an extensive, diverse, and severe social problem with a complex web of correlates.

The effort to identify and understand the causes of family abuse has led to the development of a variety of theoretical explanations. Some theories focus on psychological or sociological explanations, while others emphasize the development of multidisciplinary perspectives. The diversity of theory is due to the wide range of behaviors that encompass family abuse and the complexity of the subject. Generally, the focus of professional attention is on one theory or one type of family abuse, such as wife battering or child abuse. Often, researchers are concerned with the consequences of being abused, which may include mental illness and deviant behavior—even criminal violence.

Works on family abuse tend to have a specific emphasis. For example, the effects of child abuse and neglect can be studied through a lifespan developmental perspective (Sameroff and Emde 1989; Starr and Wolfe 1991). Another major type of work is the anthology. Most anthologies examine a general family abuse topic (family violence, child abuse) by uniting the views and theoretical slants of social science disciplines (Ohlin and Tonry 1989). Some anthologies examine the views of different disciplines, such as social science, medicine, and law (Hetherington 1975; Melton and Barry 1995). Some anthologies are devoted to the reporting of research findings in the general field of family abuse (Hotaling et al. 1988), of research findings in some particular component of the field (Horowitz et al. 1975), or of research findings combined with different theories (Cicchetti and Carlson 1989). Some anthologies are handbooks containing the contributions of those from different disciplines on a broad range of family abuse topics (for example, Van Hasselt et al. 1988). Others include works on different intervention strategies and programs designed to treat specific types of family abuse (Janko 1994).

There is almost no work aimed at synthesizing and constructively assessing current conceptions of the nature and types of family abuse. Also lacking are efforts to synthesize and assess major theoretical interpretations of family abuse and their relation to the range of policies and programs designed to reduce family abuse. An integrated approach to research findings, theory, and programs aimed at confronting the connection between types of family abuse and their diverse deviant consequences is lacking in existing works. Thus, the intent of this book is to fill these voids by integrating existing knowledge and theory concerning the extent, nature, and consequences of family abuse.

Perhaps the most significant distinction between this text and others is that it examines the relationship between family abuse and future behavior—that is, the consequences of family abuse—using an approach that integrates theory, research findings, and programmatic efforts. It is unique in that it places family abuse within a theoretical context covering sociological, psychological, and biological theories; it is analytic and not merely descriptive; and it examines treatment and prevention efforts.

The field will soon have to place research findings within a theoretical context and turn its attention to how research can most appropriately be utilized to solve the problems of family abuse and violent crime. This is especially important as there is widespread public concern over perceived increases in violent crime. At this point, theories of family abuse tend to be heavily weighted toward individualistic psychological explanations; sociological theories are in need of more development. This book offers a synthesis of a large amount of existing data, an analysis of how psychological and sociological theories examine family abuse, and treatment and social policy recommendations relevant to these concerns.

The book has five parts, most of which have several chapters. At the end of each chapter are Study Questions. The Appendix includes information on how to access the *Family Abuse: Consequences, Theories, and Responses* website. The website contains links to general sites on family violence as well as to sites on more specific topics such as sibling abuse, elder abuse, and the relationship between family abuse and mental health problems.

The aim of Part I is to define the problem, that is, to define key concepts such as family abuse; to identify the various types of abuse; and to document generally what is known about the potential negative consequences of experiencing abuse. Included in this part is consideration of the criminal consequences of victimization, especially childhood maltreatment. More specifically, Chapter 1 examines changing concepts of family abuse, available documentation as to its prevalence, and the potential connections to deviant behavior.

Part II is an overall examination of what is known about physical abuse, sexual abuse, and psychological abuse. These chapters focus on the characteristics of the specific type of abuse, the correlates of abuse, and consequences for victims. Chapter 2 addresses the various types of physical abuse. It covers what is known about the relationship of physical abuse to other types of abuse and the potential negative consequences in childhood and adulthood for its victims. Chapter 3 focuses on types of sexual abuse, such as incest, pedophilia, date rape, child care abuse, and sexual abuse by the clergy. It documents both the short- and long-term consequences of sexual abuse, including mental health problems, substance abuse, and deviant behavior. Chapter 4 defines the varieties of behaviors that make up psychological abuse and distinguishes between psychological abuse of the child and of the adult. Because psychological maltreatment is often a part of physical and sexual abuse, this chapter examines the difficulties in differentiating the effects of psychological abuse from the effects of other types of abuse. It also examines the consequences of psychological abuse for its victims.

Part III examines what light is shed on the consequences of family abuse by major sociological, psychological, and biological theories. Chapter 5 examines sociological and psychological theories of physical and sexual abuse, emphasizing theories about the causes of family abuse and theories about the impact of maltreatment on victims. Theories about the causes of physical and sexual abuse are often psychological and/or sociological in nature and include social learning theory, social exchange theory, and feminist theory. Theories about the consequences for victims of maltreatment emphasize psychological explanations for the effects of abuse and include posttraumatic stress disorder, traumagenic dynamics, and developmental theory. Special attention is given to the well-known intergenerational transmission theory of abuse, also known as the cycle of violence. Chapter 6 deals with the contributions of psychological perspectives to understand the behavioral effects of family abuse. It begins with an assessment of Freudian and behavioral views and then examines major contemporary viewpoints such as attribution theory and social learning theory. Chapter 7 reviews and synthesizes the available evidence on the forms of family abuse. This chapter also synthesizes the many theories of family abuse to make clearer the current status of theory and the theoretical work that remains to be done.

Part IV focuses on the victims and perpetrators of family abuse. The intent of this section is to provide a closer examination of the experiences of both victims and perpetrators of abuse. Chapter 8 takes a developmental perspective and examines the consequences of family abuse throughout the lifespan. This chapter focuses on children, adolescents, adults, and the elderly as both victims and perpetrators of family abuse. Chapter 9 examines critical correlates of family abuse. It focuses on the roles of gender, race, and ethnicity as factors in the development of family abuse. This chapter also examines the role of socioeconomic status as a contributing factor to family abuse.

Part V examines special populations and factors that complicate issues of family abuse. It examines what has been done and what is being contemplated concerning the efforts to prevent family abuse and treat those who abuse family members. Chapter 10 reviews special problems such as mental health and substance abuse problems and prostitution, problems often associated with family abuse. The special problems of incarcerated sex offenders and public safety issues are also examined. Chapter 11 examines key subjects such as the ethical, legal, and moral questions involving family intervention to prevent and treat family abuse, efforts to encourage early detection of abuse by school authorities and others, the attempt to deter the problem by enhancing punishment for its perpetration, and the effort to design an effective public policy to help families prevent and eliminate the problem. Chapter 11 includes the evidence concerning federal, state, and local efforts to prevent and treat family abuse.

The concluding chapter, Chapter 12, summarizes the text and what is known about the consequences of family abuse and the effectiveness of policies and programs designed to treat and prevent the problem. It also discusses the likely shape and form of future public policy and programmatic efforts.

Acknowledgments

Several reviewers provided invaluable suggestions: Eleanor D. Miller, University of Wisconsin–Milwaukee; William Farrell, University of Michigan–Flint; Gary D. Hampe, University of Wyoming; Anthony Zumpetta, West Chester University; Kenrick Thompson, Arkansas State University–Mountain Home; and Barbara Manning, formerly of Troy State University of Montgomery.

REFERENCES

Cicchetti, Dante and V. Carlson, eds. 1989. *Child Maltreatment: Theory and Research on the Causes and Consequences of Child Abuse and Neglect.* NY: Cambridge University Press.

Hetherington, E. M., ed. 1975. *Review of Child Development Research.* Chicago, IL: University of Chicago Press.

Horowitz, F., M. Hetherington, S. Scarr-Salapatek, and G. Siegel, eds. 1975. *Review of Child Development Research.* Chicago, IL: Society for Research in Child Development.

Hotaling, Gerard T., David Finkelhor, J. T. Kirkpatrick, and Murray A. Straus, eds. 1988. *Family Abuse and Its Consequences: New Directions in Research.* Newbury Park, CA: Sage.

Janko, S. 1994. *Vulnerable Children, Vulnerable Families: The Social Construction of Child Abuse.* NY: Teachers College, Columbia University.

Melton, G. B. and F. D. Barry, eds. 1995. *Protecting Children from Abuse and Neglect.* NY: Guilford Press.

Ohlin, Lloyd and Michael Tonry, eds. 1989. *Family Violence.* Chicago, IL: The University of Chicago Press.

Sameroff, A. J. and R. N. Emde, eds. 1989. *Relationship Disturbances in Early Childhood: A Developmental Approach.* NY: Basic Books.

Starr, R. H., Jr. and D. A. Wolfe, eds. 1991. *The Effects of Child Abuse and Neglect: Issues and Research.* NY: Guilford Press.

Van Hasselt, V. B., R. L. Morrison, A. S. Bellack, and M. Hersen, eds. 1988. *Handbook of Family Violence.* NY: Plenum Press.

1

The Nature, Types, and Prevalence of Family Abuse

Family abuse is an important and complex phenomenon. Its importance stems from the fact that the family is the primary social institution responsible for nurturing the young and providing intimate social bonding for all its members. Its complexity is due to the different ways family abuse may be expressed and the variety of its perpetrators.

What makes family abuse particularly insidious is that it occurs within a privileged context, one subject to highly restricted public scrutiny. To be sure, it may be subject to intervention by social service agencies and even criminal prosecution, but even in extreme circumstances it is often difficult to gain the cooperation of victims fearful of any number of imagined and real possible repercussions. An adult female victim of family abuse must consider the possibility of provoking even greater abuse on herself and her children if she reports the problem to authorities. Abused children, too, have such fears, for themselves and for their abused mother. Because intervention in family matters is highly restricted, the abuse that occurs within families may be long lasting and have the most serious individual and social consequences, from incapacitating mental problems to violent criminality.

The purpose of this initial chapter is to specify the nature of the problem—to define family abuse, to identify its various forms and types, and to document its prevalence as much as the available evidence allows. Subsequent chapters examine the diverse possible individual and social consequences of family abuse.

At the outset, it is important to acknowledge the influence of historical change, the fact that attitudes and values regarding what constitutes acceptable and unacceptable behavior alter in the course of societal evolution. Therefore, the following discussion is sensitive to the need to put the concept of family abuse in historical perspective. What, then, constitutes family abuse, and how has its meaning changed over time? Of particular concern is how family abuse is measured and whether the available evidence warrants the conclusion that it is a serious social problem.

Family Abuse

Members of a family are obliged to be highly, if not totally responsible for each other. Hardly anything of interest and concern to one member is not also of interest and concern to every other member as well. The closer the family, the greater the involvement of its members in one another's lives. Thus, family relationships may be extremely intense and of crucial importance. As intense relationships involve human emotion, including feelings of high attachment and devotion, they are vulnerable to considerable human good or ill, from loving tenderness to violent abuse. They can be the basis of the highest, most generous altruism or the lowest, most base egoistic exploitation humans are capable of.

What makes family relationships particularly susceptible to behavioral extremes is the unequal distribution of the means to enforce desires, namely, power and authority. Traditionally, males, as husbands and fathers, have been recognized as "heads of household." Wives and children have been regarded as their "property," objects over whom they have been accorded the right to exert an authoritative and controlling influence. Children, of course, have historically been treated as subordinate to the controlling influence of both parents and of a variety of other adults as well. Superordinates are in a position to impose their will on their subordinates, and subordinates are in the vulnerable position of being taken advantage of for both legitimate and illegitimate purposes. In such situations, societal intervention to protect the abused is fraught with difficulties for a number of reasons, not the least of which is the exact dividing line between generally acceptable notions of what constitutes legitimate and illegitimate physical contact between husbands and wives and parents and children.

As a rule, the use of extreme health- and life-threatening means is regarded as the dividing line. It is largely for this reason that behavioral and social scientists are inclined to address the problem of "violence and family abuse" rather than simply "family abuse." And the more extreme sounding *battering* is often used in place of *violence*. Violence and family abuse are also commonly termed d*omestic violence and abuse* and, even more dramatically, *domestic tyranny*. We prefer the term *family abuse* and regard violence as just one of the several possible means of abusing or maltreating a family member. As Frieze and Browne (1987:168) point out, "Violence connotes physical force, whereas abuse can include both nonviolent and violent interactions." Before defining family abuse and identifying its various types, it is useful and important to take brief note of historical interest in family abuse. The problem is neither new nor newly discovered (for an important discussion on this subject, see Pfohl's, "The Discovery of Child Abuse," 1977).

Family Abuse in U.S. History

Societal concern with family abuse has been expressed at various times in the history of the European settlement of North America. The seventeenth-century Puritan founders of the Massachusetts Bay Colony enacted legislation prohibiting both wife and child beating. It appears, however, that no one was ever prosecuted for violating these laws. Another period of concern dates from the mid-1870s to 1890, when societies were founded for the prevention of cruelty to children and women. (Some 300 SPCCs were in existence at the turn of the twentieth century.) The modern era is invariably traced to 1962, the year pediatrician C. Henry Kempe and several colleagues published "The Battered-Child Syndrome" in *JAMA* (*The Journal of the American Medical Association*).

Elizabeth Pleck, the source of this information, claims that public interest in family abuse has occurred "as a response to social and political conditions, or social movements, rather than to worsening conditions in the home" (1987:4–5). The Puritans' interest in domestic violence, she says, stemmed from their fundamental religious principles rather than from any particular knowledge about the extent and severity of the problem. And the rise of SPCCs, she claims, occurred when people feared the spread of crime. According to Pleck (1989:36),

> The New York millionaires who founded the world's first SPCC worried that neglected and abused boys would, as grown men, "swell the ranks of the dangerous classes," endangering "public and private security," and that similarly abused girls would soon become young women lost in "body and soul."

This second era, following the Civil War, differed from the first in that it was evident that violent crime in general and domestic violence in particular were on the rise. Pleck (1989:36) reports that figures from Philadelphia showed that husband–wife murders increased from 1 per million before the Civil War (between 1839 and 1845) to 4.1 per million afterward (between 1874 and 1890). What Pleck finds in common between the Colonial and post–Civil War eras is a heightened public sense of moral decay. Where the Puritans were ever fearful of violations of the Sabbath and other religious principles, the solid citizens of late-nineteenth-century America found their traditional rural and Protestant morality threatened by the rapid growth of cities due to an influx of immigrants from southern and eastern Europe, the growth of industry, and displacement of farmers during Reconstruction. The third and modern era grew out of a period marked by rising concern with minority rights (the Civil Rights movement in the 1950s and the Women's movement in the 1960s most of all) and by criminologists' awareness of a rise in violent crime.

Succinctly put, concern with the problem of family abuse and violence has typically occurred during times of perceived threatening social disorder or as a consequence of reform movements of one kind or another. Whether the current era of concern will follow the past in fading when worries over social order decline remains to be seen. For the present, interest in the subject is intense and, if anything, increasing. It has given rise to concerted efforts not only to document the full extent of family abuse and violence by more accurately defining it and its various forms, but also to change and create new laws, punishments, policies, and programs to treat it. The immediate problem is to define the subject and document its prevalence.

Family Abuse Types and Forms

There are two basic types of family abuse: adult abuse and child abuse. Box 1.1, based on material from an actual case, provides examples of both types and how they may be expressed in a single family. Adult family abuse encompasses the abuse of one married partner by the other, abuse between unmarried partners (either heterosexual or homosexual), and abuse of elderly parents by their children. Child abuse in the family may be perpetrated by parents, stepparents, or other family caretakers as well as by siblings or other relatives. Although not formally a family relationship, abuse between courting or dating couples is invariably included as an example of adult domestic abuse. Whether adult or child family abuse, the basic forms of abuse are physical abuse (ranging from aggressive acts such as pinching and slapping to extremely violent acts such as punching, choking, murder, and attempted murder), sexual abuse (rape, incest), emotional abuse or psychological maltreatment, and abandonment and neglect.

Accordingly, the authors of a recent report for the American Psychological Association (1996:3) say that family violence and abuse means

> the physical, sexual, and emotional maltreatment of one family member by another. The term *family violence* encompasses battering (also called spouse abuse, partner abuse, or domestic violence), marital rape, dating violence (including date rape), child sexual abuse, child physical and emotional maltreatment, and elder abuse.

By *family*, the authors mean not just those bound by blood or legal ties or the traditional nuclear family, but also stepfamilies, unmarried partners, families who live apart or together, families with or without children, people not related by blood or marriage who say they form a family, and gay and lesbian families. The report's authors (1996:5) also say that the following factors differentiate family abuse from other forms of abuse:

1. [it] occurs within ongoing relationships that are expected to be protective, supportive, and nurturing;
2. the victim wants to escape the violence but also longs to belong to a family;
3. affection and attention may coexist with violence and abuse; and
4. ongoing family relationships create opportunities for repeat victimization.

And, as family behavior is essentially a private matter, public intervention in the family's affairs requires clear and legal justification. Physical damage that is apparently the result of one family member's violence against another and brought to the attention of responsible authorities (for example, severe bruising or broken bones in a child who comes to the attention of a school nurse) is often the justification for public intervention. When the number of such instances is demonstrated to have increased or to affect what is considered a significant number of individuals, it becomes a social problem requiring governmental attention. As Elizabeth Pleck (1987:3) explains it, "Family violence violates the conditions

B O X 1.1

The Case of Linda and Gary

Linda, who has been repeatedly battered by her husband, Gary, has a daughter, Beth (age 12), by her first husband, now deceased. Linda and Gary have a son, Carl, age 5; Linda had two other pregnancies that, because of abuse, were terminated by a miscarriage and an abortion. Two years ago, Gary began drinking heavily and also became harsher with Carl, slapping the child for not waiting on his father. Gary's elderly mother moved in with the family a year ago, and, at various times since, he has abused her verbally, appropriated her Social Security checks, and withheld her medications. Ten months ago, Gary bought a gun; two months later, he forced Linda (at gunpoint) to ingest pills and alcohol, after which he called the police and reported her as being drunk, suicidal, and high. She was taken to the emergency room, interviewed, and released with prescriptions for Prozac and Xanax. Linda became increasingly anxious and fearful and, within a few months, tried to commit suicide by overdosing on these drugs.

Most recently, Linda has been uneasy about what she regards as Gary's inappropriate attention to her 12-year-old daughter. In addition, Linda learned that Gary had spent or misappropriated all of the money left to her and Beth after the death of her former husband. Finally, she worked up the courage to confront Gary with her concerns about his interest in Beth; he responded by verbally abusing Linda, raping her, breaking her jaw, and trying to drown her by shoving her head into the toilet. Beth, who was a witness to this violent scene, called the police. On their arrival, one officer seized Gary's gun (which had never been licensed), the other officer phoned for an ambulance, but neither officer arrested Gary (although there was a mandatory arrest policy in the city). Gary followed the ambulance to the hospital; although he wanted to accompany Linda into the room where she would be examined and interviewed by medical staff, he was prohibited from doing so and sent to the waiting room.

The doctor reviewed Linda's medical chart, which documented her previous suicide attempt and record of alcohol and drug usage. He and the nurse recognized that the injuries Linda had sustained were quite probably inflicted deliberately. They questioned Linda directly about a history of physical and psychological abuse, recommended that she speak to a social worker, and assured her that their major concern was to protect her and her children. Gary was told only that Linda needed an X-ray and further tests. Linda left the emergency room, picked up the children (who had been left in her mother's care), and returned home. She spent a sleepless night, thinking about what the doctor had told her. The next morning, she contacted the victim advocate whose card had been given to her at the hospital, and, together, they proceeded to court, where the advocate helped Linda obtain a 14-day court order restraining Gary from contacting her or the children.

Source: Martha B. Witmer and Cheryl A. Crawford. October 1995. "A Coordinated Approach to Reducing Family Violence: Conference Highlights," U.S. Department of Justice. Washington, DC: National Institute of Justice. Pp. 4–5.

necessary for human well-being. The individual has a fundamental right to personal safety, and one of the prime responsibilities of government is to secure that right."

Knowledge of the extent and severity of the abuse that occurs between family members is limited. Family abuse continues to be a private affair. Family members are often highly reluctant to report instances of abuse and violence to authorities for any number of reasons, some imaginary and some real (for example, fear of severe physical retaliation). Nevertheless, what is known is more than sufficient to tell us that family abuse and violence are a serious and widespread problem with far-ranging consequences. Examination of what is reported about the nature and prevalence of the types and forms of family abuse and violence demonstrates this fact.

Adult Abuse and Neglect

Observable behavioral patterns between family partners may antedate their informal or formal union. It is therefore necessary to consider abuse that occurs during the dating and courtship periods. Although knowledge is accumulating about this general subject, little is known concerning the extent to which family abuse is a unique outgrowth of the marriage experience or rather of behavioral inclinations and habits that individuals bring to a relationship. A related subject of concern is the extent to which family abuse is an expression of a "cycle of violence," the degree to which abuse is perpetuated by those who have been victimized previously as children or adults. This topic will be considered when examining the antecedents of abuse in later chapters. For the moment, we will discuss what is known about premarital abuse.

Dating and Courtship Abuse

Dating and courtship abuse may begin with verbal sparring or what the abuser may regard as inoffensive arm twisting, pushing, shoving, and other "love taps." The motivation for such acts may be to coerce a reluctant partner to have sex or to establish who will control the relationship. As can be seen in Box 1.2, sexual and nonsexual violence among dating and courting individuals occurs more often than may be assumed.

The National Center for Injury Prevention and Control (1997:1) defines dating violence

> as the perpetration or threat of an act of violence by at least one member of an unmarried couple on the other member within the context of dating or courtship. This violence encompasses any form of sexual assault, physical violence, and verbal and emotional abuse.

The bulk of what is known about the extent of dating and courtship abuse has been derived from surveys of high school and college students. Studies have found that between a half and two-thirds of respondents indicate having experienced violence in their dating relationships (Gelles & Straus 1988:63). Of special interest is the nature and prevalence of "date rape."

BOX **1.2**

Fact Sheet on Dating Violence

Violent behavior that takes place in a context of dating or courtship is not a rare event. Estimates vary because studies and surveys use different methods and definitions of the problem.

- A review of dating violence research found that prevalence rates of nonsexual, courtship violence range from 9 percent to 65 percent, depending on whether threats and emotional or verbal aggression were included in the definition.
- Data from a study of eighth- and ninth-grade male and female students indicated that 25 percent had been victims of nonsexual dating violence and 8 percent had been victims of sexual dating violence.
- Summarizing many studies, the average prevalence rate for nonsexual dating violence is 22 percent among male and female high school students and 32 percent among college students.
- Females are somewhat more likely than males to report being victims of violence.
- In a national study of college students, 27.5 percent of the women surveyed said that they had suffered rape or attempted rape at least once since age 14. Only 5 percent of those experiences were reported to the police. The term *hidden rape* has emerged because this survey and many other studies found that sexual assaults are seldom reported to the police.
- Over half of a representative sample of more than 1,000 female students at a large urban university had experienced some form of unwanted sex. Twelve percent of these acts were perpetrated by casual dates and 43 percent by steady dating partners.
- Studies of college students and high school students suggest that both males and females inflict and receive dating violence in equal proportion, but the motivation for violence by women is more often for defensive purposes. Other studies have found that women and girls were victims of dating violence twice as often as men and boys and that females suffer significantly more injuries than males.
- A recent National Crime Victimization Survey found that women were 6 times more likely than men to experience violence at the hands of an intimate partner. Intimate partners included current spouses, boyfriends, girlfriends, and dating partners, regardless of whether they are cohabiting or not.
- Nearly half of the 500,000 rapes and sexual assaults reported to the police by women of all ages were committed by friends or acquaintances. From 80 percent to 95 percent of the rapes that occur on college campuses are committed by someone known to the victim.

Source: National Center for Injury Prevention and Control, Division of Violence Prevention. Centers for Disease Control and Prevention. Atlanta, Georgia, November 3, 1997.

The most widely cited study of date rape was performed by Mary Koss and colleagues. A sample of 3,187 female college students (from technical schools, community colleges, and public and private universities) was asked questions such as "Have you had sexual intercourse with a man when you did not want to because he used some degree of force such as twisting your arm or holding you down to make you cooperate?" and "Have you had other sexual acts with a man such as oral or anal intercourse or penetration with objects when you did not want to because he used some degree of force . . . or threatened to harm you to make you cooperate?" (Koss & Harvey 1994:216). These questions parallel those of the Federal Bureau of Investigation's (FBI) Uniform Crime Reports (UCRs) reporting system. As Koss and Harvey (1994:216) state, over "a 12-month period, 76 per 1000 college women experienced one or more attempted or completed rapes defined according to the UCR definition."

The UCRs are compiled annually by the FBI and published by the U.S, Department of Justice. The UCRs contain the number of arrests in a given year and crimes determined by law enforcement agencies to have been committed. To measure the extent of serious crime, the FBI has constructed a "Crime Index." The Crime Index reports the number of known offenses in regard to seven serious crimes: the violent crimes of homicide, robbery, aggravated assault, and forcible rape and the property crimes of larceny-theft, burglary, motor vehicle theft, and arson. In a given year, some 14 million such offenses occur. For its purposes, the FBI defines forcible rape as "the carnal knowledge of a female forcibly and against her will."

Another official source of crime data is the National Crime Victimization Survey (NCVS). It is administered by the U.S. Bureau of the Census and aimed at uncovering the extent of unreported crime. A nationally representative sample of household members is interviewed annually concerning their criminal victimization during the six months preceding their interview. Homicide is obviously excluded from these surveys. Measures of violence include robbery, assaults (both simple and aggravated assault), and forcible rape. The NCVS maintains the same definition of rape as the FBI but includes both heterosexual and homosexual rape. Koss and Harvey (1994:213) find this conception somewhat troublesome for several reasons, including the fact that "men who rape other men are not always homosexual." Nonetheless, because it is based on data supplied by self-identified victims, the NCVS provides the best available information on the victim–offender relationship.

The NCVS identifies victimizations committed by intimates (spouse, ex-spouse, boyfriend, or girlfriend), other relatives (parent, child, sibling, grandparent, in-law, cousin), acquaintances (friend, someone known), and strangers. Table 1.1 identifies total self-reported victimizations in 1992 and 1993 by these categories.

As can be seen, females report a significant amount of violent victimization by intimates. Slightly more than one-fourth (26 percent) indicate being raped or sexually assaulted by an intimate, most commonly a boyfriend or an ex-boyfriend (16 percent). As measured by these data, date rape is a frequent occurrence for females. Comparable figures for male victims are not indicated because of their low number ("ten or fewer sample cases").

Overall, women are much more likely than men to be violently attacked by someone they know than by a stranger. Men, too, show a high rate of violent victimization at the hands of someone known to them, but they are much more likely than women to report victimization by strangers.

TABLE 1.1   Victim–Offender Relationship and Sex of Victim, by Type of Violent Victimization Committed by Lone Offenders, 1992–93

Victim–offender Relationship	Average Annual Percent of Victimizations				
	Total	Rape/ Sexual assault	Robbery	Aggravated assault	Simple assault
Female Victims					
Intimate	29%	26%	28%	28%	29%
Spouse	9	5	6	5	11
Ex-spouse	4	5	5	5	4
Boy/girlfriend (or ex-)	16	16	18	17	15
Other relative	9	3	5	7	11
Acquaintance/friend	40	53	19	36	41
Stranger	23	18	48	30	19
Male Victims					
Intimate	4%	*	3%	5%	3%
Spouse	1	*	*	1	1
Ex-spouse	1	*	*	*	1
Boy/girlfriend (or ex-)	2	*	2	3	1
Other relative	3	*	2	4	3
Acquaintance/friend	44	54	26	40	49
Stranger	49	46	69	51	45

Note: Excludes homicide. Intimate includes spouse or ex-spouse, boyfriend or girlfriend, and ex-boyfriend or ex-girlfriend. Detail may not add to total because of rounding.
*Ten or fewer sample cases.

Source: U.S. Department of Justice. Bureau of Justice Statistics. *Violence against Women: Estimates from the Redesigned Survey,* August 1995), Washington, DC. Table 4, P. 3.

Partner Abuse

Although the percentage of violent victimizations of females by a spouse or an ex-spouse reported in Table 1.1 is not as high as that for boyfriends or ex-boyfriends, it is still large. Based on the trend indicated by NCVS data from 1987 to 1991, the Bureau of Justice Statistics (1994a:2) reports that "on average each year, women experienced over 572,000 violent victimizations committed by an intimate, compared to approximately 49,000 incidents committed against men." Some 1,432 females were killed by an intimate. Box 1.3 shows that female victims come from all racial and ethnic groups and geographical locations. Women of higher socioeconomic standing were less likely to be victimized.

By January 1992, the NCVS was redesigned and a revised questionnaire about sexual violence (constructed to encourage respondents to report more information in greater detail) was administered. Among the major findings from the 1992 survey reported by the Bureau of Justice Statistics (see Bachman & Saltzman 1995:4) was that "Violence at the hands of an intimate involved about 9 in 1,000 women annually. This rate translates into about 1 million women who become the victims of such violence every year."

The latest comparable NCVS data (Bureau of Justice Statistics, May 2000) are for 1998. In 1998, violent intimate partner victimizations totaled 1,033,660. Female victims accounted for 85 percent of the total (or 876,340) and males 15 percent (or 157,330).

BOX 1.3

Social and Economic Characteristics of Women Victimized by Intimates

Race
White and black women had equivalent rates of violence committed by intimates and other relatives (about 5 per 1,000 persons).

Ethnicity
Hispanic and non-Hispanic females had about the same rate of violence attributable to intimates (6 per 1,000 persons).

Age
Women age 20 to 34 had the highest rates of violent victimization attributable to intimates (16 per 1,000 persons) of any age group.

Education
Women who graduated from college had the lowest rates of violence attributable to intimates (3 per 1,000 persons) compared to women with less than a high school education (5 per 1,000 high school graduates), or women with some college (6 per 1,000).

Income
Women with family incomes under $9,999 had the highest rates of violence attributable to an intimate (11 per 1,000 persons) and those with family incomes over $30,000 had the lowest rates (2 per 1,000).

Marital Status
Divorced or separated women had higher rates of violence by intimates (16 per 1,000 persons) than women who never married (7 per 1,000) or married women (1.5 per 1,000).

Location or Residence
Women living in central cities, suburban areas, and rural locations experienced similar rates of violence committed by intimates.

Source: U.S. Department of Justice. Bureau of Justice Statistics. *Selected Findings, Violence Between Intimates,* November 1994. Washington, DC. P. 2.

Trends in intimate partner violence indicate different patterns for female and male victims. Thus, between 1993 and 1998, intimate partner violence against women declined 21 percent (from over a million to less than 900,000). The rate of victimization per 1,000 women declined from 9.8 to 7.7.

The rate of victimization for males was little changed between 1993 and 1998 (from 1.6 per 1,000 males to 1.5). Male victims of intimate violence totaled 163,570 in 1993 and 157,330 in 1998.

Yet to be included in the official data is the extent of violent victimizations among same-sex partners. Thus, other sources must be sought for information about this important topic.

Same-Sex Partner Abuse

The nature and extent of abuse among same-sex partners is of concern for a number of reasons, one of the more important being the need to better understand the degree to which partner abuse is a function of gender as opposed to other elements of the relationship, such as power and control. Because crime is generally disproportionately committed by males, it may be assumed that because batterers among heterosexual partners are disproportionately male something in or about the male gender is the source of the problem. However, if battering is as frequent among same-sex (especially women) as among different-sex partners, then other factors are at play. What light, then, does the available evidence shed on this subject?

After an extensive review of the literature, Renzetti and Miley (1996) conclude that gay and lesbian couples abuse each other to the same degree as heterosexual couples. In a more recent statement, Renzetti (1997) cautions against drawing conclusions from studies of the subject as they are few and suffer from a number of methodological limitations—in particular, the fact that they have been based on self-selected rather than random samples. But as it is, the evidence is that abuse is as extensive among homosexuals as among heterosexuals and at comparable levels regardless of whether the partners are heterosexuals, gays, or lesbians. Furthermore, all three show the same forms of abuse—physical, emotional, and sexual. Same-sex partners, too, have those who batter, psychologically torment, and rape. To Renzetti and Miley, the fact of same-sex domestic violence suggests that power rather than gender is the issue. As they see it,

> A certain number of people, given the opportunity to get away with abusing their partners, will do so because they hunger for control over some part of their lives, lives over which they feel they have no control. . . . Some heterosexual men abuse their partners because they can get away with it in our sexist society, and some lesbians and gay men abuse their partners because they can get away with it in our homophobic society. (1996:3–4)

Power and control are evident in stalking, a problem involving adult domestic abuse that to date has primarily been known to plague the heterosexual community.

Stalking

As a form of domestic abuse, stalking is something that typically occurs after a female has left her partner. Some males, unwilling to accept the loss, respond by tracking and in other ways harassing, sometimes to the point of violence and murder, the departed partner. Stalking is sometimes referred to as "separation assault." Box 1.4 discusses a case of aggravated stalking.

Stalking first attracted national attention in 1989. Rebecca Shaeffer, a young actress, was murdered by a fan who stalked her for two years. Extensive media attention dramatized the need for protecting victims virtually helpless to defend themselves against an obsessive and life-threatening abuse. Stalking victims are women across the socioeconomic spectrum who share the problem of attempting to sever a relationship with a man, frequently because of his abusive ways, who refuses to accept their decision. Although a stalker may be known or unknown to the victim, someone with whom she may have had either informal (a former acquaintance or boyfriend) or formal (a husband) relations, it is estimated that as many as 80 percent of stalking cases stem from a domestic relationship. The U.S.

BOX 1.4

Aggravated Stalking

John and Edie Pallas's marriage was characterized by violence; in one episode, John beat Edie so severely he broke her jaw. When they decided to divorce, Edie moved in with her parents, but John, angered by Edie's decision to leave, began telephoning her at her parents' home and delivering threatening messages. On one Sunday in January 1993, he began calling at 7 A.M. and continued calling throughout the day, forcing Edie's parents to take the phone off the hook several times. When he did get through, he cursed and threatened Edie's parents.

Under Florida's antistalking law, John Pallas was arrested, charged with aggravated stalking, and convicted.

Florida's law states in part that "any person who willfully, maliciously, and repeatedly follows or harasses another person, and makes a credible threat with the intent to place that person in reasonable fear of death or bodily injury, commits the offense of aggravated stalking." The law further states that a person engages in harassment by "engaging in conduct directed at a specific person that causes substantial emotional distress. . . ."

On appeal, John Pallas claimed that Florida's antistalking law was vague and overly broad. However, the appellate court upheld the Florida statute and found that he had indeed unlawfully harassed and threatened his estranged wife.

Source: U.S. Department of Justice. National Institute of Justice. "Domestic Violence, Stalking, and Antistalking," April 1996. Washington, DC.

Department of Justice (1996) reports that estimates based on limited reliable sources of the number of stalkers across the nation range from 20,000 to 200,000.

Stalking was formally acknowledged as a crime by Congress when it enacted the Violence Against Women Act (VAWA), Title IV of the Violent Crime Control and Law Enforcement Act of 1994. To date, forty-nine states and the District of Columbia have enacted legislation to address the problem.

Elder Abuse

As Sandra Baron and Adele Welty (1996:33) point out, although there is no generally agreed-upon legal definition of elder abuse, "most experts would agree that elder abuse consists of harm or pain that is inflicted on persons 60 years of age or older who are unable to protect themselves." General definitions include reference to elements common to adult and child abuse, with some important variations. Like other adults and children, elders may be abused physically, sexually, emotionally, and negligently. Hence, to the American Psychological Association (1996:42) Presidential Task Force on Violence and the Family:

> Elder abuse within the family refers to physical, sexual, or emotional maltreatment. It includes psychological abuse, neglect, or financial and material exploitation of an older person by someone who has a special relationship with the elder. The abuser may be a spouse, sibling, child, grandchild, friend, or caregiver, and the violence occurs in the older person's own home or in the home of a caregiver.

Physical abuse of elders involves inflicting pain and suffering by hitting, slapping, restraining mobility, and sexual exploitation. Psychological abuse covers a range of possibilities, from subtle expressions conveying contempt and rejection to outright acts intended to humiliate and in other ways cause mental anguish (Wolf 1996:5).

Neglect of the elderly is often dichotomized as either active or passive. To Wolf and Pillemer (1989:18), for example, active neglect involves the deliberate and conscious refusal or failure of a caretaker to provide something obligated (for example, "deliberate abandonment or deliberate denial of food or health-related services"); passive neglect involves the refusal or failure of a caretaker to provide a needed function for unconscious reasons (for example, "abandonment, non-provision of food, or health-related services because of inadequate knowledge, laziness, infirmity, or disputing the value of prescribed services").

However, unlike children and other adults, elders are particularly vulnerable to financial abuse and self-neglect. Financial abuse entails the illegal exploitation or improper management and use of the funds of an elderly person by a responsible party (adult child or other relative, attorney, financial advisor, or agency).

Self-neglect among the elderly is quite pervasive. It entails refusing to eat, maintain proper hygiene, and/or seek obviously needed medical care, housing, or activities and services needed to maintain life. Mental confusion and feelings of rejection and worthlessness are often behind the situation. As Wendy Lustbader

(1996:51) describes it, "in some cases, self-neglect is best understood as disaffection from life, as loss of the will to live."

The best information available indicates that neglect is the most common form of elder abuse in domestic settings. In 1994, substantiated reports of elder abuse found 58.5 percent of the cases to be neglect, 15.7 percent physical abuse, and 12.3 percent financial abuse (American Psychological Association 1996:42). White victims accounted for 65.4 percent of the total, African Americans 21.4 percent, and Hispanics 9.6 percent, and fewer than 1 percent were Native Americans, Asians, or Pacific Islanders. Adult children of the victims were found to be the most frequent abusers. Women dominated narrowly the ranks of the abusers (52.4 percent) and clearly those of the abused (62.1 percent). The average age (median) of elder self-abusers was 76.9 years.

Elder abuse began to be recognized as a national social problem in the 1970s and attracted widespread attention in the 1980s. In 1981, the U.S.House of Representatives Select Committee on Aging released the first of its reports detailing the seriousness of the problem. Today, the federal government and all states have enacted legislation requiring reporting of instances of elder abuse and the provision of services to victims.

In 1986, all agencies combined reported 117,000 cases of elder abuse. By 1996, the number had reached 293,000—a 150 percent increase (O'Hanlon 1997). As it is generally acknowledged that elder abuse is greatly underreported, estimates of its annual frequency, depending on the methodology used, range from 700,000 to 2 million (Skabronski 1996:629).

Parental Abuse

When older nondependent children abuse elderly parents, it is called elder abuse. The abuse of nondependent parents by children is regarded as parental abuse, an important type of family abuse about which little is known. Recent awareness of the problem has been heightened by some well-publicized parricides, in particular the 1989 case of the Menendez brothers shooting their parents. The reason given by the brothers, years of abuse by their parents, is common in such cases. Sons rather than daughters have generally been the killers. As Gerald Lubenow observes,

> Almost all murders of parents are committed by sons, and in the rare cases that involve daughters, they often recruit a male agent. Usually parent killing involves a drunken, physically abusive father killed by a son who sees himself as the protector of not only himself but also of his mother and siblings. (1983:35)

Ewing (1990) details a number of such cases. He reports that in the rare instances when daughters are the instigators of a patricide, it is frequently a response to an extended pattern of sexual abuse. Often, the daughter recruits a male accomplice to assist in or perform the murder.

Although not nearly as frequently, mothers, too, are murdered by their children. According to Ewing,

> Like patricides, matricides generally appear to involve killings of abusive parents. But in cases of matricide, in contrast to patricide, the more severe abuse inflicted by the parent-victim upon the juvenile-perpetrator is frequently psychological or sexual rather than physical. (1990:38)

In a common case, a mother will persistently, thoroughly, and aggressively criticize a child's weaknesses—for example, belittling school achievement—and in other ways destroy his or her self-esteem. Often, such cases involve a combination of psychological, physical (such as slapping and beating with sticks, belts, or extension cords), and sexual abuse.

Lacking systematic and nationwide incident studies of parental abuse, one must rely on partial evidence. Ewing's analysis of UCR arrest data indicates, for example, that about 2 percent of U.S. homicides are parricides. In contrast, more than 25 percent of homicides are domestic cases involving adults. A 1994 report by the Bureau of Justice Statistics involving a survey of family murder cases in the nation's seventy-five largest counties in 1988 found that 1.9 percent (154) of the 8,063 homicide victims were murdered by their offspring. Defendants in such cases were disproportionately sons (82 percent) rather than daughters (18 percent).

Far less dramatic than parental murder, yet far more common, is the physical abuse of a parent by a child, typically an adolescent. Parental abuse is another area where there are no current estimates as to how much exists. The most common pattern is older sons hitting and abusing their mothers. Gelles and Cornell (1982) found that mothers were more likely to be hit than fathers (11 percent versus 7 percent) and were more likely than fathers to be victims of severe violence (5 percent versus 1 percent). Sons were slightly more likely to be violent and to use severe violence than daughters. The rate of severe violence by sons increased between the ages of 10 and 17, while the rate of violence by daughters fell after the age of 13. Gelles and Cornell note that sons appear to take advantage of their increased size and become more likely to engage in parental abuse.

Generally, children who murder a parent or parents have no prior criminal record of any kind. The act is heavily an internal family affair, the consequence of a lengthy pattern of abuse.

Child Abuse and Neglect

Adult family members who abuse each other also tend to abuse their children. Only in recent decades has either spousal abuse or child abuse come to be regarded as a social problem worthy of legal prohibition. As noted earlier, in the not-so-distant past wives were regarded as the property of husbands and children the property of parents. Hence, it was simply taken for granted that husbands had a right to use whatever means necessary to control their wives and parents their children. What now may be regarded as abusive and violent and legally reprehensible was viewed as acceptable disciplinary measures of no one's concern but those involved. What occurred among family members was a private affair.

In many respects, children continue to be regarded as primarily the property of their parents until they reach adulthood. As parents necessarily have considerable control over their children, they have the capacity to abuse them or not. What differentiates acceptable discipline from child abuse varies not only from society to society but also in the same society with the evolution of its child-rearing practices.

Child Abuse in Historical Perspective

What contemporary Americans regard as child battering, the early European settlers of the continent regarded as normal and expected child-rearing practice. Whipping, even to the point of what today would constitute the crime of assault and battery, was generally pervasive. It was performed by all social classes and a variety of adults. Employers, parents, preachers, relatives, and teachers could legitimately whip a child. Biblical scripture was acknowledged to justify the practice. The Old Testament contains a number of statements sanctioning the corporal punishment of children. In Proverbs, for example, one finds the following:

> The man who fails to use the stick hates his son;
> The man who is free with his correction loves him. (13:24)
> Innate in the heart of a child is folly, judicious beating will rid him of it. (12:15)

Derived from such statements is an adage that continues to be honored by segments of the population: "Spare the rod and spoil the child."

It was not until the nineteenth century, in the wake of massive industrialization and urbanization, that Western societies began to seriously question the validity of child whipping and corporal punishment generally. According to historian Lloyd de Mause (1988:42), "It was not until the nineteenth century that the old-fashioned whipping began to go out of style in most of Europe and America, continuing longest in Germany, where 80 percent of German parents still admit to beating their children, a full 35 percent with canes." The growth of industries and cities led to a gap between the rich and the poor; and the emergence of slums and tenements spurred a variety of reform activity, including the child reform movement.

Through the effort of private individuals, and modeled after earlier examples in England, the Society for the Prevention of Cruelty to Children was created in New York City in 1874. In 1912, the federal government established the Children's Bureau. It was the product of a congressional act designed to encourage research on and the distribution of accurate information about childhood development. Neither of these two precedents sparked widespread interest among the public generally or the scholarly community in particular. As previously noted, the turning point was the publication in 1962 of "The Battered-Child Syndrome" by pediatrician C. Henry Kempe and colleagues.

Kempe deliberately chose a dramatic title for his paper to call attention to the seriousness of the problem of child physical abuse, a subject he knew his pediatric colleagues had long resisted publicly acknowledging or addressing. Kempe and his colleagues (1962:105) defined *battered child syndrome* as "a term used by us to characterize a clinical condition in young children who have received serious physical abuse, generally from a parent or a foster parent." Not without a hint of criticism, they said the condition had also been referred to by radiologists, orthopedists, pediatricians, and social service workers as "unrecognized trauma." Kempe and his colleagues had to confront a number of obstacles as they tried to convince the medical community that child abuse was both sufficiently prevalent and severe enough to be regarded as worthy of greater attention (for an important account of the "discovery of child abuse," see Pfohl 1977).

Although Kempe and his colleagues said the syndrome was not age specific, they found it most discernible in children under three years of age. Physical indicators included severe bruising, broken bones, and brain damage. They admitted, however, that few hard data were available to substantiate their opinion, largely because pediatricians and others were loathe to investigate and determine the source of the problem and confront those responsible.

Today, the data indicate that physically abused children are generally under five years of age, but not infrequently much older. And even though the term *battered child syndrome* has been replaced by more general terms such as *child abuse* or *child maltreatment,* Kempe and his colleagues are credited with initiating the extensive interest and concern with child abuse that characterizes contemporary America and led to the enactment of laws requiring professionals who work with children to report instances of abuse.

Despite reporting laws across the nation, there is no exact tabulation of the extent of child abuse. Among the several reasons for this fact is the absence of consensus on exactly what constitutes child abuse. Consequently, reported instances must be verified by generally recognized overt criteria such as physical evidence rather than by precise criteria that would enable identification of the full range of types of abuse, including subtle forms of emotional and psychological abuse. The best available national data are supplied by the National Child Abuse and Neglect Data System (NCANDS). The NCANDS is a product of the National Center on Child Abuse and Neglect (NCCAN) and was created in 1974 when the U.S. Congress passed the Federal Child Abuse Prevention and Treatment Act (Public Law 93-247). The act established the National Clearinghouse on Child Abuse and Neglect and provided funds to states willing to require the reporting of instances of child abuse, research on the subject, and the development of programs to treat the problem. All states now have mandatory reporting laws, and as Sagatun and Edwards state, "Over half of the state laws provide for criminal sanctions ranging from fines to imprisonment for the failure of specified professionals to report" (1995:37). Professionals typically required to report include teachers, child care personnel, foster parents, social workers, physicians, dentists, nurses, psychologists, law enforcement, and marriage and family counselors. Depending on the state, others who may be required to report are pharmacists, clergy, attorneys, child care licensing inspectors, film or photo processors, substance abuse counselors, staff volunteers in child abuse information and referral programs, and religious healers.

The NCANDS data are based on periodic National Incidence Studies (the latest of which is NIS-3) and annual state reports. To be included, state reports must conform to the requirements of the Child Abuse Prevention and Treatment Act as frequently amended since 1974. For a number of reasons, including the fact that data-reporting requirements are subject to frequent change, not all states are represented in NCANDS tabulations.

National Incidence Studies

Periodically, the NCCAN sponsors a National Incidence Study of child abuse and neglect. Three such studies have been conducted, the first (NIS-1) was conducted in 1979 and 1980, the second (NIS-2) was conducted in 1986 and 1987, and the latest (NIS-3) was conducted in 1993 and 1994.

The NIS-3 data were supplied by a nationally representative sample of over 5,600 professionals. Two standards were used to determine child abuse—the Harm Standard and the Endangerment Standard. To be included in tabulations, reported incidents of child abuse and neglect are required to be based on evidence of demonstrable harm and substantiated evidence that a child is in danger of being abused or neglected. Thus, under the Harm Standard, some 1,533,800 children were abused or neglected in 1993. This figure represents a 67 percent increase over the NIS-2 number reported in 1986 and a 149 percent increase over the NIS-1 number reported in 1980.

Under the Endangerment Standard, 2.815 million children were either abused or neglected in 1993. The figure represents a 98 percent increase over the NIS-2 figure of 1.424 million reported in 1986. Both the number of abused children and the number of neglected children more than doubled since NIS-2. The estimated number of abused children increased from 590,800 to 1,221,800 (a 107 percent increase) and the number of neglected children from 917,200 to 1,961,300 (a 114 percent increase).

Generally acknowledged types of child abuse are specified in Box 1.5. According to the NIS-2 and NIS-3 data, based on the Harm Standard, the following increases occurred:

- The estimated number of sexually abused children rose from 119,200 in 1986 to 217,700 in 1993 (+83 percent).
- The estimated number of physically neglected children increased from 167,800 to 338,900 (+102 percent).
- The estimated number of emotionally neglected children increased from 49,200 to 212,800 (+333 percent).
- The estimated number of physically abused children increased from 269,700 to 381,700 (+42 percent).

BOX **1.5**

How Do We Define Child Abuse and Neglect?

The Child Abuse Prevention and Treatment Act (CAPTA), as amended and reauthorized in October 1996 (Public Law 104-235, Section III; 42 U.S.C. 51106g), defines child abuse and neglect as, at a minimum, any recent act or failure to act:

- Resulting in imminent risk of serious harm, death, serious physical or emotional harm, sexual abuse, or exploitation
- Of a child (a person under the age of 18, unless the child protection law of the state in which the child resides specifies a younger age for cases not involving sexual abuse)
- By a parent or caretaker (including any employee of a residential facility or any staff person providing out-of-home care) who is responsible for the child's welfare.

CAPTA defines sexual abuse as:

- Employment, use, persuasion, inducement, enticement, or coercion of any child to engage in, or assist any other person to engage in, any sexually explicit conduct or any simulation of such conduct for the purpose of producing any visual depiction of such conduct; or
- rape, and in cases of caretaker or interfamilial relationships, statutory rape, molestation, prostitution, or other form of sexual exploitation of children, or incest with children. . . .

What Are the Main Types of Maltreatment?

There are four major types of child maltreatment: physical abuse, child neglect, sexual abuse, and emotional abuse.

Physical Abuse. Physical abuse is the infliction of physical injury as a result of punching, beating, kicking, biting, burning, shaking, or otherwise harming a child. The parent or caretaker may not have intended to hurt the child, rather the injury may have resulted from overdiscipline or physical punishment.

Child Neglect. Child neglect is characterized by failure to provide for the child's basic needs. Neglect can be physical, educational, or emotional. Physical neglect includes refusal of or delay in seeking health care, abandonment, expulsion from the home or refusal to allow a runaway to return home, and inadequate supervision. Educational neglect includes the allowance of chronic truancy, failure to enroll a child of mandatory school age in school, and failure to attend to a special educational need. Emotional neglect includes such actions as marked inattention to the child's needs for affection, refusal of or failure to provide needed psychological care, spouse abuse in the child's presence, and permission of drug or alcohol use by the child. The assessment of child neglect requires consideration of cultural values and standards of care as well as recognition that the failure to provide the necessities of life may be related to poverty.

Sexual Abuse. Sexual abuse includes fondling a child's genitals, intercourse, incest, rape, sodomy, exhibitionism, and commercial exploitation through prostitution or the produc-

(continued)

BOX **1.5**   Continued

tion of pornographic materials. Many experts believe that sexual abuse is the most underreported form of child maltreatment because of the secrecy or "conspiracy of silence" that so often characterizes these cases.

Emotional Abuse (Psychological/Verbal Abuse/Mental Injury).   Emotional abuse includes acts or omissions by the parents or other caregivers that have causes, or could cause, serious behavioral, cognitive, emotional, or mental disorders. In some cases of emotional abuse, the acts of parents or other caregivers alone, without any harm evident in the child's behavior or condition, are sufficient to warrant child protective services (CPS) intervention. For example, the parents/caregivers may use extreme or bizarre forms of punishment, such as confinement of a child in a dark closet. Less severe acts, such as habitual scapegoating, belittling, or rejecting treatment, are often difficult to prove and, therefore, CPS may not be able to intervene without evidence of harm to the child.

Although any of the forms of child maltreatment may be found separately, they often occur in combination. Emotional abuse is almost always present when other forms are identified.

Source: "What Is Child Maltreatment?" Washington, DC: *National Clearinghouse on Child Abuse and Neglect Information.* March 13, 1998.

Based on the Endangerment Standard, the increases were as follows:

- The estimated number of physically abused children increased from 311,500 to 614,100 (+97 percent).
- The estimated number of sexually abused children increased from 133,600 to 300,200 (+125 percent).
- The estimated number of emotionally abused children increased from 188,100 to 532,200 (+183 percent).
- The estimated number of physically neglected children increased from 507,700 to 1,335,100 (+163 percent).
- The estimated number of emotionally neglected children increased from 203,000 to 585,100 (+188 percent).

Overall, then, the recent pattern has been that in any given year nearly 3 million instances of the major types of child abuse identified in Box 1.5 are reported nationally. Over the 1986–1995 decade, reports increased 49 percent. Notwithstanding this fact, the number of instances verified generally amounts to about 1 million annually. Verification is complicated by factors such as state differences in definitions of child abuse, the fact that child abuse reports emanate from both professional and nonprofessional sources, and verification procedures that vary from jurisdiction to jurisdiction (see Box 1.6).

BOX **1.6**

States Vary in the Standards of Proof Required to Substantiate Allegations of Child Abuse and Neglect

Level of evidence required to substantiate a report

Case worker's judgment	Some credible evidence	Credible evidence	Preponderance of evidence
Hawaii	Alaska	Alabama	District of Columbia
Mississippi	Arizona	Colorado	Georgia
Ohio	Arkansas	Connecticut	Iowa
Tennessee	California	Florida	Kansas
West Virginia	Idaho	Illinois	New Jersey
Wyoming	Kentucky	Maryland	Oklahoma
	Louisiana	Michigan	Pennsylvania
	Maine	Nebraska	Texas
	Massachusetts	Nevada	Vermont
	Missouri	Rhode Island	Virginia
	Montana	Utah	Washington
	New Hampshire		Wisconsin
	New York		
	North Carolina		
	North Dakota		
	Oregon		
	South Carolina		
	South Dakota		

Higher standards of proof result in slightly lower substantiation rates

- Where the standard of evidence is the "case worker's judgment," the substantiation rate is 49 percent.
- Where the standard of evidence is "some credible evidence," the substantiation rate is 46 percent.
- Where the standard of evidence is "credible evidence," the substantiation rate is 44 percent.
- Where the standard of evidence is "a preponderance of evidence," the substantiation rate is 43 percent.

Note: Levels of evidence required to substantiate a report of child maltreatment are established by law, regulation, policy, or custom and usage. Delaware uses "level of risk."

Source: Howard N. Snyder and Melissa Sickmund. 1995. *Juvenile Offenders and Victims: A National Report.* Washington, DC: Office of Juvenile Justice and Delinquency Prevention.

In 1995, of the approximately 1 million substantiated instances of child abuse, 54 percent were of neglect, 25 percent physical abuse, 11 percent sexual abuse, 3 percent psychological abuse, and the remaining 7 percent a mixed category of types and combinations (Office of Juvenile Justice and Delinquency Prevention, August 1997). Fifty-two percent of the victims were female and 47 percent male. Fifty-three percent were 7 years old or younger, 26 percent were aged from 8 to 12, and 21 percent were aged from 13 to 18. There were no significant differences in incidence by race or ethnicity. This is somewhat surprising in that previous evidence (for example, U.S. Department of Health & Human Services, 1996b) indicates that child abuse is higher in low- than in higher-income families and that children of single parents are much more likely than those from two-parent families to be neglected and physically abused. Lastly, in 1995, confirmed child abuse and neglect fatalities totaled 1,215.

Until NIS-2, the weakness and limitations of the NISs sponsored by NCCAN were analogous to those of the Uniform Crime Reports. Both relied on reports made to official agencies. To obtain a sense of the "dark side" of the crime problem, the National Crime Victimization Survey (NCVS) was created and NISs were expanded to include the Endangerment Standard of child abuse, data on which are obtained from nonofficial child protective service agencies such as police courts and schools. And just as the NCVS data indicate that approximately three times as much crime occurs as is reported, so too a U.S. Department of Health and Human Services press release (April 1, 1996a) stated that "results from the Third National Incidence Study of Child Abuse and Neglect (NIS-3) [indicate] that almost three times the state-reported number of children are maltreated." Nonetheless, because the NIS-3 study relies on a restricted typology and reported rather than independently empirically verified data, it, too, is regarded as most likely providing an underestimate of the actual incidence of child abuse and neglect.

State Data

Annually reported state-supplied National Child Abuse and Neglect Data System (NCANDS) data have two parts: The Summary Data Component (SDC) and the Detailed Case Data Component (DCDC). The SDC is based on the statewide reports of those individuals regarded as part of the child protective services (CPS) system. Such individuals include physicians, nurses, dentists, emergency room personnel, coroners, mental health professionals, social workers, teachers, child care providers, and law enforcement personnel.

Considering SDC data for 1998, the latest year for NCANDS-reported data, all the states plus the District of Columbia investigated the validity of some 2,806,000 total reports of alleged child abuse and neglect and substantiated the validity of some 903,000 (or about 32 percent). The rate of child maltreatment per 1,000 children in the population was 12.9, a 1 percent decline from the 1997 rate of 13.9. Figure 1.1 shows victimization rate trends from 1990 to 1998.

Fifty-three and one-half percent of the children represented by the data were victims of neglect (an additional 2.4 percent were victims of medical neglect), 22.7 percent victims of physical abuse, 11.5 percent victims of sexual abuse, and 6.0 percent victims of emotional abuse. The 1990 and 1998 rates per 1,000 children

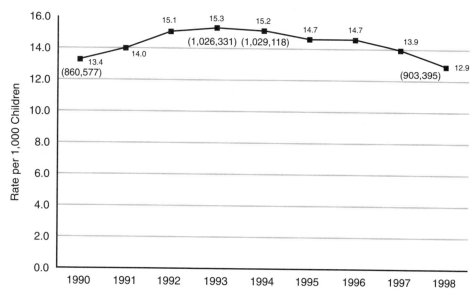

FIGURE 1.1   National Victimization Rates, 1990–1998 (SDC)

Source: U.S. Department of Health and Human Services. Administration on Children, Youth and Families. *Child Maltreatment 1998: Reports from the States to the National Child Abuse and Neglect Data System* (Washington, DC: U.S. Government Printing Office, 2000). Figure 4.1, P. 4.

of maltreatment by type are contained in Figure 1.2. As can be seen, while the rate for neglect has increased, those for physical abuse, sexual abuse, and psychological abuse have decreased. The next NIS will undoubtedly shed greater light on these data.

Organized Sadistic Abuse

A seldom-discussed type of child abuse is what the American Psychological Association's Presidential Task Force on family violence refers to as organized sadistic abuse. This is the occasionally reported instance of extreme physical abuse that are group planned, staged, or repetitive. Examples include cult-related rituals in which children may be forced to inflict violence on others and child pornography and child prostitution rings. Documentation of the extent of this type of child abuse is unavailable.

Sibling Abuse

Another type of child abuse is sibling abuse. Children may be victimized by parents and brothers and sisters. Unfortunately, little research has been conducted on this type of abuse (see Goodwin and Roscoe 1990). What work has been done suggests

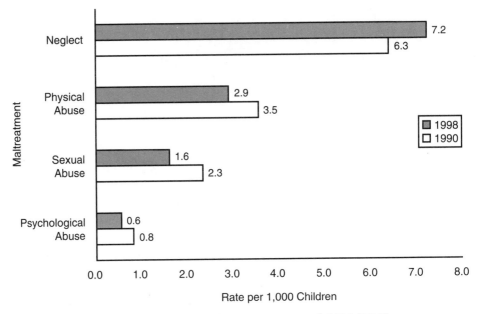

FIGURE 1.2 Rates of Maltreatment by Type, 1990 and 1998 (SDC)

Source: U.S. Department of Health and Human Services. Administration on Children, Youth and Families, *Child Maltreatment 1998: Reports from the States to the National Child Abuse and Neglect Data System* (Washington, DC: U.S. Government Printing Office, 2000), Table 4.3, Pp. 4–3.

that it is both widespread and serious. In their national violence survey, Straus and colleagues (1980) found sibling violence to be the most frequent type of family violence. Four out of five of the children surveyed admitted to performing at least one act of violence against a sibling in a given year. Extrapolated to the entire child population, this was tantamount to "over 29 million American children [engaging] in one or more acts of physical violence toward a sibling in a single year" (Straus et al. 1980:89). In a paper based on the same data, Straus (1981) reports evidence that indicates higher rates of sibling abuse in families with higher rates of child physical abuse by parents. "In general," says Straus, "the more violence experienced by the child, the higher the rate at which such children are violent towards a sibling" (1981:5). Other factors known to be associated with sibling abuse include inadequate supervision, marital problems, financial problems, parental mental disorder or substance abuse, and a negative self-image on the part of the perpetrator (Crane 1997).

Sibling abuse is often overlooked because hitting is so common that parents and others regard it as a normal part of growing up and do not actively discourage it. Because society's norms seem to encourage aggressive behavior between siblings, the subject of sibling abuse has not been considered a topic deserving of serious examination (Gelles and Cornell 1985). The question becomes how to distinguish normal sibling conflict or rivalry from sibling abuse. Wiehe (1997) describes several of the important characteristics of sibling abuse: (1) a pattern of repeatedly hurtful behavior; (2) the roles of perpetrator and victim are carried on over time; (3) the behavior of the perpetrator reflects a negative general attitude toward the sibling; (4) the intent is to harm the victim; and (5) the behavior is inappropriate for the developmental level of the perpetrator.

Sibling abuse can be any combination of physical, emotional, or sexual abuse, although emotional abuse is always a part of the other types of abuse. Physical abuse frequently consists of hitting, slapping, biting, choking, pushing, or excessive tickling. Emotional abuse includes teasing, name-calling, belittling, ridiculing, intimidating, and destruction of property.

Even less well documented than sibling physical abuse, sexual abuse among siblings may be quite common. Studies of incest, for example, have found incest among siblings to be the most frequent type of family incest. Finkelhor (1979:89–91) says, for example, that the highest reported rates of incest are those involving siblings (39 percent reported by girls and 21 percent by boys). And although slightly fewer than a third of the girls say that force or the threat of force was involved, it remains to be determined how much sibling incest is involuntary or the product of physical abuse. Incest among siblings will be discussed in more detail in Chapter 3.

Summary

This chapter illustrates the variety and extent of the problem of family abuse. Despite the fact that family affairs remain essentially private and that family abuse has been systematically studied only since the 1970s, an impressive amount of evidence on the incidence of family abuse has been amassed.

Documentation of family abuse is hindered both methodologically and conceptually. Methodologically, it is difficult to design studies to tap the depth of the problem for a number of reasons: people's reluctance to reveal personal family experiences, laws preventing and protecting individuals from unrequested intrusion, and so on. Conceptually, the problem is the lack of national consensus on the nature and types of family abuse. Different jurisdictions reserve the right to define the problem as they see fit. The federal government, through the creation of the National Center on Child Abuse and Neglect (NCCAN) by passage of the Child Abuse Prevention and Treatment Act in 1974 and its subsequent modification in 1992, has spurred the attempt at least to document and treat child abuse nationally. The act requires reports of child abuse by those professionals officially exposed to its occurrence. Data collected by these means have been used to justify enactment of legislation to facilitate local initiatives to treat the problem.

A similar effort in regard to adult family abuse is yet to be initiated. What has come to light in regard to adult abuse is the result of only piecemeal scholarly and governmental research. Notwithstanding the conceptual and methodological limitations of the evidence, it is generally agreed that family abuse is a serious and widespread social problem.

The next few chapters more thoroughly examine major types of family abuse and what is known about their causal antecedents. Succeeding chapters deal with the deviant behavioral consequences of family abuse and what has and is being done about them in terms of policy formation and programmatic treatment.

Study Questions

1. Why is it difficult to collect accurate information on the extent of family abuse in the United States?

2. When and why did family abuse emerge as a subject of serious social concern in the United States?

3. What are the basic types and forms of family abuse?

4. In what ways are adult abuse and child abuse similar and different?

5. Why is it important to study the extent of abuse among same-sex partners?

6. What is the evidence concerning the extent of family abuse in the United States?

7. Is the rate of child maltreatment increasing or decreasing? What is the evidence?

REFERENCES

American Psychological Association. 1996. *Violence and The Family: Report of The American Psychological Association Presidential Task Force on Violence and The Family.* Washington, DC.

Bachman, Ronet and Linda E. Saltzman. 1995. "Violence Against Women: Estimates from the Redesigned Survey, August, 1995." Washington, DC: U.S. Department of Justice, Bureau of Justice Statistics.

Baron, Sandra and Adele Welty. 1996. "Elder Abuse." *Journal of Gerontological Social Work,* 25:33–37.

Bureau of Justice Statistics. 1996. "Domestic Violence, Stalking, and Antistalking Legislation," April 1996. Washington, DC: U.S. Government Printing Office.

Bureau of Justice Statistics. 2000. "Intimate Partner Violence," May 2000. Washington, DC: U.S. Government Printing Office.

Crane, Mary Lou. 1997. "Childhood Sibling Abuse: A Neglected Form of Maltreatment." *Progress: Family Systems Research, and Therapy,* 6:27–41.

DeMause, Lloyd. 1988. "History of Child Abuse." *Journal of Psychohistory,* 25:41–45.

Ewing, Charles Patrick. 1990. *When Children Kill: The Dynamics of Juvenile Homicide.* Lexington, MA: Lexington Books.

Finkelhor, David. 1979. *Sexually Victimized Children.* NY: Free Press.

Frieze, Irene Hanson and Angela Browne. 1989. "Violence in Marriage." Pp. 163–218 in *Family Violence,* Volume 11 of *Crime and Justice: An Annual Review of Research,* edited by Lloyd Ohlin and Michael Tonry. Chicago, IL: University of Chicago Press.

Gelles, Richard J. and Claire Pedrick Cornell. 1982. "Adolescent-to-Parent Violence." *The Urban Social Change Review,* 15:8–14.

———. 1985. *Intimate Violence in Families.* Beverly Hills, CA: Sage Publications.

Gelles, Richard J. and Murray A. Straus. 1988. *Intimate Violence: The Causes and Consequences of Abuse in the American Family.* NY: Simon & Schuster Inc.

Goodwin, Megan P. and Bruce Roscoe. 1990. "Sibling Violence and Agonistic Interactions Among Middle Adolescents." *Adolescence,* 25:451–67.

Kempe, C. Henry, Frederic N. Silverman, Brandt F. Steele, William Droegemueller, and Henry K. Silver. 1962. "The Battered-Child Syndrome." *The Journal of the American Medical Association*, 181:105–12.

Koss, Mary P. and Mary R. Harvey. 1994. "Rape Is a Widespread Problem." Pp. 212–21 in *Violence Against Women*, edited by Karin L. Swisher and Carol Wekesser. San Diego, CA: Greenhaven Press, Inc.

Lubenow, Gerald C. 1983. "When Kids Kill Their Parents." *Newsweek*, June 27, Pp. 35–36.

Lustbader, Wendy. 1996. "Self Neglect: A Practitioner's View." *Aging Magazine*, 367:51–60.

National Center for Injury Prevention and Control. 1997. Division of Violence Prevention, Center for Disease Control and Prevention. Atlanta, Georgia.

O'Hanlon, Kevin. 1997. "Reports of Elder Abuse Rose 150% Since 1986." Bergen *Record Corporation Online*.

Pfohl, Stephen J. 1977. "The Discovery of Child Abuse." *Social Problems*, 24:310–323.

Pleck, Elizabeth. 1987. *Domestic Tyranny: The Making of Social Policy Against Family Violence from Colonial Times to the Present*. NY: Oxford University Press.

———. 1989. "Criminal Approaches to Family Violence, 1640–1980." Pp. 19–57 in *Family Violence*. Volume 11 of *Crime and Justice: An Annual Review of Research*, edited by Lloyd Ohlin and Michael Tonry. Chicago, IL: University of Chicago Press.

Renzetti, Claire M. 1997. "Violence and Abuse among Same-Sex Couples." Pp. 70–89 in *Violence between Intimate Partners*, edited by Albert P. Cardarelli. Boston, MA: Allyn and Bacon.

Renzetti, Claire M. and Charles Harvey Miley, Eds. 1996. *Violence in Gay and Lesbian Domestic Partnerships*. New York: The Haworth Press, Inc.

Sagatun, Inger J. and Leonard P. Edwards. 1995. *Child Abuse and the Legal System*. Chicago, IL: Nelson-Hall Publishers.

Skabronski, Jill C. 1996. "Elder Abuse: Washington's Repsonse to a Growing Epidemic." *Gonzaga Law Review*, 31:627–43.

Straus, Murray A. 1981. "Ordinary Violence versus Child Abuse and Wife Beating: What do They Have in Common." Paper presented at the National Conference for Family Violence Researchers, Durham, New Hampshire.

Straus, Murray A., Richard J. Gelles, and Suzanne K. Steinmetz 1980. *Behind Closed Doors: Violence in the American Family*. NY: Doubleday.

U.S. Department of Health and Human Services, Administration on Children, Youth and Families. *Child Maltreatment 1998: Reports from the States to the National Abuse and Neglect Data System*. Washington, DC: U.S. Government Printing Office, 2000.

U.S. Department of Health and Human Services Press Release. 1996. "HHS Releases New Statistics on Child Abuse and Neglect as Child Abuse and Neglect Prevention Month Begins," April 1. Washington, DC.

U.S. Department of Health and Human Services Press Release. 1996b. "Survey Shows Dramatic Increase in Child Abuse and Neglect, 1986–1993," Sept. 18, 1996. Washington, DC.

U.S. Department of Justice. Bureau of Justice Statistics. 1994. "Murder in Families," July 1994. Washington, DC.

U.S. Department of Justice. Bureau of Justice Statistics. 1997. "Sex Differences in Violent Victimization, 1994," Nov. 1997. Washington, DC.

U.S. Department of Justice. Bureau of Justice Statistics. 1994. "Violence between Intimates," Nov. 1994. Washington, DC.

U.S. Department of Justice. Office of Juvenile Justice and Delinquency Prevention. 1997. "In The Wake of Childhood Maltreatment," August 1997, Washington, DC.

Wiehe, Vernon R. 1997. *Sibling Abuse: Hidden Physical, Emotional, and Sexual Trauma*. Thousand Oaks, CA: Sage Publications.

Wolf, Rosalie S. 1996. "Elder Abuse and Neglect." *Aging Magazine*, 367:5–9.

Wolf, Rosalie S. and Karl A. Pillemer. 1989. *Helping Elderly Victims*. NY: Columbia University Press.

2 The Nature and Varieties of Physical Abuse

This chapter focuses on one of the major forms of abuse, physical abuse, and describes its varieties and prevalence. Although the various forms of abuse often blend together (American Academy of Family Physicians 1995), there are important differences between them. In this chapter, we discuss aspects of physical abuse unique to this form of abuse as well as aspects shared with other forms of abuse. Consequences of this abuse for creating or reinforcing subsequent deviant behavior are also presented.

The Nature of Physical Abuse

As defined in Box 1.5, child "physical abuse is the infliction of physical injury as a result of punching, beating, kicking, biting, burning, shaking, or otherwise harming a child." Physical abuse can range from pushing and shoving to torture and murder. It includes kicking, hitting, slapping, choking, bruising, burning, cutting, and disfigurement. Basically, any way that one person can physically injure another can be termed *physical abuse*. Such abuse includes destruction of property (for instance, smashing furniture or dishes, punching holes in walls or doors, and breaking windows) and injury to or destruction of pets (Medical College of Wisconsin 1998).

Excessive restraint of a family member is also physical abuse. Tying up a wandering child or elder is rarely necessary; and, if it is, it should be done under medical or other appropriate supervision and not in a way that cuts off circulation or leaves bruises. There are other, less injurious, ways of restraint—for example, the use of halter leashes for young children. The use of ropes, chains, handcuffs, blindfolds, or gags cannot be justified in restraining other family members. If someone is so uncontrollable that restraints are believed to be needed, professional intervention is required.

Excessive medication is another form of physical abuse. If tranquilizers are given to control behavior, there is a risk of overuse. A person may be very difficult without the medication. Sedating beyond what is medically necessary can easily occur, even without the intention to abuse. Nursing homes and long-term care facilities routinely need to administer medication to their residents. They have to be on the watch for possible overmedication and drug interaction. The dosage and choice of medications should be periodically reexamined to ensure that they are the minimum amount required with the least incapacitating effects.

Abusers do more than assault their victims. The also try to control their lives by preventing them from seeing friends or family and by keeping them from working or participating in community organizations. They may block medical or other services to reduce the chances that victims will gain help against them or create a sense of fear, danger, and entrapment to control their victims (Abbott et al. 1995).

Actions that are now regarded as physical abuse were not always thought so. How severely one punished children, especially "stubborn" children, was thought to be a family matter and not the business of society or government. Assaults against family members were not commonly treated as criminal offenses. Even when injury resulted, the assailant was not necessarily thought of as a deviant person. Only more recently have such actions been defined as "abuse" and appropriate for criminal justice intervention. The more that physical violence against family members has been studied by researchers and given play by news media, however, the more the behavior has been labeled deviant and calls for societal action against it increased. Those who commit such acts are now labeled "abusers," "perpetrators," and "offenders."

Severity and Extent

Most adult perpetrators of physical abuse are male. Although some studies suggest that 10 percent to 25 percent of wives and girlfriends may assault their husbands or boyfriends in a given year, the prevalence of men assaulting women (the number of relationships in which family violence perpetrated by men against women during a period of time) is at least twice as high. When these cases are reported to the police, 80 to 90 percent of the offenders are men (Holmes 1993; Mignon and Holmes 1995). At least 2 million women per year, and as many as 1 million men, report being assaulted by an intimate partner (American Academy of Family Physicians 1995).

The incidence (number of events in a period of time) of family violence is higher than this. A given family may have repeated violence in a given period. Studies of police reports by Dunford, Huizinga, and Elliot (1990), Holmes (1993), and Sherman (1992) suggest that as many as 60 percent of violent families repeat their violence in a given year. The National Crime Victimization Survey (Langan and Innis 1986) and National Study of Family Violence (Straus and Gelles 1986) provide similar estimates. Domestic disputes are one of the most frequent reasons police have to return to an address.

The lifetime risk (the risk of experiencing something at least once in one's life) of family violence is even higher. In some families, violence is intermittent. It may be experienced only once in several years, perhaps triggered by specific situations in which the abuser fears he or she will lose power or control. Estimates of lifetime violence in the family vary, but data from the National Study of Family Violence suggests that as many as 50 to 60 percent of families have a violent incident at least once in their lifetime (Straus et al. 1980). More conservative estimates suggest that physical assault occurs at least once in about 25 percent of all families.

Injuries from Physical Abuse

Most victims of physical abuse do not seek medical treatment for their injuries. In a study by Brookhoff and others (1997), only 22 percent of the victims studied had sought medical help. Many of those with bruises, welts, and sprains would rather suffer the pain of the injury than the embarrassment of public disclosure or the threat of more serious injury. Some may not define minor injuries as abuse but rather as "normal violence" between intimates. Those with more serious injuries are often coerced by the abuser to avoid treatment so the abuser can avoid public awareness of his or her actions.

When treatment is unavoidable, victims are coerced into passing off the injury as an accident. This is increasingly difficult to do. Medical research has identified specific injuries that are typical of assaults. Victims of physical abuse tend to have different injuries than do accident victims who fall down stairs or walk into walls (American Academy of Family Physicians 1995). Their injuries tend to concentrate in the face, neck, and trunk of the body. Nonabuse, accident victims tend more to have injured their arms, legs, or head than their face. The broken bones of abuse victims tend to be twisted fractures, rather than clean breaks. Cigarette burns should always be treated as possible abuse. Professionals in protective service agencies, medical organizations, and domestic violence centers look for these patterns of injuries in determining whether abuse has occurred. What was once thought to be a matter of opinion is now treated as a social fact.

Abuse throughout the Life Course

Newborn infants and elderly adults may be assaulted by family members. At any point in one's life, a relative may start or reactivate a pattern of assault. Physical abuse occurs in as many as one-fourth of all families. Abuse is more likely to occur when one is in a state of dependency or has few resources. Although the very young and very old are obvious targets, predatory individuals will try to undermine the power and independence of potential victims at any state of life. Seeking the weak and dependent to prey on can be a theme repeated throughout the abuser's life. Even when an abuser has not taken on the role of perpetrator, he or she may still have recurrent patterns of assaulting others.

Abuse is affected by one's life course. The very young and very old tend to be weaker and less able to defend themselves against physical abuse. Their social and economic supports often depend on those doing the abusing. Their complaints may be dismissed as exaggerated stories. With family violence between adult partners, the abuser often tries to put his or her partner in a situation of dependence, vulnerability, and isolation, not unlike that of young children and some elders.

When one partner tries to cut the other off from friends, relatives, and employment, this is a warning sign that she or he may be trying to make the other dependent.

When adults abuse their children, they tend to continue the abuse when the offspring become adults. Abusers don't stop unless the victim acquires sufficient power to force a cessation, the victim breaks off contact with the abuser, or community intervention or treatment changes the abuser. Assailants may attack elderly parents or other relatives at the same time they batter their children and their spouses. When they become older, however, they may find that their victims turn on them in a pattern of mutual assault, and abusers can then become victims. More commonly, they may be abandoned or their children may minimize contact.

This does not mean that children who are battered are doomed to become abusers. Many children grow up and reject the assaultive behavior of a parent or caretaker. Indeed, there is a whole body of research about resilient children who excel as parents despite terrible experiences as children (Gara et al. 1996; Himelein and McElrath 1996). Some abuse victims repeat the behavior of their parents or other caretakers, which has led some to talk about a cycle of violence in which persons abused as children become abusive as adults. This means that victims of family violence are faced with a challenge in dealing with their experience. It is difficult, but far from impossible, to overcome. This so-called cycle of violence will be dealt with more extensively later.

Varieties of Physical Abuse

Physical abuse is the use of force by a family member that results in pain, injury, impairment, or death. Under law, assault includes the threatened use of force, even if no injury results. Damaging property with threats to harm a person generally meets the legal standard for assault. Without injury, however, it is rarely recognized or prosecuted.

We distinguish physical assault against adults from that against children. Adult physical abuse is more likely to involve the criminal justice system. When law enforcement agencies become involved, adult cases are more likely to involve criminal charges, such as assault and battery, than are those involving children. In many states, if the physical injury to the child is not grave enough to require emergency medical attention, child victims will be referred to the child protective service system for civil action. Criminal charges may not be pursued at all.

Abuse of Children

The first risk of being a vulnerable target occurs in childhood. The social role and biological limitations of children place them in dependency; power is allocated to adult members of the family. Adults can direct violence toward children in several ways. Traditionally, child abuse involves physical assault of children. When this is done in the context of a religious cult or organized group, it becomes *organized ritual abuse*. When it is done by one's brothers and sisters (including half brothers and half sisters, stepbrothers and stepsisters, and foster or adopted brothers and sisters), it becomes *sibling abuse*. When the assailants are themselves children or adolescents who are romatically involved, it may be regarded as *dating or courtship abuse*.

Child Abuse.   Children can be abused as direct victims and as witnesses to the abuse of others (Brookhoff et al. 1997; McNeal and Amato 1998). The physical injuries of assaults upon children tend to be distinctive: broken bones that are twisted; bruises that have fingerprints; and injuries to the face, chest, or abdomen. Burns from cigarettes, ropes, and belts are also common. As noted in Chapter 1, these indicators are what was originally called the battered child syndrome (Kempe et al. 1965). There is now agreement among most professionals that they are signs of child abuse.

While many factors can produce problems in social and psychological development, physical abuse can severely disable and impair the emotional, intellectual, and social growth of children (Utech 1994). Developmental delays in these areas, when combined with evidence of injury, are warning signs that a child may be physically abused. Such injuries may also intensify the abuse: The impairments of the child become excuses for the parent to punish the child further.

Witnessing assault against other family members affects children in a way very similar to being the victim (McNeal and Amato 1998). Emotional trauma and fear of the abuser often result. This is intended by perpetrators. They want the children to be afraid and to bend to their will. A child's experience of a threat to another is as much an assault on the child as on the victim threatened. Young witnesses are controlled as much by fear resulting from vicarious experience of violence as by being victims themselves.

Physical abuse of children is often excused as justified corporal punishment. Until recently, it was not even defined as deviant behavior unless permanent injury to the child resulted. All 50 states allow parents to use some level of physical discipline of their children. Some, like Texas, specifically exempt corporal punishment as a valid charge of child abuse. Any physical assault against one's children is permitted if it doesn't result in severe, permanent injury. Other states limit physical punishment to use of an open hand on a child's seat. They explicitly prohibit use of belts, ropes, cords, whips, fists, feet, or any other weapon for physical punishment. Many, however, disagree on where to draw the line. There is not a high level of national social consensus on where to draw the line between acceptable corporal punishment and physical abuse. Many child psychologists, however, say that strategies such as using time out or withdrawal of rewards is more effective than corporal punishment.

There is research on corporal punishment that indicates when it is more likely to harm a child (Deater-Deckard and Dodge 1977; Lopez and Holmes 1983). Whippings or spankings that leave welts or bruises are harmful and meet the legal standards in most states for child abuse. Factors affecting the harmfulness of corporal punishment are discussed in Box 2.1.

Laws in every state mandate that certain professionals must report child abuse to protective service agencies, even if it is only suspected, not verified. Doctors,

BOX **2.1**

When Is Corporal Punishment Harmful?

Research has rarely shown harm resulting from discipline in the following circumstances:

- It results in no welts, bruises, or physical injury.
- It contains no threats of producing injury.
- It is consistently applied using standards appropriate to the developmental level of the child.

Research does suggest circumstances in which corporal punishment is likely to result in physical or psychological harm to the child:

- It produces welts, bruises, or physical injury.
- Explicit threat of future injury is made.
- The standards are applied inconsistently or are inappropriate for the developmental level of the child.
- The parent doing the discipline is perceived as distant or uncaring.
- The cultural context of the family doesn't have clearly defined traditional rules for punishment.
- The parent and the child are of the same sex.

When any of these circumstances are present, the risk of harming the child is increased. Some of these circumstances, by themselves, do not guarantee the child will be harmed. The presence of several of these factors, however, is a cause for concern.

---

nurses, teachers, police, social workers, psychologists, and child care workers are required to report such suspicions. In many states, even lawyers and clergy are required to break confidentiality to report child abuse. Box 2.2 discusses a controversy regarding the mandatory reporting laws.

Organized Ritualistic Abuse.   Ritual abuse tends to occur in religious cults or sects that stress patriarchy, obedience to authority, submission of women to men, and physical punishment for religious infractions (Bottoms et al. 1995; Copps 1992; Pritt 1998). Such groups tend to be regarded as deviant in modern societies and are commonly labeled by others as cults. Intervention against family violence in such groups, however, raises a question as to whether the action is based on stopping child abuse and domestic violence or on prejudice against deviant religious beliefs. Are they labeled as abusive because their beliefs and practices are deviant or because they injure their children? Under law, the line is drawn when punishment results in physical or emotional trauma (or imminent threat of injury). Religious beliefs are no legal justification for family violence or injuring children. Allowing a different standard for violence in the home because of one's religious

---

BOX **2.2**

Mandated Reporting: Child Protection or Parental Intrusion?

Most people support the principle that children ought to be protected from brutal assault. Most accept the idea that professionals who have responsibility for caring for children or for enforcing the laws ought to report child abuse when it comes to their attention. It doesn't seem unreasonable that these persons have a professional obligation to report such cases. This professional obligation has been codified into law in every state. Doctors, nurses, social workers, police, teachers, and school administrators in every state are required to report cases they suspect of being child abuse to the state's Child Protection Service (CPS) agency. Hundreds of thousands of families every year are investigated by CPS workers to determine whether abuse or neglect has really occurred. Several thousand children each year are found to be in life-threatening situations and might have died had their cases not been reported.

On the other hand, 40 percent of all cases investigated are not found to involve abuse or neglect. Several hundred thousand families each year are scrutinized and, often, stigmatized, even though there is no finding of abuse. This has led some to believe that the threshold for reporting suspected cases ought to be raised. Why should families be needlessly subjected to humiliation and public ostracism based on tenuous, and sometimes groundless, suspicions? This accusation may even be used by parties in a child custody dispute to deny one parent custody of or visitation rights to his or her children.

If the standard of evidence for mandated reporting is too high, many cases will go unreported and children will be injured with no one held responsible. Some children will even die as a result of failure to report. If the standard for reporting is too low, families can be needlessly destroyed with little gain in protection of children. One approach to this dilemma is to provide training to mandated reporters so they may more easily distinguish between groundless accusations and possible problems needing investigation. Others have proposed changing the standard for reporting. The debate over how to deal with this issue continues.

---

beliefs is an unconstitutional violation of the separation of church and state (MacLean-Mossie 1994). On the other hand, religious freedom requires allowing parents to discipline as their religion dictates, so long as it is short of the standard for child abuse.

Religious organizations such as Children of God, Iskcon Gurukulas (Hare Krishna schools), the Branch Davidians, and the Identity Church have been charged with tolerating or promoting abuse of children, particularly physical abuse done in the name of corporal punishment ("Youth Cult" 1992)—although such charges have been vigorously disputed. As discussed in Chapter 1, when physical punishment results in injury to a child—including bruises, welts, burns, broken bones, or scars—it goes beyond corporal punishment as a free expression of religious beliefs. It is child abuse. Similarly, if the punishment leaves emotional trauma in the child, it is child abuse. Evidence of emotional trauma can be shown by frequent bad dreams, extreme fear of strangers or authority figures, bed-wetting, fire-starting, self-mutilation, or violence toward other children or pets. An example of ritualistic abuse is given in Box 2.3.

Historically, religious groups defined as deviant or a threat to the established order have often been accused of ritual abuse of children. The same accusations against contemporary witches and Branch Davidians of torture and murder of children were previously made against Mormons, Jews, and early Christians (Bottoms et al. 1995; Pritt 1998). One must be careful to distinguish between unsubstantiated allegations or acts of disturbed individuals who belong to a church and acts that are condoned by an organized religious belief.

Abuse within Satanic cults is believed by some to be increasing among people with severe dissociative disorders (Kendler et al. 1997; Young 1993). Similar accusations have been made against those who follow a Gothic lifestyle or listen to heavy metal rock. Evidence that Satanism is increasing or that it commonly involves ritualistic abuse of children has, however, proven sparse. Such reports tend to be based on guided memories, which a working group of the American Psychological Association has indicated could be fallible (American Psychological Association 1994). Forensic evidence of such abuse exists (Mulhern 1994), but has been more limited. However some cases have had sufficient evidence to warrant criminal prosecution. The alleged perpetrators in the criminal cases tend to be adults, although the media have given much attention to rumors and allegations against adolescents (La Fontaine 1997). The presence of psychiatric disorders has not proven an effective defense against criminal charges for the perpetrators in such cases, nor has a defense based on religious freedom.

The fact that some religious cults promote physical abuse of children by no means implies that most do. Some religious organizations work quite specifically

---

BOX 2.3

Mormon Polygamists Accused of Child Abuse

Members of the Church of Jesus Christ of Christian Saints, a break-away splinter group from the Church of Jesus Christ of Latter Day Saints (the Mormon church), have been accused of and charged with child abuse. Criminal charges of assault, false imprisonment, incest, kidnapping, and bigamy are also pending. This group espouses polygamy and strong patriarchical rule in families. The Mormon church itself has rejected polygamy. Wives and children of a man in the sect who disobeyed his wishes were taken to a secluded ranch in Idaho, where they were kept prisoner and beaten into compliance. Girls aged sixteen and seventeen were forced by their parents to marry whomever their parents designated. In some cases, this was a close male relative, such as an uncle or a half brother. Members of the group say polygamy and physical punishment of wives and children are justified by their religion. They claim the charges are a result of prejudice against their different religious beliefs and that they should be allowed to discipline and restrain their members as they wish.

against violence (CTAC 1998). Many churches sponsor Parents' Anonymous meetings or offer shelter to battered women and children. Some of these are listed as resources in the appendix.

Sibling Abuse.   Many families accept fights between siblings as perfectly normal. While there is no agreed-upon definition of sibling abuse, fighting or play that results in serious injury is usually regarded as deviant. For this discussion, the intentional inflicting of harm by a sibling will be regarded as sibling abuse. Even then, it may still be dismissed as "sibling rivalry" or as a normal fight that has gotten out of hand (Wiehe 1997).

Research shows that sibling assault is a pervasive social problem (Reid and Donovan 1990; Straus et al. 1980). Assault of siblings may be even more common than physical abuse perpetrated by parents (Straus et al. 1980:77). A national survey by Straus, Gelles, and Steinmetz (1980) found that more than half of all children had been attacked by a brother or sister during the preceding year. A similar percentage acknowledged attacking their sibling in turn. Despite its prevalence, sibling abuse is not always recognized as a problem. Wilson and Fromuth (1997) found that 65 percent of college students had been kicked, bitten, hit, or choked by a brother or sister. Sixty percent reported doing the same to their siblings. Only about 25 percent regarded this as abuse.

Recognizing sibling abuse is more difficult because some forms of abuse may be dismissed as play. Tying up a brother or sister may resemble a game of cops and robbers or cowboys and Indians. When it is accompanied by taunts, threats, assaults, or exploitation, it crosses the line and becomes sibling abuse—even though the children involved may regard it as normal. Tickling a child, despite requests to stop, until he or she becomes angry or cries is also abusive. Too often this kind of play is regarded as a normal way to treat a brother or sister.

Play can be distinguished from abuse because it involves trust (Wiehe 1997). The "aggressor" will stop when asked by the "victim" or when pain or suffering is obvious. In play, the dominant sibling doesn't laugh at the pain or suffering of the brother or sister. Any injury or pain that results is not part of a repeated pattern or behavior. That behavior may even be abandoned in the future to avoid further injury or suffering. If the behavior is continued despite the pleas of or injury to the victim, it is sibling abuse.

Like other forms of abuse, the principal issues in sibling abuse are power and control. Siblings torment each other when they fear they can't control a brother or sister they believe should bend to their will. Older siblings tend to imitate abusive parents with respect to younger siblings. Brothers try to dominate sisters when they accept traditional sexist attitudes, often learned from their father. When such persons are concerned about their ability to control their lives and those of subordinates, abusing siblings become a way of reassuring themselves that they can control someone and that they are not alone and powerless.

Adolescents are more likely to abuse their brothers and sisters than are younger children (Utech 1994). Conflict between siblings may increase as teens challenge their roles in the family as well as in society. Those who imitate violent behavior are acquiring the physical strength to use it effectively. Those who have been suppressing their anger at victimization, and who have not learned positive ways to channel it, may no longer be able to restrain it. Societal norms also favor older children having authority over younger children.

When young children hit, kick, pinch, or assault a brother or sister, they may not fully appreciate that their actions may cause harm or suffering. They may, however, imitate the actions of others. For most, it is not part of a repeated pattern of behavior. When it does become a pattern, however, it is a cause for concern.

Dating and Courtship Abuse. Physical assault between teens is portrayed by media as common and relatively harmless (Reisman 1998). Common, it is. Harmless, it's not. Violence between teens who are dating or courting often precedes domestic violence or marital rape if the couple should marry (McLaughlin et al. 1992; Straus et al. 1980). The young males are practicing their skills at sexual dominance and testing the boundaries of acceptable behavior. Patterns of physical assault among those dating prior to marriage are very similar to those after marriage. It is usually wishful thinking that a violent boyfriend or girlfriend will change after marriage. Only if he or she is willing to complete therapeutic intervention is there hope.

Schools, including colleges, are required to report such behavior to law enforcement agencies, but underreporting is a severe problem. Victims may be afraid of being ostracized by their schoolmates or of suffering retaliation from their abuser. Many parents don't want to think their teen is abusive. They vigorously defend their child and attack the accuser as lying and unreliable. Many officials don't want their school to get the reputation that their students are victimized by violence. Even so, many schools have begun antiviolence programs directed at dating violence and date rape. Research discussed in later chapters provides hope for these efforts.

Abuse of Adults

Reaching adulthood and leaving an abusive family does not necessarily mean that one escapes family abuse. Some adults repeat behavior learned from their parents or siblings and reinforced by media images of violence. Adult victims of child abuse may be sought out as victims by perpetrators or become perpetrators themselves. Other adults may have had the good fortune to grow up in nonabusive families and become trapped in an adult abusive relationship. This section describes ways in which adults continue to be involved in abuse.

Abuse can be directed toward spouses or ex-spouses, same-sex partners, and elders (by adult family members) and toward parents in the family (by children). Victims can have more than one of these roles. Abuse of adults also tends to depend on the sex of the victim. Women are physically abused by men more often than by other women. Although some researchers have claimed that women and men abuse each other with equal frequency (Gelles and Straus 1988), serious abuse that comes to the attention of police and hospital emergency rooms is overwhelmingly perpetrated by men against women (Harlow 1991; Holmes 1993; Isaac et al. 1994; Mignon and Holmes 1995; Sherman 1992; Stark and Fletcroft 1988).

Spouse Abuse. Spouse assault occurs in official marriages and common-law marriages and between couples living together. This is the common conception of domestic violence. It is the single most common cause of injury to women (Stark and Fletcroft 1988). It is the most common form of assault encountered by police (Sherman et al. 1992). One is far more likely to be attacked by one's spouse or domestic partner than by a complete stranger. Three out of four offenders assaulting women have a domestic relationship with the victim (Harlow 1991). A quarter of women report physical violence during their marriage (Medical College of Wisconsin 1998).

Assault is highly likely to be repeated. Between 60 and 80 percent of domestic violence offenders repeat their violence within a year, some numerous times (Holmes 1993; Sherman et al. 1992; Thistlethwaite et al. 1998). The repetitive nature of this offense is one of the principal reasons it is of such concern to police, physicians, social workers, and therapists.

Spouse abuse is also the greatest risk factor in child abuse. At least 70 percent of men who batter women also batter their children (Bower et al. 1989). Even when they don't hit the children, witnessing the abuse of their mother is psychologically damaging to the children (McNeal and Amato 1998).

Spouse abusers typically report their violence to researchers as being less than that reported by the victims (Langhinrichsen-Rohling and Vivian 1994; McLaughlin et al. 1992; Szinovacz and Egley 1995). The assailant's view is that the abuse doesn't

---

BOX 2.4
Why Don't Victims Leave?

Why don't spouse abuse victims leave their spouses? If they really don't want to be abused, why don't they just leave? There are five important reasons why many abuse victims don't leave their abusers:

- They fear for their lives if they leave.
- They've been kept from economic resources that would allow them to leave.
- They've been cut off from friends, family, and social supports that would help them leave.
- Attitudes by other people say, "It's a family matter, and no one else should get involved."
- The number of beds in available shelters is far fewer than the number of victims needing shelter protection.

Each of these reasons acts as a barrier to leaving. Those who do leave are the fortunate ones who find support for their departure or are so desperate that even the prospect of being homeless and destitute is a preferable alternative.

really happen. If it does happen, it's not very serious. If it's serious, then it's the victim's fault. They do this for three reasons. First, they may not perceive the abuse as physical assault. Their experience and education may have taught them that this is something other than assault, such as "love taps," discipline, or controlling behavior. When they recognize it as violence, they may define it as normal behavior: "Everyone does it." "It's our own private business." "There's nothing wrong with it." "She deserves it." When they recognize that it is violence and wrong, they want to preserve their self-image and avoid the legal consequences of their behavior. Such individuals are often manipulators who can come up with an excuse or an explanation that either puts the blame on others or minimizes the blame on themselves. This ability to minimize, excuse, and explain is known as denial and minimization. Often, it is extremely difficult for such offenders to admit how wrong their behavior was. They resist being labeled an abuser quite vigorously. Tactics to overcome this wall of defense are discussed in Chapter 11.

The emotional intensity and negative attitudes of physical abusers toward their spouses have led some states to consider repeated spouse abuse as a type of hate crime. Box 2.5 examines spousal assault as a hate crime.

Same-Sex Partner Abuse. In some states, assault of same-sex partners qualifies as spousal or domestic assault. In other states, violence by same-sex partners may not fall under domestic violence statutes. The social definition of abuse for same-sex partners is not always the same as that for heterosexual partners. This variety of family violence shares much with spouse abuse, however. The basic drive of the

---

BOX 2.5

Is Spouse Assault a Hate Crime?

A hate crime is any criminal offense that is motivated by hatred of another. Additional penalties can be imposed if the offender is found guilty of committing a hate crime. The hate crime statutes in most states include hatred of another's race, religion, national origin, or sexual orientation as a necessary element in definition of a hate crime. In some states, hatred of another's gender has been added: The definition of a hate crime based on gender requires that the criminal offense, such as assault or mayhem, be motivated by hatred of the victim's gender; it is not a hate crime if the physical abuse is based on hatred of the other as a person. If a case of spouse abuse is defined as a hate crime, the penalties can be significantly greater than if the same assault is not so defined.

How can investigators tell whether an assault is a hate crime? There has to be a pattern of behavior or other evidence indicating hatred of the other's gender. For example, if the assailant says, "I can't stand your incompetence!" this indicates hatred of the other's behavior, not his or her gender. If the assailant says, "You're just like every other woman. You're all alike!" this indicates that the victim's gender is the target of hatred. Similarly, if there is a pattern of court protection orders taken out against the same offender by more than one female victim, this could indicate a pattern of behavior against women in general.

abuser to dominate and control is the same, whether the relationship is heterosexual or homosexual. The basic tactics of violence, threats, cajoling, and isolating the victim are the same. However, homosexual partners are often treated differently from heterosexual partners by society and by social institutions. This produces aspects of same-sex partner abuse that are not found in traditional spouse abuse (Allison 1998; Klinger 1995; Renzetti 1992).

A same-sex relationship marred by violence is especially difficult to leave because of prejudice and discrimination that may result. The partners may not be publicly known as homosexual. The abuser may threaten to "out" the victim if he or she leaves. Police and shelter personnel may be prejudiced against gays and lesbians and give their cases minimal effort (Allison 1998), or they may be denied access to such shelters altogether. Homophobic individuals may say the victims are only getting what they deserve. Legal statutes and court rulings often give same-sex partners fewer rights to division of common assets. "Palimony" for homosexual relationships is extremely rare, and legal practice may not assume that shared property is jointly owned.

Parental Abuse. Sometimes parents are abused by their children, most often teenagers (Utech 1994). Although the rate of assault on parents by children is lower than that of child abuse by parents, perhaps 10 percent of families have a parent assaulted by a child in the family (Utech 1994). When such assaults do occur, the parent victim is often in fear for his or her life.

Parental assault is serious because it devastates the family relationships. Normal parent–child interaction and child rearing cannot occur when one's child is being physically violent. The trauma from such assaults lingers for years. In addition, it can lead to parricide, in which the family bonds (and members) are destroyed altogether. Children who assault their parents are often kicked out of their homes, even if they are underage. When they remain in the home without therapeutic intervention, sibling abuse may also occur.

Parent abuse may begin in response to a parent's violent use of corporal punishment. As the child becomes an adolescent, the parent may increase the violence to control a stronger and bigger teen. The adolescent may then respond by assaulting the parent to defend him- or herself or others (Utech 1994). The violence experienced as a child may also become part of the teen's routine coping strategies when faced with threats or frustration. In either case, the child may start a pattern of assault against the parent, occasionally leading to death of a parent. Parent abuse can also result from the teen's drug use, mental illness, or involvement in gangs.

Elder Abuse. As noted in Chapter 1, elders are less likely to be physically assaulted than are young adults, but the consequences of such assault are more grave. Elders have less strength to defend themselves, and their injuries may have more severe consequences and be slower to heal.

Assault of one's aging parents, grandparents, or other elder relatives can be a continuation of parent or caretaker abuse, or it may originate as an aging relative begins to lose power and authority in a household. Elder abuse is not just retaliation for the elder's past abuse of his or her children. Many times, there was no past child abuse. Frequently, the adult children have emotional and financial difficulty in caring for an elderly parent. Adult children faced with caring for their own children and their parents may have difficulty coping with the stress and may lack the skills or resources needed to reduce the stress. The coping skills of the children may be inadequate to deal with the situation, and deviant behavior in the form of physical abuse may result. Assaulting one's parents has been thought deviant long before it was called elder abuse. Social embarrassment at being a victim of such deviance by a family member, as well as direct threats, has prevented many elders from reporting their situation.

Identifying elder abuse is complicated by the elder's shame at being assaulted by one's own children, fear of retaliation or loss of needed support, or dementia. In the latter case, the elder may not be able to describe the event adequately or give credible testimony. When the elder is delusional and paranoid and is easily bruised by acts of daily living, it can be very difficult to know what really happened. Older adults are also more likely to believe that such issues are a private family matter that they don't wish to discuss with outsiders. Identifying elder abuse is also difficult due to uncertainty concerning the balance between an adult's right to autonomy and the desire to protect a frail elder, as discussed in Box 2.6.

Deviant Consequences of Physical Abuse

It should be emphasized at the outset that not every abuse victim has deviant outcomes. Many victims are resilient and have internal strength that allows them to overcome the effects of the abuse. As discussed in later chapters, if abuse victims have positive, supportive role models and other resources available to them, the deviant and criminal consequences of physical abuse are by no means certain.

Many victims, however, do suffer deviant consequences. Some possible consequences of physical and sexual abuse are the same. Other possible consequences are unique to each type of abuse. Either type can encourage emotional and behavioral problems, low self-esteem, depression, substance abuse, suicide, posttraumatic stress disorder, running away, aggressive behavior, delinquency, and criminal behavior. Although there are other factors that also encourage these problems, research shows consistent correlations between physical abuse and these problems.

Victims of physical abuse tend to view the world as a dangerous place in which violence, force, and aggression are used to take what one wants or needs. When coping with problems, they are more likely either to strike out or to become extremely passive. They are more likely to be concerned with their physical strength or skill or lack thereof than are sexual abuse victims. Some of the strongest proponents of the view that "It's a dog-eat-dog world and you have to look out for yourself" are victims of physical abuse who have rationalized their experience and deceived themselves into believing that such behavior is normal and acceptable. With such beliefs, they are more easily led into criminal activity or to take advantage of opportunities that arise.

BOX 2.6

Elder Protection: Autonomy versus Support

Most states have elder abuse reporting laws similar to those for child abuse. An important difference, however, is that the elders are adults. They are presumed under law to be able to make their own decisions, care for themselves, and take responsibility for the consequences of their own actions. If adults knowingly fail to take action to prevent an injury, the law presumes that was their choice; a bad choice, but theirs. This is the principle of autonomy. Adults can make their own decisions and the legal system will not intervene, unless laws are broken. Exceptions to the principle of autonomy are made for coercion or for dementia. If an elder is forced to accept abuse or no longer has the mental capacity to defend him- or herself against abuse, the courts can step in.

Determining coercion is sometimes easier than determining dementia. If an elder shows signs of physical abuse and complains of physical attacks, the case can be investigated similar to other domestic violence cases. If the mental status of the elder is not clear, however, there may be ambiguity about what happened and how competent the elder is to explain and deal with the situation. Dementia is a gradual process. In its early stages, outbursts of violence by the elder or periods of paranoid delusions may be rare. The first occurrence might even seem credible. What actions should be taken against alleged assailants? How much should the state intervene? How much of the autonomy of the elder should be taken away to protect her or him and to protect others? What should one look for in making that decision?

Three principles are especially important to apply in these cases: competent assessment, periodic review, and providing the least restrictive environment. "Competent assessment" means that professionals should be brought in when there are questions regarding dementia and potential injury. "Periodic review" means that the situation could change over time and needs to be reexamined to address new needs or issues. Providing the "least restrictive environment" means that elders should be allowed as much autonomy as they can exercise without being a danger to themselves or others. Using these principles will help produce decisions that respect the autonomy of elders while providing support where it is essential.

The various types of deviance associated with physical abuse are not equally likely. Serial murder and cult involvement, for example, are not commonplace and involve more factors than physical abuse alone. A pattern of aggressive behavior or retreat from social interaction are more commonly associated with physical abuse.

Physical Abuse and Types of Deviance

There are a variety of possible deviant consequences of physical abuse. It may encourage family conflict, educational failure, substance abuse, mental health problems, delinquency, assaultive behavior, criminality, cult involvement, and serial murder. More than one of these possibilities can happen at the same time.

Family Conflict and Revictimization. Research has raised questions regarding how many violent adults were themselves abuse victims. Incarcerated offenders often report being abused as children. The extent to which this is true, however, is debated, as some prisoners may claim abuse as a way to manipulate the system and win sympathy. The body of research findings does suggest that many who experience violence and conflict in their families of origin tend to express violence in subsequent relationships and intensify existing family conflicts (Fitzpatrick 1997; McNeal and Amato 1998). Their adult families often have problems of disorganization, low cohesion, poor parental supervision, and inconsistent or meager supports, rules, or expectations.

The disorganization and low cohesion often seen in such families is consistent with the abusers wanting to control the family members. The victims are denied power to order their own lives. The perpetrators are mainly concerned with order in their own lives, not in others'. The conflicting expectations and demands by the perpetrator tend to result in confused role boundaries and inappropriate role behavior by many family members. In addition, isolation of the family and inefficient use of available resources exacerbate family conflicts.

Children who are abused sometimes become involved in abusive relationships when they get older. Such persons may have acquired habits, ways of thinking, or coping strategies that put them at greater risk of being revictimized. As noted above, one possible coping response to physical abuse is that the person may become more passive when faced with threats or problems. Those who develop this response are easier victims for assaultive types than those who have other coping strategies.

This does not mean that the victim is to blame for the revictimization. Physical abusers may seek out potential victims. They may watch for potential targets or take advantage of situations that they find. They may even manipulate events to place their victims in a weaker situation. It is the abusers who are responsible for their behavior.

Educational Failure. Studies show that physical abuse is associated with school truancy (Rich and Gutierres 1979), difficulty concentrating, and academic failure. Victims also tend to suffer intellectual impairment (Utech 1994). Although there are many societal and organizational factors that contribute to educational failure, problems associated with victimization also seem to increase the risk of educational problems and make it more difficult for victims of physical abuse to succeed in school (Fitzpatrick 1997). Early school problems may lead to further academic failure and aggressive behavior. Having school problems is also a risk factor for delinquency, substance abuse, and criminality.

There are several reasons why physical abuse is associated with educational difficulties. A chaotic family environment makes study difficult. Depression and low self-esteem reduce motivation. Brain injury and unmet medical needs impair performance. Fear of social relationships undermines group learning and collaborative education. Too good a performance may also single a child out as a target for abuse.

Substance Abuse. Alcoholism is one of the most common substance abuse problems associated with family violence (Gaudry 1988; O'Farrell and Murphy 1995). In Massachusetts, one-fourth of persons with a domestic violence court protection order against them had prior arrests for drunk driving (Isaac et al. 1994). In one study, a majority of county prisoners in that state had evidence of alcohol problems (Holmes and Reibel 1992).

Victims, too, are likely to have substance abuse problems. In a Colorado study of emergency room patients, more than 70 percent of domestic violence victims had an alcohol problem, compared with 50 percent of nondomestic violence victims—a 40 percent increase in risk for domestic violence victims (Abbott et al. 1995). An Illinois study of elder abuse found a significant relationship between assault on elders and substance abuse (Hwalek et al. 1996). Other studies have found both alcohol and other drug abuse a greater risk among domestic violence victims (El-Bassel et al. 1995; Miller 1990; Plichita 1992).

The substance abuse may also be reinforced by other consequences of physical abuse. The increased risks of somatic complaints and depression resulting from physical abuse are associated with risk of substance abuse (Jaffe et al. 1986; Ratner 1993). One explanation for this linkage is that the substance abuse is used as a form of self-medication: Using alcohol and other drugs may be a way of trying to cope with the physical and mental health problems resulting from physical abuse. The substance abuse, in turn, may intensify other deviant behaviors resulting from physical abuse. It can easily lead to being labeled a deviant and require the person to engage in criminal activity to meet the need for the substance.

Mental Health Problems. Shame, guilt, anger, and low self-esteem are some of the more common problems correlated with abusive family situations (Hoglund and Nicholas 1995; McNeal and Amato 1998). Victims may also withdraw from social interaction. Sometimes, however, the trauma may lead to a serious mental illness. There is evidence that major depression, posttraumatic stress disorder, and multiple personalities can be produced by more extreme physical violence (Frazer 1995). It may also lead to suicide (Abbott et al. 1995).

Major Depression. This problem has social, psychological, and biological roots. Rarely is there a single cause. When victims of physical abuse repress their anger, however, and are constantly reminded of their powerlessness, it is not surprising that severe depression can result (Forsstron-Cohen and Rosenbaum 1985; McNeal and Amato 1998). When physical abuse is one of the causes of depression, community service agencies need to be involved to stop ongoing abuse and deal with its consequences.

Posttraumatic Stress Disorder. Posttraumatic stress disorder (PTSD) is a major mental health problem experienced by people who undergo repetitive exposure to violent, stressful situations having high uncertainty of outcome. Terms such as *shell-shock* and *battle fatigue* from the First and Second World Wars presaged recognition of this problem. It wasn't really recognized as a major mental health problem, however, until after the Vietnam War.

Individuals suffering from PTSD have reduced ability to cope with additional stress. They may lash out at those producing stress. They may experience flashbacks and imagine they are still in the earlier violent situation. They may abuse alcohol and other drugs to dull the memories and the pain of their experiences. Victims who have PTSD, however, should not be regarded as inherently violent persons. Often, they are withdrawn and not violent at all.

More recently, it has been recognized that victims of family violence may experience PTSD. Particularly when the violence is frequent, unpredictable, and uncertain in outcome, victims may develop this problem. It is a particularly poignant problem for victims of physical abuse because their experience of PTSD in their families of origin may reinforce family violence and lead to violence in new families they join.

Multiple Personalities. It has already been noted that there may be a link between multiple personality disorder (or dissociative personality disorder, as it is also known) and an increase in cult ritualistic abuse on the part of abusers (Mulhern 1994). Although the research evidence is not extensive, it appears that extreme trauma experienced by such victims is associated with an increased risk of this disorder. In rare cases, there can be a macabre process of sadistic multiple personality abusers who produce a new generation of disturbed persons with multiple personalities.

Suicidal Behavior. The psychological trauma of physical abuse is also associated with suicidal behavior (Fabian 1986; Frazer 1995). The risk of suicide is compounded by the additional risks of depression, substance abuse, and low self-esteem (McNeal and Amato 1998)—all of which increase the risks of suicide. One study of women receiving emergency room treatment (not necessarily for a domestic assault) found that 80 percent of women with a history of suicide attempts had experienced domestic violence (Abbott et al. 1995). Suicide attempters often are asking for help to deal with the traumatic effects of physical abuse.

Delinquent and Criminal Consequences. Several delinquent or criminal consequences may result from physical abuse. Victims are more likely to express delinquent or assaultive behavior, to commit criminal acts, or, in rare cases, even to become serial murderers.

Delinquency. Children who have been abused or who have witnessed violence in their families are more likely to wind up in court for delinquent acts (Knudsen 1992; Sexton 1998). For some, this is how they learned to cope in their families when faced with life problems. For others, anger at those who abused them or other family members may become displaced onto everyone else in society. Such individuals often espouse a rhetoric of retribution against those who commit real or imagined offenses against them. The delinquency is an expression of rage at how they were treated and a naive attempt to assert control over their environment.

Assaultive Behavior.   Reviews of the literature on the consequences of physical abuse clearly show a link with some victims becoming assaultive in their behavior toward others, both within and outside the home (Becker 1964; Koski 1987; Tavris 1989). Individuals with criminal histories of multiple assault charges often report having witnessed or been victimized by physical abuse when they were young. These individuals have learned that violence can sometimes get them what they want. They haven't learned the price they pay in damaged relationships, loss of trust, and lost opportunities for mutual support or help from others.

Criminality.   Juveniles who have been abused have an increased risk of committing criminal behavior (Satterfield and Schell 1997). In some cases, they may perpetrate extreme violence without remorse, having lost much of their capacity for empathy as a result of being victimized themselves. Those who grow up in violent homes are more likely to start committing crimes earlier, be arrested earlier, continue crimes into adulthood, and become repeat offenders (Satterfield and Schell 1997).

   The existence of repeat violent juvenile offenders has led some states to treat more teens as "hardened criminals." California, for example, has created a special category for juveniles of "violent dangerous offenders"(California State Legislature 1996) and can delay release of youth who lack remorse for their crimes or show violent or threatening behavior—even if they have served their sentence and have committed no crimes while in custody. Such states are also trying more juveniles in adult criminal courts, giving them adult sentences, and incarcerating them with adults—despite research showing this is likely to worsen their criminal behavior, not deter it. The difficulty in accurately identifying "dangerous offenders" among adults applies even more to juveniles, who have more capacity to change than do career adult offenders.

   Adults who commit domestic violence are likely to commit other violent crimes. In Massachusetts, half of all persons who had domestic violence restraining orders taken out on them also had a history of violent criminal offenses (Isaac et al. 1994). Three-fourths had a prior criminal history record. In every state where this has been studied, it has been found that those who commit family violence are likely to commit violent crimes against others as well.

   Criminality is aggravated when family abuse also involves substance abuse. According to a study on substance abuse and America's prisons by the National Center on Addiction and Substance Abuse (CTAC 1998):

- Involvement in criminal activity varies directly with the prevalence, frequency, and seriousness of drug use.
- Persons testing positive for drugs at the time of arrest have a higher probability of being rearrested (and more quickly) than those who do not test positive.
- Addicted offenders who receive little or no treatment show an accelerating pattern of criminal activity over time.

The physical abuse and the substance abuse may both reinforce subsequent criminal behavior.

Serial Murder.   Research on serial killers has many problems. Much of it is anecdotal or case studies. Fox and Levin (1990), however, were able to use data from a national database of homicide reports to develop a profile of serial killers. This was supplemented by interviews with many of these murderers in prison. Such offenders usually report being physically abused as children. This research is not without criticism, however. The population of convicted serial killers may not represent the population of serial murderers who are never arrested. It isn't known what percentage of all serial murderers are eventually arrested and convicted. It is also difficult to corroborate these reports of abuse as a child. Serial killers may reconstruct their childhood history to elicit sympathy. Records and witnesses may no longer exist. When records regarding child abuse are available, however, they generally support a history of abuse.

The study by Fox and Levin indicates that this outcome of abuse is not very common. The number of serial murderers is small compared to the number of those who kill for financial gain. Domestic homicides far exceed the number of serial murder victims. Yet, when this is an outcome, it exacts a heavy toll. Some serial killers claim to have murdered several hundred victims before they were caught. One of these killers is discussed in Box 2.7.

B O X 2.7

Portrait of a Serial Killer

Henry Lee Lucas may have been the most prolific serial killer in America. He confessed to over 600 murders in 26 states (Mendoza 1998). One of his alleged victims, said to have been killed by his partner Ottis Toole, was six-year-old Adam Walsh, about whom a TV special was made. Lucas also claimed to have carried poison to Guyana for Reverend Jim Jones to bring about the Jonestown massive murder-suicides, though there is no proof he ever left the United States. He later recanted as false his confessions of some of his alleged murders. But he was linked by evidence to over 200 of the 600 confessed murders.

Lucas was physically abused throughout his childhood, primarily by his mother. She repeatedly humiliated him and his father, whom she called No Legs because of a train accident. His alcoholic father was driven to suicide by her abuse. Once, his mother beat Henry with a wooden board so badly that he was semiconscious for three days before her boyfriend took him to a hospital. On another occasion, she forced him to go to school in a dress with his hair in curls. Eventually, he killed his mother with a knife. For this he served ten years of a forty-year sentence.

After serving time for the matricide, he joined up with a violent paranoid schizophrenic, Ottis Toole, to carry out numerous homicides. Many of their victims were hitchhikers. Sometimes, they would run the victims over in their car without stopping. Other times, they would stop so Ottis could cut up the bodies and occasionally taste the remains.

Summary

This chapter looks at varieties of physical abuse. It considers varieties of physical abuse of children, adults, and elders. It discusses child abuse, ritual abuse, sibling abuse, and dating assaults. It examines domestic abuse, parent abuse, and elder abuse. For each variety of abuse the precipitating factors, the nature of the violence, and the social and psychological issues involved could vary.

The chapter also examines consequences of physical abuse. These include family conflict, educational failure, substance abuse, mental health problems, delinquency, assaultive behavior, criminality, cult involvement, and serial murder. Several of these consequences could occur simultaneously. Some may aggravate the family abuse or lead to other deviant or criminal consequences.

Study Questions

1. Why can tickling a child be regarded as a form of physical abuse?

2. What factors seem to motivate abusers in their violence toward family members?

3. Do you think elder abuse is committed more often by adult victims of child abuse or by adults who have poor coping skills for dealing with stress? Why?

4. What are some of the reasons sibling abuse is underreported?

5. How can you tell whether conflict in a dating relationship is a precursor to courtship violence or domestic violence?

6. Why do you think child abuse is reported more often for preschool-age children than for school-age children?

7. If a child hasn't been abused by his or her parents, why would he or she start abusing them as a teenager?

REFERENCES

Abbott, Jean, Robin Johnson, Jane Koziol-McLain, and Steven R. Lowenstein. 1995. "Domestic Violence Against Women: Incidence and Prevalence in an Emergency Department Population." *JAMA, The Journal of the American Medical Association.* 273:1763–68.

Allison. 1998. "Domestic Violence in Lesbian Relationships" (WWW document, URL=http://www. en.com/users/allison/l_dv.html.).

American Academy of Family Physicians. 1995. "ACOG Issues Technical Bulletin on Domestic Violence." *American Family Physician.* 52:2387–90.

American Psychological Association. 1994. "Interim Report of the APA Working Group on Investigation of Memories of Childhood Abuse." (WWW document, URL=http://www.apa. org/releases/interim.html).

Becker, W. C. 1964. "Consequences of Different Kinds of Parental Discipline." Pp. 169–208 in M. L. Hoffman and L. W. Hoffman, eds. *Review of Child Development Research.* NY: Russell Sage.

Bottoms, Bette L., Roxanne Shaver, and Quanjian Qin. 1995. "In the Name of God: A Profile of Religion-Related Child Abuse." *Journal of Social Issues.* 51:85.

Bower, Arsbitell, and McFerran. 1989. "On the Relationship Between Wife Beating and Child Abuse." In *Feminist Perspectives of Wife Abuse*. NY: Free Press.

Boyle, Maureen. 1995. "State Study Shatters Stereotype About Abusers." *The Standard Times* (WWW document, URL=http://www.s-t.com/projects/DomVio/statestudy.html).

Brookhoff, Daniel, Kimberly K. O'Brien, Charles S. Cook, Terry D. Thompson, and Charles Williams. 1997. "Characteristics of Participants in Domestic Violence: Assessment at the Scene of Domestic Assault." *Journal of the American Medical Association*. 277:1369–74.

California State Legislature. 1996. "It's too Late." Committee Report 352. (WWW document. URL=http://www.parl.gc.ca/committees352/jula/eviden.html).

Copps, Donald. 1992. "Religion and Child Abuse: Perfect Together." *Journal for Scientific Study of Religion*. 31:35–46.

CTAC 1998. "CTAC—Churches Take a Corner" (WWW document. URL=http://www.ctac-usa.org).

Deater-Deckard, K. and K. A. Dodge. 1977. "Externalizing Behavior Problems and Discipline Revisited: Nonlinear Effects and Variation by Culture, Context, and Gender." *Psychological Inquiry*. 8:161–75.

Dunford, F., D. Huizinga, and D. S. Elliott. 1989. "The Omaha Domestic Violence Police Experiment." (final report) Washington, DC: National Institute of Justice.

El-Bassel, N., A. Ivanoff, and R. F. Schilling. 1995. "Correlates of Problem Drinking Among Drug-Using Incarcerated Women." *Addiction Behavior*. 20:359–69.

Fabian, S. 1986. *The Last Taboo: Suicide and Attempted Suicide Among Children and Adolescents*. NY: Penguin.

Fitzpatrick, K. M. 1997. "Fighting Among America's Youth: A Risk and Protective Factors Approach." *Journal of Health and Social Behavior*. 38:131–48.

Forsstron-Cohen, B. and A. Rosenbaum. 1985. "The Effects of Parental Marital Violence on Young Adults: An Exploratory Investigation." *Journal of Marriage and the Family*. 45:405–10.

Fox, James A. and Jack Levin. 1990. *Mass Murder*. NY: Free Press.

Frazer, Judy. 1995. "COMMUNITY JUSTICE COURSE (Overview and Learning Outcomes)" (WWW document, URL= http://wwwtafe.lib.rmit.edu.au/judy/overview.html).

Gara, Michael A., Seymour Rosenberg, and Elaine P. Herzog. 1996. "The Abused Child as Parent." *Child Abuse & Neglect*. 20:797–809.

Gaudry, E. 1988. *Recovery from Alcoholism*. NY: Collins Dove.

Gelles, Richard and Murray A. Straus. 1988. *Intimate Violence*. NY: Simon & Schuster.

Harlow, C. W. 1991. "Female Victims of Violent Crimes." Bureau of Justice Statistics. Washington, DC: U.S. Department of Justice.

Himelein, Melissa J., and Jo Ann V. McElrath. 1996. "Child Sexual Abuse Survivors: Cognitive Coping and Illusion. *Child Abuse & Neglect*. 20:747–66.

Hoglund, Collete L. and Karen B. Nicholas. 1995. "Shame, Guilt, and Anger in College Students Exposed to Abusive Family Environments." *Journal of Family Violence*. 10:141–58.

Holmes, William. 1993. "Police Arrests for Domestic Violence." *American Journal of Police*. 12,4:101–25.

Holmes, William and Michael Reibel. 1992. "Drug Offenders in County Jails," paper presented at meetings of Academy of Criminal Justice Sciences, Pittsburgh, PA.

Hwalek, Melanie A., Anne Victoria Neal, Carolyn Stahl Goodrich, and Kathleen Quinn. 1996. "The Association of Elder Abuse and Substance Abuse in the IlliINNis elder abuse system." *The Gerontologist*. 36:694–701.

Isaac, Nancy, Donald Cochran, Marjarie Brown, and Sandra Adams. 1994. "Men Who Batter: Profile from a Restraining Order Database." *Archives of Family Medicine*. 3:50–54.

Jaffe, P., D. Wolfe, and L. Zak. 1986. "Emotional and Physical Health Problems of Battered Women." *Canadian Journal of Psychiatry*. 31:625–29.

Kempe, C. Henry, Frederic N. Silverman, Brandt F. Steele, William Droegemueller, and Henry K. Silver. 1962. "The Battered-Child Syndrome," *The Journal of American Medical Association*, 181:105–12.

Kendler, Kenneth S., Charles Gardner, and Carol A. Prescott. 1997. "Religion, Psychiatry, and Substance Use and Abuse." *American Journal of Psychiatry*. 154:322.

Klinger, Rochelle L. 1995. "Gay Violence." *Journal of Gay & Lesbian Psychotheraphy*. 2:119–35.

Koski, P. R. 1987. "Family Violence and Nonfamily Deviance: Taking Stock of the Literature." Pp. 23–46 in F. Hagan and M. Sussman, eds. *Deviance and the Family*. NY: Hayworth Press.

LaFontaine, J. S. 1997. "Allegations of Sexual Abuse in Satanic Rituals." *Religion*. 24:181.

Langan, P. and C. A. Innes. 1986. "Preventing Domestic Violence Against Women. (Special Report, NCJ-102037) Washington, DC: U.S. Department of Justice, Bureau of Justice Statistics.

Langhinrichsen-Rohling, J. And D. Vivian. 1994. "The Correlates of Spouses' Incongruent Reports of Marital Aggression." *Journal of Family Violence*. 9:265–83.

Lopez, Linda and William Holmes. 1983. "Maternal Involvement and Academic Success for Kindergarten Pupils," *Reading Improvement*. 20,4:248–51.

MacLean-Mossie, Ann. 1994. "Medical Decisions and the Constitution." *Hastings Constitutional Law Quarterly*. 21:725.

McLaughlin, I. G., K. E. Leonard, and M. Senchak. 1992. "Prevalence and Distribution of Premarital Aggression Among Couples Applying for a Marriage License." *Journal of Family Violence*. 7:309–19.

McNeal, Cosandra and Paul R. Amato. 1998. "Parents' Marital Violence: Long-Term Consequences for Children." *Journal of Family Issues*. 19:123–40.

Medical College of Wisconsin. 1998. "Family Violence Fact Sheet for Community Leaders." Department of Family Medicine. (WWW document, URL=http://www.family.mcw.edu/ahec/ec/factshe.html).

Mendoza, J. 1999. "Serial Killer Hit List." (World Wide Web document) URL=www.mayhen.net/crime/serial.htm.

Mignon, Sylvia and William Holmes. 1995. "Police Response to Mandatory Arrest Laws." *Crime and Delinquency*. 41:430–42.

Miller, B. 1990. "The Interrelationships between Alcohol and Drugs and Family Violence." *National Institute of Drug Abuse Monograph*. 103:177–207.

Mulhern, Sherrill. 1994. "Satanism, Ritual Abuse, and Multiple Personality Disorder: A Sociohistorical Perspective." *International Journal of Clinical and Experimental Psychology*. 42:265–76.

O'Farrell, Timothy J. and Christopher M. Murphy. 1995. "Marital Violence Before and After Alcoholism Treatment." *Journal of Consulting and Clinical Psychology*. 63:257–63.

Office of Child Development. 1994. *National Incidence Study of Family Violence*. Washington, DC.

Plichita, S. 1992. "The Effects of Woman Abuse on Health Care Utilization and Health Status: A Literature Review." *Women's Health Issues*. 2:154–63.

Pritt, Ann F. 1998. "Spiritual Correlates of Reported Sexual Abuse among Mormon Women." *Journal for the Scientific Study of Religion*. 37:273.

Ratner, P. 1993. "The Incidence of Wife Abuse and Mental Health Status in Abused Wives in Edmonton, Alberta." *Canadian Journal of Public Health*. 84:246–49.

Reid, W. J. and T. Donovan. 1990. "Treating Sibling Violence." *Family Therapy*. 17:49–59.

Reisman, Judith. 1998. "Images of Children, Crime and Violence in Playboy, Penthouse, and Hustler." Abstract of final report for OJJDP grant 84-JN-AX-K007. (WWW document, URL=http://www.iglou.com/first-principles/abstract.html).

Renzetti, Claire. 1992. *Violent Betrayal: Partner Abuse in Lesbian Relationships*. Newbury Park, CA: Sage Publications.

Rich, J. W. and Gutierres, S. E. 1979. "Escape/Aggression in Sexually Abused Juvenile Delinquents." *Criminal Justice and Behavior*. 6:239–43.

Satterfield, J. H. and A. Schell. 1997. "A Prospective Study of Hyperactive Boys with Conduct Problems and Normal Boys' Adolescent and Adult Criminality." *Journal of the American Academy of Child and Adolescent Psychiatry*. 36:1726–35.

Sexton, Elizabeth. 1998. "Harmed Children: Delinquency, Child Abuse, and School." *Reclaiming Children and Youth: Journal of Emotional and Behavioral Problems*.

Sherman, Lawrence. 1992. *Understanding Violent Families*. NY: Free Press.

Sherman, Lawrence, Janell Schmidt, and Dennis Rogan. 1992. *Policing Domestic Violence: Experience and Dilemmas*. NY: Free Press.

Stark, E. and A. Fletcroft. 1988. "Violence Among Intimates: an Epidemiological Review." Pp. 293–318 in V. N. Hasselt et al., eds. *Handbook of Family Violence*. NY: Plenem.

Straus, Murray A. and Richard J. Gelles. 1986. "Societal Changes and Change in Family Violence from 1975 to 1985 as Revealed by Two National Surveys." *Journal of Marriage and the Family.* 48:465–79.

Straus, Murray, Richard Gelles, and Suzanne Steinmetz. 1980. *Behind Closed Doors: Violence in the American Family*. NY: Doubleday.

Szinovacz, M. F. and L. C. Egley. 1995. "Comparing One-Partner and Couple Data on Sensitive Marital Behaviors: The Case of Marital Violence." *Journal of Marriage and the Family.* 57:995–1010.

Tavris, C. 1989. *Anger: The Misunderstood Emotion*. NY: Simon & Schuster.

Thistlethwaite, Amy, John Wooldredge, and David Gibbs. 1998. "Severity of Dispositions and Domestic Violence Recidivism." *Crime & Delinquency.* 44:388–98.

Utech, Myron R. 1994. *Violence, Abuse, and Neglect: The American Home*. Dix Hills, NY: General Hall.

Wiehe, Vernon R. 1997. *Sibling Abuse: Hidden Physical, Emotional, and Sexual Trauma*. Thousand Oaks, CA: Sage Publications.

Wilson, Carol D. and Mary Ellen Fromuth. 1997. "Characteristics of Abusive Sibling Relationships and Correlations with Later Relationships." Paper presented at meetings of the American Psychological Association, Chicago.

Young, Walter C. 1993. "Sadistic Ritual Abuse: An Overview in Detection and Management." *Primary Care: Clinics in Office Practice.* 20:447–49.

"Youth Cult." 1992. *Social Work Today.* 23:10.

CHAPTER

3 The Nature and Varieties of Sexual Abuse

Sexual abuse is the most emotionally charged form of abuse and therefore the most difficult for people to acknowledge and discuss. Even so, there is general public awareness that this is a very important issue because victims of sexual abuse can bear lifelong consequences of their victimization.

Sexual abuse encompasses a wide variety of behaviors. Perhaps the most disturbing form is child sexual abuse, which may be perpetrated by a relative or by someone outside the family, even a stranger. The term *sexual abuse* also applies to the sexual assault or rape of an adult when, as also in the case of child sex abuse, it involves the abuse of power over the victim and violation of the victim's right to normal and healthy relationships.

There are a number of areas of disagreement in the field, especially regarding definitions of sexual abuse, which will be discussed later. One area of contention is whether those who have endured sexual abuse should be referred to as "victims" or "survivors." The term *victim* connotes that the individual is passive and helpless, clearly an appropriate designation for a child who has been sexually abused. The term *survivor* connotes that the individual has overcome a traumatic experience and is probably a more appropriate term for an adult who has endured sexual abuse. Some prefer to use the term *resilient adult* because it connotes increased strength gained from enduring traumatic events. (See Lam 1998:26–27 for a good discussion of sexual abuse terminology.) We concur with Lam (1998) that children are more appropriately considered "victims" while adults are "survivors" of sexual abuse.

This chapter reviews the types and extent of sexual abuse and examines the short- and long-term consequences of victimization, including the potential deviant and criminal consequences. This chapter reflects more a psychological than a sociological perspective because psychology has made stronger contributions to the field in terms of definitions and treatment. It is also easier to examine these important issues when looking at individual perpetrators and victims rather than trying to examine sociological factors that may underlie family abuse.

Child Sexual Abuse

Sexual abuse of a child can be physical, verbal, or emotional in nature. It includes a wide variety of behavior: adult nudity in front of the child, disrobing, spying on a child in the bathroom or bedroom, kissing, fondling, and masturbation. Sexual abuse also includes having children pose in sexual positions for someone who will see them in person or on film, exposing children to pornographic movies or photographs, touching children sexually in ways such as digital penetration of the vagina or rectum, and attempting or completing intercourse with children (Finkelhor 1986; Gilmartin 1994; Sgroi 1982).

Paraphilia is the broad category of sexual activity involving nonconsenting persons, whether children or adults; it includes a wide variety of behaviors such as pedophilia and exhibitionism. *Incest, pedophilia, intrafamilial,* and *extrafamilial sexual abuse* are all terms used to refer to the relationship between the victim and the perpetrator of sexual abuse. *Pedophilia* is used by some to refer to sexual abuse by a perpetrator who is not part of the family. Some use the term to refer to any sexual activity between an adult and a child, related or unrelated. Some prefer to use the term *incest* for sexual abuse that occurs between relatives. Incest takes place within the family boundaries, and is therefore often referred to as intrafamilial abuse, while sexual abuse by someone outside the family is called extrafamilial abuse.

Araji and Finkelhor (1986:89) point out that the term *pedophilia* is useful because "it suggests an internal predisposition that is independent of an actual offense." Rather than referring to specific sexually abusive behaviors, this definition emphasizes that the pedophile has an ongoing sexual attraction to children. *Pedophilia* refers to looking to children for sexual gratification while sexual abuse or child molestation are the activities in which pedophiles engage.

The *Diagnostic and Statistical Manual of Mental Disorders,* fourth edition (American Psychiatric Association 1994) uses the term *pedophilia* for perpetrators who are either related or unrelated to the child. This is the most widely used manual of diagnoses used by mental health professionals and so it is easy to see the psychological rather than sociological perspective of this work. The diagnostic criteria for pedophilia are as follows:

A) Over a period of at least 6 months, recurrent, intense sexually arousing fantasies, sexual urges, or behaviors involving sexual activity with a prepubescent child or children (generally age 13 years or younger).

B) The fantasies, sexual urges, or behaviors cause clinically significant distress or impairment in social, occupational, or other important areas of functioning.

C) The person is at least age 16 years and at least 5 years older than the child or children in Criterion A (American Psychiatric Association 1994:528).

A number of strategies can be used by the perpetrator to get children to engage in sexual behavior. These can include pressuring, seducing, bribing, and forcing a child to participate in the abuse. The perpetrator may also use the threat of force. Box 3.1 reviews signs and symptoms of child sexual abuse.

Although research findings have been inconsistent, some generalizations can be made about child sexual abuse. Child sexual abuse knows no boundaries in terms of age, gender, race/ethnicity, and psychological characteristics (Lam 1998). It does appear that sexual abuse is more closely associated with lower social class (Schneider 1997). The notion that most sexual abuse is committed by strangers is incorrect: It is more frequently committed by family members and those who know the child (Schneider 1997). Although both males and females are victims of sexual abuse, the majority of victims are female (Chesney-Lind and Shelden 1998; Finkelhor 1984). Finkelhor and Baron (1986) estimated from their review of the research that approximately 71 percent of child sexual abuse victims are female. Stepfathers are the most likely perpetrators of incest. Finkelhor (1984) found that a stepfather was five times more likely than a biological father to victimize a daughter, a finding similar to those of other research.

Some common characteristics of families in which there is incest include frequent marital conflict and single parenthood. These families are often grappling

---

BOX **3.1**
Signs and Symptoms of Child Sexual Abuse

- Persistent sexual play with themselves, toys, or other children
- Language or behavior that reflects sexual knowledge beyond the normal for the age group
- Unexplained pain, bleeding, or swelling of the mouth, genitals, or rectal area
- Urinary tract infections
- Sexually transmitted diseases
- Physical complaints including headaches and/or stomach aches
- Bedwetting
- Excessive bathing or poor hygiene
- Eating disorders
- Anxiety and/or depression including suicide attempts
- Sleep disturbances
- School problems
- Discipline problems including running away
- Aggressive or self-destructive behavior
- Substance abuse problems
- Sexual activity at an early age
- Early pregnancy

Source: The Sexual Assault Crisis Center of Knoxville, Tennessee. Child Sexual Abuse. 1998. (www http://www.cs.utk.edu/~bartley/sacc/childabuse.html).

with substance abuse problems, depression, and violence (Beitchman et al. 1992; Lam 1998). In their review of the literature, Finkelhor and Baron (1986) offered a picture of those children at highest risk of incest. Children most likely to be victimized are preadolescent girls. They are not likely to live with their biological father and may live with a stepfather. They are more likely to have sick or disabled mothers or mothers who work outside the home. They are more likely to witness conflict between their parents and to report a poor relationship with one of their parents.

Most literature examines characteristics of either the perpetrators or the victims of sexual abuse, giving little attention to the strategies used by the perpetrator in sexually exploiting children (Young 1997). It is known that sexual abuse of children is likely to evolve over a period of time rather than be a one-time occurrence. Indeed, the perpetrator usually progresses slowly and "grooms" the child, so that the sexual behavior can be felt to be an appropriate activity by the victim. This is known as the normalization process.

In a review of 45 cases in which perpetrators and victims were related or acquainted, Young (1997) found that there were a variety of strategies employed by the perpetrator to engage the child in sexual activity. One strategy was for perpetrators outside of the family to become incorporated into the family as a babysitter, boarder, or "courtesy uncle." Some perpetrators used "accidental" touching while playing games. Some used the strategy of offering help to the child, such as tutoring, and expecting sexual activity in return. Sexual activity between a parent and child was incorporated into caretaking and socialization, such as bathing a child and "educating" the child about body parts and functions. Box 3.2 provides an example of the experiences of a child sexual abuse victim.

The Extent of Child Sexual Abuse

While the true extent of child sexual abuse remains unknown, several studies have documented the fact that this is not an uncommon problem. Studies have reported rates of child sexual abuse to be between 6 and 62 percent for women and between 3 and 31 percent for men (Peters, Wyatt, and Finkelhor 1986). The wide variation in estimates of sexual abuse for both males and females reaffirms the difficulty in gathering data on sexual abuse. A recent study of women found the prevalence of childhood sexual abuse to be 21 to 32 percent if a broad definition of sexual abuse was used and 15 to 26 percent if a less inclusive definition of sexual abuse was used (Vogeltanz et al. 1999). The National Center on Child Abuse and Neglect estimated that the number of sexually abused children increased from 119,200 in 1986 to 217,700 in 1993, an increase of 83 percent (Sedlak and Broadhurst 1996). This increase was attributed to real increases in sexual abuse and to greater awareness of the problem. This picture is changing, however. Finkelhor (1998), citing Wang and Daro (1998), stated that estimates of substantiated cases of child sexual abuse in 1997 fell to 84,000, a reduction of 40 percent from the early 1990s, with sexual abuse accounting for approximately 8 percent of all child maltreatment cases.

BOX **3.2**

A Case of Childhood Sexual Abuse

The words of a girl who endured years of sexual abuse by her father:

I touched the cold sheets. His touch was cold, too, his sloppy groping gestures hidden under the sheets. The touch of his hanging belly on top of mine. The smell of Old Spice and Canadian Club breathing down on me from his sloppy open mouth. He wasn't drunk. He was never drunk, just undignified. He felt my [vagina] with his fingers and then, like a doctor prescribing a medicine, he said, "We'll just get some baby oil and then it won't hurt at all. You're lucky I am doing this for you the first time and not some punk in the back seat of a car."

I was beyond thinking and feeling then.

I remember the putrid smell of baby oil and the cold wet oil dripping from my thighs. I remember saying over and over to myself, It will be over soon, it will be over soon, it will be over. . . .

The shock of the searing pain so deep inside me, I knew no one had a right to that. I pulled away, furiously struggling to get free. I screamed. He looked at me with contempt.

"It doesn't hurt that much. I used the baby oil so I know."

It was then that I started screaming, "No, *get off me! get off me!*"

He seemed shocked. "Take it easy now. Well, maybe it does hurt the first time a little. Okay, calm down, okay."

His body slid across me like a great lumpy slug.

I closed my eyes for a second to squeeze the tears back.

He went to touch me but I jerked away.

I crawled from the bed, my [vagina] aching like it had been sliced open. I walked slowly to the bathroom, a trickle of blood running in a thin, delicate line down my thigh.

Source: Maggie Hoyal. 1995. "These Are the Things I Remember." Pp. 119–28 in *Rape and Society,* Patricia Searles and Ronald J. Berger, eds. Boulder, CO: Westview Press.

Jones' and Finkelhor's (2001) most recent review reveals a national decline of substantiated cases of child sexual abuse of 31 percent from 1992 through 1993. Finkelhor offers several reasons for the decline of sexual abuse:

The decline in child sexual abuse may be due to a new caution among and perhaps some intimidation of professionals and the public at large in the face of publicity about false reports, misguided prosecutions, and civil lawsuits. It may also reflect the adoption of sounder, more conservative standards in the investigation of abuse. But the decline also could be due to some real abatement of the problem, related to factors such as increased public awareness and vigilance, the wide-spread adoption of prevention programs, incarceration of many offenders, and even a general upward trend in the economy and social well-being. (1998:1864)

There are several key reasons for varying rates of child sexual abuse. One difficulty is that there is not an agreed-upon definition of sexual abuse. Depending on the study, *sexual abuse* can refer to exhibitionism, watching pornographic videos, fondling, oral sex, or sexual intercourse. Some studies focus only on adult-to-child sexual abuse and ignore other types, including abuse by peers (Peters et al. 1986). The difficulties in definition make it hard to determine how much of each type of sexual victimization occurs. Clearly, there is a need to work toward an operational definition of sexual abuse that can be applied consistently in research. There is also the discrepancy between a legal definition of child sexual abuse and an operational definition. Legal definitions of sexual abuse are for the purposes of prosecuting perpetrators of child sexual abuse: Operational definitions are designed to make research findings comparative so knowledge can accumulate and lead to more appropriate treatment and prevention strategies (Lam 1998).

Perhaps the major issue in defining and learning the extent of child sexual abuse is the fact that victims are not likely to disclose their abuse. In a national survey, Finkelhor et al. (1990) found that 33 percent of male victims and 42 percent of female victims told no one of their abuse. Gomes-Schwartz et al. (1990) found that a child telling about abuse was the most common way sexual abuse was discovered. The reality is that unless a child is able and willing to disclose abuse, it is not likely to be discovered another way. In fact, unlike physical and emotional abuse or neglect, sexual abuse is "defined and divulged at the discretion of the child" (Knudsen 1992:132).

It is highly unlikely that the perpetrator will disclose the abuse. The reasons are obvious: the risk of legal repercussions and the severe stigma society will impose. Legal or child protective interventions are also likely to have an impact and can curtail the abuse, which the perpetrator will probably not want. For these reasons, perpetrators may not define their behavior as abuse. One study found that of self-reported perpetrators of child sexual abuse who had been sexually victimized themselves, only 35 percent labeled their own victimization as abuse (Fromuth and Conn 1997).

Some differences in research findings can be attributed to the wording of specific questions. To ask, "Were you sexually abused as a child?" is different from asking, "Before you were sixteen, did anyone try to have contact with your genitals or try to get you to touch his or her genitals?" It is obvious that the more specific the questions, the more likely the researcher is to elicit detailed information.

With these cautions in mind, there are still some interesting and important findings. A number of studies have reported relatively high rates of sexual abuse using the method of self-report on the part of victims. A Los Angeles Times national survey in 1985 found that 27 percent of women and 16 percent of men reported sexual abuse before they turned 18 years old (Finkelhor 1986). In an eighteen-year longitudinal study of 1,000 children in New Zealand, at age 18, 17.3 percent of girls and 3.4 percent of boys reported a history of child sexual abuse before the age of sixteen. Those at highest risk were girls exposed to a number of serious family problems: considerable marital conflict, low parental attachment, high level of paternal overprotection, and parental alcohol problems (Fergusson et al. 1996).

Sexual abuse is a significant international problem, as discussed in Box 3.3. Physical abuse has received more attention than sexual abuse on an international level, and the United States has led the way in acknowledging sexual abuse as an important social problem (Finkelhor 1984).

Male Victims of Sexual Abuse

Sexual abuse of boys has received little attention until recently and is even more underreported than sexual abuse of girls (Becker 1988; Holmes and Slap 1998; Watkins and Bentovim 1992). Finkelhor's (1984) review of the research found estimates of men sexually abused as children ranging from 2.5 to 8.7 percent. Mendel's (1995) review of studies of prevalence found that between 3 and 16 percent of the male general population have been sexually victimized, while a review of studies of undergraduates found rates of between 4.8 and 33 percent. A study by Fromuth, Burkhart, and Jones (1991) found that 3 percent of a sample of male college students fit the criteria for sexually abusing a child. Most studies find age of onset to be between seven and ten years. A recent review of 166 studies (from 1985 to 1997) of sexual abuse of boys found prevalence estimates ranging from 4 to 76 percent (Holmes and Slap 1998).

The underreporting of male child sexual abuse has been attributed to the male ethic of self-reliance, the stigma of homosexuality, and an unwillingness to see that sexual activity with older females can be abusive. Underreporting can also be due to the victim's sense that his circumstances are extremely rare and that the relative freedom boys have, compared with girls, could be curtailed if the abuse became known (Finkelhor 1984; Mendel 1995). One study reported that only one man in a sample of 25 told of the abuse at the time it occurred (Dimock 1988).

BOX **3.3**
World Congress Against Sexual Exploitation of Children

The first-ever World Congress Against Sexual Exploitation of children met in Stockholm, Sweden, in August 1996. It was organized by the Philippine agency, End Child Prostitution in Asian Tourism, and more than 1,200 delegates from governments and private organizations from around the world were in attendance.

It was estimated that more than 1 million children under the age of 16 are sold for sexual favors and that during the 5-day conference these children will have served more than 12 million "customers."

Source: Bruce Harris. 1996. "Sexual Abuse Is Not Just a Plague of the So Called Third World." *One World News Service.* (www http://www.oneworld.org/news/partner_newsaug1996_children2.html).

In their review of the literature, Watkins and Bentovim (1992) state that extrafamilial abuse such as sexual activity perpetrated by clergy or coaches is more common than incest among male victims and more likely to be reported to the police as a crime. Intrafamilial abuse or incest is more likely to be reported to child protective agencies, so these agencies are more aware of girls as sexual abuse victims (Finkelhor 1984).

In general, boys, in common with girls, are most likely to be victimized by men. Boys are more likely to be victims of extrafamilial abuse and are more likely than girls to be one of a number of victims of the same perpetrator. Boys are more likely than girls to be victims of physical as well as sexual abuse. They are also more likely to be subjected to anal abuse than are girls (Watkins and Bentovim 1992).

Female Perpetrators of Child Sexual Abuse

There is little information available on female perpetrators of sexual abuse, and it is only since the late 1980s that much work has been done in this area (Fromuth and Conn 1997; Jennings 1993; Watkins and Bentovim 1992). Although there are no clear statistics on its prevalence, female sexual abuse of children may not be as rare as imagined and may account for 5 percent or more of child sexual abuse. Finkelhor's (1984) review of the literature led him to suggest that women are perpetrators in 5 percent of cases of sexual abuse of girls and 20 percent of cases of sexual abuse of boys. Dimock (1988) found that of his sample of 25 men abused as children, 28 percent were victimized by women. A literature review by Watkins and Bentovim (1992) found that of female perpetrators of male victims, only 5 to 15 percent come to professional attention. Some suggest that female perpetration has not been acknowledged and studied in the same way as male perpetration because it undermines our notions of how women should relate to children—as mothers, nurturers, and caretakers (Elliott 1993).

The victims of young female sexual offenders tend to be under the age of six and have some relationship to the offender (Hunter et al. 1993). In a sample of 546 female college students, 4 percent met the criteria for sexually abusing a younger child. Only 4 percent of this group considered their behavior to be child sexual abuse. Victims were most likely to be boys and to be related to the perpetrator. Although few differences between perpetrators and nonperpetrators were found on psychological and background variables, perpetrators were more likely to have been sexually abused as children and to report sexual interest in children (Fromuth and Conn 1997).

Mother–son incest is a specific type of female perpetration that has received little professional attention (Bachmann, Moggi, and Stirnemann-Lewis 1994). Watkins and Bentovim (1992) point out the complexity of mother–son incest: "Because the sexual act generally requires the male taking the initiative or being 'active,' confusion may exist in mother–son incest as to whether the abuse was perpetrated by the boy against his mother, or mother against the son" (35). However, even though at times the son may feel he is the active partner, the discrepancy in sexual knowledge and issues of responsibility determine that the mother is the abuser.

It has been suggested that being a victim of a female perpetrator is even harder to cope with than being victimized by a male. This form of abuse may be the source of even greater shame and stigma because it is regarded as highly unusual. Such victims may take longer to disclose their abuse in the treatment setting than children victimized by male perpetrators (Sgroi and Sargent 1993).

Sibling Sexual Abuse

Very little is known about the extent of sibling sexual abuse, although it has been suggested that it may be the most common form of incest (De Jong 1989). Such sexual abuse is typically at the hands of an older brother or sister and can extend over long periods of time (Cafaro and Conn-Cafaro 1998). Finkelhor (1980) found that 15 percent of college women and 10 percent of college men reported sexual activity with a sibling. Fondling and touching of the genitals were the most frequent activities among all age groups. According to Wiehe, reported cases "barely represent the tip of the iceberg, since most incidents of sexual abuse by siblings go not only unreported but undetected by parents" (1997:60). Wiehe's own research with a clinical sample found that 33 percent had been physically and/or emotionally abused by a sibling, while 76 percent of respondents indicated that they had been victims of sibling sexual abuse. As with other types of intrafamilial child sexual abuse, girls are more likely to be the victims and the abuse is likely to continue over a period of time. Box 3.4 offers examples of what victims of sibling abuse endure.

Wiehe (1997) also stated that other forms of abuse are likely to occur at the same time. He found that 3 percent of victims had been abused physically and sexually, 11 percent had been abused emotionally and sexually, and 37 percent had been abused physically, emotionally, and sexually. Wiehe offered several possible explanations of why many more respondents experienced sexual abuse. Respondents were people in treatment programs; sexual abuse victims may be more likely to seek professional help than are victims of emotional or physical abuse. This may be because the impact of sexual abuse on their lives was more traumatic than the impact of other types of abuse. According to Wiehe, definitions of sexual abuse tend to be clearer than definitions of other kinds of abuse so that acknowledging sexual abuse from a sibling may be easier than determining that one has been subject to emotional and physical abuse.

Child Care Abuse

Child care abuse is especially disturbing because it can affect large numbers of children at the same time. The need for quality child care is obvious, but it has not been a high priority in terms of social policy and funding. In general, child care issues tend not to attract much attention. The exception is child care abuse: the media widely publicize reported cases. Faller (1990) reviewed Finkelhor et al.'s

B O X **3.4**

Examples of Sibling Abuse

In Sterling Heights, Michigan, a 12-year-old girl was allegedly raped by her 17-year-old brother. They had been sharing a bedroom in their parents' 2-bedroom apartment. The girl became pregnant and at 29 weeks into the pregnancy had a legal abortion in Kansas. Michigan law prohibits abortion after 24 weeks unless the woman's (or girl's) life is endangered. Despite complaints of vomiting and difficulty eating, four previous medical examinations failed to determine the girl was pregnant until an advanced stage.

Prosecutors expect to charge the brother with first-degree criminal sexual conduct, which could lead to a life sentence. Prosecutors indicated a willingness to pursue a lesser sentence if the boy "obtains psychological treatment."

"Prosecutors Postpone Incest-Rape Charges." 1998. *The Boston Herald,* August 1, 13.

• • •

A woman talking about sexual abuse by her older brother:

He started the activity by fondling me and progressed to having me manually stimulate his penis. After the initial two incidents, I refused to cooperate further. He then began to expose himself to me when we were alone and tried to force me to participate. My refusal led to a stage of terrorism, where he would chase me and threaten me.

Another woman talking about being sexually victimized by her older brother:

He made it into an experiment. He would have me undress and he would look and touch me—especially my vagina. I was frequently required to touch his penis. He would have me in the playhouse or basement room. At age 9 or 10, he started penetrating me—again as an experiment. No emotions or feelings. I was told not to tell because it was an experiment and if I told it would fail. There was more to his convoluted logic, but that was the gist of it.

Source: Vernon R. Wiehe. 1997. *Sibling Abuse,* 2nd ed. Thousand Oaks, CA: Sage Publications, Inc. Pp. 74–75.

(1988) examination of cases of reported child care abuse in 1985, which found that 1,300 children in 267 child care centers (out of 229,000 total centers) had been sexually abused. Finkelhor et al. estimated that 5.5 of every 10,000 children enrolled in child care are abused; in comparison 8.9 children of every 10,000 children under the age of six are sexually abused at home.

Faller (1990) described two general categories of sexual abuse in child care: unplanned sex with children and planned sex with children. *Unplanned sex* with children can involve *circumstantial sexual abuse* when a perpetrator who has no past history of sexual activity with children, because of life circumstances, engages in sex with a child. *Naive pedophilic abuse* refers to those perpetrators who like children and only after they begin working with children begin to experience sexual attraction. Some perpetrators are coerced into sexual abuse by others in authority at the child care center; this is known as *induced sexual abuse.*

Four types of *planned sexual abuse* are described by Faller (1990). *Calculated pedophilic abuse* is committed by those whose primary sexual orientation is to children and who seek out this work to have access to victims. *Entrepreneurial sexual abuse* is committed for profit and includes pornography and child prostitution. *Sexual abuse by people who hate children* may be especially cruel in its effort to intentionally terrorize. *Ritualistic abuse* is related to some rite of a religion, satanism, or cult.

Two nationally known cases of suspected child care abuse are described in some detail. Both child care abuse cases received considerable media attention and both raise the question of whether the extraordinary events occurred at all. Johnson (1995) reported that child abuse cases, as human interest stories, "have become increasingly important to the organizational needs and interests of mass media" (28).

The McMartin Pre-School case in California is considered an example of satanic sexual abuse in a case that played out from 1983 to 1990. The mother of a two-and-a-half-year-old boy accused a teacher, Raymond Buckey, of making her son ride a horse while naked and sodomizing him while he stuck the boy's head in a toilet. Reportedly, the mother had made similar accusations against her estranged husband and three health club employees. Other children in the school were interviewed, and they said they had been raped and sodomized by Raymond Buckey as well as tied up, drugged, and sexually abused by other teachers. There were reports that children were forced to drink the blood of rabbits and dig up the bodies in cemeteries for Buckey to cut up. There were accounts that men in black robes carried black candles, a suggestion that satanism was practiced. In all, 400 children were interviewed and 350 were thought to be victims of abuse (MacDonald 1995).

These charges resulted in the arrest of Buckey; his mother, grandmother, and sister; and three other teachers. The charges against the others were dropped in 1986 due to lack of evidence, but Buckey and his mother went to trial. The trial lasted two years and nine months, and in 1990 Buckey and his mother were acquitted of 52 criminal charges. The jury did not reach a verdict on thirteen remaining charges, and these charges were not pursued. Jurors were concerned that questionable methods had been used to obtain evidence from the children, specifically, that questions were too leading. Reportedly, children who acknowledged abuse received some reward while those who denied abuse were criticized. Seven jurors stated that they thought some abuse had occurred but that they were unable to sort out fact from fantasy. This was certainly an extremely difficult situation for the children to cope with; they also had to endure cross-examination by the defense attorneys. The judge in this case summed it up with these words: "The case has poisoned everyone who had contact with it" (MacDonald 1995:115). One lasting effect of the McMartin case is the concern over the reliability of child victim-court witnesses.

Another high-profile child care sexual abuse case, the Fells Acres case in Massachusetts, began with accusations in 1984. Three child care providers in Malden, Massachusetts, a mother and her son and daughter, were convicted of molesting approximately 40 children between the ages of three and six. The mother and daughter were sentenced to 8 to 20 years, while the son received a 30- to 40-year sentence. The mother, Violet Amirault, and daughter, Cheryl Amirault LeFave, were released from prison in 1995 when a judge overturned their convictions. The Massachusetts Supreme Judicial Court twice upheld the convictions and rejected requests for a new trial. Violet Amirault died in 1997. The son remains incarcerated, and LeFave was expected to return to prison ("Editorial Criticizes SJC" 1999). The final outcome for LeFave was decided in October 1999 by a Massachusetts Superior Court judge (Rakowsky 1999). In a deal between defense lawyers and prosecutors, it was determined that she would not have to return to the prison where she had already served eight years. In exchange for her freedom, LeFave agreed to drop her 15-year effort to clear her name of the sexual abuse charges. She also agreed not to make television appearances and not to profit from the case during the 10 years she must remain on probation. After all these years, the controversy remains as to whether child sexual abuse actually took place. Those who feel there was no abuse point to suggestive interviewing of the children, police actions that spread panic among parents, and media sensationalism as responsible for the court convictions (Shalit 1995).

Ritual Sexual Abuse

A controversial issue is the sexual exploitation of children by satanic groups. These stories are very difficult to sort out and the bizarre circumstances surrounding the types of crimes committed—rape, torture, and murder—almost defy description (MacDonald 1995). There is considerable controversy among law enforcement and mental health professionals as to whether and how much ritual sexual abuse actually exists. Some who write on this topic maintain that these experiences are fantasy or delusion; others maintain that ritualized trauma is of such significant proportions that it should be considered a newly identified psychiatric syndrome (Noblitt 1995). Some have said that the reasons these groups can operate so successfully in such secrecy is that adult members must commit a serious crime in order to be admitted into the satanic cult. Reportedly, the commission of a crime serves as a guarantee that participants will not at a later date seek law enforcement assistance if they want to leave the cult. Some who deny the existence of ritual abuse claim that allegations of ritual abuse are concocted by those who are on a "moral crusade" against satanism (Victor 1992).

Edwards (1990) described the signs and symptoms of ritual sexual abuse as panic at the sight of blood, difficulty with menstrual periods, artwork using unusual symbols, and a preoccupation with death and dying and phases of the moon. Fear of the dark, nightmares, eating disorders, self-mutilation, and very negative attitudes toward authority figures may also be symptoms. It has also been noted that victims of ritual abuse have a higher rate of multiple personality disorder, attributable to the severe abuse they have endured (Cozolino 1989; Gould 1992; Young 1993).

Shaffer and Cozolino (1992) interviewed 20 adults in outpatient counseling who described memories of childhood ritual abuse. Respondents reported emotional and physical problems, including eating disorders. Although only one respondent remembered the ritual abuse before entering therapy, respondents reported these experiences had permeated their lives as adults.

An accusation of ritual sexual and other types of abuse is currently unfolding (Parrott 2000). A $400-million lawsuit was filed in 2000 in federal court in Dallas, Texas, by 44 people who were former students at Hare Krishna boarding schools in the United States and India. The attorney who filed the lawsuit against the International Society of Krishna Consciousness stated that the case involved "the most unthinkable abuse and maltreatment of little children we have seen. It includes rape, sexual abuse, physical torture, and emotional terror of children as young as three years of age" (Parrott 2000:A17). A Hare Krishna spokesperson bemoaned the fact that a lawsuit had been filed and acknowledged that abuse had taken place in the boarding schools but that the organization had provided therapy and monetary support for victims.

Weir and Wheatcroft (1995), using a tool for assessing the validity of allegations in ritual sexual abuse cases, found that in only one-quarter of the 20 cases studied were the allegations true. The authors noted that this finding was in strong contrast to their prior clinical experience with cases of other types of sexual abuse, in which the rate of false allegations is significantly lower. While more is becoming known about ritual sexual abuse, the topic will likely continue to be controversial.

Sexual Abuse by Clergy

Although clergy sexual abuse is not a new problem, it is a relatively new area of study. The actual extent of clergy sexual abuse is unknown, but Father Stephen J. Rossetti (1994), a licensed clinical psychologist specializing in child sexual abuse, estimates that 3 to 7 percent of Catholic clergy have had sexual involvement with children. In his work with over 500 clergy in residential treatment for sexual abuse, Hands (1998) found that approximately 10 percent had sexually abused a child and that the majority of victims were adolescent boys. While those clergy offenders who sexually abused adults came from a variety of church denominations and were both single and married, Hands found that those who sexually abused boys were predominantly from the Roman Catholic and Episcopal churches and were unmarried (Wages of Sin 1997). Jenkins's (1995) review found that "by far the largest number of stories have involved the Roman Catholic Church" (106). Since 1985, the Catholic Church has paid $640 million in sexual abuse settlements (Wages of Sin 1997).

Some have acknowledged that churches have been slow to respond to and secretive in dealing with allegations of clergy sexual abuse. The first public case of clergy sexual abuse was brought in 1984 against Father Gilbert Gauthe, a Catholic priest in Louisiana who received a prison sentence of twenty years. This case initiated the precedent that failure to intervene in cases of clergy sexual abuse would result in financial penalties, including compensatory damages and payment for psychotherapy for victims (Jenkins 1995). However, it took until 1993 for the American Bishops of the Roman Catholic Church to convene a committee to publicly investigate the problem of sexual abuse by the clergy (Rossetti 1993, 1994). The secrecy with which sexual abuse by the clergy has been handled can have a severe impact as it erodes the trust parishioners have in the priesthood and the church (Kaiser 1996; Rosetti 1993). A recent book, *The Changing Face of the Priesthood,* by Rev. Donald B. Cozzens, states that "the scandal of clergy misconduct with minors has cast a long shadow on the credibility and authority of priests and bishops" which will remain into the next century (Paulsen 2000:A1).

While the church may be invested in keeping these cases secret, when they do become known, cases of clergy sexual abuse tend to receive considerable media attention. Box 3.5 provides an example of clergy sexual abuse.

Adult Sexual Abuse

Like child sexual abuse, the sexual abuse of adults results in consequences that can last a lifetime. Ideas about sexual assault have changed over time, especially with the relatively recent acknowledgment that marital rape does exist. Also, the meaning of the term *rape* has changed over time. The legal definition, in most states,

---

BOX **3.5**

An Example of Clergy Sexual Abuse

One of the best-known cases of clergy sexual abuse is that of Father James R. Porter, who sexually abused at least 50 boys and girls, and perhaps as many as 100, between 1960 and 1967 in the area of Fall River, Massachusetts. Porter left the priesthood in 1967. One of Father Porter's victims, a private investigator, tracked him down in 1992, only to find James R. Porter living in Minnesota with his wife and four children. His crimes against children while a priest included fondling, masturbation, sex games, and rape. Investigation of the abuses found that other clergy were aware of Porter's sexual abuse of children and that the Catholic Church failed to respond to complaints that were made. Porter pleaded guilty to 41 charges and in 1993 received an 18- to 20-year prison sentence. After serving 6 years in prison, Porter was denied parole in April 2000.

Sources: Linda Matchan. 1992. "Ex-Priest's Accuser Tell of the Damage." *The Boston Globe,* June 8:1, 8. Linda Matchan. 1992. "Diocese Allegedly Was Told of Abuse: Man Says Then Msgr. Medeiros Heard Claim About Priest." *The Boston Globe,* June 10:1, 17. James L. Franklin and Linda Matchan. 1993. "Porter Gets 18–20 Years." *The Boston Globe,* December 7; Metro/Region:1. Johanna Weiss. 2000. "Former Priest Denied Parole in Sex Abuse." *The Boston Globe.* April 8:B3.

is "the penetration of the penis into the vagina under force or the threat of force" (Wiehe 1997:73). The definition of rape has recently been broadened to include any type of sexual activity involving force or threat of force. The issue of consent becomes paramount—rape occurs when the victim does not give consent or cannot give consent. Of course, in cases in which the victim is a child, the child, by definition, cannot give consent.

Wiehe (1997) comments on the importance of the more inclusive definition of rape:

> This broadening of the meaning of the term *rape* has important implications both for the prosecution of perpetrators and for the treatment of sexual abuse survivors. In terms of prosecuting perpetrators, a perpetrator's use of aggression, force, or threats brings his or her behavior into the realm of rape, regardless of the nature of the activity. For example, fondling a victim's genitals can no longer be labeled as less harmful than sexual intercourse (although pregnancy could occur as a result of the latter but not the former) because the consequences are essentially the same: the victim's rights to privacy have been abused by means of an aggressive act. In other words, the victim has been raped. Likewise, the implications for the treatment of sexual abuse are that regardless of the nature of the activity, a victim of sexual abuse is a victim of an aggressive act. (73)

Rape is currently understood as a crime that does not necessarily focus on sex and sexual gratification, but instead on power and exploitation. According to Groth et al. (1997):

> Rape is a pseudo-sexual act, a pattern of sexual behavior that is concerned much more with status, aggression, control, and dominance than with sensual pleasure or sexual satisfaction. It is sexual behavior in the service of nonsexual needs, and in this sense, is clearly sexual deviation. (1240)

Sexual Abuse in the Dating Relationship: Acquaintance and Date Rape

Acquaintance rape is committed by a perpetrator who is not a stranger to the victim (Koss and Cook 1993). Date rape is a specific form of acquaintance rape and involves some level of romantic involvement.

Date and acquaintance rape are concerns for adolescents as well as adults. But, for adolescents, date and acquaintance rape may be even more difficult to recognize and acknowledge because high school students have had less social and dating experience than college students and adults. There may be less clear boundaries of appropriate and inappropriate sexual behavior.

Bergman's (1992) study of dating violence among high school students found that it occurred in long-term relationships, was repeated, and did not cause the termination of the relationship. In his review of the literature, Ferguson (1998) found that researchers generally agree that young people do not define dating violence as a problem. In common with older victims of dating violence, adolescents may not recognize that they are victims of abuse.

While there is controversy over whether men or women commit more dating violence, it is clear that sexual abuse in the dating relationship almost always has a male perpetrator and a female victim. The concept of date rape emerged in the 1980s as a special case of dating violence. It can include being forced to have sex or being afraid to say no to sex (Ferguson 1998). Date rape, perhaps more than other rapes, is not likely to be officially reported. Victims may not recognize the behavior as rape. They can blame themselves for misjudging the character of the perpetrator, may feel too embarrassed, or believe that nothing will come of a legal case (MacDonald 1995).

There is no clear notion of how much date rape exists. In their review of the literature regarding prevalence of sexual assault, including date rape, Lundberg-Love and Geffer (1989) found that studies have reported that as few as 2 percent or as many as 77 percent of women are victimized. Kanin (1984) found that 25 percent of women in the study reported sexual assault—rape or attempted rape. Koss et al. (1987) found that in a sample of 3,187 college women, 27.5 percent had been the victims of rape or attempted rape since the age of fourteen. Eighty-four percent knew the men who raped them. Fifty-seven percent were victims of date rape. Mills and Granoff (1992) found that 28 percent of female college students in their sample has been victims of rape or attempted rape. One-sixth of the male college students admitted to behavior that met the legal definition of sexual assault, while 29 percent admitted to continuing sexual advances after a woman had said no.

Many rapes, far more than come to the attention of law enforcement and the public, occur in fraternities and on college campuses. The research of Martin and Hummer (1989) found that the organization of fraternities contributes to coercive and often violent sex. Fraternities are very concerned with expressions of masculinity and by nature seek to elevate the status of men above that of women. Martin and Hummer state, "In claiming that women are treated by fraternities as commodities, we mean that fraternities knowingly, and intentionally, *use* women for their benefit. Fraternities use women as bait for new members, as servers of brothers' needs, and as sexual prey" (466). The fact that "sticking together" is so important and that there is little oversight by college administrators creates a climate such that rapes can occur with few opportunities for intervention. Colleges are now making a stronger effort to educate students about sexual harassment and sexual assault on campus.

In the 1990s, the use of Rohypnol, the "date rape drug," came to public attention. Currently, Rohypnol is used on many college campuses. The drug is in pill form and can easily be slipped unnoticed into a drink (Hanson and Venturelli 1998). The combination of the drug with the alcohol produces such intense intoxication that after waking from sleep, the victim is unable to remember what has happened. In response to the problem of Rohypnol use, Congress passed the Drug-Induced Rape Prevention and Punishment Act in 1996, making it a federal crime to give someone a controlled substance without his or her knowledge with the intent of committing a violent crime. Under current federal law, a person found guilty can receive up to 20 years in prison and a $250,000 fine (Ray and Ksir 1999).

Spousal Sexual Abuse

While many women fear rape by a stranger, in reality, most sexual abuse of women is committed by current or former male intimate partners (Browne 1997). However, it is only recently that spousal sexual assault, or marital rape, has come to be seen as a legitimate topic for study and intervention. This is clearly tied to the long history of wives being considered the property of their husbands. The feminist movement of the 1970s has had some success in changing laws so that a husband can now be prosecuted for the rape of his wife (Wallace 1996).

In their research, Finkelhor and Yllo (1995) describe a rather blasé attitude toward marital rape: study respondents saw it as a matter of "He wants to. She doesn't. He says, 'That's tough, I'm going to anyway,' and he does" (152). Such attitudes make it difficult for victims to come forward. The shame felt by the victims and the intimidation of the victim by the perpetrator make it even more difficult. Spousal sexual abuse often occurs within the context of a generally abusive and exploitive relationship. Finkelhor and Yllo characterize marital sexual abuse as having little to do with sex and much more to do with "humiliation, degradation, anger, and resentment" (152).

Finkelhor and Yllo (1995) described three types of marital rape. The first type, *battering rape,* occurred in one-half of the marital-rape cases in their study. The rape essentially is a continuation of battering behavior. *Force-only rape* occurs in relationships with little or no other types of violence. Perpetrators use only as much force as needed to get their wives to have sex with them; the purpose was to have sex and not to hurt the woman. *Obsessive rape* involves a preoccupation with sex. It usually includes a desire for unusual sexual activity such as anal intercourse, bondage, and insertion of objects into the vagina.

Same-Sex Sexual Abuse

Less is known about family violence among homosexual couples than among heterosexual couples. Sexual abuse receives even less attention than other forms of same-sex abuse. Same-sex victims of sexual abuse can find it even more difficult to disclose than heterosexual victims because there is little support for the lesbian or gay lifestyle. Sexual abuse can take a number of forms. A lesbian may force her partner into unwanted sexual activity such as fondling, oral sex, or penetration. The perpetrator may force her partner to watch or engage in pornography and/or may make negative comments about her partner's sexual performance (Jackson 1998). Bologna, Waterman, and Dawson (1987) found that 26 percent of lesbian partners had been victims of sexual violence at least once during their relationship. In his review of male-to-male gay domestic violence, Burke (1998) described behaviors including forced sexual activity such as rape or sodomy, assaulting genitals with objects, forced nonmonogamy, and forced sexual contact with animals.

Elder Sexual Abuse

While increasing attention has been given to physical and emotional abuse of the elderly, not much is known about elder sexual abuse. It is, however, likely to go hand-in-hand with physical abuse. Elder sexual abuse refers to "touching or physically forced sexual activities with an older person without consent or understanding" (Hill and Amuwo 1998: 200). A 1999 study of elder abuse in Massachusetts found that sexual abuse accounted for 1 percent (27 cases) of elder abuse reports (Scheible 2000).

Although reports of sexual abuse are relatively rare, there are some rapists who single out the elderly as their victims. For example, in Attleboro, Massachusetts, a 77-year-old woman was raped, beaten, and robbed by a 33-year-old neighbor ("Elderly Woman Raped in Attleboro" 1998). The alleged perpetrator was charged with aggravated rape, sodomy, assault and battery on a person over 65, burglary, and armed robbery.

Parental Sexual Abuse

Literature on sexual abuse of a parent does not appear to exist. When such abuse does occur, it is likely to occur between mother and son. Watkins and Bentovim (1992) caution that although the boy may feel he is the aggressor in sexual activity with his mother, the mother is the one who bears culpability for this form of sexual abuse. The mother is responsible for her son and the fact that she has more sexual experience means the accountability rests with her.

Child Sexual Abuse and Adult Rape: A Comparison

Finkelhor (1979) described the similarities and differences between sexual child abuse and rape. There are a number of similarities. Both are sex crimes involving the genitals of the offender or the victim. Victims experience a trauma unique to sexual offenses. In addition to the trauma of their victimization, they may feel humiliation and shame, as though they are responsible for bringing the victimization on themselves. Unfortunately, others may also hold this view. Survivors of both rape and child sexual abuse can have difficulty with subsequent sexual adjustment. Although Finkelhor (1979) stated that "The offenders are almost all men" (3), more recent research shows that female perpetrators may be more common than currently acknowledged. Finkelhor pointed out that, historically, both types of offenses were treated similarly—denying the importance of the occurrences and blaming the victim.

Finkelhor (1979) also pointed out the major differences between child sexual abuse and rape. Both females and males are the victims of child sexual abuse, while the vast majority of rape victims tend to be female. (Men can be raped—this is known to be a significant problem among prison inmates.) The pattern of sexual abuse is such that the relationship between the perpetrator and the victim tends to be much closer than in rape. Although more recent research shows that date rape and acquaintance rape are not uncommon, rape is more likely to be committed by a stranger than is sexual abuse. Sexual abuse of children is more likely than rape to occur over a period of time and to constitute a pattern of behavior. In contrast, rape, with the exception of marital rape, is likely to occur only once. Sexual abuse of children usually involves less physical force than does rape. Although victims of child sexual abuse do endure coercion, such abuse is not likely to involve the depth of coercion or the use of weapons often involved in rape. Sexual abuse of children often involves exhibition and touching and does not necessarily include sexual intercourse. The legal definition of rape is typically completed intercourse or attempted intercourse.

Finkelhor (1979) further noted that sexual abuse of children and rape are likely to receive different professional interventions. Sexual abuse, if detected, is more likely to receive a response from the state child welfare organization, while rape is more likely to receive a law enforcement and legal response. Since the publication of Finkelhor's book (1979), the legal response to sexual abuse of children has improved, although the capacity of the criminal justice system to respond to sexual abuse remains a murky issue.

Deviant and Criminal Consequences of Sexual Abuse

What are the effects of sexual abuse on the victim? How can the complexities of abuse and the consequences be understood by the victim and others? These are complex questions with no clear and simple answers. Much more attention must be paid to sorting out the relationships between sexual abuse and deviant and criminal behavior.

Finkelhor and Browne (1985) formulated a model for understanding how and why sexual abuse can result in trauma for the child. They describe *traumagenic dynamics*—the interaction of four factors that can cause the major trauma often associated with child sexual abuse: traumatic sexualization, betrayal, powerlessness, and stigmatization. *Traumatic sexualization* refers to the process by which the child's normal sexual development becomes distorted as a result of the abuse. *Betrayal* refers to the child's discovery that a person on whom she has been dependent has actually done her harm. *Powerlessness* is the process by which the child feels no control over his life. *Stigmatization* focuses on the shame, guilt, and feelings of worthlessness that the child may endure and that may become part of her self-image. Traumagenic dynamics offers an important framework for understanding the personal experience of child sexual abuse. It also serves both as a conceptual framework for research on child sexual abuse and as a framework that clinicians can use in their treatment of victims. The work of Finkelhor will be examined in more detail in Chapter 5.

Because sexual abuse does not always or even frequently come to official attention, much remains to be known about perpetrators. Many studies tend to focus on clinical samples, or incarcerated offenders, and there is a need to examine characteristics of perpetrators who do not get caught (Fromuth et al. 1991).

Consequences of Victimization

It can be difficult to measure the effects of child sexual abuse because the problems often associated with it may be experienced by children who also have other kinds of family or personal problems (Knudsen 1992). There is, however, clear agreement among researchers and clinicians that the effects of victimization can permeate an individual's life. Bass (1995) gives a picture of the enormity of the consequences of sexual abuse, which are likely to color a child's entire life:

> When a man sexually uses a child, he is giving that child a strong message about her world: He is telling her that she is important because of her sexuality, that men want sex from girls, and that relationships are insufficient without sex. He is telling her that she can use her sexuality as a way to get the attention and affection she genuinely needs, that sex is a tool. When he tells her not to tell, she learns there is something about sex that is shameful and bad; and that she, because she is a part of it, is shameful and bad; and that he, because he is a part of it, is shameful and bad. She learns that the world is full of sex and is shameful and bad and not to be trusted, that even those entrusted with her care will betray her; that she will betray herself. (116)

Short-Term Consequences of Child Sexual Abuse. The consequences of child sexual abuse for the victim can depend on a variety of factors (Gomes-Schwartz et al. 1990; Lam 1998). It may depend on the age of the child and the length of time over which the abuse took place. It may depend on the victim's relationship to the perpetrator, the age difference between the two, and the type of sexual abuse that occurred. For instance, it is not surprising that forced intercourse can be more damaging to a child than exhibitionism; the degree of physical violence used may be more compelling than the sex act itself. The reactions of others when the abuse is disclosed can also have a bearing on the child's adjustment: Those who have family support tend to do better. Box 3.6 reviews the factors that can affect a child's adjustment after disclosure.

In their study of the initial effects of sexual abuse, Gomes-Schwartz et al. (1990) found that the victim's age at the onset of sexual abuse and the duration of abuse had no bearing on the effects the experience had on the child. Findings supported the idea that sexual abuse by someone in a parental role is more damaging than other types of sexual abuse. They also found that children who had not told about the sexual abuse before entering a treatment program were less anxious and hostile than those who had disclosed. This suggests that disclosure does not necessarily provide relief for the child and indeed may be very stressful. The concern expressed by the mother for her child was not related to the level of distress experienced by the victim. However, if the mother expressed anger toward the

---

BOX 3.6

Adjustment after the Disclosure of Sexual Abuse

Factors affecting a child's adjustment after sexual abuse is disclosed:

1. The nature and duration of the relationship of the victim to the offender
2. The duration of the sexual abuse activities
3. The type of sexual abuse activities imposed upon the victim (i.e., exhibitionism or more extreme behaviors such as sexual intercourse)
4. The degree of aggression or severity of force the child endured
5. The victim's developmental state or maturity at onset of the sexual abuse
6. The age difference between the victim and the offender (the greater the age difference, the greater the trauma)
7. The sophistication of the child about sexual abuse
8. The environment or context of the sexual abuse
9. The degree of the victim's participation
10. The gender of the victim and perpetrator
11. The degree of support from the family and professionals on disclosure of the sexual abuse

Source: Judy N. Lam. 1998. "Child Sexual Abuse." Pp. 25–55 in *Violence in Intimate Relationships: Examining Sociological and Psychological Issues,* Nicky Ali Jackson and Gisele Casanova Oates, eds. Boston, MA: Butterworth-Heinemann.

---

child, the child was likely to have lower self-esteem and exhibit behavioral problems.

Children who are victimized can be overwhelmed by the emotions accompanying the sexual abuse: fear, anger, isolation, sadness, guilt, confusion, and shame (Child Sexual Abuse 1998). Teenagers with a history of sexual abuse and a parent with an alcohol problem show higher rates of substance abuse, eating disorders, pregnancy risk, and suicidal ideation (Chandy, Blum, and Resnick 1996). Luster and Small (1997) looked at the effect of sexual abuse on teenage involvement in binge drinking and thoughts of suicide. Adolescents who had been both physically and sexually abused had more problems than those who experienced just one kind of abuse. Intense parental monitoring and support reduced problem outcomes among sexually abused adolescents.

A sample of 745 students age 12 to 19 who reported a history of sexual abuse was compared with 745 students with no history of sexual abuse (Garneski and Deikstra 1997). A significantly larger proportion of students with a sexual abuse history reported more emotional problems, aggressive/criminal behaviors, substance abuse, and suicide. Sexually abused boys had more combinations of problems. The strongest combination was that of emotional problems and suicidal thoughts—this combination occurred 20 times more often among sexually abused boys than among nonsexually abused boys.

A study of the impact of sexual abuse on adoption found that those children who experienced sexual abuse were more likely to have behavioral problems and emotional attachment problems than the comparison group (Smith and Howard 1994). Children who had been sexually abused had more frequent moves while in placement and were more likely to experience the disruption of the adoption.

Not surprisingly, young female victims of sexual abuse are at higher risk of pregnancy (Elders and Albert 1998) than their peers. Sexual abuse contributes to adolescent pregnancy by increasing the probability that adolescents will have intercourse earlier and with more partners and decreasing the likelihood that birth control will be used (Stock et al. 1997). Sexually abused pregnant adolescents are also more likely than nonabused pregnant adolescents to experience thoughts of suicide (Elders and Albert 1998).

Rape by acquaintances, dates, or relatives can have more negative effects than rape by a stranger (Karp et al. 1995). For victims of all types of rape, the immediate effects can include crying, anxiety, sadness, moodiness, fear, guilt, shock, and humiliation (Gilmartin 1994). Physical symptoms can include abdominal pain or discomfort, disrupted sleep, headaches, and muscular tension. Behavioral changes can include difficulty in maintaining obligations (indicated, for instance, by absenteeism from work or school) and excessive time spent either alone or with others. Interpersonal problems can include difficulty trusting others. Rape victims may also undergo a change in their self-image, experiencing problems especially with self-esteem and self-blame. They may also have difficulty in sexual functioning and experience less interest in sex and less sexual satisfaction.

Long-Term Consequences of Sexual Abuse. A history of child sexual abuse places victims at risk for a range of difficulties later in life, including emotional and behavioral problems, low self-esteem, sexual dysfunction, substance abuse, eating disorders, involvement in further abusive relationships, depression, and suicide (Beitchman et al. 1992; Browne and Finkelhor 1986; Finkelhor 1984; Langeland and Hartgers 1998; Romans et al. 1995; Wonderlich et al. 1997). A study of those with borderline personality disorder found that sexual abuse may be a strong determinant in the development of the disorder (Silk et al. 1995). Feinauer et al. (1996) found that women whose childhood sexual abuse was more frequent and occurred over a longer period of time had more symptoms of emotional trauma. In a sample of 45 women who experienced childhood sexual abuse, 86.7 percent met the *Diagnostic and Statistical Manual* (DSM III-R) criteria for posttraumatic stress disorder (Rodriguez et al. 1997). This compared with 19.4 percent of women who were in outpatient treatment for relationship problems but had no history of sexual abuse. Eighty-nine percent of the sexually abused women reported childhood physical abuse. There is also an association between childhood sexual abuse and chronic physical problems in adult women (Farley and Keaney 1997).

Substance abuse is also associated with a history of child sexual abuse, especially for women. A 1991 study of 1,099 women found that experiencing sexual abuse as a child was linked with substance abuse problems, sexual dysfunction, and depression (Wilsnak et al. 1997). Victims started having consensual sex at an earlier age. Substance abusing women in recovery with a history of sexual abuse may be at greater risk of relapse than those without a history of sexual trauma (Wadsworth, Spampnet, and Halbrook 1995). The relationship between sexual abuse and substance abuse is explored in more detail in Chapter 10.

For rape survivors, psychological problems are the most frequent long-term consequences (Gilmartin 1994). Anger, hostility, depression, phobias, nightmares, and suicidal ideation may persist. Physical complaints may continue over a period of time and can include fatigue and pain during intercourse. Survivors of rape may experience difficulties in maintaining intimate relationships and long-term issues with trust. They may experience confusion and a distorted view of the world. The loss of a sense of security in the world and a strong sense of vulnerability may occur. Rape survivors also tend to have more weight problems and more substance abuse problems (Karp et al. 1995). Burgess and Holmstrom (1974, 1979) described a *Rape Trauma Syndrome*; their book is now considered a classic work in the field. Initially, the woman experiences the psychological and physical symptoms described previously and then over time deals with the reorganization of her disrupted life.

There is also an association between sexual assault and pornography. In the late 1970s, there was a rapid increase in the amount of child pornography produced (Finkelhor 1984). In the age of the Internet, child pornography is flourishing. Pedophiles are increasingly luring children through chat rooms. According to the U.S. Customs Service, there were 35 convictions in 1995 for possession of child pornography used on the Internet. During the first eight months of 1998, there were 189 convictions (Heslam 1998). Box 3.7 gives an illustration of the international scope of pornography on the Internet. In 2000 the U.S. Department of Justice

---

BOX **3.7**

Child Pornography, the Government, and the Internet

Hard-core pornography is an international problem and can involve high-ranking government officials. Pornography on computer drives and diskettes was seized from an apartment in Zandvoort, Netherlands. The resident, a 49-year-old convicted pedophile, was shot to death in June 1998, reportedly by a rival gang member. Confiscated materials included digital photos and videos of children as young as 12 months old being raped and sodomized.

An official with the Justice Ministry, the organization charged with investigating the child pornography case, was terminated for downloading child pornography from his office computer for his personal use.

Authorities claimed that few of the seized materials were produced in the Netherlands. They probably came from central and eastern Europe and were originally posted on the World Wide Web in the United States.

Source: Associated Press. 1998. "Scandal Grips Netherlands," *The Boston Sunday Globe,* August 2:A29.

Bureau of Justice Statistics developed a statistical program to track the types, amounts, and consequences of cybercrime, including pornography (Statistics at a Glance 2000).

Another area of research is the complex relationship between the person the victim "blames" or holds responsible for the sexual abuse and subsequent adjustment in adulthood. McMillen and Zuravin (1997) found that women who had high levels of self-blame for their sexual abuse tended to have lower self-esteem, less comfort with closeness to others, and more relationship anxiety. Those women with high levels of blaming the family for their sexual abuse had more relationship anxiety and an increased likelihood of having a maltreated child. Placing the blame for the sexual abuse on the perpetrator was not associated with adult adjustment variables.

Consequences for Male Victims. Less is known about the consequences for male victims of sexual abuse than for female victims. A problem unique to male victims that is known concerns the fact that images of masculinity in U.S. culture can compound the consequences of victimization. Watkins and Bentovim (1992) reviewed the work of Rogers and Terry (1984) on the consequences of victimization for boys and found that the most common reaction of boys is to try to reassert their masculinity, often inappropriately. This behavior can take the form of disobedience, hostile attitude, aggression, fighting, and destructiveness. Boy victims may experience confusion concerning their sexual identity: For instance, a boy may see himself as being selected for victimization because the perpetrator thought him effeminate. If the boy does not physically resist the abuse, he may think of himself as not masculine. The male victim may find that he experienced sexual arousal, which conflicts with his sexual identity and may lead him to define himself as homosexual. A less common reaction is the "recapitulation of the victimizing experience." This means that the boy replays the victimization with himself as the perpetrator. Finkelhor (1984) found that boys who were victimized by "much older men were over four times more likely to be engaged in homosexual activity than were nonvictims" (195). Luster and Small (1997) found that males who had been or were being sexually abused had greater suicidal ideation than did female abuse victims.

Delinquency and Criminality. Childhood abuse and neglect have a significant impact on the likelihood of being arrested for delinquency, adult criminality, and violence, although the relationship is quite complex. Maxfield and Widom (1996) found that childhood victims of abuse/neglect were more likely than controls to have nontraffic juvenile or adult arrests (49 percent vs. 38 percent). They were more likely to have arrests for violent crimes (18 percent vs. 14 percent), even controlling for age, race, and sex.

One of the most difficult research and policy issues to grapple with is the question of whether having been sexually victimized as a child sets the scene for becoming a sexual offender in adolescence or adulthood. Becker (1988) found that in a sample of juvenile sex offenders, 19 percent indicated during an initial interview that they were victims of sexual abuse. Eleven percent had been victimized by strangers and 89 percent by people they knew.

There is some evidence that adult perpetrators of child sexual abuse usually begin their activity during adolescence (Longo and Groth 1983; Watkins and Bentovim 1992). Abel and colleagues (1987) found that 59 percent of adult sex offenders in one study began offending in their adolescent years. In another sample, Sansonnet-Hayden and colleagues (1987) reported that three out of six abused boys later became perpetrators themselves.

There is also evidence that some abuse victims may become perpetrators at very early ages. Friedrich, Beilke, and Urquiza (1988) reported that 13 percent (4) of 31 boys in one study who were victims of sexual abuse became perpetrators themselves by the age of 8. Chasnoff and colleagues (1986) reported on 3 baby boys whose victimization stopped at 4, 9, and 18 months, respectively. Two of these boys were sexually molesting other children before they were three years old.

In almost all areas of family violence, it has been debated whether being a victim of one form of abuse will lead to victimizing others in the same way. This concern is alive and well when it comes to child sexual abuse. While Finkelhor (1986) and Straus and Gelles (1988) caution that this is not inevitable—victims do not have to become abusers themselves—there does seem to be compelling evidence of a relationship. There are similarities between the experiences of those victimized by childhood sexual abuse and the forms their own adult perpetration of sexual abuse takes (Romano and DeLuca 1997). However, we must keep in mind that the majority of male sexual abuse victims do not become perpetrators (Becker 1988). It is also true that abusers are not necessarily abuse victims (Watkins and Bentovim 1992).

Juvenile sex offenders are more likely to have been victims of physical and sexual abuse than nonoffenders (Zgourides, Monto, and Harris 1997). In another study, juvenile sex offenders who have been arrested were more likely to report sexual victimization by a male perpetrator (Spaccarelli et al. 1997). In comparing a group of juvenile sex offenders with a low-violence control group, Spaccarelli et al. (1997) found that sex offenders experienced more exposure to physical abuse, family violence involving weapons, greater acceptance of physical and sexual aggression, and responded to stress with more aggressive control-seeking behavior.

In a study of 42 male sex offenders it was found that sex offenders are likely to have been victims of sexual abuse as children. The abuse is likely to have been severe and to have been perpetrated by several offenders (Romano and DeLuca 1997).

The relationship between physical and sexual abuse among females and their delinquent behavior is strong. Female runaways are especially prone to sexual abuse. Until recently, the juvenile justice system has ignored complaints of sexual abuse (Chesney-Lind and Shelden 1998). Girls who were sexually abused were found to be significantly more likely to be substance abusers and to engage in petty theft and prostitution. This pattern was not found among male runaways (McCormack, Janus, and Burgess 1986).

Child sexual abuse is also associated with the most extreme forms of criminal behavior. As discussed in the previous chapter, serial killers have often been victims of childhood physical abuse and also victims of sexual abuse. Box 3.8 gives a description of one of the most notorious serial killers in the world.

To further our understanding of child sexual abuse, its prevalence and its effects, much more work needs to be done. Some of the problems in research methodology could be solved by using standardized research designs, large representative samples, comparison groups, and the use of agreed-upon definitions of sexual abuse, as well as better record keeping (Browne and Finkelhor 1986; Lam 1998).

Alternative Views of Child Sexual Abuse

There are individuals and organizations that actually seek to promote sexual relations between adults and children. Richard A. Gardner (1992), a prominent child psychiatrist, described what he claims are the positive aspects of pedophilia. According to Gardner, children who become sexually active at an early age are likely to maintain an active sex life. This will increase the length of time they can have children and increase the likelihood they will have children. Therefore, according to Gardner, pedophilia serves the purpose of procreation (Dallam 1998).

The North American Man/Boy Love Association (NAMBLA), an organization devoted to sexual activity between boys and adult males, was formed in 1978. The NAMBLA website describes the organization as a "political, civil rights, and educational organization." Their mission is to "provide factual information and help educate society about the positive and beneficial nature of man/boy love." While claiming to condemn sexual abuse and coercive sex, NAMBLA claims that male children are capable of appropriate decision making regarding sexual relationships

BOX **3.8**

The Monster of the Andes

Pedro Alonso Lopez, known as the "monster of the Andes," was one of the most notorious serial killers in the world. He was born in Colombia, South America. His early family life was characterized by poverty, abuse, and neglect. His mother, a prostitute, kicked him out of the house for fondling his younger sister. Lopez was 8 years old at the time. He was then sodomized by a pedophile. At age 18, while incarcerated, Lopez was gang raped. He killed 3 of his attackers. Upon his release from prison, Lopez began a spree of killing girls. By 1978 he had murdered 100 girls in Peru. Very likely Lopz was responsible for the deaths of over 300 victims.

Source: Internet Crime Archives. (www http://www.mayhem.net/crime/serial.html).

with adult males. Not surprisingly, NAMBLA is strongly opposed to age-of-consent laws.

NAMBLA made the news in 2000 in Massachusetts when the organization was sued by the parents of a 10-year-old boy murdered by two men (Rakowsky 2000). One of the men serving a life sentence for the torture and murder of Jeffrey Curley was a member of NAMBLA. The $200 million suit alleges that the perpetrator was a heterosexual before joining NAMBLA in 1997 and that he then became obsessed with raping boys. The suit alleges that the perpetrator accessed the NAMBLA website just before he killed Curley in October of 1997.

What is so bad about child sexual abuse? Why do the vast majority of us see sexual abuse as such abhorrent behavior? Finkelhor (1984) offers the following insight:

> The basic proposition here is that adult-child sex is wrong because the fundamental conditions of consent cannot prevail in the relationship between an adult and a child. The proposition seems to be an important supplement to other arguments, particularly the argument that such acts are wrong solely because they harm the child. It adds a moral dimension to the empirical one. Thus even if someone could demonstrate many cases where children were not harmed by such experiences, one could still argue that the experiences were wrong because the child could not consent. The wrongness is not contingent upon proof of a harmful outcome. (18)

Physical and Sexual Abuse: A Comparison

Finkelhor (1979) describes the similarities and differences between physical and sexual abuse. He sees that some of the characteristics of sexual abuse that distinguish it from rape make it similar to physical abuse. Sexual abuse is at the juncture of physical abuse and rape. Both are very serious and one should not be considered more serious than the other. They are similar in that the children are victimized by adults who are responsible for them. Both kinds of abusive relationships can continue over many years. Both fall into the category of child protection, involving an agency that is charged with protecting the child.

There are also a number of important differences between physical and sexual abuse. Physical and sexual abuse may not occur at the same time and there are different dynamics in each type of abuse. In his more recent work, Finkelhor (1984) finds that physical and sexual abuse are not as closely related as some think. In his sample, sexually abused girls did not report greater levels of violence within the families than nonvictimized girls. This is an area in which there is not general agreement among researchers. Although there is little clinical or research evidence that addresses concurrent physical and sexual abuse (Stermac, Davidson, and Sheridan 1995), more recent findings are that physical and sexual abuse *are* related. For example, Rodriguez et al. (1997) found that 89 percent of women who were sexually abused also were victims of childhood physical abuse. In a comparison of incest offenders with non–sex offenders, Stermac et al. (1995) found that both groups utilized physical violence toward partners and children in the home. (See Stermac et al. [1995] for a continued discussion of the association between physical and sexual abuse.)

The trauma of each type of abuse is different: Sexual abuse is primarily psychological trauma while physical abuse is physically damaging and sometimes life-threatening. There certainly are cases where a child endures physical damage to the genital area or a sexually transmitted disease; however, the lives of most sexual abuse victims are not in danger. It also may be the case that the victim is threatened with physical harm, or harm to another family member, if the sexual abuse is disclosed.

Finkelhor (1979) describes different motivations for each type of abuse. Sexual abuse may or may not be hostile; it may emerge from a desire for sexual gratification. Physical abuse is motivated by the desire to harm the child, at least during the time it occurs. Social attitudes toward each type of abuse are different. Society is much more intolerant of sexual abuse while violence is much more acceptable, and for some, physical discipline is considered an appropriate part of parenting.

There are differences in vulnerability as well. Preadolescents (8–12) are those most vulnerable to sexual abuse while younger children are the most vulnerable to physical abuse. This, of course, does not mean physical and sexual abuse cannot occur over the entire range of childhood and adolescence.

Another difference may be in the reactions of health professionals. Finkelhor (1984) suggests that sexual abuse does not get the same attention as physical abuse from physicians. One reason is the emotionalism attached to sexual abuse, another is that victims may not show physical trauma from the abuse. Since physicians are trained to deal with physical problems, sexual abuse falls outside their field of interest. While physicians have played an important role in bringing attention to physical abuse, this has not happened in the area of sexual abuse. Social workers and psychologists are the professionals much more likely to work in this area.

Summary

Sexual abuse is the most difficult of all forms of abuse to acknowledge. It can be physical, verbal, or emotional in nature. There is much secrecy surrounding both child and adult sexual abuse. Secrecy regarding sexual abuse impedes our ability to learn more about victims and perpetrators and therefore impedes our ability to prevent sexual abuse.

Pedophilia is the term used to refer to sexual activity between an adult and child. *Incest* is the term used when the sexual activity takes place within the family and is also referred to as *intrafamilial abuse*. Sexual abuse by someone outside of the family is called *extrafamilial abuse*.

The majority of child sexual abuse is perpetrated by men against girls with stepfathers being the most likely perpetrators. Women who are perpetrators of sexual abuse and boys who are victims of sexual abuse have been given little research attention until recently. Sexual abuse of siblings is probably the most common form of sexual abuse. Ritual sexual abuse of children is a very controversial topic—some see ritual sexual abuse as nonexistent while others see it as a major problem. But most experts agree that sexual abuse of children by day care providers and by the clergy are important areas of concern.

Adult sexual abuse includes rape by a stranger, acquaintance or date rape, partner or spousal sexual abuse, and elder sexual abuse. Same-sex sexual abuse has recently started to receive more professional attention.

Short-term consequences of child sexual abuse include fear, anger, isolation, confusion, guilt, self-blame, shame, and early pregnancy. Long-term consequences of child sexual abuse are very powerful. A sexual abuse history can be associated with psychological and physical problems, depression, substance abuse, sexual dysfunction, eating disorders, suicide, and aggressive/criminal behaviors. For adults who are victims of sexual abuse, short-term consequences can include anger, depression, suicidal ideation, nightmares, sexual dysfunction, and physical problems. Long-term consequences include weight problems and substance abuse.

Child sexual abuse is associated with perpetrating sexually abusive behavior. But it is important to note that most individuals who have been sexually abused do not go on to become perpetrators of sexual abuse.

Study Questions

1. Why is it so difficult to disclose sexual abuse?

2. What are the short-term consequences of suffering child sexual abuse?

3. What are the long-term consequences of suffering child sexual abuse?

4. What characteristics do child sexual abuse and adult sexual abuse have in common?

5. Why is it difficult to acknowledge that women can be perpetrators of sexual abuse?

6. What are the factors that make sexual abuse by the clergy difficult to acknowledge?

7. Compare and contrast child sexual abuse with adult sexual abuse.

8. What are the similarities and differences between physical and sexual abuse?

REFERENCES

Abel, G. G., J. V. Becker, M. Mittelman, J. Cunningham-Rathier, J. Rouleau, and W. Murphy. 1987. "Self-Reported Sex Crimes in Nonincarcerated Paraphilias." *Journal of Interpersonal Violence.* 2:3–25.

American Psychiatric Association. 1994. *Diagnostic and Statistical Manual of Mental Disorders,* 4th ed. Washington, DC: Author.

Araji, Sharon and David Finkelhor. 1986. "Abusers: A Review of the Research." Pp. 60–88 in *A Sourcebook on Child Sexual Abuse,* David Finkelhor, ed. Beverly Hills, CA: Sage Publications.

Bachmann, K. M., F. Moggi, and F. Stirnemann-Lewis. 1994. "Mother-Son Incest and Its Long-Term Consequences: A Neglected Phenomenon in Psychiatric Practice." *Journal of Nervous and Mental Diseases.* 182:723–25.

Bass, Ellen. 1995. "Child Sexual Abuse." Pp. 115–18 in *Rape and Society,* Patricia Searles and Ronald J. Berger, eds. Boulder, CO: Westview Press.

Becker, Judith V. 1988. "The Effects of Child Sexual Abuse on Adolescent Sexual Offenders." Pp. 193–207 in *Lasting Effects of Child Sexual Abuse,* Gail Elizabeth Wyatt and Gloria Johnson Powell, eds. Newbury Park, CA: Sage Publications.

Beitchman, J. H., K. J. Zucker, J. E. Hood, G. A. da Costa, D. Akman, and E. Cassavia, 1992. "A Review of the Long-Term Effects of Child Sexual Abuse." *Child Abuse and Neglect.* 16:101–17.

Bergman, L. 1992. "Dating Violence Among High School Students." *Social Work.* 37:21–7.

Bologna, M. J., C. K. Waterman and L. J. Dawson. 1987. "Violence in Gay Male and Lesbian Relationships: Implications for Practitioners and Policy Makers." Paper presented at the Third National Conference for Family Violence Researchers, Durham, NH.

Browne, Angela. 1997. "Violence in Marriage: Until Death Do Us Part?" Pp. 48–69 in *Violence Between Intimate Partners: Patterns, Causes, and Effects,* Albert P. Cardarelli, ed. Needham Heights, MA: Allyn and Bacon.

Browne, Angela and David Finkelhor. 1986. "Impact of Sexual Abuse: A Review of the Research." *Psychological Bulletin.* 99:66–77.

Burgess, Ann Wolbert and Lynda Lytle Holmstrom. 1974. "Rape Trauma Syndrome." *American Journal of Psychiatry.* 131:981–86.

———. 1979. *Rape: Crisis and Recovery.* Bowie, MD: Robert J. Brady.

Burke, Tod W. 1998. "Male-to-Male Gay Domestic Violence: The Dark Closet." Pp. 161–79 in *Violence in Intimate Relationships: Examining Sociological and Psychological Issues,* Nicky Ali Jackson and Gisele Casanova Oates, eds. Boston, MA: Butterworth-Heinemann.

Cafaro, John V. and Allison Conn-Caffaro. 1998. *Sibling Abuse Trauma: Assessment and Intervention Strategies for Children, Families, and Adults.* Binghamton, NY: The Haworth Maltreatment and Trauma Press.

Chandy, Joseph M., Robert W. Blum, and Michael D. Resnick. 1996. "History of Sexual Abuse and Parental Alcohol Misuse: Risk, Outcomes and Protective Factors in Adolescents." *Child and Adolescent Social Work Journal.* 13:411–34.

Chasnoff, M. D., W. J. Burns, S. H. Schnoll, K. Burns, G. Chisum, and K. Kyle-Spore. 1986. "Maternal-Neonatal Incest." *American Journal of Orthopsychiatry.* 56:577–80.

Chesney-Lind, Meda and Randall G. Sheldon. 1998. *Girls, Delinquency, and Juvenile Justice,* 2nd edition. Belmont, CA: Wadsworth.

Child Sexual Abuse. 1998. The Sexual Assault Crisis Center of Knoxville, Tennessee. (WWW http://www.cs.utk.edu/~bartley/sacc/childabuse.html).

Cozolino, Louis J. 1989. "The Ritual Abuse of Children: Implications for Clinical Practice and Research." *Journal of Sex Research.* 26:131–38.

Dallam, Stephanie J. 1998. "Dr. Richard Gardner: A Review of His Theories and Opinions on Atypical Sexuality, Pedophilia, and Treatment Issues." *Treating Abuse Today.* 8:15–23 (WWW http://idealist.com/tat/subscribe.shtml).

De Jong, A. R. 1989. "Sexual Interaction Among Siblings and Cousins: Experimentation or Exploitation?" *Child Abuse and Neglect.* 13:271–79.

Dimock, P. T. 1988. "Adult Males Sexually Abused as Children." *Journal of Interpersonal Violence.* 3:203–21.

"Editorial Criticizes SJC on Fells Acre Case Ruling." 1999. *The Boston Globe,* September 14, 1999, p. B4.

"Elderly Woman Raped in Attleboro." 1998. *The Boston Globe,* February 1, B, 3:1.

Elders, M. Joycelyn and Alexa E. Albert. 1998. "Adolescent Pregnancy and Sexual Abuse." *Journal of the American Medical Association.* 280:648–49.

Elliott, Michelle. 1993. "What Survivors Tell Us—An Overview." Pp. 5–13 in *Female Sexual Abuse of Children,* Michelle Elliott, ed. NY: The Guilford Press.

Faller, Kathleen Coulborn. 1990. *Understanding Child Sexual Maltreatment.* Newbury Park, CA: Sage Publications.

Farley, Melissa, and Joanne Keaney. 1997. "Physical Symptoms, Somatization, and Dissociation in Women Survivors of Childhood Sexual Assault." *Women and Health.* 25:33–45.

Feinhauer, Leslie L., Jill Mitchell, James M. Harper, and Skip Dane. 1996. "The Impact of Hardiness and Severity of Childhood Sexual Abuse on Adult Adjustment." *The American Journal of Family Therapy.* 24:206–14.

Ferguson, Carroy U. 1998. "Dating Violence as a Social Phenomenon." Pp. 83–118 in *Violence in Intimate Relationships: Examining Sociological and Psychological Issues,* Nicky Ali Jackson and Gisele Casanova Oates, eds. Boston, MA: Butterworth-Heinemann.

Fergusson, David M., Michael T. Lynskey, and L. John Horwood. 1996. "Prevalence of Sexual Abuse and Factors Associated with Sexual Abuse." *Journal of the American Academy of Child and Adolescent Psychiatry.* 35:1355–56.

Finkelhor, David. 1979. *Sexually Victimized Children.* NY: The Free Press.

———. 1980. "Sex Among Siblings: A Survey of Prevalence, Variety, and Effects." *Archives of Sexual Behavior.* 171–93.

———. 1984. *Child Sexual Abuse: New Theory and Research.* NY: The Free Press.

———. 1986. *A Sourcebook on Child Sexual Abuse.* Newbury Park, CA: Sage Publications.

———. 1998. "Improving Research, Policy, and Practice to Understand Child Sexual Abuse." *JAMA: Journal of the American Medical Association.* 280:1864–65.

Finkelhor, David and L. Baron. 1986. "Risk Factors for Child Sexual Abuse." *Journal of Interpersonal Violence.* 1:43–71.

Finklehor, David and Angela Browne. 1985. "The Traumatic Impact of Child Sexual Abuse: A Conceptualization." *American Journal of Orthopsychiatry.* 55:530–49.

Finkelhor, David, Gerard Hotaling, I. A. Lewis, and C. Smith. 1990. "Sexual Abuse in a National Survey of Adult Men and Women: Prevalence, Characteristics, and Risk Factors." *Child Abuse and Neglect.* 14–19-28.

Finkelhor, David, Linda Williams, and Nanci Burns. 1988. *Nursery Crimes: Sexual Abuse in Day Care.* Newbury Park, CA: Sage Publications.

Finkelhor, David and Kersti Yllo. 1995. "Types of Marital Rape." Pp. 152–59 in *Rape and Society: Readings on the Problem of Sexual Assault.* Patricia Searles and Ronald J. Berger. Boulder, CO: Westview Press.

Fromuth, Mary Ellen, B. R. Burkhart, and Catherine Webb Jones. 1991. "Hidden Child Molestation: An Investigation of Adolescent Perpetrators in a Nonclinical Sample." *Journal of Interpersonal Violence.* 6:37.

Fromuth, Mary Ellen and Victoria E. Conn. 1997. "Hidden Perpetrators: Sexual Molestation in a Nonclinical Sample of College Women." *Journal of Interpersonal Violence.* 12:456–65.

Gardner, Richard A. 1992. *True and False Accusations of Child Sexual Abuse.* Cresskill, NJ: Creative Therapeutics.

Garneski, Nadia and Rene F. W. Deikstra. 1997. "Child Sexual Abuse and Emotional and Behavioral Problems in Adolescence: Gender Differences." *Journal of the American Academy of Child and Adolescent Psychiatry.* 36:323–40.

Gilmartin, Pat. 1994. *Rape, Incest, and Child Sexual Abuse: Consequences and Recovery.* NY: Garland Publishing, Inc.

Gomes-Schwartz, Beverly, Jonathan M. Horowitz, and Albert P. Cardarelli. 1990. *Child Sexual Abuse: The Initial Effects.* Newbury Park, CA: Sage Publications.

Gould, Catherine. 1992. "Ritual Abuse, Multiplicity, and Mind-Control." *Journal of Psychology and Theology.* 20:194–96.

Groth, A. Nicholas, Ann Wolbert Burgess, and Lynda Lytle Holmstrom. 1977. "Rape: Power, Anger and Sexuality." *American Journal of Psychiatry.* 134:1239–43.

Hands, Donald R. 1998. "Cognitive Distortions of Clergy Sex Offenders." *The Association for the Treatment of Sexual Abusers,* (Spring), 9.

Hanson, Glenn and Peter Venturelli. 1998. *Drugs and Society,* 5th ed. Boston, MA: Jones and Bartlett Publishers.

Heslam, Jessica. 1998. "Child Pornographers Increasingly Using the Internet." *The Patriot Ledger.* September 4, 1, 11.

Hill, Jacqueline B. and Shaffdeen A. Amuwo. 1998. "Understanding Elder Abuse and Neglect." Pp. 195–223 in *Violence in Intimate Relationships: Examining Sociological and Psychological Issues,* Nicky Ali Jackson and Gisele Casanova Oates, eds. Boston, MA: Butterworth-Heinemann.

Holmes, William C. and Gail B. Slap. 1998. "Sexual Abuse of Boys: Definition, Prevalence, Correlates, Sequelae, and Management." *JAMA: Journal of the American Medical Association.* 280:1855–61.

Hunter, J. A., Jr., L. J. Lexier, D. W. Goodwin, P. A. Browne, and C. Dennis. 1993. "Psychosexual, Attitudinal, and Developmental Characteristics of Juvenile Female Sexual Perpetrators in a Residential Treatment Setting." *Journal of Interpersonal Violence.* 12:456–65.

Jackson, Nicky Ali. 1998. "Lesbian Battering: The Other Closet." Pp. 181–94 in *Violence in Intimate Relationships: Examining Sociological and Psychological Issues,* Nicky Ali Jackson and Gisele Casanova Oates, eds. Boston, MA: Butterworth-Heinemann.

Jenkins, Philip. 1995. "Clergy Sexual Abuse: The Symbolic Politics of a Social Problem." Pp. 105–30 in *Images of Issues: Typifying Contemporary Social Problems,* Joel Best, ed. NY: Aldine de Gruyter.

Jennings, Kathryn T. 1993. "Female Child Molesters: A Review of the Literature." Pp. 219–34 in *Female Sexual Abuse of Children,* Michele Elliott, ed. NY: Guilford Press.

Johnson, John M. 1995. "Horror Stories and the Construction of Child Abuse." Pp. 17–31 in *Images of Issues: Typifying Contemporary Social Problems,* Joel Best, ed. NY: Aldine de Gruyter.

Jones, Lisa and David Finkelhor. 2001. "The Decline in Child Sexual Abuse Cases." *Juvenile Justice Bulletin,* January. Washington, DC: U.S. Department of Justice.

Kaiser, Hilary. 1996. "Clergy Sexual Abuse in U.S. Mainline Churches." *American Studies International.* 34:30–42.

Kanin, E. J. 1984. "Date Rape: Unofficial Criminals and Victims." *Victimology: an International Journal.* 9:93–108.

Karp, Stephen A., David E. Silber, Robert W. Holmstrom, and Lisa J. Stock. 1995. "Personality of Rape Survivors as a Group and by Relation of Survivor to Perpetrator." *Journal of Clinical Psychology.* 51:587–92.

Knudsen, Dean D. 1992. *Child Maltreatment: Emerging Perspectives.* Dix Hills, NY: General Hall, Inc.

Koss, Mary K. and Sarah L. Cook. 1993. "Facing the Facts: Date and Acquaintance Rape Are Significant Problems for Women." Pp. 104–19 in *Current Controversies on Family Violence,* Richard J. Gelles and Donileen R. Loseke, eds. Newbury Park, CA: Sage Publications.

Koss, Mary P., C. A. Gidycz, and N. Wisniewski. 1987. "The Scope of Rape: Incidence and Prevalence of Sexual Aggression and Victimization in National Sample of Higher Education Students." *Journal of Consulting and Clinical Psychology.* 55:162–70.

Lam, Judy N. 1998. "Child Sexual Abuse." Pp. 25–55 in *Violence in Intimate Relationships: Examining Sociological and Psychological Issues,* Nicky Ali Jackson and Gisele Casanova Oates, eds. Boston, MA: Butterworth-Heinemann.

Langeland, Willie and Christina Hartgers. 1998. "Child Sexual and Physical Abuse and Alcoholism: A Review." *Journal of Studies on Alcohol.* 59:336–48.

Longo, R. and A. N. Groth. 1983. "Juvenile Sexual Offences in the Histories of Adult Rapists and Child Molesters." *International Journal of Offender Therapy and Comparative Criminology.* 27:235–41.

Lundberg-Love, P. and R. Geffer. (1989). "Date Rape: Prevalence, Risk Factors, and a Posed Model." Pp. 166–84 in *Violence in Dating Relationships: Emerging Social Issues,* M. A. Pirog-Good and J. E. Stets, eds. NY: Praeger.

Luster, Tom and Stephen A. Small. 1997. "Sexual Abuse History and Problems in Adolescence: Exploring the Effects of Moderating Variables." *Journal of Marriage and the Family.* 59:131–42.

MacDonald, John M. 1995. *Rape: Controversial Issues, Criminal Profiles, Date Rape, False Reports and False Memories.* Springfield, IL: Charles C. Thomas.

Martin, Patricia Yancy and Robert A. Hummer. 1989. "Fraternities and Rape on Campus." *Gender and Society.* 3:457–73.

Maxfield, M. G. and C. S. Widom. 1996. "The Cycle of Violence: Revisited 6 years Later." *JAMA: The Journal of the American Medical Association.* 275:1708.

McCormack, A., M. Janus, and A. Burgess. 1986. "Runaway Youths and Sexual Victimization: Gender Differences in an Adolescent Runaway Population." *Child Abuse and Neglect.* 10:387–95.

McMillen, Curtis and Susan Zuravin. 1997. "Attributions of Blame and Responsiblity for Child Sexual Abuse and Adult Adjustment." *Journal Interpersonal Violence.* 12:30–38.

Mendel, Matthew Parynik. 1995. *The Male Survivor: The Impact of Sexual Abuse.* Thousand Oaks, CA: Sage Publications.

Mills, Crystal S. and Barbara J. Granoff. 1992. "Date and Acquaintance Rape among a Sample of College Students." *Social Work.* 37:504–09.

Noblitt, James Randall. 1995. "Psychometric Measures of Trauma Among Psychiatric Patients Reporting Ritual Abuse." *Psych Reports.* 77:743–47.

North American Man/Boy Love Association. (WWW http: www.nambla.org/).

Nugent, Patricia M. and Daryl G. Kroner. 1996. "Denial, Response Styles, and Admittance of Offenses Among Child Molesters and Rapists." *Journal of Interpersonal Violence.* 11:475–86.

Parrott, Susan. 2000. "Hare Krishna Boarding Schools Sued in Child-Sex Abuse Case." *The Boston Globe,* Associated Press, June 13: A17.

Paulsen, Michael. 2000. "Rector's Book on Clergy, Sex Is Bestseller—Among Priests." *The Boston Globe,* June 3:A1, A6.

Peters, Stefani Doyle, Gail Elizabeth Wyatt, and David Finkelhor. 1986. "Prevalence." Pp. 15–59 in *A Sourcebook on Child Sexual Abuse,* David Finkelhor, ed. Beverly Hills, CA: Sage Publications.

Rakowsky, Judy. 1999. "LeFave Granted Freedom: Striking Deal She Drops Bid to Overturn Fells Acres Conviction." *The Boston Globe,* October 22:A1, A18.

———. 2000. "Curley Parents Sue Man-Boy 'Love' Group, Web Site." *The Boston Globe,* May 17:B1, B5.

Ray, Oakley and Charles Ksir. 1999. *Drugs, Society, and Human Behavior,* 8th ed. Boston, MA: WCB/McGraw-Hill.

Rodriguez, Ned, Hedrika Vand Kemp, Susan W. Ryan, and David W. Foy. 1997. "Posttraumatic Stress Disorder in Adult Female Survivors of Childhood Sexual Abuse: A Comparison Study." *Journal of Consulting and Clinical Psychology.* 65,1:53–59.

Rogers, C. N. and T. Terry. 1984. "Clinical Interventions with Boy Victims of Sexual Abuse." In *Victims of Sexual Aggression: Treatment of Children, Women, and Men,* I. R. Stuart and J. G. Greer, eds. NY: Van Nostrand Reinhold.

Romano, Elisa and Rayleen V. DeLuca. 1997. "Exploring the Relationship Between Childhood Sexual Abuse and Adult Sexual Perpetration." *Journal of Family Violence.* 12:85–98.

Romans, Sara E., Judy L. Martin, Jessie C. Anderson, G. Peter Herbison, and Paul E. Mullen. 1995. "Sexual Abuse in Childhood and Deliberate Self-Harm." *American Journal of Psychiatry.* 152:1336–42.

Rossetti, Stephen J. 1993. "Parishes As Victims of Abuse." *Human Development.* 14:15–20.

———. 1994. "Child Sexual Abuse in the Church." *The Priest,* (January), 33–37.

Sansonnet-Hayden, H. G. Haley, C. Marriage, and S. Fine. 1987. "Sexual Abuse and Psychopathology in Hospitalized Adolescents." *Journal of the American Academy of Child and Adolescent Psychiatry.* 26:753–57.

Scheible, Sue. 2000. "Elder Abuse: Reports of Neglect Rising in Massachusetts." *The Patriot Ledger,* June 14:A1, A2.

Schneider, H. J. 1997. "Sexual Abuse of Children: Strengths and Weaknesses of Current Criminology." *International Journal of Offender Therapy and Comparative Criminology,* 41:324.

Sedlak, Andrea J. and Diane D. Broadhurst. 1996. *Executive Summary of the Third National Incidence Study of Child Abuse and Neglect.* (WWW http://www.casanet.org/library/abuse/stabuse.htm).

Shaffer, Ruth and Louis Cozolino. 1992. "Adults Who Report Childhood Ritualistic Abuse." *Journal of Psychology and Theology.* 20:188–93.

Sgroi, Suzanne M., ed. 1982. *Handbook of Clinical Intervention in Child Sexual Abuse.* Lexington, MA: D. C. Heath.

Sgroi, Suzanne M. and Norah M. Sargent. 1993. "Impact and Treatment Issues for Victims of Childhood Sexual Abuse by Female Perpetrators." Pp. 14–36 in *Female Sexual Abuse of Children,* Michelle Elliott, ed. NY: The Guilford Press.

Shalit, Ruth. 1995. "Witch Hunt: The McMartin Child Abuse Case, The Sequel." *The New Republic.* 212:14–15.

Silk, Kenneth R., Sharon Lee, Elizabeth M. Hill, and Naomi E. Lohr. 1995. "Borderline Personality Disorder Symptoms and Severity of Sexual Abuse." *American Journal of Psychiatry.* 152:1059–64.

Smith, Susan Livingston and Jeanne A. Howard. 1994. "The Impact of Previous Sexual Abuse on Children's Adjustment in Adoptive Placement." *Social Work.* 39:491–501.

Spaccarelli, Steven, Blake Bowden, J. Douglas Coatsworth, and Soni Kim. 1997. "Psychosocial Correlates of Male Sexual Aggression in a Chronic Delinquent Sample." *Criminal Justice and Behavior.* 24:71–95.

Statistics at a Glance. 2000. Washington, DC: U.S. Department of Justice, Bureau of Justice Statistics. (www.ojp.usdoj.gov/bjs).

Stermac, Lana, Alison Davidson, and Peter M. Sheridan. 1995. "Incidence of Nonsexual Violence in Incest Offenders." *International Journal of Offender Therapy and Comparative Criminology.* 39:167–78.

Straus, Murray A. and Richard Gelles. 1988. *Intimate Violence.* NY: Simon and Schuster.

Stock, Jacqueline L., Michelle A. Bell, Debra K. Boyer, and Frederick A. Connell. 1997. "Adolescent Pregnancy and Sexual Risk-Taking Among Abused Girls." *Family Planning Perspectives.* 29:200–03.

U.S. Department of Health and Human Services. 2000. *Child Maltreatment: Reports from the States to the National Child Abuse and Neglect Data System.* Washington, DC: U.S. Government Printing Office.

Victor, Jeffrey S. 1992. "Ritual Abuse and the Moral Crusade Against Satanism." *Psychology and Theology.* 20:248–53.

Vogeltanz, Nancy D., Sharon C. Wilsnack, T. Robert Harris, Richard W. Wilsnack, Stephen A. Wonderlich, and Arlinda F. Kristjanson. 1999. "Prevalence and Risk Factors for Childhood Sexual Abuse in Women: National Survey Findings." *Child Abuse and Neglect.* 23:579–92.

Wadsworth, Rick, Alana M. Spampnet, and Bernadette M. Halbrook. 1995. "The Role of Sexual Trauma in the Treatment of Chemically Dependent Women: Addressing the Relapse Issue." *Journal of Counseling and Development.* 73:401–06.

"Wages of Sin: The Catholic Church." 1997. *The Economist.* 344:18.

Wallace, Harvey. 1996. *Family Violence: Legal, Medical, and Social Perspectives.* Needham Heights, MA: Allyn and Bacon.

Wang, C. and D. Daro. 1998. *Current Trends in Child Abuse Reporting and Fatalities: The Results of the 1997 Annual Fifty State Survey.* Chicago, IL: Center on Child Abuse Prevention Research.

Watkins, Bill and Arnon Bentovim. 1992. "Male Children and Adolescents as Victims: A Review of Current Knowledge." Pp. 27–66 in *Male Victims of Sexual Assault,* Gillian C. Mezey and Michael B. King, eds. Oxford, Cambridge: Oxford University Press.

Weir, I. Kirk and M. S. Wheatcroft. 1995. "Allegation of Children's Involvement in Ritual Sexual Abuse: Clinical Experience of 20 cases." *Child Abuse and Neglect.* 19:491–505.

Wiehe, Vernon R. 1997. *Sibling Abuse: Hidden Physical, Emotional and Sexual Trauma,* 2nd ed. Thousand Oak, CA: Sage Publications.

Wilsnak, Sharon C., Nancy D. Vogeltanz, Albert D. Klassen, and T. Robert Harris. 1997. "Childhood Sexual Abuse and Women's Substance Abuse: National Survey Findings." *Journal of Studies on Alcohol.* 58:264–72.

Wonderlich, Stephen A., Timothy D. Brewerton, Zeljko Jocic, Bonnie S. Dansky, and David W. Abbott. 1997. "Relationship of Childhood Sexual Abuse and Eating Disorders." *Journal of the American Academy of Child and Adolescent Psychiatry.* 36:1107–15.

Young, Shelley. 1997. "The Use of Normalization as a Strategy in the Sexual Exploitation of Children by Adult Offenders." *The Canadian Journal of Human Sexuality.* 6:285–95.

Young, Walter C. 1993. "Sadistic Ritual Abuse. An Overview in Detection and Management." *Primary Care.* 20:447–58.

Zgourides, George, Martin Monto, and Richard Harris. 1997. "Correlates of Adolescent Male Sexual Offense: Prior Adult Sexual Contact, Sexual Attitudes, and Use of Sexually Explicit Materials." *International Journal of Offender Therapy and Comparative Criminology.* 41:272–83.

4 The Nature and Varieties of Psychological Abuse

Psychological maltreatment is regarded by many as the most prevalent of the major forms of family abuse. It is also generally assumed that all forms of abuse are likely to entail psychological and emotional repercussions. As Brassard, Germain, and Hart (1987) put it, "experts generally believe that psychological maltreatment almost always accompanies other forms of abuse and neglect, is more prevalent than other forms of maltreatment, and is often more destructive in its impact on the lives of young people" (3).

Psychological maltreatment is a complex subject, particularly because it may be perpetrated directly or indirectly, blatantly or subtly and because victims often have difficulty discerning its effects. For some victims, it is only in adulthood, once they have gained physical and social distance from the perpetrator, that they recognize that they have been psychologically or emotionally abused. For these reasons alone, it is difficult to gauge the extent, depth, and effects of the problem.

The difficulty of specifying the nature of psychological maltreatment is reflected in the inability to construct generally acceptable definitions of key terms such as *psychological maltreatment, psychological abuse,* and *emotional abuse.* Some use them interchangeably, while others feel that one is the better umbrella term. The result is an ambiguity that hinders research and knowledge accumulation. Hence, the first subject of concern here is the conceptual problem: specifying the key terms that define the subject. Subsequent sections of this chapter examine the ways in which psychological maltreatment may be imposed, what is known about its prevalence, and its personal and deviant consequences.

The Conceptual Problem

Problems of definition can occur both when people use different words or concepts to describe the same thing and when people use the same word or concept to describe different things. In the present context, for example, some use all of the following terms synonymously: *emotional abuse, mental abuse, mental cruelty, mental injury, psychological abuse,* and *psychological maltreatment.* The tendency has been to use either *emotional abuse* or *psychological abuse* as the inclusive term, and this has provoked critical reaction.

Kieran O'Hagan (1995), for example, shows that emotional abuse and psychological abuse may be quite independent of each other. He calls attention to the different meanings of persons' emotional life and psychological life. Whereas one's emotional life is based on feelings such as love, affection, fear, and hate, one's psychological life is based on factors that influence mental development, for example, the impact of perception and cognition on one's ability to develop language facility. O'Hagan provides two case examples from biographical literature: one demonstrates that emotional abuse may not have debilitating cognitive consequences (the case of "Dibs"); the other demonstrates that psychological abuse may not have debilitating emotional consequences (the case of "Gosse"). According to O'Hagan (1995),

> Dibs was severely emotionally abused, and this had serious adverse effects upon his emotional and social development. He was not psychologically (mentally) abused. His mental development was neither impeded nor impaired. Gosse was severely psychologically abused (by parents who had not the slightest notion they were doing so). He was not emotionally abused; on the contrary, his parents ensured the highest quality of emotional life and development during his infancy and early childhood. (452)

Accordingly, O'Hagan defines *emotional abuse* as "the sustained, repetitive, inappropriate emotional response to the child's experience of emotion and its accompanying expressive behavior" (456). *Psychological abuse* he defines as "the sustained, repetitive, inappropriate behavior which damages or substantially reduces the creative and developmental potential or crucially important mental faculties and mental processes of a child; these faculties and processes include intelligence, memory, recognition, perception, attention, imagination, and moral development" (458).

To be sure, says O'Hagan, the two forms of abuse are often interrelated. The perpetration of the one invariably entails perpetration of the other. Nevertheless, the point he stresses is the need to be aware of the fact that psychological maltreatment results in not just one, but at least two different possible effects: "Emotional abuse impairs the emotional life and impedes emotional development; psychological abuse impairs the mental life and impedes mental development" (458–59).

It is for reasons such as O'Hagan's that others have made the case for employing *psychological maltreatment* as the basic concept. The major advocates of this position have been Brassard, Germain, and Hart (1987), experts in the field of child abuse. As they point out, the 1983 International Conference on Psychological Abuse of Children and Youth identified the following eight "domains of psychological abuse": mental cruelty (verbal abuse); sexual abuse and exploitation (the psychological effects of incest, rape, and so on); living in dangerous and unstable environments (for example, living in a war zone); drug and substance abuse (psychological effects of misuse of drugs provided or abetted by others); influence by negative and limiting models (role models in and outside the home whose example is psychologically debilitating); cultural bias and prejudice (the psychological effects of minority group membership); emotional neglect and stimulation deprivation (rejection, failure to provide warmth and affection); and institutional abuse (for example, a nursery school in which children may be sexually abused by a caretaker). To Brassard, Germain, and Hart, psychological maltreatment stands "for all affective and cognitive aspects of child maltreatment including both acts of omission and commission" (4).

To minimize confusion, we think it best to follow the lead of Brassard, Germain, and Hart as well as of O'Hagan. The subject of concern is psychological actions that fundamentally abuse the individual's mind, leading to problematic feelings, attitudes, and behavior. The term *psychological abuse* may suggest a more restricted subject, the content of the mind exclusive of its behavioral consequences. *Psychological maltreatment* appears to us to be the more neutral and less ambiguous term, encompassing the content of the mind and its behavioral effects. It allows for the separation of the two major possible effects of abuse, the affective or emotional and the cognitive or developmental, or some combination of the two. Further, it appears to be the best option to minimize confusing the causal agent and its effects. Such confusion occurs when *emotional abuse* is employed as the general term, for it then must be used to describe both a type of abuse and its consequences. Lacking clarification, the reader may be left to determine whether the subject of concern is a particular type of abuse and how it is perpetrated or one of the effects of a singular type or different types of abuse.

Mindful of the conceptual problem, particularly the need to differentiate the ways abuse may be perpetrated from its effects, we now ask, What is known about child and adult psychological maltreatment? What are their basic similarities and differences? How are they imposed and with what psychological and behavioral consequences?

Child Psychological Maltreatment

The 1983 International Conference on Psychological Abuse of Children and Youth generated the following definition of psychological maltreatment:

> Psychological maltreatment of children and youth consists of acts of omission and commission which are judged by community standards and professional expertise to be psychologically damaging. Such acts are committed by individuals, singly or collectively, who by their characteristics (e.g., age, status, knowledge, organizational form) are in a position of differential power that renders a child vulnerable. Such acts damage immediately or ultimately the behavioral, cognitive, affective, or physical functioning of the child. Examples of psychological maltreatment include acts of rejecting, terrorizing, isolating, exploiting, and mis-socializing. (cited in Brassard and Gelardo 1987:128)

Clinicians, who treat clients, generally emphasize the need for accurate diagnosis of the problem prior to effective treatment intervention. Academic scholars, who study the problem for basic knowledge acquisition, stress the need for precise documentation of the variety and extent of the problem. Clinicians and scholars share the view that psychological maltreatment requires serious examination because of its potential negative developmental consequences. As Judy Keith-Oaks (1990) sees it, "while the effects of emotional abuse are less visible than physical bruises, over the long term the consequences are far greater because the results are dysfunctional behaviors that may interfere with successful development" (33). Of particular concern to students of the subject are questions concerning what types of psychological maltreatment exist, how they are imposed, and with what effects.

Types of Child Psychological Maltreatment

Children may be maltreated or abused directly or indirectly. They may be harmed by what caregivers do to them and what they do not do for them (see Box 4.1). Abuse is thought of as harm that is deliberately, or at least knowingly, imposed and neglect as something that essentially occurs primarily because of ignorance or indifference. Although this distinction is meaningful, it simplifies a more complicated reality. In fact, the two terms are intimately connected. Abusive behavior often entails negligence, and certainly negligence may be defined as abusive if unduly prolonged and harmful. Further, both abuse and neglect may be imposed in different degrees and by intention or ignorance. Perception plays a key part in any given situation. Abusers often think that their treatment of the victim is justified and therefore not abusive. Victims, too, may perceive what has happened to them as something normal and deserved. Practitioners, then, have the challenging task of sorting out the particulars and accurately diagnosing a given situation and of having to convince one or both parties involved that they have a serious problem requiring treatment.

Dorota Iwaniec (1995), an experienced pediatric social worker, has written sensitively about the complexities of child abuse and neglect, especially their mixture. For her, the basic concept is emotional abuse, which she says may take the form of either "overtly rejecting behavior" or "passive neglect" (5). Parents and other caretakers who are persistently critical and negative as well as those who deliberately ignore a child's basic needs are equally emotionally abusive.

Rather than identify types of emotional abuse and neglect, Iwaniec provides a list of twenty-one types of parental behaviors that indicate its occurrence. Prime examples include humiliating, terrorizing, ignoring, isolating, persistent ridiculing and criticizing, shaming in front of peers and siblings, corruption (by drugs, prostitution, crime), and not permitting the expression of emotion.

Iwaniec's list of items is similar to that delineated by scholars more concerned with specifying psychological maltreatment's bearing on child development than emotional affect per se. James Garbarino (1993), for example, identifies five categories of psychological maltreatment that threaten child development:

B O X **4.1**

Psychological Maltreatment

[Psychological maltreatment is the] willful infliction by a parent or other caretaker of mental, emotional, or psychological harm or anguish. Often called psychological abuse, such maltreatment can be directly inflicted by parents, siblings, other family members, and caretakers. It also can be inflicted indirectly through children's exposure to violence in the home. Witnessing or other exposure to abuse of a parent is a form of psychological maltreatment.

Psychological maltreatment is often a pattern of interaction. It includes a range of behavior: terrorizing, threatening, isolating, exploiting or corrupting, spurning, rejecting, denying emotional responsiveness, or neglecting mental health, medical, or educational care. Included are humiliation, abusive gestures or words, confinement, or withholding sleep, food, or shelter, when these actions are meant to humiliate or cause fear or anguish in the child.

Although psychological abuse may occur without other types of abuse, frequently it accompanies other types of child abuse.

Neglect also is psychological maltreatment. It includes experiences in which a caretaker either deliberately or by extraordinary inattentiveness permits the child to experience avoidable suffering or fails to provide one or more of the ingredients generally essential for nurturing the development of the child's physical, intellectual, and emotional capabilities.

The term *neglect* is used even when the parent or caretaker fails to provide for the child's needs solely because of lack of means. A parent without health insurance, for example, who fails to provide health care for a sick child may be considered neglectful. Parents who lack resources, therefore, are in a no-win situation; this helps explain why more parents living in poverty are reported as abusers.

Source: American Psychological Association. 1996. *Violence and The Family: Report of The American Psychological Association Presidential Task Force on Violence and The Family.* Washington, DC. P. 50.

Rejecting: refusing to acknowledge the child's worth and the legitimacy of the child's needs.

Isolating: cutting the child off from normal social experiences.

Terrorizing: verbally assaulting the child, creating a climate of fear.

Ignoring: being psychologically unavailable to the child.

Corrupting: missocializing the child, stimulating the child to engage in destructive and antisocial behavior. (308)

Garbarino stresses the relative importance of the five across the life span, particularly during the key developmental stages of infancy, early childhood, school age, and adolescence. For instance, it is difficult to terrorize an infant verbally because symbolic meanings are yet to be learned.

> [E]ven a monstrous threat [to the infant] is not terrorizing. Smile and say sweetly, "Hello baby, I'm going to cut your heart out and feed it to my dog." The appropriate infant response is "Goo-goo." . . . The child's vulnerability to terrorizing really comes to fruition with the development of language and the capacity for fantasy play. Now, the threat to "cut your heart out and feed it to my dog" becomes vividly terrorizing. (310)

Others stress the more subtle, but no less psychologically devastating, side of emotional abuse. To Gregory Jantz (1995), for example, emotional abuse may be expressed through words, actions, or indifference. He identifies a number of examples from clinical experience. Examples of perpetrators of abuse expressed through words include "the person who is always right," who believes that others are entitled to their opinions as long as they agree with his or hers; "the great guilt-giver," the parent or spouse who always blames the victim for his or her faults; and "the historian," the person who remembers everything negative that has ever happened to the victim. Examples of emotional abuse expressed through actions include physical intimidation, manipulation, and physical threats. Emotional abuse expressed through indifference is perpetrated through inaction. It occurs when something should be said or done but isn't. "As damaging as the other types of emotional abuse, it is the *absence* of the expected that wounds" (Jantz 1995:76). Examples include "the absent caregiver," the parent who is always away from home, and "the M.I.A. parent," the parent who never takes the time to make a timely telephone call or respond to letters.

As Iwaniec indicates, legislative acknowledgment of the problem of child emotional abuse occurred in Britain in 1980 and the United States in 1977. In Britain, she says that legislation was first written to permit intervention only after abuse occurred but was later amended to permit timely intervention. The same pattern has not been followed in the United States.

As of December 31, 1996, twenty-two states had enacted child abuse legislation encompassing emotional abuse. The laws are concerned with punishing offenders after the fact rather than permitting preventive intervention. In California, for example, the law reads:

> Any person who, under circumstances or conditions likely to produce great bodily harm or death, willfully causes or permits any child to suffer, or inflicts thereon unjustifiable physical pain or mental suffering, or having the care or custody of any child, willfully causes or permits the person or health of that child to be injured, or willfully causes or permits that child to be placed in a situation where his or her person or health is endangered, shall be punished by imprisonment in a county jail not exceeding one year, or in the state prison for 2, 4, or 6 years.

The problem has not been so much the writing and passing of legislation as law enforcement. One would assume that it is only the rare perpetrator or perpetrators who voluntarily confess culpability and seek treatment. To combat the problem effectively, to document the fact of psychological maltreatment, the cooperation of witnesses and verifiable evidence are needed. As the victim of such abuse does not typically bear outward signs of abuse, law enforcement agencies must rely on the views of those who know about the situation and are willing to testify in a court of law, as well as whatever evidence they can muster from qualified professionals (for example, psychologists or social workers) and others (for example, school nurses and teachers). Notwithstanding the difficulty of collecting data about an inadequately defined, difficult-to-verify subject, the available evidence indicates that child psychological maltreatment is extensive.

The Incidence of Child Psychological Maltreatment and Neglect

As indicated in Chapter 1, the Third National Incidence Study of Child Abuse and Neglect (NIS-3) reported increases in all measured types of child maltreatment. Published in 1996, the NIS-3 is based on data collected in 1993. The previous study, NIS-2, was based on data amassed in 1986. As previously indicated, two measures of abuse were used: the Harm Standard (an act or omission that evidences demonstrable harm to a child) and the Endangerment Standard (which adds to those acts or omissions identified by the Harm Standard those that qualified reporting professionals believe may lead to abuse). Thus, using the broader Endangerment Standard, the estimated number of children emotionally abused increased from 188,100 in 1986 to 532,200 in 1993 (a 183 percent increase). The estimated number of emotionally neglected children rose from 203,000 in 1986 to 585,100 in 1993 (a 188 percent increase).

The NIS-3 found the primary perpetrators of all types of child maltreatment to be parents (77 percent) and other relatives (12 percent). Chief among the "other relatives" are siblings. In a nonrandom sample of some 150 individuals who responded to a newspaper advertisement for respondents, Vernon Wiehe (1990) found 11 (or 7 percent) who admitted to being only emotionally abused by a sibling. But 107 (71 percent) reported being emotionally maltreated while being physically or sexually abused by a sibling. As Wiehe states, "This means that 78 percent or 118 of the 150 persons in the sample had been emotionally abused" by a sibling (1990:26).

The question is, what are the psychological and behavioral effects of child psychological maltreatment? If child psychological maltreatment is the most prevalent of the varieties of abuse, does it generate a greater variety of negative consequences for its victims? To what extent does it lead to serious individual reactions, such as mental illness, as well as acts of social deviancy, such as substance abuse and criminality? While the available evidence is not sufficient in quality or quantity to provide clear answers to such questions, it is supportive of a connection between psychological maltreatment and a number of personal problems and some forms of social deviancy.

Personal and Deviant Consequences

Several pronounced symptoms of child psychological maltreatment and neglect have been identified. Among the most consistent are low self-esteem and self-confidence, feeling unworthy of the respect and attention of others and, therefore, feeling incompetent and irrelevant. In addition, Jantz lists the problems of perfectionism, a chronic sense of failure, guilt, a crisis orientation, and anger and resentment as further consequences (1995:88–95). Similarly, others, most notably the American Humane Association and the National Center for Child Abuse and Neglect, list the following consequences of psychological maltreatment: behavior extremes, habit disorders, conduct disorders, neurotic traits, psychoneurotic reactions, overly adaptive behaviors, lags in development, and attempted suicide (cited by Brassard, Hart, and Hardy 1991:257). Still others emphasize depressive consequences (Gross and Keller 1992; Cerezo and Frias 1994). Such lists describe individuals capable of either directing their problematic feelings inward (mental illness, substance abuse, suicide) or outward (aggression and violence).

Nonetheless, lacking are detailed studies of the bearing of different types of child or adult psychological maltreatment on problematic and deviant outcomes. The slight evidence available on these subjects must be culled from studies of other, more attention attracting types of abuse (physical and sexual), which sometimes include examination of the effects of child neglect.

The problem has been that when child neglect has been included in a study it has been correlated with physical abuse. A noteworthy exception is the work of Cathy Spatz Widom, who has studied the validity of the assumption that "violence begets violence," or the "cycle of violence" hypothesis.

The outcome of child abuse that has been of major concern to Widom is whether or not physically abused children are more likely than nonabused children to be physically aggressive and involved in crime. Upon reviewing the evidence, she found that few studies separately examined the bearing of child neglect on the subject. But those that did indicated that neglected children demonstrated "high rates of physical aggression" (1989:19). Widom's own research sponsored by the National Institute of Justice (NIJ) has highlighted the connection between child neglect and criminal behavior (as indicated by arrest record). Her research, based on following 1,575 cases from childhood to young adulthood, led to the conclusion that in addition to a childhood history of physical abuse,

> victims of neglect are also more likely to develop later criminal violent behavior as well. . . . If it is not only violence that begets violence, but also neglect, far more attention needs to be devoted to the families of children whose "beatings" are forms of abandonment and severe malnutrition. (1992:1)

Widom's definition of child neglect was strictly physical, namely, caretaker failure to provide children with the basic necessities of life (food, shelter, clothing, medical attention). Why physical neglect should generate as much physical aggression and involvement in adult criminality as physical abuse was not examined. One might assume it's likely that a physically neglected child also would be emotionally neglected. But this remains to be determined. However, the evidence of other research supports the evidence from clinical experiences such as Jantz's reported above that child emotional abuse may generate physical aggression and deviancy.

The study in question involved interviews with 3,346 parents with at least one child under 18 in residence. According to Wiehe (1996:146), those children, regardless of gender or educational level (preschool, elementary, high school), who were found to be the victims of parental verbal aggression were more likely than other children to be physically aggressive, inclined to be officially delinquent, with evidence of interpersonal problems.

The possible deviant expressions of physical aggression and other consequences of child psychological maltreatment are yet to be determined. As gender differences have been found in regard to the effects of other types of abuse, they should be expected in regard to psychological maltreatment. Widom, for example, points out that her findings indicate that abused or neglected males are more likely to be arrested for street violence and girls for nonviolent offenses such as disorderly conduct, curfew violations, or loitering (1992:2). But, again, as Widom confined her analysis to physical neglect, her findings must be viewed as merely suggestive of a likely connection between emotional neglect and criminality.

The effect of different types of emotional abusers on the victim is also a little studied subject. The abuser is generally taken to be a caretaker—parents or their surrogates. Comparisons are not routinely made between parents, fathers and mothers, and other caretakers (siblings and nonrelatives) and what difference this might make in terms of consequences. Some attention has been given to sibling perpetrated emotional abuse.

In a pioneering work on the subject, Wiehe (1990) refers to sibling abuse as "an undetected problem." It has been undetected largely because it has been rationalized as something other than what it is. As he says, "The teasing and verbal put-downs in which siblings engage with each other and with children in general, although disliked by parents, is often accepted as normal behavior, and between siblings, it is simply excused as sibling rivalry" (1990:28). Wiehe found 118 (79 percent) of his 150 respondents to have been emotionally abused as a consequence of being either physically or sexually maltreated by a sibling.

Wiehe tells us that victims of sibling abuse often refer to what was done to them as *teasing,* a word that connotes something irritating but not very serious. But as he says, more accurate contemporary synonyms for sibling teasing include: belittle, ridicule, intimidate, annoy, scorn, provoke, and harass (1990:25).

The perpetrator of sibling abuse is often the oldest child in a family given the responsibility of caring for its younger member or members. The motivation for sibling perpetrated psychological abuse has been traced to resentment over a younger sibling perceived as the family favorite, an opportunity for expressing anger and hostility accumulated for any number of reasons, and a way of dealing with their own abuse by adhering to the parental example (Whipple and Finton 1995:138). Crittenden's (1984) work suggests that sibling abuse is related to the parental style of childrearing. In regard to both abusive and nonabusive sibling families, her data "suggest that parental style of childrearing begins to influence the child at a very early age and that most children are influenced to be similar to their parents" (1984:438).

Whipple and Finton list the following possible psychological consequences of sibling psychological maltreatment: somatic symptoms, nightmares, phobias, academic underachievement, aggressiveness, withdrawal, depression, feelings of worthlessness, confusion, apathy, isolation (1995:139–40). Low self-esteem is generally identified as the most frequent consequence of sibling psychological maltreatment.

The effects of child abuse of any kind are to a considerable degree dependent on the victim's maturation level. For students of deviant behavior, adolescence is of special concern because it is during this period that serious and dangerous personal and social repercussions emerge. The destructive effects of child psychological maltreatment may be self or other directed. The two alternative reactions are captured in the following description of the psychologically maltreated adolescent:

> Adolescents may become truant or runaways, get involved with delinquency or substance abuse, rebel against authority, or even become purposefully destructive. Alternatively, they may become depressed, attempt suicide, develop eating or other somatic disturbances, and become emotionally troubled and unstable. (Garbarino, Guttmann, and Seeley 1986:64)

Do the effects of child psychological maltreatment tend to diminish or persist into adulthood? Is adult psychological "battering" any more or less prevalent or serious than child psychological maltreatment? Are the deviant behavioral outcomes of adult psychological maltreatment basically similar to or different from those of children? Unfortunately, as will be explained in the following section, the prevalence of adult psychological maltreatment is even less well documented than child psychological maltreatment. It will also become evident in the discussion that the means used and their effects are basically the same whether the victim of psychological maltreatment is a child or an adult.

Adult Psychological Maltreatment

In their study of the effects of different types of child abuse on 133 undergraduate females, Sappington et al. found that verbal child abuse was associated with "an increased risk of later date abuse and psychological problems" (1997:319). Possible explanations, they suggest, include an attempt to recreate learned family interaction patterns in intimate relationships, the possibility that victims suffer a degree of low self-esteem that makes them more vulnerable to later acceptance of abuse and that victims of childhood abuse have a reservoir of anger that induces them to lash out at others and provoke retaliation. Each of these possibilities remains to be empirically assessed.

Other research indicates that childhood psychological maltreatment may have long-term health consequences. Gross and Keller examined the possible long-term health effects of childhood physical and psychological abuse on 260 undergraduates. Their measures of long-term health consequences were depression, low self-esteem, and maladaptive attributional style (for example, the inclination to attribute behavioral problems to factors beyond one's ability to understand and control). They found that when compared to those who reported not being abused, those who reported being either physically or psychologically abused as children suffered more depression, had lower self-esteem but no greater tendency to a maladaptive attributional style. More important, after controlling for the effects of physical abuse, "Multiple linear regression analyses pointed to psychological abuse as a critical variable in predicting levels of depression, self-esteem, and attributional style" (1992:171).

Lastly, Moeller and Bachmann also studied the long-term health conse-quences of the major types of child abuse. Their sample was 668 women in a gynecological practice who responded to a mailed questionnaire. More than half (53 percent) reported being abused as a child physically, sexually, or emotionally. Emotional abuse was the most frequently reported type of abuse. More than a third (37.4 percent) of the total sample indicated experiencing "severe emotional distress in childhood." The effects of the major types of child abuse were not separately analyzed. Rather, the authors examined the combined health consequences of physical, sexual, and emotional abuse. Compared to those who did not report being abused as a child, "The abused reported significantly more hospitalizations for illnesses, a greater number of physical and psychological problems, and lower ratings of their overall health" (1993:623). Furthermore, frequency of reported instances of child abuse was associated with poorer health as an adult and increased risk of suffering abuse.

Actually, adult psychological maltreatment is not a precisely defined field. This is in good measure due to the fact that interest in it is of recent origin and the tendency of investigators to focus their attention and theoretical conceptions on certain groups (student populations, women in counseling or therapy) or contexts (dating or marital relationships). There is recognition of some general types of adult psychological maltreatment, but not an overall guiding framework that connects the work of all who study its manifestations.

The first part of the next section deals with the various types of adult psychological maltreatment that have been identified. Subsequent sections exam-ine the forms, incidence, and consequences of adult psychological maltreatment in dating relationships, marital and partner relationships, and in treatment of the elderly.

Varieties of Adult Psychological Maltreatment

Generally, adult psychological maltreatment includes all forms of abuse perpetrated by nonphysical contact. The most widely agreed on type is verbal abuse or verbal aggression. The use of words to belittle, coerce, intimidate, provoke, and the like are prime examples. One can also produce these effects nonverbally by facial expression, body posture, and gestures. Such means may be used to convey the likely use of physical means unless certain results transpire, or they may be the preliminary signals of physical violence. As Jantz (1995:58) indicates, abusers who combine verbal threats with actions increase their ability to control people and circumstances.

DeGregoria (1987:228) identifies the following three other "yet to be widely agreed upon" types of adult psychological maltreatment: (1) economic deprivation (the use of income to coerce, threaten, or control a partner); (2) social humiliation (publicly embarrassing a partner to intimidate or coerce a partner); and (3) social isolation (the limiting of contacts and friendship choices by a partner). Other possibilities, such as the expression of psychological aggression toward another or others to coerce or provoke desired responses such as sympathy or understanding, have not been identified, presumably because they have not yet been regarded as falling within the abusive category.

Common to all the above conceptions of psychological maltreatment is the loss or gain of power and control depending on whether or not one is looking at the subject from the vantage point of the perpetrator or the victim. Abusers have various ways of psychologically maltreating their victims. Jantz (1995:128) identifies several ways verbal psychological abusers accomplish their ends (for example, by means of "the overbearing opinion"—one who always has the better view of a subject, constantly uses "put-downs," or always devalues the victim's accomplishments—and "the great guilt-giver," one who always makes the victim the reason for his failures). Abusers, says Jantz, psychologically maltreat their victims through actions (for example, "the screamer," one who yells to emotionally intimidate and control; "the person who plays favorites," one who consistently makes the victim feel inferior to a favored person; and "the Dr. Jekyll and Mr. Hyde," the person whose public behavior masks his true private character).

The study of adult psychological maltreatment and its consequences has focused on dating relationships, marital and partner relationships, and on the treatment of the elderly.

Psychological Maltreatment During Dating

To understand what lies behind the expression of abuse among adults, it is important to consider what individuals bring to their relationship. Patterns of behavior learned in the socialization process, the different ways males and females are taught and learn to regard themselves and others, especially those of the opposite gender, are of particular concern to students of adult abuse. Behind this interest is the fact that the perpetrators of interpersonal violence and abuse of all kinds are predominantly men. What is it, then, about the socialization of men that makes them more likely than women to abuse another, psychologically and otherwise?

Typically, males more than females have been socialized to be simultaneously more aggressive, socially distant, and less vulnerable emotionally. The consequence, as Lisak, Hopper, and Song (1996) point out, is a level of "empathy deficits," a reduced ability to sympathetically identify with others. As they say, research on gender differences in development has yielded the consistent finding that males "learn to neutralize the expression of most emotions over the course of development" (1996:725). The evidence is that by early childhood, males become much less inclined to be expressive emotionally than females.

Of particular concern to Lisak, Hopper, and Song is the effect of the experience of abuse during the socialization process. If males being taught to suppress their emotions become the victims of abuse they are likely to experience fear and helplessness, emotions generally associated with being abused. One response "entails the rigid adherence to masculine gender norms, a resolution which requires the forceful suppression and repression of abuse-related emotions" (1996:725). Citing the work of Mosher and Tomkins (1988), Lisak, Hopper, and Song state that males who respond in this way tend to convert feelings of fear and helplessness into anger. And from their reading of the research evidence, "The gender-rigid, emotionally constricted individual is less likely to be able to tolerate approaching the negative emotional states evoked by trauma, and more likely to avoid them, either by using psychological defenses, or by converting them to aggressive action" (1996:725). The aggressive action the authors have in mind is, of course, the abuse of another.

To Lisak, Hopper, and Song, then, males, victimized by the socialization process and their caretakers, react to aroused conflicted feelings by developing rigid notions about gender roles and a reduced capacity to identify with the plight of others. Such individuals, it is assumed, are much more likely than others to be the perpetrators of abuse, the precise form of which may vary depending on personal experience and individual character traits.

A related and more common interpretation is that males are socialized by the tenets of patriarchal society. Patriarchal theorists postulate that male-female partner aggression is a product of a social norm subordinating women to the control of men. In this perspective, perceived female partner assertiveness is viewed by the male as a challenge to his right to control, to his power and authority. If one has learned this example from parental conduct or has experienced physical aggression in this context, one is likely to consider physical aggression a legitimate way of responding to challenges to authority in a dating (or marriage) relationship.

Following this lead, Stets (1991), concerned with developing a theoretical scheme to analyze psychological aggression in dating relationships, hypothesizes that those who accept the legitimacy of physical aggression may also accept the legitimacy of psychological aggression. Accordingly,

> those who inflict psychological aggression will be more accepting of physical aggression. Those who sustain psychological aggression will also be more accepting of physical aggression, otherwise they would not tolerate such aggression. (99)

Stets also suggests that the expression of and submission to aggressiveness in dating relationships is influenced by an individual's self-image. For example, a male with low self-esteem may become aggressive to bolster his self-image. And a female with low self-esteem may accept aggression as her just desserts.

Lastly, Stets, taking a further cue from research on physical aggression, hypothesizes that psychological aggression is more likely to occur in serious than in casual dating relationships. "Dating relationships in which there is high behavioral involvement (time spent with one's partner is large) may be characterized by an increased change that conflict will arise over such issues as fidelity or how to spend time together" (1991:100).

Stets tested his hypotheses on a sample of upper-division students in a midwestern university. The variable interpersonal control ("the degree to which one person controls another in a relationship") was measured by responding to assertions such as "I keep my partner in line," "I am successful in imposing my will onto my partner." Similar measures were constructed for the other independent variables ("Witnessing and Experiencing Physical Violence," "Self-Esteem," "Acceptance of Violence," and "Behavioral Involvement"). Contrary to hypothesized expectations, Stets found no difference in either the amount of control or aggression expressed by males and females across their relationships. He did find a correlation between interpersonal control and the infliction of psychological aggression. As he states:

> After controlling for all other factors, interpersonal control positively influences inflicting and sustaining psychological aggression in dating relationships. These effects are large relative to the other facts . . . , and they hold for both men and women. These findings, in combination with the lack of gender difference in either level of control or level of aggression, suggest that it is interpersonal control rather than structural positions in society which account for psychological abuse. (1991:108)

In a more recent study focusing on date abuse, and also based on a sample of undergraduates, Sappington et al. found that:

> Verbal abuse by a date was associated with an increased risk that the woman would experience emotional problems, drug problems, and would receive treatment. While verbal abuse may sound like a trivial problem next to sexual or physical abuse, it appears to be equally serious in terms of the problems associated with it. (1997:326)

Similar effects have been noted among married and common law partners. One would, however, expect the effects to be more serious among the former, if for no other reason than the greater difficulty of dissolving the relationship without risking legal repercussions.

Psychological Maltreatment of Partners

A prevailing assumption is that abuse generally is more likely in relationships where partners are unequal in physical power and economic independence. The greater the physical and economic inequality between partners, the greater the vulnerability of the weaker of the two to the expectations, demands, and disciplinary sanctions of the other. In such situations, what may constitute just grounds for punishment to one partner may be viewed by the other as unjustifiable and abusive. Most healthy relationships entail a semblance of this possibility in certain instances

because of different partner strengths and weaknesses, the inevitability of disagreements and disputes, and the complexity of effective conflict resolution. In the
healthy situation, disagreements are as likely to be resolved in favor of one partner
as the other depending on the circumstances. In the truly abusive situation, one
partner is the constant loser, the perpetual target of the controlling other.

Jantz feels that what is so damaging about emotional abuse is its far-reaching,
long-lasting effects. As he observes:

> Not only does it damage a person's self-esteem at the time that it is done, it also sets
> up a life pattern that daily assaults the inner-being. Present events and relationships
> are filtered through the negative messages and events of the past. Behavior is
> unknowingly modified to produce results consistent with the established life-
> pattern. Through continued emotional assault, even a healthy life pattern can be
> subverted by an abusive one. (1995:31–32)

Valerie Nash Chang puts it this way:

> Any relationship that forces adaptation to another person will lead to some loss of
> sense of self. Women who have experienced on-going psychological abuse give voice
> to this process. In their attempt to please him and avoid criticism, they vigilantly
> censor their actions, adapting until all sense of unique self is lost. (1996:109)

In general, the greater the loss of self, the greater the dependency. Associated
with heightened dependency is vulnerability to increased rather than decreased
bonding with the perpetrator. The effect is similar to what is referred to as the
Stockholm syndrome, the tendency of hostages to develop psychological attachment to their captors. Loring refers to the effect as "traumatic bonding." As she
describes it, "Loss of self leaves the victim vulnerable to traumatic bonding, a type
of attachment that intensifies the loss of selfhood. . . . Fear and terror render the
emotionally abused woman incapable of detaching herself from the relationship
with the abuser, for she has no separate and cohesive self to detach" (1994:45).

Traumatic bonding is not simply one-way, the attachment of the victim to the
perpetrator. The perpetrator too becomes dependent on the victim. The relationship
between the victim and the perpetrator becomes one of "codependency." "A
characteristic kind of attachment binds victim and abuser . . . the abuser perceives
the victim in terms of his own needs and wishes, while the victim struggles to
connect with him in a mutually validating and emphatic manner" (Loring:16).

Loring emphasizes that psychological maltreatment of female by male adult
partners is accomplished by overt and covert means. She provides a list of 23 ways
of effecting overt psychological abuse, including belittling, yelling, criticizing,
slamming doors, and withholding of affection. She describes covert abuse as
consisting of "an insidious, sometimes complex pattern of negative feedback." The
means, often unrecognized for what they are, include discounting the victim's
needs and feelings, constantly reminding the victim of her intellectual and social

inferiority, and threatening physical and emotional abandonment. The message to the woman is that she, not he, is the cause of her own abuse.

Conveying the idea that the victim rather than the abuser is the problem is also readily apparent in the psychological maltreatment of the elderly. But here, too, emotional abuse may be perpetrated by both covert and overt, direct and indirect, means.

Psychological Maltreatment of the Elderly

Psychological maltreatment is extremely prevalent among the elderly. Some studies (Block and Sinnott 1979; Boydstron and McNairn 1981; Wolf and Pillemer 1989) have found it to be the most frequent type of elder abuse. Even when not found to be the primary type, it is invariably found to be associated with all other major types of abuse (physical, sexual, neglect).

Commonly, psychological maltreatment of the elderly is conceptualized as causing "mental anguish," especially stress and confusion that undermines self-confidence and promotes dependency. Mental anguish is often described as the result of three factors: humiliation, harassment, and manipulation. To Tanya Johnson (1986), for example, humiliation can occur by making elders feel ashamed of their behavior, by blaming elders for attitudes and behavior so as to make them feel guilty, and by ridiculing the thoughts and actions of elders. Harassment, she says, is accomplished by bullying, intimidating, and in other ways threatening older people. Finally, she says, mental anguish can be the result of manipulative behavior.

> Manipulation can be experienced by an elder by . . . being denied access to information, being given false information, being forced to rely on others so that a situation of unreasonable dependence is created. . . . (187–88)

Pillemer and Wolf define elder psychological abuse as "the infliction of mental anguish, e.g., called names, treated as a child, frightened, humiliated, intimidated, threatened, isolated, etc." (1986:220). Their research, conducted in the early 1980s and sponsored by the U.S. Administration on Aging, surveyed elder abuse in three geographical areas: Worcester, Massachusetts; Syracuse, New York; and Rhode Island. The three areas yielded a total of 328 substantiated cases of elder abuse. Psychological abuse was the most prevalent, and constituted 72 percent (236) of the total. The means of effecting psychological abuse assumed the following rank order: intimidation, verbal assault, humiliation, threats, isolation, and "other manifestations." More than one means invariably was used.

More recently, Peretti and Majecen (1991) sought to determine the factors that affect elder emotional abuse in home interviews with 58 individuals age 68 to 87. In rank order by frequency of response, the following 9 variables were identified: lack of attention, lack of affection, neglect, derogatory naming, demeaning commentary, exploitation, threats of violence, loud talking, and confinement.

Lack of attention referred to being ignored and made to feel unimportant, the effect of which was to make the individual feel isolated and alone. By *lack of affection* respondents meant the failure of family members to kiss, hug, squeeze, and generally provide "tactile stimulation." *Neglect* meant ignoring essential bodily needs by failing to provide timely assistance in eating, drinking, and eliminating. *Derogatory naming* referred to the use of "pernicious names or labels." No examples were provided. *Demeaning commentary* was basically defined as the use of language conveying a low opinion of the individual. *Exploitation* referred to feelings of being taken advantage of financially by friends and relatives. *Threats of violence* included both verbal and actual physical assault. *Loud talking* meant being addressed in such a loud way as to indicate anger and hostility. *Confinement* referred to being restricted in terms of movement about their own home (confinement to certain rooms) and not being allowed outdoors by themselves (1991:258–60).

The picture conveyed is one in which victims are confused as to why they are being abused and helpless to do much, if anything, about it. Because of their limitations—physical, psychological, financial, and so on—the elderly victim is inevitably forced to internalize a good deal of the resulting frustration and anger. The psychological and behavioral consequences are discussed in the next section.

The Incidence of Adult Psychological Maltreatment

The prevalence of adult psychological maltreatment and neglect is even less well documented than that for children. A national incident study comparable to that for children is yet to be conducted. This is the case even though it is commonly assumed to be the most extensive of the major forms of maltreatment. A major obstacle to accurate data collection is the absence of an accepted operational definition of the concept, a term that investigators can use with confidence to guide their research. Consequently, as Follingstad et al. state, psychological maltreatment "has not been an area in which researchers have appeared eager to delve, perhaps because it is so difficult to define" (1990:108). As it is, one cannot be sure that those who use and study the subject of psychological maltreatment are examining the same thing or different things. Exactly what does and does not constitute psychological maltreatment remains something of a mystery. As Follingstad et al. indicate, the available evidence as to its prevalence is noteworthy for being anecdotal and fragmentary.

Some suggestive data are available concerning the psychological maltreatment of the elderly, the most helpless and dependent of the adult population. In the late 1980s, Pillemer and Finkelhor (1988) reported the results of their study of a random sample of the elderly population (those 65 years of age and older) of the Boston metropolitan area. Some 2,020 people were asked to report the extent of their neglect and physical and psychological abuse. Psychological abuse was defined as repeated verbal insults and threats and classified for data analysis as "chronic verbal aggression." Indicators of neglect included failure to provide certain personal services such as meals, housework, haircuts, and so on. The frequency of physical violence was the highest, a rate of 20 per 1,000 members of the population. Next came chronic verbal aggression at 11 per 1,000 and neglect at 4 per 1,000.

Inspired by the Boston study, researchers in Britain conducted a small-scale national survey to determine the extent of elder abuse. A questionnaire was administered in 1992 to a random sample of 2,130 individuals 60 years of age and older. Three categories of abuse were specified, verbal (defined comparably to that used in the Boston survey), physical, and financial. As reported by Bennett and Kingston (1993), verbal abuse ranked the highest (5 percent, or 32 of the 593 individuals in the sample 65 years of age or older). Further, "more women (7 percent) than men (4 percent) are verbally abused, although there is a slightly higher proportion of men who reported physical and financial abuse (3 percent) than women (1 percent)" (148).

Comparable surveys for nonelderly adults by status (dating, married) and gender are not available. What piecemeal evidence there is suggests that psychological maltreatment is highly prevalent and seriously damaging to its victims. Some contend that its effects are just as, if not more, devastating than those of physical abuse. To Valerie Nash Chang, "Because the erosion of self-esteem, self-confidence, and self-concept that results from psychological abuse is slow to heal, psychic bruises are often deeper, more lasting, and more devastating than physical bruises" (1996:12).

Behavioral Consequences of Psychological Maltreatment

The most consistently mentioned psychological effect of psychological maltreatment in adults or children is loss of self, or low self-esteem, the feeling that one is inferior, inadequate, a failure, and impotent in all major respects. According to Loring and Myers the major means of effecting low self-esteem, humiliation and degradation, destroy the victim's ability to communicate, his or her sense of values and dreams and very reason for living. This form of violence, they say, "Can bring on profound depression and illness, automobile accidents, suicide, and murder of the abuser" (1994:15).

Jantz emphasizes that the concomitants of psychological maltreatment are anxiety, frustration, and hopelessness. When such emotions are constant and intense, he says, they cause the body to produce chemicals that encourage fight or flight. The problem is, of course, that most of the time, neither of the two is perceived as a valid option. The result, according to Jantz, is that the chemical imbalance encourages options such as: addictions, allergies/asthma, depression, digestive disturbances, eating disorders, free-floating anxiety, hypochondria, migraine headaches, panic attacks, phobias, and unexplained skin rashes (1995:98).

Not surprisingly, posttraumatic stress disorder (PTSD) has been correlated with psychological maltreatment. The American Psychiatric Association describes PTSD as follows:

> The essential feature of Posttraumatic Stress Disorder is the development of characteristic symptoms following exposure to an extreme traumatic stressor involving direct personal experience of an event that involves actual or threatened death or serious injury, or other threat to one's physical integrity; or witnessing an event that

involves death, injury, or a threat to the physical integrity of another person; or learning about unexpected or violent death, serious harm, or threat of death or injury experienced by a family member or other close associate. (1994:424)

As the description suggests, PTSD is typically thought of as a response to an extremely distressing psychological event that happens all at once such as being forcibly raped or witnessing a brutal murder. However, PTSD may also be the cumulative product of subtle and indirect actions and threats such as those integral to psychological maltreatment, persistent verbal abuse generating overwhelming distress, and the diverse personal and socially aberrant consequences cited above.

It is important to be mindful not only of the possibility of the same effect being produced by either dramatic instances or accumulative effect, but also by non-abusive and abusive antecedents. Sensitivity to these complexities is particularly important in the study of the aging population.

Aging Americans are particularly sensitive to their physical appearance, many feeling so humiliated by their "looks" as to feel ashamed to appear in public. Elderly people are also prone to being depressed and experiencing low self-esteem due to declining physical ability and sense of social usefulness. As noted above, major means of effecting low self-esteem by psychological maltreatment include persistent acts that shame and humiliate. How much the low self-esteem associated with individual and social pathologies among the elderly is the consequence of impersonal cultural values or psychological maltreatment is unknown. Nonetheless, it is an important subject because of the ever-growing elderly population and its vulnerability to stress and maltreatment.

Summary

Psychological maltreatment is regarded by many as the most important variety of family abuse. Its importance lies not so much in the way it is imposed as in its consequences. Its nonphysical, primarily verbal, and often subtle means of perpetration belies its power to devastate the victim's self-esteem and sense of autonomy. The abuser is always right, the victim always wrong. By persistently undermining self-confidence, by publicly humiliating and constantly correcting and belittling the victim, the abuser becomes the controlling authority and the victim his or her subject to treat in any way desired. But the reaction is not simple, untroubled compliance. Those victimized by psychological maltreatment have been found to exhibit a wide range of aberrant responses, most of which are self-directed: eating disorders (bulimia, anorexia, compulsive overeating); substance abuse; and psychological problems (depression, hypochondria, migraine headaches, phobias, skin rashes). Some exhibit posttraumatic stress disorder, all the symptoms of having been victimized by a supremely threatening experience. Sometimes, however, the response has been other directed. Some victims have been found to murder their abusers.

The effects of psychological maltreatment parallel those identified for the other major types of abuse (physical, sexual). This indicates that the effective locus of all forms of abuse is the mind, the directing center of individual thought and action. The difficulty specifying the exact content of the human mind and how it operates is behind the complexity of the study of psychological maltreatment and specifying exactly what it is and is not. The subject has been variously referred to as psychological abuse, emotional abuse, verbal aggression, controlling behaviors, psychological torture, and even brainwashing. The trend has been to subsume all under the neutral sounding term *psychological maltreatment.*

A problem for researchers is the differentiation of psychological maltreatment as a form of abuse from the central effect of all forms of abuse. Yet to be clarified is whether or not different types of abuse (physical, sexual, psychological) yield different measurable behavioral effects. It is not known whether all forms of abuse constitute simply different ways of influencing the same "thing" (the mind) or distinct causes of different types of behavior. Researchers have yet to conduct studies controlling for the different possible comparative effects of different types of abuse. A direct connection between a certain type of abuse, and only that type of abuse, and a distinct behavioral effect is yet to be determined. What we do seem sure of is that suffering persistent abuse is associated with a range of aberrant possibilities, depending on age, developmental stage of life, and a number of individual (gender, past experiences) and social (socioeconomic status, marital status) factors. The contributions of biological factors such as so-called genetic predisposition have yet to be included in the examination of factors that influence the perpetration and effects of abuse.

Finally, the available evidence suggests the durability of suffering childhood psychological maltreatment. Adults have been found to suffer long-term health consequences (physical and psychological) of being psychologically and otherwise abused as children. Compared to those who have not, those psychologically maltreated as children also have been found to be more susceptible to later abuse as adults. The different theoretical explanations for these findings remain to be validated by empirical testing.

Study Questions

1. Why is it important to keep in mind possible differences between the meaning of terms such as *emotional maltreatment* and *psychological abuse*?

2. What are the major forms of child psychological maltreatment?

3. How prevalent is child psychological maltreatment and neglect?

4. What are some of the adult consequences of suffering childhood psychological maltreatment?

5. What are the major forms of adult psychological maltreatment and neglect?

6. What is known about the personal and deviant consequences of child and adult psychological maltreatment?

7. Why is psychological maltreatment considered by many to be the most important of the major types of abuse?

REFERENCES

American Psychiatric Association. 1994. *Diagnostic and Statistical Manual of Mental Disorders,* 4th ed. Washington, DC: Author.

Bennett, Gerald and Paul Kingston. 1993. *Elder Abuse: Concepts, Theories, and Interventions.* London: Chapman & Hall.

Block, M. R. and J. D. Sinnott, eds. 1979. *The Battered Elder Syndrome: An Exploratory Study.* College Park: University of Maryland, Center for Aging.

Boydstron, L. S. and J. A. McNairn. 1981. "Elder Abuse by Adult Caretakers." In *Physical and Financial Abuse of the Elderly.* Pub. No. 97–297. Washington, DC: U.S. House of Representatives, Select Committee on Aging, San Francisco.

Brassard, Marla B. and M. Gelardo. 1987. "Psychological Maltreatment: The Unifying Concept in Child Abuse and Neglect." *School Psychology Review.* 16:127–36.

Brassard, Marla B., Robert Germain, and Stuart N. Hart. 1987. *Psychological Maltreatment of Children and Youth.* NY: Pergamon Press.

Brassard, Marla B., Stuart N. Hart, and David B. Hardy. 1991. "Psychological and Emotional Abuse of Children." Pp. 255–70 in *Case Studies in Family Violence,* Robert T. Ammerman and Michel Hersen, eds. NY: Plenum Press.

Cerezo, M. Angeles and Dolores Frias. 1994. "Emotional and Cognitive Adjustment in Abused Children." *Child Abuse & Neglect.* 18:923–32.

Chang, Valerie Nash (1996). *I Just Lost Myself: Psychological Abuse of Women in Marriage.* Westport, CT: Praeger.

Crittenden, Patricia M. 1984. "Sibling Interaction: Evidence of a Generational Effect in Maltreating Infants." *Child Abuse & Nelect.* 8:433–38.

DeGregoria, Barbara. 1987. "Sex Role Attitude and Perception of Psychological Abuse." *Sex Roles.* 16:227–35.

Follingstad, Diane R., Larry L. Rutledge, Barbara J. Berg, Elizabeth S. Hause, and Darlene S. Polek. 1990. "The Role of Emotional Abuse in Physically Abusive Relationships." *Journal of Family Violence.* 5:107–20.

Garbarino, James. 1993. "Psychological Child Maltreatment: A Developmental View." *Primary Care.* 20:307–15.

Garbarino, James, Edna Guttmann, and Janis Wilson Seeley. 1986. *The Psychologically Battered Child.* San Francisco, CA: Jossey-Bass Publishers.

Gross, Amy B. and Harold R. Keller. 1992. "Long-Term Consequences of Childhood Physical and Psychological Maltreatment." *The Journal of Aggressive Behavior.* 18:171–85.

Iwaniec, Dorota. 1995. *The Emotionally Abused and Neglected Child: Identification, Assessment and Intervention.* NY: John Wiley & Sons.

Jantz, Gregory L. 1995. *Healing the Scars of Emotional Abuse.* Grand Rapids, MI: Fleming H. Revell.

Johnson, Tanya. 1986. "Critical Issues in the Definition of Elder Mistreatment." Pp. 167–96 in *Elder Abuse: Conflict in the Family,* Karl A. Pillemer and Rosalie S. Wolf, eds. Dover, MA: Auburn House Publishing Company.

Keith-Oaks, Judy. 1990. "Emotional Abuse: Destruction of the Spirit and the Sense Self." *The Clearing House.* 64:31–5.

Lisak, David, Jim Hopper, and Pat Song. 1996. "Factors in the Cycle of Violence: Gender Rigidity and Emotional Constriction." *Journal of Traumatic Stress.* 9:721–43.

Loring, Marti Tamm. 1994. *Emotional Abuse.* NY: Lexington Books.

Loring, Marti Tamm and David L. Myers. 1994. "Differentiating Emotional Abuse." Pp. 15–24 in *Emotional Abuse.* NY: Lexington Books.

Moeller, Tamerra P. and Gloria A. Bachmann. 1993. "The Combined Effects of Physical, Sexual, and Emotional Abuse During Childhood: Long-Term Health Consequences for Women." *Child Abuse & Neglect.* 17:623–40.

Mosher, D. L. and S. S. Tomkins. 1988. "Scripting the Macho Man: Hypermasculine Socialization and Enculturation." *The Journal of Sex Research.* 25:60–84.

O'Hagan, Kieran P. 1995. "Emotional and Psychological Abuse: Problems of Definition." *Child Abuse & Neglect*. 19:449–61.

Peretti, Peter O. and Kris G. Majecen. 1991. "Emotional Abuse Among the Elderly: Affecting Behavioral Variables." *Social Behavior and Personality*. 19:255–61.

Pillemer, Karl A. and D. Finkelhor. 1988. "The Prevalence of Elder Abuse: A Random Survey Sample." *The Gerontologist*. 28:51–57.

Pillemer, Karl A. and Rosalie S. Wolf, eds. 1986. *Elder Abuse: Conflict in the Family*. Dover, MA: Auburn House Publishing Company.

Sappington, A. A., Robert Pharr, Ashley Tunstall, and Edward Rickert. 1997. "Relationships Among Child Abuse, Date Abuse, and Psychological Problems." *Journal of Clinical Psychology*. 53:319–29.

Stets, Jan E. 1991. "Psychological Aggression in Dating Relationships: The Role of Interpersonal Control." *Journal of Family Violence*. 6:97–114.

Whipple, Ellen E. and Sara E. Finton. 1995. "Psychological Maltreatment by Siblings: An Unrecognized Form of Abuse." *Child and Adolescent Social Work Journal*. 12:135–46.

Widom, Cathy Spatz. 1989. "Does Violence Beget Violence? A Critical Examination of the Literature." *Psychological Bulletin*. 106:3–28.

——— . 1992. "The Cycle of Violence." National Institute of Justice. Washington, DC: U.S. Department of Justice.

Wiehe, Vernon R. 1990. *Sibling Abuse: Hidden Physical, Emotional, and Sexual Trauma*. Lexington, MA: Lexington Books.

——— . 1996. *Working With Child Abuse and Neglect*. Thousand Oaks, CA: Sage Publications.

Wolf, Rosalie S. and Karl A. Pillemer. 1989. *Helping Elderly Victims*. NY: Columbia University Press.

5 Physical Abuse, Sexual Abuse, and Deviancy: Theoretical Interpretations

While much attention may be focused on sexual abuse, perpetrators, and victims, Finkelhor (1979) points out that more is known about sexual deviance than healthy sexuality and how it develops. While theory development in general is not sufficiently developed, sexual abuse may be the area where theory is least developed (Hudson and Ward 1997).

Whether the field of family violence should search for one theory to explain all types of family abuse or whether several special theories are preferable to explain some types is an important issue. A single theory would allow cutting through a mass of confusing and contradictory opinions about why people commit physical and sexual abuse. It could also lead to a coordinated and consistent strategy for dealing with the problem. On the other hand, it may be that one theory about both physical and sexual abuse would be too broad and of limited use in explaining specific types of family abuse and too general to lead to a specific treatment and prevention strategy. Thus there are three reasons for theory development: explanation, understanding, and application. In addition, well-developed theory can replace the prejudicial opinions and wild speculation of some social commentators and political pundits that often prevent effective action meant to prevent further abuse.

Mendel (1995) provides a succinct statement regarding the importance of theory to the understanding of sexual abuse, which can also be applied to physical abuse:

> Conceptual frameworks provide a lens through which to view the disparate phenomena that comprise child sexual abuse. It is only through creating such a lens—and then continually honing and polishing it—that our understanding of child sexual abuse is advanced. There is, or must be, a recursive mutual feedback loop between data collection and analysis on the one hand, the theory formation

on the other. Optimally, the model or framework should guide us in our choices of questions and research strategies; the resultant data should then be fed back into the loop and our theories revised accordingly. Out of the meld of theory and research arises increased knowledge of child sexual abuse and, thus, more effective avenues of intervention. (74)

Theories of childhood maltreatment are of two basic types—theories that seek to explain why physical and sexual abuse occur and theories that examine the effects of abuse on the victim. The first type of theory, for example, tries to explain why fathers have sexual intercourse with their daughters. The second type of theory examines the effects of the abuse on the daughter. The intergenerational transmission theory of abuse focuses on victims becoming abusers and is an integration of the two types. This chapter reviews theories that examine the causes and effects of physical and sexual abuse. Special attention is given to intergenerational transmission theory, also known as the "cycle of violence" theory.

Marshall (1997) describes three levels of theory in an examination of deviant behavior: the *macrolevel, midlevel,* and *microlevel.* The macrolevel is the broadest and tends to focus on the development of all types of abuse. For example, macrolevel theory may focus on how the individual becomes a perpetrator of abuse. According to Marshall, the best use of a macrolevel theory is to point to issues that need further explanation and empirical evidence. A midlevel theory focuses on one type of deviant behavior, such as pedophilia. For example, a midlevel theory may try to explain the sexual abuse of children. Finally, microlevel theory examines a particular aspect of a specific type of deviance—such as empathy in perpetrators. Microlevel theories, because they are specific, are more likely to be used in specific research. Ideally, the results of microlevel work can then feed theories at the midlevel and macrolevel.

The following will review older and more current theories regarding the development of physical and sexual abuse. It will include coverage of psychological, sociological, and social psychological theories of abuse. See Box 5.1 for a review of the major assumptions in theories of the development of physical and sexual abuse. The latter part of the chapter will discuss theories of the consequences of abuse.

Psychological Theories

Psychological theories locate the source of abuse within the individual perpetrator. Three approaches to psychological theories of physical and sexual abuse predominate: *psychiatric, behavioral,* and *cognitive.* The first emphasizes the role of mental illness. The second emphasizes rewards and punishments. The third focuses on how cognitive images, especially fantasy and media images, may lead to deviant behavior. Psychological theories of abuse have focused much more on the psychiatric approach of understanding underlying emotional conflicts than on the behavioral or cognitive approaches.

B O X 5.1
Theories of Causes of Physical and Sexual Abuse

Theory	Major Assumptions
Psychological Theories	The source of the abuse is located within the individual perpetrator or individual victim.
a. Psychiatric theories	Abuse occurs because of deviant personality traits that result from problems in the completion of childhood developmental stages.
b. Behavioral theories	Abuse occurs because it has rewards for the abuser or its avoidance resulted in punishment.
c. Cognitive theories	Abuse occurs because the perpetrator acts on fantasies of abuse or is trying to resolve dissonance in self–image.
Sociological Theories	Abuse is caused by societal factors.
a. Subculture of violence theory	Abusive behavior occurs regularly and is considered acceptable to perpetrators and victims within a specific subculture.
b. Feminist theory	Abuse occurs because women are considered subordinate to men and a patriarchal society encourages violence toward women.
c. Sex role socialization theory	Men are socialized to be more aggressive than women and sexual aggressiveness bolsters men's sense of masculinity. Male victims are assaulted when they have feminine roles.
d. Social learning theory	Abusers have learned their behavior by being witness to or victims of abuse themselves and have received approval for abusing others.
e. Resource theory	Abusers have more resources (social, financial, psychological), they devalue the victims, and they are able to impose their will on victims.
f. Social exchange theory	Abusers have the power to exploit victims while victims lack sufficient power to rebuff the abuse and lack sufficient resources to offer alternative rewards.
g. Family systems theory	The source of abuse is located within imbalances in dynamics and relationships among family members.
Social/Psychological Theories	Abuse occurs because of a combination of factors including characteristics of abusers and environmental influences.
a. Finkelhor's four pre-conditions model of sexual abuse	For child abuse to occur there must be motivation, overcoming internal and external inhibitors, and overcoming the resistance of the child.
b. Attachment theory	Abuse occurs because of inadequate or inappropriate relationships with parents, which prevents a loving bond from developing between the parent figure and the child.

Psychiatric Theories

While there are differences between psychoanalytic and psychiatric theories, they will be jointly discussed. (See Tzeng, Jackson, and Karlson [1991] for further discussion of the distinctions between psychoanalytic and psychiatric theories.)

These theories, especially psychoanalytic theory, have their basis in the work of Sigmund Freud. (See Box 5.2.) Psychoanalytic theory focuses on development through psychosexual stages. According to Freud, these stages are the oral stage, the anal stage, the phallic stage, latency, and the genital stage. (See any introductory psychology textbook for a review of these stages. See also Hall [1954].) Problems can arise in the completion of these developmental stages. Experiencing childhood trauma and failure to resolve conflicts are thought to lead to problems in becoming a fully functioning adult. Freud also developed a theory of personality he claimed is divided into three parts. The *id* is governed by the "pleasure principle" and has no regard for responsible behavior. The *ego* is governed by the "reality principle," which allows the individual to make appropriate and rational decisions. The *superego* is known as the "conscience" and governs ethical standards—it is also the source of guilt. A deficiency in the development of the ego or superego was thought to be associated with deviant behavior (Masters and Roberson 1990). Obviously, the inability to feel guilt (today known as antisocial personality disorder) can set the scene for serious criminal offending including family abuse.

Finkelhor (1979) points out that early theories of sexual abuse were in the psychopathology model; that is, perpetrators of abuse were considered physical and moral degenerates who had personality disorders. If the failure to deal with issues of psychological development results in anger displaced toward others, then sexual and physical abuse of others can result.

One explanation of sexual abuse consistent with psychoanalytic theory is that abusers are not able to fulfill their needs in adult relationships and, therefore, turn to children (Tzeng et al. 1991). Gleuck (1954) felt that perpetrators of child sexual

B O X **5.2**

Freud, Psychoanalytic Theory, and Incest

Freud developed his seduction theory in the mid-1890s. Seduction theory claimed that all neuroses are the result of childhood sexual abuse. Freud committed himself to seduction theory before a professional audience in 1896 and his theory was not well received. Freud then rejected seduction theory as the explanation for *all* neuroses. He began saying that some reports of incest by young women were hysterical fantasies, that their unresolved castration anxiety and "Electra Complex" led girls to fantasize about having sex with their fathers. However, Freud did not feel the theory deserved total rejection. He continued to feel some neurotics were sexually victimized by their fathers.

Source: Peter Gay. 1988. *Freud: A Life for Our Time.* NY: W. W. Norton and Company.

abuse had seductive mothers, which led to incest anxiety, failure to deal with Oedipal conflicts, and a fear of women and sexuality.

The psychoanalytic and psychiatric theories have been widely accepted, in part, because they fit the notion that abusers are sick individuals, apart from normal people. The evidence to support these theories, however, is considered very weak and these theories have fallen from favor (Tzeng et al. 1991). Kline (1987) argues that while psychoanalytic theories may not have much empirical support, it is possible to conduct research that will show the strength of these theories. In their review of the literature, however, Tzeng et al. (1991) found that research documented few personality traits shared by child sexual abusers. There is evidence that perpetrators of sexual abuse tend to be shy, passive, and less assertive than the average person. However, these are hardly characteristics that can easily distinguish the abuser from the nonabuser. Psychological theories can also ignore other critical factors such as family, community, and other social factors (Gelles 1993). Gelles points out that there

> continues to be a heavy psychological bias in most theoretical conceptualizations about the causes and explanations of child abuse, wife abuse, elder abuse, and other forms of family violence. The enduring stereotype of family violence is that the abuser is mentally disturbed or truly psychotic and that the victim is a defenseless innocent. The typical reaction to a description of a case of domestic violence or a photo of an abused woman or child is that "only a sick person" would do such a thing. (40)

According to Gelles, "Only about 10 percent of abusive incidents are caused by mental illness" (41). Yllo (1993), in discussing wife battering, cautions that "it is crucial that psychological *explanations* of battering not serve as *excuses* for battering" (59). Yllo also cautions that the psychological problems of women have been inappropriately seen as the cause of their victimization. In effect, the problems resulting from abuse are cast as a "victim personality," in which personality traits and/or poor judgment put the woman at risk of abuse. This explanation can be seen as a sophisticated form of victim blaming.

Another theory that examines individual pathology is that sex offenders may have deviant sexual arousal. This means that they have a physical response to inappropriate sexual objects such as children. This is not a theory about the cause of sexual abuse, but rather an effort to objectively measure sexual arousal that reflects an underlying problem. Phallometric assessments (a process known as phallometry) measure erectile responses in the effort to determine whether offenders have abnormal sexual attractions to children.

This is a controversial subject with conflicting research results regarding the usefulness of phallometry. Some have concluded that the use of phallometry does not clearly support the notion of deviant sexual arousal (Marshall 1997). Marshall discusses the ethical difficulties of using this method with juvenile offenders, noting this has been used with offenders as young as 10: "It seems to me that presenting such young boys with clearly sexually erotic images of younger children might actually encourage deviance" (165). Operant conditioning programs designed to reduce arousal by applying electrical shocks are based, in part, on this notion. Even in the presence of deviant sexual arousal, however, there is a difference between feeling aroused and doing something about it.

Some theories of sexual abuse focus on characteristics of the victim to explain sexual abuse. Finkelhor (1979) reminds us that through the years some have thought that children can behave in seductive ways and actually encourage sexual activity to take place. Emotionally needy children who have poor relationships with their parents have found they can receive attention by appealing to the sexuality of adults. The "sexually defenseless child" is vulnerable and may appear to readily accept the sexual activity. Known as a "victim precipitation" theory, it examines the ways in which children are seen as responsible for their own sexual abuse. Finkelhor states: "The idea that children are responsible for their own seduction has been at the center of almost all writing on sexual abuse since the topic was first broached" (1979:24). He notes that the concept is poorly defined and can certainly lead to concerns about blaming the victim.

Psychological characteristics of the victim have also been used to explain physical abuse. The use of "victim personality" was mentioned above. In addition, family members who are seen as annoying or whose psychological problems impair their interactions with the family may be said to be "asking for trouble." The victims may even be said to be seeking the abuse as a warped form of attention-getting or as a misunderstood form of expressed love.

Behavioral Theories

This approach to psychological theory explains behavior as a result of rewards and punishments. With respect to physical and sexual abuse, the thought is that individuals who abuse family members receive rewards from abusing or (less often) experience punishments if they refrain from abusing. The rewards may be behavioral (compliance with the abuser's wishes), emotional (sadistic pleasure), or social (affirmation of power and authority). They may even be economic if the abuser financially exploits the victim, as with prostitution or confiscation of income of the victim.

Little research has been done on the behavioral psychology of physical and sexual abuse. The most powerful research tool of behavioral psychology, experimental psychology, cannot be ethically or legally used to produce abusive outcomes. There has, however, been some work done with "token economies." A token economy occurs when someone receives a token (a gold star, a plastic chip, a check mark on a chart) for good behavior. In this case, abusers receive rewards if they refrain from their abusive behavior. It has mainly been tested with respect to physical abuse by children. It is more difficult to test this theory with respect to sexual abuse because of the difficulty of observing and tracking the behavior. If experimenters observed the behavior, they would be obliged to immediately intervene; but perhaps this could be built into the experimental protocol as part of the "punishment" procedures.

Behavioral research has primarily been done with children and its generalizability to real life situations or to adults is unclear. The use of electrical shocks as part of behavioral conditioning to reduce sexual arousal among adults is consistent with behavioral theory as well as arousal theory. However, the procedure is controversial and the ability to generalize the results to the real world is not well documented.

Cognitive Theories

Cognitive psychological theories of physical and sexual abuse concentrate on how fantasies and media images act as a cognitive rehearsal for subsequent behavior. Fantasies of sexual domination and physical aggression are seen as precursors to sexual and physical violence. Media images of sexual violence and physical aggression are thought to encourage these fantasies. Experimental research with films and comic books that portray such abuse has clearly shown a correlation between exposure to these images and abusive behavior.

The media and authors who write for them have generally discounted the voluminous research showing this association. The counterargument is that such images only reflect the violence of society. Little rigorous research has been done supporting this view. Many have also resisted attempts to reduce images of sexual and physical violence as infringing on the rights of free speech and journalistic autonomy.

While psychological theories are not especially helpful in explaining why sexual and physical abuse occurs, they have contributed to efforts to treat offenders (Gelles 1993). The majority of treatment efforts have their basis in the psychological perspective as they focus on altering the thoughts, feelings, and behavior of the individual perpetrator. These psychologically based interventions will be discussed in Chapter 11 on treatment of family abusers.

Sociological Theories

Sociological theories offer the widest perspective for explaining physical and sexual abuse. According to Gelles: "A sociological perspective neither excludes nor diminishes the contributions of psychological or social psychological variables; rather, it places these variables within a wider explanatory framework that considers the impact of social institutions and social structures on social behavior" (1993:43). However, the sociological perspective is not without flaws. Sociological theories are complex as they examine many factors. They do not lead to simple solutions to family violence. Sociological theories, therefore, do not easily provide guidance for clinical interventions.

Several different sociological theories of physical and sexual abuse have been proposed. These include theories about resource control, subcultures of violence, feminism and patriarchy, sex role socialization, social learning, social exchange, and family systems. Each of the sociological theories has a different view of social systems and how they produce abusive behavior. They are not mutually exclusive and do overlap. All of these theories may explain different aspects of family abuse.

Subculture of Violence Theory

Gelles (1993) considers the subculture of violence theory to be the most fully developed and widely used theory. Wolfgang and Ferracuti (1967) explain why certain groups in our society have different levels of violence by saying the offenders come from specific groups that have norms and values that encourage violence. This view is supported by the fact that violence is not randomly distributed throughout the country, or even within a single city. It tends to be concentrated in limited geographic areas. More important, official records suggest that it is more likely in some ethnic or racial groups than others; but these records have been criticized as potentially reflecting the prejudice of the record keepers by overlooking violence in geographic areas or social groups of those having economic or political power. With respect to sexual abuse, a similar argument is made that for some groups sexual coercion is normatively accepted not only by the perpetrators, but by the victims as well. This comes close to blaming the victim for living in a violent and coercive environment.

The subculture of violence hypothesis has a lot of popular support, in part, because it allows many people to say that violent people are not like themselves. The violent are said to have different norms and values, not shared with peaceable citizens like themselves. The leap from believing abusers are part of a subculture of violence to believing they are part of a deviant subculture is a small one. These beliefs, then, justify treating abusers differently. Why should they be treated humanely if they don't share the humane norms and values that we do? This view is, of course, based on beliefs and opinions about other groups. Except for members of criminal gangs and certain religious cults, however, there is scant research evidence of clearly identifiable violent subcultures. There is certainly no scientific evidence that those engaged in physical and sexual abuse come primarily from such groups. The vast majority of abusers come from the same cultural groups we do.

Feminist Theory

The feminist perspective focuses on power and gender issues when dealing with family violence (Yllo 1993). The key to this approach is understanding the historical subordination of women to men. While women have made significant historical contributions to society, men have been the ones to record and interpret history— the patriarchal tradition (Lerner 1986). The feminist perspective encourages an examination of the societal structure that is designed to condone, perhaps encourage, and perpetuate the superordination of men over women. Dobash and Dobash (1979) have long been known for their view that a patriarchal society encourages violence toward women, and Herman showed that male supremacy is a critical factor in father-daughter incest:

> Whereas male supremacy creates the social conditions that favor development of father-daughter incest, the sexual division of labor creates the psychological conditions that lead to the same result. Male supremacy invests fathers with immense

powers over their children, especially their daughters. The sexual division of labor, in which women nurture children and men do not, produces fathers who are predisposed to use their power exploitatively. The rearing of children by subordinate women ensures the reproduction in each generation of the psychology of male supremacy. It produces sexually aggressive men with little capacity to nurture, nurturant women with undeveloped sexual capacities, and children of both sexes who stand in awe of the power of father.

Wherever these conditions obtain, father-daughter incest is likely to be a common occurrence. In any culture, the greater the degree of male supremacy and the more rigid the sexual division of labor, the more frequently one might expect the taboo on father-daughter incest to be violated. (1981:62)

According to Gelles, the feminist approach "focuses only on the influence of gender and gender-structured relations on the institution of the family and the violence and abuse therein" (1993:35). One strength of feminist theory is that it "provides the explanation and the formulation to both explain and end violence toward women" (41). That is, feminist theory is not content with explaining the behavior but seeks an advocacy approach to stop the violence. Another strength of feminist theory, according to Gelles (1993), is that varying types of research, using different methodologies, offer support that inequality between the sexes explains violence against women.

As with any theory, there are limitations to the feminist theory. The major problem, according to Gelles, is that it focuses exclusively on patriarchy as the cause of violence toward women. The feminist perspective has not been applied to other forms of abuse and does not explain some complexities of family violence. It does not, for example, easily explain physical and sexual abuse within single headed households. Gelles states: "Feminist theory offers a single-variable analysis, albeit a powerful one, in a multivariable world" (1993:42–43). Yllo, in the same volume, disagrees that patriarchy is a single variable, rather it "is very complex and multidimensional" (1993:49). It includes cultural, economic, social, political, and legal factors that support patriarchy. Yllo also points out that other sociological theories are sharpened by the feminist perspective, including resource theory, social exchange theory, and family systems theory.

Sex Role Socialization Theory

Sex role socialization theory can be seen as part of or an offshoot of feminist theory. Sex role socialization may be an important factor in understanding why, among people with similar backgrounds, some become perpetrators and some do not (Gilgun 1991). This theory is supported by the fact that men are much more likely to be perpetrators of sexual and physical abuse than women and women are much more likely to be victims. Men are taught to be much more aggressive than women. They are given the message that sexual relations and physical domination bolster their masculinity. Since males are not encouraged to talk about feelings when they experience difficulty in their lives; they may rely on sexual activity or aggression to express their feelings and deal with problems.

Women do not receive the same messages encouraging physically and sexually aggressive behavior. Our cultural images place women in the nurturing role of taking care of husbands and children. (Women do, however, see women as sexual objects of men.) Women are encouraged to express their feelings and confide in others. Women, thus, "May be less likely than men to act out in sexual ways or with physical and sexual violence because they have more exposure to models of nurturing. They are given more permission than males to express personal and painful feelings" (Gilgun 1991:102). The difference between sex role socialization theory and feminist theory is that sex role socialization emphasizes the individual consequences of differences in gender socialization and feminism focuses more on the institutional consequences.

Social Learning Theory

Judith V. Becker (1988) points out that the mental health field lacks a theory of sexual abuse that is widely accepted and empirically derived. Becker feels that the social learning model can be appropriately applied to sexual abuse and "would appear to explain the phenomenon and is waiting validation" (205). Very simply, the social learning model involves a process of learning behaviors. In focusing on juvenile offenders, Becker emphasizes that social isolation is likely to be a contributor: Adolescents who do not have age-appropriate friends and the skills to make those friends may "befriend younger children and then sexualize those relationships" (201).

Becker went on to hypothesize that a model that includes different factors, such as individual characteristics, family issues, and environmental issues, can help to explain sexual abuse by juveniles:

> Individual characteristics might include an impulse control disorder, a conduct disorder, limited cognitive abilities, and a history of physical or sexual abuse. Family variables include (a) residing in a family where parents or parent surrogates engage in either coercive sexual or physical behavior toward each other, the children, or others; (b) residing in a family in which the belief system of one or both parents is supportive of coercive sexual behaviors; and (c) having parents who are lacking in empathy and in functional interpersonal skills experiencing emotional and/or physical neglect within the family. Social factors include a society that is supportive of coercive sexual behavior and the sexualization of children and/or bonding with a peer group that engages in antisocial behavior. (1988:201–02)

Social learning theory has also been applied to physical abuse. The only difference is that the content of one's experience is presumed to be dominated by physical aggression, rather than sexuality and sexual domination. Those who physically abuse family members are thought to have witnessed abuse by others and incorporated it into their own patterns of behavior. This theory helps explain why physical and sexual abuse tends to represent behavior of multiple members within a family. The theory does less well in explaining why siblings growing up in the same abusive environment may turn out very differently behaviorally.

The typical explanation of such diverse outcomes usually involves saying the siblings didn't actually have the same experiences in growing up. Older siblings may have shielded younger siblings from the physical or sexual abuse. Empirical support for this explanation of different outcomes in the same households has been weak.

Resource Theory

Resource theory assumes that all social systems revolve around threats or use of force. The more resources a person has, the more force he or she has and the more likely people will comply with the threat of force. This is why William J. Goode (1971) says that the more resources a person has, the less likely he is to use force. The implied threat may be sufficient to obtain compliance. For families in which there are few financial resources, Gelles (1993) says there is a higher likelihood of violence. This may be due to threats not being as credible when made by persons having few resources. Yllo (1993) says that resource theory does not take into account the fact the women have less access to resources than men and, therefore, it could be expected that women are more violent. In reality, this is not the case. However, resource theory attempts to explain violence by those having more resources than their victims, even though the perpetrator may have few resources to begin with. All that is needed is that he or she has more resources than the victim.

Social Exchange Theory

Social exchange theory focuses on a system of rewards and negative sanctions in human relations. Simply put, people will engage in behaviors that are likely to bring positive rewards and avoid behaviors that are likely to bring a negative sanction. It differs from behavioral conditioning, however, in that the rewards and sanctions are thought to be rationally evaluated according to the values of those experiencing the rewards and sanctions.

In examining physical and sexual abuse, social exchange theory can offer an explanation for why perpetrators engage in abusive behavior. Since exchange theory focuses on power—who has it and who doesn't—it is easy to see how this theory is relevant to physical and sexual abuse. That is, the abuser is the one with the power to exploit while the victim does not have sufficient power to thwart the perpetrator's advances, nor resources to offer an alternative exchange. Social exchange theory can also be used to explain why victims of abuse may have considerable difficulty in disclosing abuse—they fear that disclosure will make the situation worse and that, indeed, is what can happen.

Gelles (1983; 1993) supported the use of what he calls exchange/social control theory by noting the factors involved in having the costs lower than the rewards of family violence. It is the concern for family privacy and the hesitation of social agencies to become involved that can reduce the costs of family violence. Gelles pointed out that the views of physical discipline of children by parents and a general cultural approval for violence contribute to the rewards for violence.

Elizabeth Leonard (1996) applied social exchange theory to Summit's child sexual abuse accommodation syndrome. Summit's (1983) work is an effort to describe the pattern of common responses of victims of childhood sexual abuse. Leonard stated that one advantage of applying exchange theory to sexual abuse is that it "encourages a broader, multidisciplinary understanding of the phenomenon" (108). Leonard reviewed each of the five stages of the sexual abuse accommodation syndrome: (1) secrecy, (2) helplessness, (3) entrapment and accommodation, (4) delayed, conflicted, and unconvincing disclosure, and (5) retraction.

1. *Secrecy.* Most experts agree that secrecy is the hallmark of sexual abuse. The child is likely confused about the appropriateness of the behavior, not having previous knowledge or experience with sexual abuse. Victims may be told that this behavior is "special" and that no one else should be told. Some perpetrators ensure secrecy by making threats to the life of the child or other family members or loved ones. Exchange theory explains that the child may find it less costly to keep the secret. If the secret is told, the child fears that the threats will come true and that worse things will befall him or her.

2. *Helplessness.* It is obvious that children are subordinate to adults and are expected to do as they are told by trusted adults. Adult perpetrators of abuse learn how to exploit the helplessness of children. Perpetrators focus on the rewards of sexual abuse while there are unlikely costs to them. In reality, the helplessness of the child is part of the reward sought by the perpetrator.

3. *Entrapment and Accommodation.* When the child is caught in a pattern of sexually abusive behavior, she or he must try to survive. Exchange theory says that when there is inequity in the relationship the child may try to restore some sense of equity by the way he views the situation. This means that children may try to restore equity by convincing themselves they are to blame for the abuse. Indeed, this attitude is likely to be fostered by the abuser. The dynamics are very confusing as the child learns to be "good" by acquiescing to the sexual abuse. The reward to the child is that conflict is avoided, the family stays intact, and the abuser approves of the behavior.

4. *Delayed, Conflicted, and Unconvincing Disclosure.* Summit (1983) found that circumstances may change to the point where the child becomes able to make the disclosure of abuse. This can occur because the child may be getting older and more independent or because the child tells in response to escalating violence in the home. According to exchange theory, the child feels that new rewards associated with a change in circumstance may make disclosure less costly than was previously the case. The changed circumstance may be the entrance of an alternative power source into the family situation (police, social workers, teachers, relatives, friends) or a decline in the power of the abuser (divorce, illness, growth of the victim). Whatever the motivation for disclosure, the results are extremely difficult for all concerned. For the spouse of the abuser, most often the wife, this is a no-win situation. Either her child is a liar or her husband is a despicable person. Social exchange theory reminds us that wives and mothers are in the position of having to weigh the costs in

terms of whom to believe. If she is financially and socially dependent on the abuser, the scales could be tipped toward disbelieving her child.

5. *Retraction.* In the terrible aftermath of disclosure, Summit describes the intense pressure placed on the child to take back the disclosure in an effort to preserve the family. In exchange terms, the child learns the benefits of disclosure did not outweigh the cost. According to Leonard, "Once again the child takes on the burden of preserving the family at his or her own cost" (1996:115). Indeed, the child is likely to find that adults offer rewards for the retraction. Family relationships are then renegotiated within this system of costs and rewards.

In sum, social exchange theory as applied to Summit's child sexual abuse accommodation syndrome reminds us that the issues of costs and rewards are present throughout the stages of sexual abuse. The child faces very difficult choices about how to manage the abuse and its disclosure. Understanding these choices requires knowledge of what the different costs and rewards are that result from the child's actions.

Exchange theory has also been applied to physical abuse of elders. Dowd (1975) argues that as family members age, they tend to have a decline in their power resources. The reduction in power is thought to create an imbalance in the relationships between the elders and other family members. Being at a power disadvantage, they may then be exploited and abused by other family members. This theory, however, rests on the assumption of "disengagement"; that is, as people get older their earnings decline and they become more isolated. With growing discussion of "productive aging" it remains to be seen how useful this theory will be in the future.

Family Systems Theory

Family systems theory locates the source of abuse within the dynamics of the family. Straus (1973) developed the social system approach as it applies to the family. This theory examines how violence is used within the family and how violence is maintained, reduced, or increased in the family (Gelles 1993). (See Box 5.3 for the factors that relate general systems theory to family violence.)

Finkelhor (1984) describes family systems theory as "one of the most eagerly welcomed theoretical developments in the field of mental health in generations" (226). It focuses on father-daughter incest because that is the form of sexual abuse it best explains. Family systems theory centers on a poor marital relationship in which the mother does not adequately function as wife and mother. The father then establishes a relationship with usually the oldest daughter that becomes sexual. Finkelhor criticizes this theory on several grounds. First, it tends to blame the mother and the daughter for the incest. Second, it makes a theoretical distinction between abuse within the family and abuse outside of the family. Finkelhor feels this results in a lack of attention to theory in abuse outside of the family. Third, since the emphasis is placed on family relationships, this can mean less attention to the offender. If the focus of theory is only on family dynamics that contribute to

---

B O X **5.3**

The Relationship of General Systems Theory to Family Violence

1. Violence between family members has many causes and roots. Normative structures, personality traits, frustrations, and conflicts are only some examples.
2. More family violence occurs than is reported.
3. Most family violence is either denied or ignored.
4. Stereotyped family violence imagery is learned in early childhood from parents, siblings, and other children.
5. The family violence stereotypes are continually reaffirmed for adults and children through ordinary social interactions and the mass media.
6. Violent acts by violent persons may generate positive feedback; that is, these acts may produce desired results.
7. Use of violence, when contrary to family norms, creates additional conflicts over ordinary violence.
8. Persons who are labeled violent may be encouraged to play out a violent role, either to live up to the expectations of others or to fulfill their own self-concepts of being violent or dangerous.

Source: Richard Gelles. 1993. P. 37 citing Murray A. Straus, 1973. "A General System Theory Approach to a Theory of Violence Between Family Members." *Social Science Information.* 12:105–25.

---

abuse, there is less attention to the characteristics, attitudes, and motivations of offenders. Yllo (1993) agrees and states that gender issues are ignored. In reality, it is the behavior of the male that should be the source of concern.

An alternative family systems theory, the Circumplex Theory (Sprenkle and Olson 1978), goes beyond a focus on the mother's functioning to examine the overall structure and function of the family. Those families that are isolated and heavily focused on each member's lives are said to be enmeshed. The rules are also highly rigid and tend to give disproportionate power to the father who may use physical or sexual abuse to maintain the system and prevent members from becoming more involved outside of the family system. The rules are very unclear or contradictory and may lead to problems of setting boundaries for appropriate behavior. Without clear boundaries to the roles of the family members, children can become exploited and violence may be an accepted behavior. This version of family systems theory does not lead to blaming the mother and it gives more emphasis to the role of the father in accounting for the abuse.

Social/Psychological Theories

Some theories seek to incorporate both sociological and psychological perspectives in explaining physical and sexual abuse. Finkelhor (1984) offers a sociological/psychological model for addressing sexual abuse that emphasizes the need for a "multifactor analysis" (36). Finkelhor seeks a framework by which to organize existing sexual abuse theory and describes four factors that explain why perpetrators sexually abuse children. The factors of emotional congruence, sexual arousal to children, and blockage refer to explanations for how perpetrators develop their sexual interest in children. The fourth factor—disinhibition—refers to how the interest in the child leads to sexually abusive behavior.

1. *Emotional congruence* explains why perpetrators find it satisfying to have sex with a child. This examines the psychological needs of the perpetrator. This includes research that suggests the perpetrator is childlike and immature himself. Perpetration may be seen as a way to cope with the perpetrator's own past victimization. Other explanations of emotional congruence include low self-esteem on the part of the perpetrator and feelings of inadequacy in adult relationships.

2. *Sexual arousal to children* explains the reason the perpetrator's sexual preference is for children. This includes research that shows perpetrators have a stronger physiological response to children. According to Finkelhor, some explain this with social learning theory—sexual arousal occurs under certain conditions. Some theories focus on the victimization of the perpetrator—that there is conditioning regarding the sexually abusive behavior. For some there may be modeling—the victim becomes a perpetrator after his own experience of seeing a perpetrator find him sexually appealing. The process of finding children sexually appealing can have a social component as child pornography may play a role.

3. *Blockage* examines the issues that prevent the perpetrator from getting his needs met in adult relationships. This category includes psychological theories. Perpetrators can lack social skills, feel inadequate, and be unassertive. Incest theories tend to fall into the blockage model as the emphasis is on family dynamics in which the marital relationship is poor. Since there are blocks to getting his needs met, the perpetrator father seeks gratification through a sexual relationship with his daughter. Finkelhor says that blockage theories can be of two types. *Developmental blockages* focus on a Freudian view of the Oedipal conflicts in which the person is blocked from achieving a mature level of sexual development. *Situational blockages* focus on social or family problems that act as barriers to a normal sexual relationship.

4. *Disinhibition* refers to the conditions that allow a perpetrator to overcome his inhibitions and engage in sexual activity with a child. It includes strategies to overcome the child's resistance. The perpetrator may use alcohol and/or drugs as a disinhibitor and may distort his perceptions of the child to think the child desires this contact. That is, disinhibition is anything that serves as an excuse for making sexual activity with a child acceptable. Incest theories often fall into the disinhibition category.

The value of this typology is that it is an effort to organize existing theories on sexual abuse of children. It is an effort to make more manageable and understandable very complex information and theories. Finkelhor's model has gained widespread acceptance and has encouraged research in these areas (Marshall 1997). For an alternative typology of sexual abusers and serial rapists developed by the FBI's National Center for the Analysis of Violent Crime, see Box 5.4.

Finkelhor (1984) says that the four factors can also be used to generate new theory. His model points out that existing theories rely on other processes that are not necessarily explained. While theories of emotional congruence can take for granted that sexual arousal occurs, the sexual arousal itself is in need of explanation. Blockage theories may explain why appropriate sexual outlets are not available but do not explain why children become the replacement.

Finkelhor's (1984) model points out that adequate theory needs several different levels of explanation. Theory should be able to explain why the perpetrator is sexually aroused by a child, as well as why inhibitions are absent. Adults may have barriers to emotional and sexual satisfaction and still not have an attraction to a child and may not act on those feelings even if they did have them. Finally, Finkelhor's model implies that many adults may have some of the characteristics of perpetrators and yet do not become sexual abusers. Theory has to develop in a way to discriminate between perpetrators and nonabusers. Finkelhor also believes that there is no compelling reason that theories of sexual abuse should distinguish between incest and sexual abuse outside of the family.

Four Preconditions Model of Sexual Abuse

Finkelhor (1984) devised a model for understanding sexual abuse between an adult and a child, with particular attention to the process by which abuse occurs. The Four Preconditions Model of Sexual Abuse is designed to incorporate information about both sexual offenders and victims. Four preconditions must be met before abuse occurs:

1. *Motivation to Sexually Abuse.* The potential perpetrator must have some motivation for sexually abusing a child. The source of the motivation can be emotional congruence, sexual arousal by a child, and being unable to have needs met in appropriate ways. The motivation to sexually abuse can come from one or more of these factors.
2. *Overcoming Internal Inhibitors.* The potential perpetrator must overcome internal inhibitions against following through on this motivation. This precondition is the equivalent of disinhibition, as previously discussed. It does not describe the motivations for abuse but accounts for why the desire can be acted on. Disinhibition is a requirement for abuse to occur.
3. *Overcoming External Inhibitors.* The potential perpetrator must overcome external barriers to following through on this motivation. The most important issue is the amount of supervision the child receives from other adults. Extensive supervision of a child means less access for the perpetrator. Children are more vulnerable to abuse when the mother is absent or incapacitated in some way, for example, by physical or mental illness.

BOX 5.4

FBI Crime Classification of Serial Rapists

According to the FBI's *Crime Classification Manual* (1992), there are four basic types of sexually violent offenders: power-reassurance, exploitative, angry, and sadistic offenders. The power-reassurance perpetrators feel inadequate. They are motivated primarily by a need to be reassured of their power and sexual potency. They may have their victims stage and enact fantasies that they planned in advance. Their sexual abuse may involve voyeurism, exhibitionism, or seduction, as well as coercion. The exploitative sexual abusers are motivated primarily by a need to dominate others and exercise control. Their actions tend to be impulsive. They take advantage of opportunities that present themselves, but they rarely plan something in advance. Anger rapists use sex to express rage at others. The victim is not the source of the rage, but his or her behavior may precipitate or act as an excuse for sexual domination. Sexual abuse is episodic, whenever the rage or anger spills out or stressful events occur. The victim is usually humiliated or degraded in some way. The sadistic offenders are the most extreme. They experience sexually violent fantasies and act them out on their victims. Mental and physical torture may occur. Their abuse tends to become increasingly violent.

Each of these types exhibits a different pattern of abuse. The most common, the power-reassurance type, may involve little actual violence—although the threat of violence is certainly present. They plan their abuse in advance and force victims to excuse their behavior. The exploitative abusers depend on circumstances of opportunity. While they seek out potential circumstances, they can be thwarted if denied easy opportunity. The anger abuse tends to be associated with the occurrence of life stresses. They may go for long periods without any acts of abuse. Their acts rarely are planned nor do these offenders seek opportunities to commit the abuse. The sadistic offenders are the rarest type, but the most dangerous. The more violent their acts, the more pleasure they get from it. Their actions correspond more to the common image of the psychopath.

Source: FBI. 1992. *Crime Classificaton Manual.* Washington, DC: U.S. Department of Justice.

4. *Overcoming the Resistance of the Child.* The potential perpetrator must overcome a child's possible resistance to the sexual abuse. Children at risk for sexual abuse may have poor family relationships and lack emotional security. Children may lack knowledge of sexual abuse. There may be a strong trust relationship prior to the onset of the abuse and coercion may also be a factor.

For sexual abuse to occur all four preconditions must be met in the order outlined. Finkelhor says the Preconditions Model is valuable because it includes both psychological and sociological perspectives—it incorporates individual perpetrator characteristics, family dynamics, and cultural factors. The model also places responsibility for the abuse with the perpetrator and avoids blaming the victim. The Four Preconditions Model can also be helpful in the treatment of sexual abuse. Professionals can evaluate victims and their families using the model to determine strengths and to develop treatment plans to help overcome weaknesses.

Attachment Theory

Attachment theory is another theory that incorporates both psychological and sociological components. Developed by John Bowlby (1969, 1973, 1980), attachment refers to the bond a child develops with the caregiver. This chapter reviews how attachment theory explains physical and sexual abuse. (See Chapter 6 for an extensive review of Bowlby's work.)

Attachment theory has been used extensively for understanding the antecedents and consequences of physical abuse. Egeland and his colleagues (1981, 1988) have argued that physical abuse is strongly influenced by problems of attachment of the abusers. As explained in Chapter 6, individuals who grow up in families without close attachments to their parents will have problems developing appropriate mental images of parent-child interaction. Such individuals tend not to have strong feelings for protecting and empathizing with their own children. In fact, they tend to feel rejection for the children and express that rejection through violence. Egeland, Jacobvitz, and Stroufe (1988) have also argued that physical abuse of the children creates attachment problems in those children that may perpetuate the violence in the next generation.

Pamela Alexander (1992) has developed the attachment perspective on sexual abuse. In the sexual abuse context, attachment theory focuses on incest and not on other types of sexual abuse. Attachment theory is concerned both with the pathology of the perpetrator of sexual abuse as well as family relationships that can predict increased risk of sexual abuse. Secure attachment refers to feeling loved and protected and provides the strong foundation from which a child can view the world. It is associated with good self-esteem and positive peer relationships and empathy.

Insecure attachment is generally associated with avoidance, resistance, and disorganization. Alexander (1992) reviews the findings of Stroufe (1988). *Avoidant attachment* is characterized by attention-seeking or aggressive behavior and a lack of empathy. *Resistant attachment* in infancy sets the scene for helplessness, neediness, passivity, and impulsivity. These forms of insecure psychological attachment frequently occur prior to sexual abuse. Also, a history of attachment can reduce the long-term effects of sexual abuse. Another form of insecure attachment *disorganized/disoriented* was identified by Main and Solomon (1986, 1990). For this child the attachment figure, the adult caregiver, is both the source of anxiety to the child as well as the solution to the anxiety. The child does not have a strategy for coping and engages in a variety of behaviors including both strong attachment and strong avoidance of the caregiver. The child may appear stressed and fearful and apprehensive when in the company of the caregiver.

According to Alexander, "Sexual abuse is frequently associated with the intergenerational transmission of insecure attachment" (1992:188). Alexander reviews several themes that frequently characterize sexually abusive families. Rejection of the child is associated with avoidant attachment. The child feels unloved and unwanted in response to the parent who is physically and psychologically unavailable. A second theme in sexually abusive families is the notion of role reversal or parentification in which the child becomes the responsible one in the family. Adults who have been parentified as children may expect their children to meet their needs as they tried to meet their own parents' needs. It may be likely that the parentified child in adulthood is still trying to meet the needs of the parents and for that reason is unavailable to their children. The third theme of insecure attachment in families described by Alexander is that of fear and unresolved trauma that is associated with disorganized attachment. This can occur in families with many problems including substance abuse, physical abuse, and few limits on sexual behavior. The lack of coping strategies can increase the impact of child sexual abuse. In sum, if family members are not able to meet their needs in appropriate ways and do not provide adequate supervision, insecure attachment can open the door for sexually abusive behavior.

Attachment problems in childhood set the scene for difficulties in intimate relationships in adulthood. This can take the form of an inability to trust or an inappropriate dependency or the person might even become a victim of abuse in adulthood. Adults with insecure attachment as children can also experience difficulties in their own parenting roles. Another form of difficulty often found in women who were sexually abused as children is problems with anxiety, depression, and posttraumatic stress disorder. Attachment theory suggests that mechanisms used by children to deal with anxiety associated with attachment continue to be used into adulthood. Another group of symptoms in adults that can be traced to insecure attachment is poor self-image and self-esteem. It can also be associated with mental disorders, including borderline personality disorder, which is characterized by abrupt mood changes, intense personal relationships that are seen in black-or-white terms, and risk-taking behavior.

In sum, attachment theory is useful in explaining both the causes and the consequences of physically and sexually abusive behavior. It predicts that children in abusive families will be at risk of expressing that abuse when they become adults. Since attachment theory has value in explaining the effects of physical and sexual abuse, it may help in predicting the symptoms associated with physical and sexual abuse and understanding its consequences. However, more studies are needed to show the relationship between early attachment issues and specific subsequent difficulties (Parker and Parker 1986).

Theories about the Impact of Abuse

While some theories seek to explain the causes of physical and sexual abuse, other theories examine the effects of such abuse. Theories of posttraumatic stress disorder (PTSD), Traumagenic Dynamics, Developmental Theory, and Intergenerational Transmission of Abuse have identified some of the consequences of physical and sexual abuse. See Box 5.5 for a review of the major assumptions in theories about the impact abuse.

Posttraumatic Stress Disorder

The theory of posttraumatic stress disorder is taken from the psychological perspective and was first used to explain the effects of war on its veterans. The *Diagnostic*

BOX **5.5**

Theories about the Impact of Physical and Sexual Abuse

Posttraumatic stress disorder	Abuse is a traumatic event that evokes intense fear and helplessness. Symptoms continue to occur over time, including flashbacks and violence displaced on others.
Traumagenic dynamics (Finkelhor and Browne 1985)	Sexual abuse results in an inappropriate view of sexuality, strong feelings of betrayal of trust, powerlessness, and stigma.
Developmental theory	Abuse interferes with the physical, psychological, and social development of victims.
Intergenerational trans-mission of abuse	Abusive parents can produce abusive children.

---

and Statistical Manual IV (American Psychiatric Association 1994) defines PTSD as occurring when a person has experienced events that involve serious injury or death (actual or threatened) and then responds with extreme fear or helplessness. The traumatic event can be reexperienced in a number of ways including recurrent thoughts, dreams, flashbacks, psychological distress, and physiological reaction to events that resemble or symbolize the original event. See Box 5.6 for the *Diagnostic and Statistical Manual (DSM–IV)* criteria for posttraumatic stress disorder.

In the 1980s PTSD was applied to sexual abuse as survivors of abuse experienced similar symptoms to war victims including recurrent thoughts, flashbacks to the events, and psychological disturbance. The concept of PTSD has also been applied to police, emergency medical technicians, prison employees, and others in high-intensity jobs. There are variations on the theme of PTSD; however, they have several things in common. There is agreement that the cause of the stress is uncommon or unusual, that high levels of anxiety result, and the stress is greater than the coping skills of the victim (Spaccarelli 1994). PTSD does explain some of the response to sexual abuse, but "it does not have a great deal to say about the unique nature of sexual abuse" (Mendel 1995:78).

Mendel (1995) says that sexual abuse does have important distinctions from the PTSD associated with war experiences. In contrast, sexual abuse often occurs in childhood, is often an ongoing pattern rather than one traumatic event, and sexual abuse is often at the hands of trusted adults. Physical abuse has obvious parallels with sexual abuse in these same characteristics. It, too, often occurs in childhood, is ongoing, and is at the hands of trusted adults. In both cases, the victims may have recurrent nightmares, heightened vigilance or passivity, depression, mistrust of adults or authority figures, and difficulty interacting with others. The problems of interaction may be especially strong with respect to behaviors similar to the type of abuse experienced, such as difficulties about sexuality or physical aggression. Such individuals also are at greater risk of developing substance abuse problems and may have suicidal ideation.

BOX **5.6**

DSM-IV Criteria for Posttraumatic Stress Disorder

A. The person has been exposed to a traumatic event in which both of the following were present:

1. The person experienced, witnessed, or was confronted with an event or events that involved death or serious injury (actual or threatened) or a threat to the physical integrity of self or others.

2. The person's response involved intense fear, helplessness, or horror.

B. The traumatic event is persistently reexperienced in one or more of the following ways:

1. Recurrent and intrusive distressing recollections of the event, including images, thoughts, or perceptions.

2. Recurrent distressing dreams of the event.

3. Acting or feeling as if the traumatic event were recurring (includes a sense of reliving the experience, illusions, hallucinations, and dissociative flashback episodes, including those that occur on awakening or when intoxicated).

4. Intense psychological distress at exposure to internal or external cues that symbolize or resemble an aspect of the traumatic event.

5. Physiological reactivity on exposure to internal or external cues that symbolize or resemble an aspect of the traumatic event.

C. Persistent avoidance of stimuli associated with the trauma and numbing of general responsiveness (not present before the trauma), as indicated by three or more of the following:

1. Efforts to avoid thoughts, feeling, or conversations associated with the trauma.

2. Efforts to avoid activities, places, or people that arouse recollections of the trauma.

3. Inability to recall an important aspect of the trauma.

4. Markedly diminished interest or participation in significant activities.

5. Feeling of detachment or estrangement from others.

6. Restricted range of affect (e.g., unable to have loving feelings).

7. Sense of a foreshortened future (does not expect to have a career, marriage, children, or a normal life span).

D. Persistent symptoms of increased arousal (not present before the trauma), as indicated by two or more of the following:

1. Difficulty falling or staying asleep.

2. Irritability or outbursts of anger.

3. Difficulty concentrating.

4. Hypervigilance.

5. Exaggerated startle response.

E. Duration of the disturbance (symptoms in Criteria B, C, and D) is more than one month.

F. The disturbance causes clinically significant distress or impairment in social, occupational, or other important areas of functioning.

Source: Reprinted with permission from the American Psychiatric Association. *Diagnostic and Statistical Manual of Mental Disorders,* 4th ed. Copyright 1994, American Psychiatric Association. Pp. 427–29.

The PTSD model has been criticized for not being able to explain the differences between individuals' responses to similar sources of stress. For example, if two young women of similar backgrounds were both victims of incest perpetrated by their fathers, why does one become a respected high school teacher and the other, a drug addicted prostitute? Spaccarelli points out that PTSD models have not made much progress in answering these critical questions: "How much do personality, coping style, or temperament variables contribute to abuse victims' perceptions of abuse-related threat and to their coping responses? Are these effects independent of the severity of the abuse?" (1994:341)

Traumagenic Dynamics

Finkelhor and Browne (1985) devised a model for understanding the long-term effects of sexual abuse further discussed in Finkelhor (1988). These four traumagenic dynamics are *traumatic sexualization, betrayal, powerlessness,* and *stigmatization.*

1. *Traumatic sexualization.* This dynamic refers to the victim of sexual abuse developing an inappropriate view of sexuality as a result of the sexual abuse. This can result in early sexual activity, promiscuity, prostitution, and sexual dysfunction in adulthood.
2. *Betrayal.* This refers to the dynamic that shows the child that he or she has been harmed by someone trusted, an especially strong dynamic within the family. The results can be serious difficulties in trusting others, isolation, depression, vulnerability to abuse in adulthood, and general difficulty in intimate relationships.
3. *Powerlessness.* This dynamic refers to the inability of the child to protect himself or herself from the perpetrator. The child's emotional and physical boundaries are overrun. This can lead to fear, anxiety, poor self-esteem, or a need to control and to identify with the aggressor. Behavior problems can include eating or sleep disorders, depression, running away, aggression, delinquency, and becoming an abuser.
4. *Stigmatization.* This dynamic refers to the guilt and shame that surround sexual abuse. The secrecy involved in sexual abuse can foster the feeling of stigma as the child feels different from others. The feelings of being different from others can continue into adulthood engendering poor self-esteem. Behavior problems can include social isolation, self-abusing behaviors, substance abuse, criminal activity, and suicide.

Finkelhor and Browne's (1985) theory of traumagenic dynamics is especially useful in explaining the effects of sexual abuse on women. According to Spaccarelli, the strengths of the traumagenic dynamics model are:

> It makes an attempt to clearly identify the most stressful or dangerous aspects of the abuse situation and seems to go further than most PTSD models in conceptualizing the types of threat perceptions that might be related to symptomatology. (1994:342)

The theory of traumagenic dynamics would seem to be applicable to physical abuse as well. If one replaces the traumatic sexualization with traumatic physical aggression, the abuse leads to an inappropriate understanding of the use of physical aggression. This would lead to assaultive behavior, acceptance of violence, or extreme fear of violence. Similarly, the dynamic of betrayal in physical abuse can also lead to difficulties in trusting others, isolation, depression, and generalized difficulty in intimate relationships. The experience of powerlessness may result in similar problems of vulnerability, fear, anxiety, or poor self-esteem. The victim may develop a high need to control or may identify with the aggressor. Behavior problems may develop, including eating or sleep disorders, running away, delinquency, and becoming an abuser. The experience of stigmatization in physical abuse can also lead to guilt, poor self-esteem, social isolation, self-abusing behaviors, substance abuse, criminal activity, and suicide.

There are also weaknesses to the traumagenic dynamic model. It does not make a distinction between the acute and chronic abusive events and the relationship between them. It does not discuss the factors that can support or refute the development of each of the four dynamics. It does not clearly distinguish between the abusive events and the victim's response to the abuse. It is also difficult to verify through research (Green 1993; Spaccarelli 1994).

Developmental and Transactional Theory

The developmental model focuses on the physical, social, and psychological development of victims of child maltreatment. Child maltreatment interferes with the healthy development of the child leading to problems that can be experienced immediately or later in the growth process from adolescence into adulthood and throughout the life course. The focus, then, is on understanding the effects of the abuse on the child when it occurs and whether the age of the child at the onset of abuse has an impact on the short- and long-term consequences of maltreatment. This issue of the impact of age on response to the maltreatment is explored in detail in Chapter 9.

Spaccarelli (1994) discusses the work of Cole and Putnam (1992) and Alexander (1992) as examples of work in the developmental perspective. We have already discussed Alexander's work in some detail. As indicated previously, attachment problems in childhood can be carried into adulthood and manifest in difficulties in adult intimate relationships. The work of Cole and Putnam (1992) supports the view that the age and emotional development of the child are related to the child's ability to cope with maltreatment. Younger children with limited coping skills may rely more on denial. School-age children with stronger coping abilities and greater likelihood of examining behavior and relationships may be more likely to feel guilt and shame. Adolescents are more likely to cope with maltreatment through behavior problems such as aggression, sexual behavior, or substance abuse. Cole and Putnam state:

> Incest interferes with typical self- and social development, and the psychiatric disorders most closely associated with a childhood history of incest reflect these

impairments in self- and social functioning. Research in developmental psychology reveals that self- and social development are important continuing themes throughout infancy, childhood, adolescence, and adulthood and that each developmental transition is associated with revision and change in one's self-definition, and integration, in the self-regulation of behavior and affect, and in the scope and quality of one's social relationships. The incest experience interferes with these necessary developmental transitions in a manner that increases the risk of serious psychopathology. (1992:179–180)

Transactional theory, a variation on developmental theory, is concerned with examining the effects of maltreatment by looking at both the individual and the environment. The impact of the abuse must be examined within the context of the child's family and community, taking into consideration the developmental stage of the child.

As developed by Spaccarelli (1994), the model acknowledges that victims of abuse face considerable stress: from the abuse itself, from changes in the family (more fighting or family separation), and from the consequences if the community learns about the maltreatment. The model states that abuse results in negative consequences for the victim—low self-esteem, self–blame, loss of trust, and impaired relationships with others, although Spaccarelli acknowledges the resilience of some victims. The concept of resilience is discussed in the next section. The child's reaction to the abuse must also be placed within the broader context; personality characteristics as well as characteristics of the child's environment are important factors in determining how the child will cope with the abuse.

In sum, the transactional model emphasizes the importance of the stressful abusive events, the child's own appraisal of the situation, the coping strategies used by the child, and the possible moderators to maltreatment such as family response. While Spaccarelli developed the model to further our understanding of sexual abuse, it can also be applied to physical abuse. The model is a holistic approach that speaks to the importance of integrating the individual abuse victim's experience within the larger social world.

Intergenerational Transmission of Abuse

The theory that physical and sexual abuse is transmitted from one generation to the next has received support. Perpetrators of sexual abuse and physical abuse often have a history of being abused themselves. It is also true that some perpetrators of abuse have not been victimized as children in the same way, although they may have been victims of other forms of abuse. This suggests that factors other than being a victim can be important (Gilgun 1991). Finkelhor points out that a simple explanation of intergenerational transmission is problematic:

It appears plausible that a history of molesting may play a role in the creation of some child molester. However, such a theory quickly becomes an all-encompassing explanation. Why is someone a child molester? Why, because he himself was abused. But fortunately for society and unfortunately for such a simple theory, most children who are molested do not go on to become molesters themselves. This is particularly true among women, who whether victimized or not rarely become offenders. Obviously, if victimization is a causal factor it interacts with some other factors. (1984:47)

The intergenerational transmission theory or cycle of violence theory has been very difficult to empirically test. Widom (1989) reviewed the methodological problems that plague the literature on the cycle of violence. See Box 5.7 for a review of common problems in research on intergenerational transmission theory.

. Various theories of physical and sexual abuse suggest intergenerational transmission. Psychoanalytic theory tells us that perpetrators of sexual abuse who were themselves victimized as children "identify with the aggressor" as a way to overcome their sense of powerlessness (Tzeng et al. 1991). The social exchange perspective addresses intergenerational transmission through the eyes of child victims of adult sexual perpetrators who later themselves become perpetrators. As victimized children they learn that there may be no sanction at all for adult offenders. Thus there may be rewards for the adult perpetrator and few, if any, costs (Leonard 1996).

The literature on resilience adds a broader picture to the intergenerational transmission theory (Gilgun 1991). Resilience refers to the ability to overcome a difficult childhood. This can include living with few financial resources, having inadequate parents, or living in institutional care. Those children who are not resilient may be unable to overcome their harsh or negative beginnings. They have

---

BOX **5.7**

Methodological Problems in Research on Intergenerational Transmission Theory

1. Questionable criteria for abuse and neglect, including use of nonsubstantiated cases.
2. Designs weakened by inaccurate information due to retrospective data or reliance on second-hand information.
3. Weak sampling techniques, including convenience or opportunity samples.
4. Ex post facto nature of studies, offering little predictive power.
5. Reliance on correlational studies at one point in time.
6. Failure to distinguish between abused and neglected children, treating them as one group.
7. Lack of appropriate comparison or control groups and failure to consider statistical base rates.
8. Tendency to examine generalized delinquent behavior, with less focus on violent criminal behavior.
9. Lack of knowledge of long-term consequences of abuse and neglect into adulthood.

Source: Cathy Spatz Widom. 1989. P. 28. "Does Violence Beget Violence? A Critical Examination of the Literature." *Psychological Bulletin.* 106:3–28.

not been able to make connections with others and receive the support they need. Their lives may be such that they did not learn to trust others.

Children are considered resilient when they can maintain self-esteem, positive relationships with peers, and function well in school despite family and financial problems. Some of the mechanisms that foster resilience, as shown by research, include an affectionate relationship with at least one parent, a strong marital relationship between parents, a family member or others outside the family who take an interest in the child and who encourage positive values. Also important are the personal qualities of the individual child—the ability to express feelings and empathize with others (Gilgun 1991). Gilgun conducted in-depth interviews with 48 victims of the various types of child abuse and concluded "that the existence of confidant relationships may be the single most important factor associated with breaking the cycle of abuse" (1991:102).

The intergenerational transmission theory helps us understand why physical and sexual abuse tends to run in families. It does not explain why men victimize far more often than women. It does not explain why women are the primary victims of abuse (Finkelhor 1984; Tzeng et al. 1991), nor does it explain how and why the majority of victims do not become abusers as adults. Clearly, more is going on than just an intergenerational cycle of violence.

The number and complexity of theories of physical and sexual abuse make it difficult to develop clear and specific explanations of physically and sexually abusive behavior. There are many different kinds of abuse, making it unlikely that one or two theories will suffice. Different theories may prove to each explain a part of the picture.

Finkelhor says that theories of child sexual abuse have developed at such a slow pace that this has impeded research and clinical practice. New theories, according to Finkelhor, can generate "a sense of intellectual excitement as well as practical activity—two developments the field could desperately use" (1984:221).

Referring to the broader category of sexual deviance, Hudson and Ward point to the lack of an integrated approach to development of theory building: "The lack of an organizing framework, or meta-theory, has resulted in the ad hoc proliferation of theories that often overlap, confuse levels of theory, and frequently neglect each other's existence" (1997:481). The problem of overlapping theories is especially true for those that seek to explain the consequences of abuse. Several different theories predict outcomes of depression, poor self-esteem, aggressive behavior (sexual or physical), passivity, problems in intimacy and social interaction, substance abuse, mental illness, delinquency, and criminality. How is one to know what is going on if different theories produce the same result? The empirical result will not be able to tell them apart. To advance theory in this area, research will need to be designed to study situations in which the theories predict different consequences.

Summary

Theories of maltreatment are important for understanding both the causes and the consequences of physical and sexual abuse. Psychological theories focus on individual characteristics of perpetrators of abuse with the assumption that abusers have abnormal personalities. Sociological theories offer the widest perspective for explaining physical and sexual abuse. They are especially complex because they examine human behavior within a broader social context. Sociological theories examined in this chapter are: subculture of violence theory, feminist theory, sex role socialization theory, social learning theory, resource theory, social exchange theory, and family systems theory. Social/psychological theories are an effort to integrate the characteristics of the perpetrators and victims of physical and sexual abuse with the characteristics of the surrounding environment. The four preconditions model of sexual abuse and attachment theory are examples. Theories that focus on the impact of physical and sexual abuse are examined. They include posttraumatic stress disorder, traumagenic dynamics, and developmental theories. Finally, the theory of intergenerational transmission of abuse is examined.

Study Questions

1. What are the factors that make defining family abuse theory difficult?

2. What do theories of physical and sexual abuse have in common?

3. What are the differences between theories of physical and sexual abuse?

4. What are the differences between psychological and sociological theories of physical and sexual abuse?

5. How does the traumagenic dynamics model help to explain sexual abuse?

6. How can attachment theory be applied to physical and sexual abuse?

7. How does the concept of posttraumatic stress disorder help to explain the effects of maltreatment?

8. How useful is the intergenerational transmission of abuse theory?

REFERENCES

Alexander, Pamela. 1992. "Application of Attachment Theory to the Study of Sexual Abuse," *Journal of Consulting and Clinical Psychology.* 60:185–95.

American Psychiatric Association. 1994. *Diagnostic and Statistical Manual of Mental Disorders,* 4th ed. Washington, DC: Author.

Becker, Judith V. 1988. "The Effects of Child Sexual Abuse on Adolescent Sexual Offenders." Pp. 193–207 in *Lasting Effects of Child Sexual Abuse,* Gail Elizabeth Wyatt and Gloria Johnson Powell, eds. Newbury Park, CA: Sage Publications.

Bowlby, John. 1969. *Attachment and Loss, Volume I, Attachment.* NY: Basic Books, Inc.

———. 1973. *Attachment and Loss, Volume II, Separation, Anxiety and Anger.* NY: Basic Books, Inc.

———. 1980. *Attachment and Loss, Volume III, Loss, Sadness, and Depression.* NY: Basic Books, Inc.

Cole, P. M. and F. W. Putnam. 1992. "Effect of Incest on Self and Social Functioning: A Developmental Psychopathology Perspective." *Journal of Consulting and Clinical Psychology.* 60:174–84.

Dobash, R. Emerson and Russell P. Dobash. 1979. *Violence Against Wives: A Case Against the Patriarchy.* NY: Free Press.

Dowd, James J. 1975. "Aging as Exchange: A Preface to Theory." *Journal of Gerontology.* 30:584–94.

Egeland, B., D. Jacobvitz, and L. A. Stroufe. 1988. "Breaking the Cycle of Abuse." *Child Development.* 59:1080–88.

Egeland, B. and L. A. Stroufe. 1981. "Attachment and Early Maltreatment." *Child Development.* 52:44–52.

Finkelhor, David. 1979. *Sexually Victimized Children.* NY: The Free Press.

———. 1984. *Child Sexual Abuse: New Theory and Research.* NY: The Free Press.

———. 1988. "The Trauma of Sexual Abuse: Two Models." Pp. 61–82 in *Lasting Effects of Child Sexual Abuse,* Gail Elizabeth Wyatt and Gloria Johnson Powell, eds. Newbury Park, CA: Sage Publications.

Finkelhor, David and Angela Browne. 1985. "The Traumatic Impact of Child Sexual Abuse: A Conceptualization." *American Journal of Orthopsychiatry.* 55:530–49.

Gay, Peter. 1988. *Freud: A Life for Our Time.* NY: W. W. Norton and Company.

Gelles, Richard J. 1983. "An Exchange/Social Control Theory." Pp. 151–65 in *The Dark Side of Families: Current Family Violence Research,* David Finkelhor, Richard J. Gelles, Gerard T. Hotaling, and Murray A. Straus, eds. Beverly Hills, CA: Sage Publications.

———. 1993. "Through a Sociological Lens: Social Structure and Family Violence." Pp. 31–62 in *Current Controversies on Family Violence,* Richard J. Gelles and Donileen R. Loseke, eds. Newbury Park, CA: Sage Publications.

Gilgun, Jane F. 1991. "Resilience and the Intergenerational Transmission of Child Sexual Abuse." Pp. 93–105 in *Family Sexual Abuse: Frontline Research and Evaluation,* Michael Quinn Patton, ed. Newbury Park, CA: Sage Publications.

Glueck, B. C. 1954. "Psychodynamic Patterns in Sex Offenders." *Psychiatric Quarterly.* 28:1.

Goode, William J. 1971. "Force and Violence in the Family." *Journal of Marriage and the Family.* 33:624–36.

Green, Arthur H. 1993. "Child Sexual Abuse: Immediate and Long-Term Effects and Intervention." *Journal of the American Academy of Child and Adolescent Psychiatry.* 32:890–902.

Hall, Calvin S. 1954. *A Primer of Freudian Psychology.* NY: The World Publishing Company.

Herman, Judith Lewis. 1981. *Father-Daughter Incest.* Cambridge, MA: Harvard University Press.

Hudson, Stephen M. and Tony Ward. 1997. "Future Directions." Pp. 481–500 in *Sexual Deviance: Theory, Assessment, and Treatment,* D. Richard Laws and William O'Donohue, eds. NY: Guilford Press.

Kline, Paul. 1987. "Sexual Deviation: Psychoanalytic Research and Theory." Pp. 150–75 in *Variant Sexuality: Research and Theory,* Glenn D. Wilson, ed. Baltimore, MD: The Johns Hopkins University Press.

Leonard, Elizabeth D. 1996. "A Social Exchange Explanation for the Child Sexual Abuse." *Journal of Interpersonal Violence.* 11:107–17.

Lerner, Gerda. 1986. *The Creation of Patriarchy.* NY: Oxford University Press.

Main, M. and J. Solomon. 1986. "Discovery of an Insecure-Disorganized/Disoriented Attachment Pattern." Pp. 95–124 in *Affective Development in Infancy,* T. B. Brazelton and M. W. Yogman, eds. Norwood, NJ: Ablex Publishing.

———. 1990. "Procedures for Identifying Infants as Disorganized/Disoriented During the Aimsworth Strange Situation." Pp. 121–60 in *Attachment in the Preschool Years,* M. Greenberg, D. Cicchetti, and M. Cummings, eds. Chicago, IL: University of Chicago Press.

Marshall, W. L. 1997. "Pedophilia: Psychopathology and Theory." Pp. 152–74 in *Sexual Deviance: Theory, Assessment and Treatment,* D. Richard Laws and William O'Donohue, eds. NY: Guilford Press.

Masters, Ruth and Cliff Roberson. 1990. *Inside Criminology.* Englewood Cliffs, NJ: Prentice Hall.

Mendel, Matthew Parynik. 1995. *The Male Survivor: The Impact of Sexual Abuse.* Thousand Oaks, CA: Sage Publications.

Parker, Hilda and Seymour Parker. 1986. "Father-Daughter Sexual Abuse: An Emerging Perspective." *American Journal of Orthopsychiatry.* 56:531–48.

Spaccarelli, Steve. 1994. "Stress, Appraisal, and Coping in Child Sexual Abuse: A Theoretical and Empirical Review." *Psychological Bulletin.* 116:340–62.

Sprenkle, Douglas H. and David H. Olson. 1978. "A Circumplex Model of Marital Systems: An Empirical Study of Clinic and Non-Clinic Couples." *Journal of Marriage and Family Counseling.* 4:59–74.

Straus, Murray. 1973. "A General Systems Theory Approach to a Theory of Violence Between Family Members." *Social Science Information.* 12:105–25.

Stroufe, L. A. 1988. "The Role of Infant-Caregiver Attachment in Development." Pp. 18–38 in *Clinical Implications of Attachment,* J. Belsky and T. Nezworski, eds. Hillsdale, NJ: Erlbaum.

Summit, R. C. 1983. "The Child Sexual Abuse Accommodation Syndrome." *Child Abuse and Neglect.* 7:177–93.

Tzeng, Oliver C. S., Jay W. Jackson, and Henry C. Karlson. 1991. *Theories of Child Abuse and Neglect: Differential Perspectives, Summaries, and Evaluations.* NY: Praeger.

Widom, Cathy Spatz. 1989. "Does Violence Beget Violence? A Critical Examination of the Literature." *Psychological Bulletin.* 106:3–28.

Wolfgang, Marvin and Franco Ferracuti. 1967. *The Subculture of Violence.* London: Tavistock.

Yllo, Kersti. 1993. "Through a Feminist Lens: Gender, Power, and Violence." Pp. 47–52 in *Current Controversies on Family Violence,* Richard J. Gelles and Donileen R. Loseke, eds. Newbury Park, CA: Sage Publications.

6 Psychological Maltreatment and Its Consequences: Theoretical Interpretations

Theory building is dependent on a clearly specified subject whose components can be interpreted and examined by available means of measurement. Unfortunately, and despite the fact that many regard it as a basic if not the most important of the major types of family abuse, psychological maltreatment lacks this prerequisite. General definitions of the term abound, but an agreed on operational definition, an established conception guiding basic research enabling the collection of systematic knowledge, is yet to be achieved. Basic reasons for this situation and efforts to identify an acceptable operational definition are discussed in the opening pages of this chapter.

The lack of an acceptable and precise definition of psychological maltreatment does not mean that attempts have not been made to theorize about its nature, causal antecedents, and behavioral consequences. Indeed, a considerable range of perspectives has been brought to bear on the subject, and the bulk of this chapter is devoted to the identification and assessment of psychological maltreatment theories.

As will become evident, theories of psychological maltreatment involve different ideas as to what the proper subject of attention should be (for example, the causal antecedents of its perpetration versus the extent and seriousness of its effects). The difficulties that differences of opinion about both the proper means and aims of theory building and knowledge accumulation about psychological maltreatment present to those wishing to develop a unified perspective and research agenda are an integral part of the discussion. The concluding section is devoted to a consideration of the obstacles that must be overcome if advancement in psychological maltreatment theory is to occur.

Defining Psychological Maltreatment: What's the Problem?

Garbarino, Eckenrode, and Bolger (1997) refer to psychological maltreatment as an "elusive crime," a deviant act that has avoided, despite the best efforts of many, precise delineation. Among the several reasons for this fact are the basic difficulty of specifying anything alleged to be psychological (something in the nonobservable minds of people rather than in the physically observable world) and the natural tendency to theorize about a perceived subject or problem prior to and independently of knowledge collection. In any scientific endeavor, theorizing at some level must inevitably precede data collection as one must at least have some preliminary notions as to why, where, and how to collect relevant information. Problems occur when theorists begin to draw conclusions and develop explanations without, or prior to, subjecting their assumptions to empirical validation. To validate a theory (for example, a hypothetical assumption about the causal antecedents of psychological maltreatment), the scientist must devise a means of objectively testing it by collecting information that may or may not confirm it. It is a canon of what is regarded as science that between a theory and a conclusion there must be supporting evidence collected by methods that can be repeated or independently verified by any qualified scientist. A necessary prerequisite for this to occur is an operational definition of a basic concept such as psychological maltreatment. An operational definition of a concept is one that includes a set of defined ways (for example, observations to be made or physical actions to undertake) that enables others to independently confirm what it is said to mean. Students of psychological maltreatment have attempted its operational definition, but they have yet to accomplish the goal.

The most serious effort to date to begin the process of identifying an operational definition of psychological maltreatment was proposed by McGee and Wolfe (1991). The first problem they confront is the failure of those who have provided basic definitions to specify what is meant by "psychological." As they see it, the reference to something psychological in child abuse research is generally meant to differentiate the nonphysical from the physical. But the fact is, as those who study the subject are inclined to point out, something nonphysical (psychological maltreatment) may have physical consequences (ulcers, skin rashes). To deal with this problem, McGee and Wolfe feel it necessary to clarify whether or not the term *psychological* in *psychological maltreatment* refers to "parent behaviors" or "child outcomes." As they indicate, the tendency is to stress child outcomes, that is, psychological maltreatment as an effect of either or both nonphysical and physical parental or caregiver behaviors. They provide a number of examples, including the views of leading experts such as Brassard, Germain, and Hart (1987) who say that "psychological maltreatment consists of acts which deny or frustrate efforts on the part of an individual to satisfy his/her basic psychological needs to the degree that the individual's functioning becomes maladaptively deviant" (8). To these authors, psychological maltreatment refers to child outcomes that may stem from either or both nonphysical (negligent) or physical (corporal punishment or sexual abuse) caregiver behaviors.

McGee and Wolfe cite other sources, the National Incidence Study conducted by the National Center on Child Abuse and Neglect in particular, to show that others stress a more limiting conception, a definition that stresses the nonphysical in caregiver actions as well as the nonphysical in child outcomes. After reviewing the range of conceptions, McGee and Wolfe (1991) find that "no overall consensus exists as to whether psychological maltreatment includes parent behaviors involving physical or sexual contact with the child" (6).

In effect, there is no clear agreement as to whether or not psychological maltreatment is to be viewed as an essentially independent phenomenon (something with its own causes and effects) or a consequence of physical and sexual abuse. This is not to suggest that McGee and Wolfe believe that the different types of abuse may or should not be interrelated. Their point is rather that if psychological maltreatment is a separate type of abuse, it must be defined so as to clearly differentiate it from other types and studied to reveal its own particular dynamics (antecedents and consequences).

Prevailing definitions of psychological maltreatment that emphasize victim outcomes manifest another problem identified by McGee and Wolfe. In their view, "Operational definitions of psychological maltreatment that focus on outcome are inherently tautological" (1991:8). A tautological statement is true by definition. A dictionary example is the statement: "Either it will rain tomorrow or it will not rain tomorrow." McGee and Wolfe see a parallel in such statements and definitions of psychological maltreatment that do not make a distinction between the predictor (for example, parent behavior) and the criterion (for example, psychological harm). One might be led to incorrectly posit, for example, that if a child evidences psychological problems he or she has been psychologically maltreated. The cause and effect are predetermined by definition rather than by an independent test capable of generating results contrary to expectations. In science, the predictor, for example, parental behavior, must be allowed to have more than one possible effect, including no effect at all.

Succinctly put, an objectively useful operational definition of psychological maltreatment must contain the potential for various outcomes (abusive and non-abusive effects) to what may be assumed as causally antecedent (parental behaviors). Without doubt, it is important to determine which parental behaviors have abusive effects. But as McGee and Wolfe (1991) remind us, "Researchers must first precisely define and measure parent behaviors *independently* of those effects" (10).

Accordingly, McGee and Wolfe propose the development of an operational definition of psychological maltreatment that focuses attention on potentially harmful parent to child communication. By communication they have in mind direct (for example, verbal statements and physical actions) and indirect (for example, neglect and indifference) messages that negatively affect a child psychologically. They acknowledge that their conception is similar to others but that the critical distinction is that the acts imply *potential* harm to the child. Our primary point is that psychological maltreatment should not be defined or diagnosed to have occurred using retrospective evidence of psychological damage. (1991:10)

Critical evaluations of McGee and Wolfe's position were published in immediately succeeding articles in the same publication. In the first, Barnett, Manly, and Cicchetti take issue with a number of points. They feel it important that if physical types of abusive causes and effects are to be excluded from an operational definition of psychological maltreatment, some clear guidelines for specifying what is and is not physical abuse must be identified. As they indicate, even though restraining actions such as "locking-in or tying-up" may have harmful physical effects, they are usually classified as indicators of psychological rather than physical abuse. As far as they are concerned such examples indicate that "an adequate operational definition of psychological maltreatment cannot be developed separately from definitions of other forms of maltreatment" (1991:20).

Barnett, Manly, and Cicchetti are similarly critical of two other key elements of McGee and Wolfe's conception. The first concerns the emphasis placed on excluding from an operational conception of psychological maltreatment actions that "are far removed from" interpersonal behavior. They provide the examples of a child witnessing spousal abuse and parent tendencies to show a clear preference for one child over another. As the possible negative consequences of such actions may not be the result of direct communication, they would seem to be unqualified for classification as types of psychological maltreatment. Thus, here too, they criticize McGee and Wolfe for not providing the criteria for determining what is and is not a "far removed" act of psychological maltreatment.

The second subject of concern involves McGee and Wolfe's emphasis on including under psychological maltreatment verbal and nonverbal "parent to child communications that may potentially damage the child psychologically." Barnett, Manly, and Cicchetti stress that here too guidelines are needed to clearly identify what McGee and Wolfe have in mind by potentially damaging communications. In the absence of clear guidelines, they fear that psychological maltreatment might become a "catch-all" for actions that should be excluded. As they state, "Divorce and parental psychopathology have been empirically associated with child dysfunction, but by themselves should not be considered maltreatment" (1991:22).

In the second critique, Jay Belsky questions the validity of McGee and Wolfe's emphasis on including acts of *potential harm* in their definition of psychological maltreatment. In his view, this contradicts their stated desire to shift analytical attention away from victim outcomes to potentially abusive parental actions. "If the concern is with nonphysical behavior by the parent that has the potential for psychologically harming the child," he says, "then why is it necessary to include in the definition characteristics of the child that will increase or decrease the likelihood that he or she will be harmed by the parent's behavior?" (1991:33).

Belsky also calls attention to the proper meaning of what McGee and Wolfe have in mind by the undefined term *harm.* He wonders, for example, if pain should also be included in the definition of psychological maltreatment. By pain he has in mind something "immediate" that may or may not have enduring effects. "Perhaps," says Belsky, "psychological maltreatment should be defined in terms of the *immediate pain* it causes the child and its *potential* for *lasting harm*" (1991:33). As he adds, such a definition enables intentional acts whose effects are short-lived and remedied to qualify as psychological maltreatment.

Although the importance of McGee and Wolfe's conception of psychological maltreatment is generally acknowledged, neither they nor anyone else has systematically refined it in light of the criticism that it has attracted. An operational definition of the term, one that is generally acceptable to those who research and theorize about its dynamics and manifestations, continues to be something desired but unrealized. Psychological maltreatment remains an elusive concept about which there is substantial discussion and intense opinion but little systematically amassed information.

A subject that has been generally ignored is the need to develop an operational definition of psychological maltreatment that includes both child and adult perpetrators and victims. Parental abuse of children has occupied the attention of conceptualizers to the virtual neglect of abuse of adults by their children. Also not sufficiently taken into account is psychological maltreatment perpetrated by nonrelatives (for example, teachers, child care providers, doctors, nurses, and nursing home staff). As it is, those who study adults rather than children, and situations involving nonrelative rather than relative perpetrators, must develop their own definition and theoretical slants. Lacking common concepts, theories, and methods, the knowledge gained by those in one camp does not have any necessary relevance for those in the other. Those in the field evidence greater concern with obtaining specialized knowledge of a particular subject (child abuse in particular) within a particular theoretical orientation (for example, psychopathology) rather than basic knowledge of all related subjects within a general theoretical perspective. The available theoretical slants on psychological maltreatment reflect this interest specialization.

Child Psychological Maltreatment Theory

Theory is a complex term. It has a number of components (for example, concepts, conceptual schemes, constructed types, frames-of-reference, hypotheses, propositions, axioms), each of which may be referred to as theory. It is, furthermore, constructed and employed for a range of purposes, from an effort to specify basic concepts (ideas and key terms) to attempts to develop a detailed explanation of a subject such as psychological maltreatment. In any scientific endeavor, theory is prerequisite to the systematic study and interpretation of phenomena. It is the necessary means of making sense of factual detail. With theory, a group of scientists is able to pursue research and collect interrelated data. Without it, the meaning of data is at best irrelevant and at worst meaningless.

Matching the complex meaning of theory is the complexity of the general subject of child maltreatment. Child maltreatment too is a complex whole composed of four interrelated subtypes—neglect, and physical, sexual, and psychological abuse. Spearheading efforts to develop specific theories of each and a general theory subsuming all have been primarily those in fields whose practitioners are particularly sensitive to or exposed to the problem of child maltreatment; these include pediatricians, social workers, developmental psychologists, and sociologists. Psychologists have been primarily responsible for introducing the greatest variety of particular and general theories of child maltreatment—the ecological and developmental perspectives. Both perspectives are sensitive to the interests and contributions of medical experts such as pediatricians and geriatric social workers. Social learning theory, another general perspective, emanates from the social psychologically oriented, primarily psychologists and sociologists.

In addition to general theories, there are other more disciplinary confined theories such as attachment theory in psychology and social change theory in sociology. Whatever the type or source of psychological maltreatment theory, the subject of concern has been the child. A specifically adult-oriented psychological maltreatment theory remains to be developed. Thus, we will begin by examining general theories concerned with child psychological maltreatment.

General Theories of Child Psychological Maltreatment

Ecological Theory

An ecological orientation is currently the most influential attempt to integrate the study of child maltreatment. Ecology is the study of the bearing of environment on plant and animal life. Developed by botanists and animal biologists, it was adapted for the study of human social organization by sociologists at the University of Chicago during the 1920s (Park and Burgess 1925). Chicago sociologists sought to understand how people are physically distributed in urban areas and how their particular habitats (blocks, neighborhoods, communities) influence their behavior. They were especially interested in the bearing of environmental influences on deviant behavior (juvenile delinquency and adult criminality in particular). Their leadership and interests were behind the establishment of and the type of data collected every 10 years by the U.S.Bureau of the Census.

Psychologist Urie Bronfenbrenner (1977, 1979) proposed an ecological perspective to bring theoretical unity to the study of human development. His ideas in turn have been developed by others to do the same thing for the study of child maltreatment.

Bronfenbrenner looks at the nuclear family as part of a topographical area that includes the dwelling area (block, neighborhood), the local community, the state, the region, the larger culture. Each of the spatial units is viewed as part of an interrelated complex. Individual development (the psychological and behavioral evolution of a person) is thought of, then, as something influenced by a number of extra-individual factors (local norms, state laws, regional history, larger cultural values, and social institutions), all of which must be taken into account to fully understand its particular form and diverse possibilities. As Bronfenbrenner puts it,

"The understanding of human development demands going beyond the direct observation of behavior on the part of one or two persons in the same place; it requires examination of multiperson systems of interactions not limited to a single setting and must take into account aspects of the environment beyond the immediate situation containing the subject" (1977:514).

To Bronfenbrenner, ecological space is composed of four overlapping system layers ("a nested arrangement of structures"). The first, that is, the most immediate, is the *microsystem*. The microsystem is an individual's immediate setting, the places where his daily interactions occur (home, day care facility, play area). The elements, or units of analysis of a setting, says Bronfenbrenner, are "the factors of activity, role, and interpersonal relation" (1979:22). In other words, these are the several variables that must be examined in a given situation to understand why and how individuals become the way they are, form their attitudes, values, and behavioral patterns.

Impinging on the microsystem is a *mesosystem*. A mesosystem denotes those structures that influence individuals at particular times in their development. At different times, for example, the teenage years, the interaction of family, school, and peer group may become of heightened importance. Church and camp may be added to the mix. Essentially, then, "a mesosystem is a system of microsystems" (1977:515).

Beyond a mesosystem is an *exosystem*. An exosystem, unlike a microsystem or a mesosystem, does not directly impinge on the individual. It is the larger societal structures and institutions that influence the local area, or, in ecological terms, the individual's habitat (for example, the employment situation, the mass media, governmental structures—local, state, and national—and the available means of communication and transportation).

The overarching layer is a *macrosystem*. A macrosystem is the larger culture, its essential values and how they are conveyed to the individual by the other systems. Of particular interest to the student of individual development, for example, is the cultural value placed on childrearing. "What place or priority children and those responsible for their care have in such macrosystems is of special importance in determining how a child and his or her caretakers are treated and interact with each other in different types of settings" (1977:515).

Bronfenbrenner, then, proposes a theoretical slant to analyze the course of human development as it is influenced by the social and cultural factors (groups, social institutions, cultural values) that structure individuals' life space and variously come into play at different times and stages in the maturation process. To be sure, the family and its influence on the child is at the center of Bronfenbrenner's scheme, but he insists that it be regarded as a component of a larger whole rather than an isolated entity. It is not so much who family members are that attracts his attention, but how the attitudes, values, and actions of its members are conditioned and patterned by key groups and institutions (in particular, the school, the workplace, the church, the economy, and the mass media).

It should be noted that methodologically, Bronfenbrenner does not regard either of the two basic types of research (laboratory or natural field settings) as more superior than the other. Each is regarded as the source of valuable albeit different types of information. People behave differently in different situations and settings, and the laboratory, he feels, is no less an important behavioral setting than any other.

Bronfenbrenner's perspective has been adapted for analysis of child maltreatment, most notably by Jay Belsky who finds it wanting in one major respect; namely, consideration of the individual background of adult family members responsible for child rearing. As he indicates, in the study of child maltreatment one must take into account ontogenic development, "how a particular parent grows up to behave in an abusive or neglectful manner" (1980:321). Thus, Belsky's framework for the analysis of child maltreatment is a modified version of Bronfenbrenner's and is based on four levels of analysis: (1) ontogenic development (parental background), (2) the microsystem (the family setting), (3) the exosystem (neighborhood, community, workplace), and (4) the macrosystem (cultural values and belief systems).

Belsky contends that his ecological perspective facilitates both the integration of existing data on child maltreatment and the guidance of future research. By focusing attention on interrelated causal sources of the problem, he feels that his perspective "should stimulate investigators to move beyond the mere identification of individual variables that are correlated with child abuse and neglect to the study of relationships among variables" (1980:321).

Belsky examines the available evidence indicating influential variables at each of the four ecological layers. At the ontogenic level, for example, he singles out parents' socialization history, the consistent finding of an abusive history of maltreatment in parents who maltreat children. But as it is also a consistent finding that not all those who have been abused become abusive parents, Belsky suggests the need to determine why those who have been abused do not become abusers, and what it is that leads those with nonabusive backgrounds to become abusers. Clues, he feels, must be sought in analyses of the interaction of ontogenic and the other ecological strata.

At the microsystem level, Belsky considers findings indicating that children often contribute to their own maltreatment. Research indicates that children vulnerable to abuse include both those who are hyperactive as well as those who are particularly passive and indifferent to parental expectations and disciplinary measures. As Belsky reminds us, however, "Child maltreatment must be considered an interactive process; although children may play a role in their own abuse or neglect, they cannot cause it by themselves" (1980:324).

At the exosystem level, Belsky identifies two factors particularly associated with the expression of child maltreatment: parental employment situation and the neighborhood.

Unemployment, for example, has been identified as a factor differentiating the abusive from the nonabusive family. And higher incidents of child maltreatment have been found in neighborhoods containing more "isolated" than nonisolated families. Isolated families are those lacking support in time of need (for example, in coping with a hyperactive or highly passive child) from relatives and others (friends and professionals).

At the macrosystem level, Belsky points to cultural factors such as the acceptance of violence and aggression as legitimate ways of responding to interaction challenges and provocations, including child resistance to discipline. Comparative international crime data, for example, indicate that the United States is a particularly violent nation. Violent crime in the United States (murder, forcible rape, aggravated assault, robbery) outdistances all industrially advanced nations.

In brief, Belsky advocates a general (the ecological perspective) frame of reference and a conceptual scheme (the four layers of analysis) for the study of child maltreatment, more specifically, the interrelated factors behind its perpetration by parents. As shown in Figure 6.1, parents are assumed to be the primary perpetrators of child maltreatment. In addition to what parents bring to their parenthood, three other factors are considered to be of central importance in influencing possible child abuse: the family system (the microsystem), the neighborhood and workplace situation (the exosystem), and cultural beliefs and values.

Belsky does not consider the different types of child maltreatment and how they fit into his scheme. Others, however, have applied the ecological perspective to the different types, including psychological maltreatment.

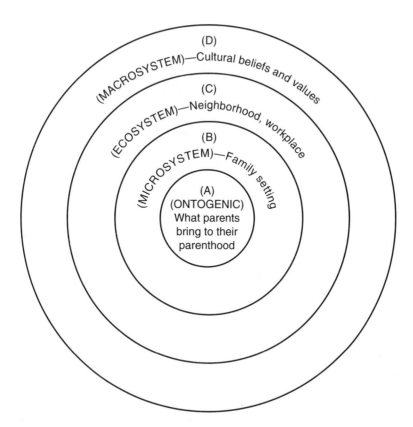

FIGURE 6.1 Belsky's Ecological Frame of Reference for the Analysis of Child Maltreatment

Sociologist Geoff Preston, for example, takes the view that child abuse in Western societies is in good measure the product of social and cultural forces and changes that have complicated and altered family structure. He argues that "since the seventeenth century the family has been progressively transformed in such a way as to create social conditions conducive to an emotionally abusive family ecology" (1986:42). He has in mind the changes wrought by the processes of industrialization and urbanization and their attendant scientific and technological innovations. Work, which for most of humankind's history took place within the family, was transformed into something occurring outside its confines. The rise of compulsory education and public welfare institutions also removed responsibilities previously confined to the family. Having been taken away from much of the family's productive and emotional life, says Preston, children have become alienated and individualized. "Hence family ecologies which are abusive are not so much a consequence of parental failure or a lack of interest and concern for children, but of larger social changes which are fundamentally beyond parental control" (1986:43).

Preston contends that from the ecological perspective, the view of child abuse as the product of an abuser and an abusee is basically irrelevant and a distraction. From his ecological vantage point, emotional abuse is "the result of the child inhabiting a situation or ecology characterized by patterns of interpersonal and intersystem relationships which have an influential and detrimental effect on the child's emotional development" (1986:43). Chief among these factors, he feels, is family breakdown, parental divisiveness leading to violence, separation, and divorce.

Citing evidence showing that the emotional effects of family breakdowns may be short or long term, Preston focuses on its long-term consequences. Some stem from the failure of anyone to provide children with an explanation for the parental split. Lacking an explanation, many children feel a strong sense of blame for their parents' behavior and divorce and develop fantasies indicative of hope for parental reconciliation. Serious emotional personality consequences may include "wariness of relationships with adults, vicarious affection, depression and withdrawal, difficulties with trust, an externalized locus of control, pseudo-maturity, emotional-cognitive splitting, over- or underperformance at school, low self-esteem, difficulties over intimacy in adulthood and psychiatric symptoms" (1986:44).

Preston differentiates the degree of child emotional abuse by four different types of separated families: nonabusive, mildly emotionally abusive, moderately emotionally abusive, severely emotionally abusive.

Data from a survey of some 98 families revealed certain differences in the four family types. Thus, the nonabusive family tended to be smaller, the parental split and divorce by mutual consent, with no evidence of child exposure to or involvement in parental conflict. The mildly emotionally abusive family evidenced a higher frequency of parental conflict, custodial disputes, parental insensivity to children's needs, and unresolved issues prior to the split. The moderately emotionally abusive family evidenced a higher degree of parental conflict than the mildly emotionally abusive family, parental emotional dependence on the children, evidence of severe parental emotional disorder, and the rejection of one child or another by either parent. The severely emotionally abusive family evidenced the following: intense and escalating conflict, siblings split between mother or father households, children involved in giving emotional support to one or both parents, and involvement in prolonged litigation.

One of the shortcomings of Preston's theory is that it does not, as Tzeng, Jackman, and Karlson (1991:180) point out, explore the reasons behind family separation. The specific ecological factors impinging on the different family types as well as the characteristics of family members (their ontogenic background) are not considered. Another shortcoming is the failure to compare the consequences of different types of abuse so as to shed light on the possible uniqueness of the emotionally abusive family. Lastly, Preston's family typology is not based on a clear separation of the exclusively emotionally abusive from the physically abusive family. No mention is made of a determined effort to confront and solve this confounding difficulty. Hence, one must, as Tzeng et al. caution, take Preston's typology as suggestive but needing further testing to clarify its meaning and validity.

Child Needs Theory

Hart, Germain, and Brassard (1987) have developed a perspective on child psychological maltreatment emphasizing its need depriving effects. In their view:

> Psychological maltreatment consists of acts which deny or frustrate efforts on the part of an individual to satisfy his/her basic psychological needs to the degree that the individual's functioning becomes maladaptively deviant. (8)

They emphasize that the validity of their viewpoint rests on certain basic assumptions: the ability of psychological needs theory to satisfactorily explain "important aspects" of human motivation and behavior, that given acts of psychological maltreatment may hinder or prevent essential psychological need fulfillment, and that frustrating or preventing psychological need fulfillment leads to psychological maladjustment and social deviancy.

Hart, Germain, and Brassard acknowledge the fact that their viewpoint and assumptions are rooted in the work of Abraham Maslow. Maslow, a psychologist who sought to reconcile Freudian and behavioral theory, was both highly theoretically and empirically oriented. He was also inclined to tackle the large problem of human nature, what it is and what makes it unique, what motivates people and how their personalities are formed.

Maslow's theory of motivation, what makes people act, think, and feel in some ways rather than others, is based on need gratification. As in the case of all organisms, humans must satisfy certain compelling demands, or basic needs, in order to exist. To Maslow, these include the physiological needs (food, water), the safety needs (physical and psychological security), the belongingness and love needs, the self-esteem needs, and the self-actualization needs.

To Maslow, all needs are thought of as existing in some general prioritized order or being hierarchically arrayed. Once certain needs are met, others rise to the fore. According to Maslow:

> The basic needs arrange themselves in a fairly definite hierarchy on the basis of relative potency. . . . In this sense, the physiological needs . . . are stronger than the safety needs, which are stronger than the love needs, which in turn are stronger than the esteem needs, which are stronger than . . . the need for self-actualization. (1987:56–57)

Maslow used his needs theory to account for neuroses and to define the psychologically healthy personality. Essentially, he views the neurotic as one who is need deprived. In his view, "most neuroses" involve "ungratified wishes for safety, for belongingness and identification, for close love relationships and for respect and prestige" (1968:21). Out of his experience as a psychotherapist, Maslow found that many psychological problems tended to disappear when the identified need deficiencies were overcome. In his view, then, basic need gratification is prerequisite to a healthy personality. A healthy personality is one capable of "self-actualization," affirmation of his or her unique abilities and interests.

To Hart, Germain, and Brassard, Maslow's needs deficiency account of the origins of the psychologically troubled is of fundamental importance. As they see it, "It is logically supportable to hypothesize that psychological maltreatment is a direct attack on psychological need fulfillment, and that this is what produces its destructive power" (1987:8). In their view, acts of psychological maltreatment include terrorizing, verbal assault, physical abuse, threatened withdrawal of love, emotional neglect, scapegoating, and physical exploitation. Accordingly, Hart, Germain, and Brassard point out that

> [t]errorizing, verbal assault, and physical abuse would be in conflict with safety, and in some cases, physiological needs. Threatened withdrawal of love, inattention to nurturing, rejecting, and denying emotional responsiveness would be in conflict with belongingness and love needs, and would also interfere with fulfillment of physiological and safety needs. Scapegoating, exploiting, knowingly permitting maladaptive behavior, berating and disparaging would be in conflict with esteem needs. (1987:9)

As in the case of ecological theories of child psychological maltreatment, child needs theory is much in need of empirical testing to determine its strengths and weaknesses. A conceptual strength of the theory lies in its clear analytical focus—the extent to which blood parents or other child rearers attend to the basic needs of their children. But in emphasizing one side of an interaction process (the child as virtually passive recipient of the child rearer's demands), it tends to minimize the influence of the other, the child's possible role in the expression of psychological maltreatment. Thus, the theory, as currently articulated, does not provide for the possibility that child psychological maltreatment may be something that gradually emerges in the socialization process, or something that occurs to some children in one family but not to all. Furthermore, nothing is provided concerning possible differences in effecting child psychological maltreatment by child rearers of the same and opposite gender as their charges. Neither is attention given to the possibility of the need deprivation inflicted by one parent being compensated for by the other or others (in particular, uncles, aunts, grandparents).

A perspective of emerging relevance in the broad field of child maltreatment that addresses the interaction side of the subject is attachment theory. Although it has not been applied to analysis of the specific problem of emotional maltreatment, attachment theory, as will become evident, is highly relevant to an understanding of the meaning of emotional maltreatment and its effects.

Attachment Theory

Attachment theory has been mostly developed by John Bowlby (1969, 1973, 1980). Psychoanalytically trained, Bowlby traces the source of personality strengths and weaknesses to social bonding—the nature and strength of the tie between the child and its mother (or mother substitute) above all. He outlined his theoretical perspective in the third volume of his trilogy, *Loss, Sadness and Depression* (1980).

Bowlby defines attachment as behavior that stems from the maintenance of proximity to a "preferred individual," especially during the first five years of life. Generally, of course, although hardly exclusively, a child's "preferred individual" is his or her mother. Although interested in adult attachments and their behavioral effects, Bowlby gave primary attention to childhood attachments, how they develop in the interaction process, and how they are maintained or become attenuated or broken with what behavioral consequences.

Bowlby believed that attachment behavior was a distinctive class of behavior separate from but equal in importance to feeding and sexual behavior. He thought the impetus to attachment behavior was instinctive but mediated by culturally varied social systems that specify acceptable behavioral aims and goals as well as the proper means for their attainment. Attachment behavior, he says, arises in the course of a species' evolution to further its members' survival and security. And in Bowlby's view, an individual's psychological health or pathology is causally related to attachment to or loss or lack of attachment to an important other or others.

Clearly, then, Bowlby's concept of attachment is fundamentally an emotionally driven need, a need to be cared for. Put this way, one might be tempted to infer that what he has in mind is some version of the traditional concept of psychological dependence. This would be a mistake as he took pains to differentiate the concepts of attachment and dependence. To Bowlby:

> Logically, the word "dependence" refers to the extent to which one individual relies on another for his existence, and so has a functional reference; whereas attachment as used here refers to a form of behavior and is purely descriptive. As a consequence of these different meanings, we find that, whereas dependence is maximum at birth and diminishes more or less steadily until maturity is reached, attachment is altogether absent at birth and is not strongly in evidence until after an infant is past six months. The words are far from synonymous. (1969:228)

The point that Bowlby stresses is that "intimate attachments to other human beings are the hub around which a person's life revolves," and that "from these intimate attachments a person draws his strength and enjoyment of life and through what he contributes, he gives strength and enjoyment to others" (1980:442).

To determine the importance of intimate attachment, Bowlby studied the emotional and behavioral effects of disruptions or threatened disruptions of bonds between parents and children and between adults. These included analyses of the consequences of temporary separations between parent and child (nursery schools in particular), the loss by death of a parent or child, and the loss of a mate via death and otherwise (separation, divorce). He found clear evidence of a range of clinical and nonclinical problems, from anxieties, phobias, depression, and suicide to "disturbances of parenting and marriage" (1980:441). What remained to be determined, he said, was the precise causal bearing of social bond disruptions on specific emotional and behavioral manifestations.

Certain of Bowlby's concepts demonstrate the relevance of attachment theory to the study of childhood emotional maltreatment. One of the more important of these is his notion of anxious attachment. As he points out, some people seem to be unusually dependent on another, to cling to him or her as if their life depended on it. But rather than describe the phenomenon by use of pejorative terms such as "over dependent" or "childishly dependent," terms that express the "norms and values of the observer using them," Bowlby introduced the more value neutral sounding "anxious attachment" or "insecure attachment." "Anxious attachment," he says, "respects the person's natural desire for a close relationship with an attachment figure, and recognizes that he is apprehensive lest the relationship be ended" (1973:213).

Bowlby found evidence of a causal connection between a number of factors and expressions of "anxious attachment" by young children. Children living in nursery homes and lacking a permanent attachment figure as well as those living at home but experiencing regular periods of separation (both short and long term) from their mothers or main caregivers evidenced higher anxiety about their attachments and greater fear of strangers than those having more steady attachments. An even stronger relation was found between parental threats to abandon a child or withhold love if he or she did not behave and expressions of "attachment anxiety."

Repeated over a period of years, threats of abandonment and rejection may give rise to feelings of anger and hostility toward attachment figures that may erupt into violence. "It seems not unlikely," says Bowlby, "that a number of individuals who become literally murderous towards a parent are to be understood as having become so in reaction to threats of desertion that have been repeated relentlessly over many years" (1973:250). Of course, anger and hostility may be redirected, that is, displaced onto others, perhaps a mate or even a casual acquaintance.

In summary, "attachment anxiety" may be thought of as a form of emotional abuse, one perpetrated by a pattern of intended or unintended distancing by a key attachment figure or figures that threatens the security, self-confidence, and very emotional well-being of the victim. Bowlby was well aware that the problem may persist into adulthood and pose any manner of problems for the individual and those with whom he or she seeks intimacy, especially an inability to trust others and express unreserved love and affection.

The pioneering research of Ainsworth (1967, 1978) and more recent work by others (Crittenden 1988; Carlson et al. 1990; and Allen, Hauser, and Borman-Spurrell 1996) have yielded some important evidence on the relevance of attachment theory to an understanding of child maltreatment and possible adult problems. For example, when compared to families where child maltreatment is not in evidence, families with reported and verified instances of child maltreatment (physical, sexual, and emotional) have been found to have a much greater degree of inconsistent child care. As Carlson et al. state, "Maltreated infants are much more likely than comparison infants to be rated as insecurely attached to their caregivers, and are particularly likely to demonstrate a disorganized/disoriented attachment" (1990:514).

As Allen et al. (1996:255) point out, insecure attachments during both childhood and adolescence are associated with depression and a variety of behavior problems (delinquency, substance abuse, suicide). Allen and colleagues investigated the possible long-term adult effects of childhood insecure attachments. Their study entailed interviews with 142 adolescents (71 males and 71 females) hospitalized at age 14 for a variety of mental problems. Eleven years later they were reinterviewed. The results were compared to a demographically matched group from a high school located in the same residential area as those hospitalized. As they report, in contrast to the control group that evidenced a "typical mixture" of security and insecurity, "virtually all" of those adolescents previously hospitalized evidenced insecure attachments in young adulthood. This was, in their view, largely the result of unresolved childhood insecurity. Lastly, "Insecurity in adult attachment organization at age 25 was also linked to self-reported criminal behavior and use of hard drugs in adulthood" (1996:254).

The link between attachment and criminality has been stressed by sociologist and control theorist Travis Hirschi. Control theorists hypothesize that delinquency is associated with the absence of social bonding, or, as Bowlby would have it, the absence of secure attachments to parents or caregivers.

To Hirschi, social bonding is prerequisite to the development of moral restraint and the controlling influence of conscience directed behavior. From the vantage point of control theory, effective deviancy prevention is dependent on bonding with positive role models, caregivers who teach and practice moral sensitivity. In Hirschi's words:

> Control theory assumes that the bond of affection for conventional persons is a major deterrent to crime. The stronger this bond, the more likely the person is to take it into account when and if he contemplates a criminal act. (1969:83)

From the above, then, it is apparent that a number of general perspectives have been used to account for various aspects of child psychological maltreatment. However, an equivalent amount of theoretical attention has not been accorded the problem of adult psychological maltreatment. Whatever the reasons for this fact a specifically adult oriented theory of psychological maltreatment does not exist. As will be seen, theorizing about the subject takes the form of a patchwork of concepts and assumptions borrowed from theories mainly developed for other purposes.

Adult Psychological Maltreatment Theory

As noted above, a theory focusing on the nature of adult psychological maltreatment is yet to be identified. For a variety of reasons, some valid and others less so, this has not inhibited theorizing about the subject. The problem is that such theorizing tends to be ex post facto, attempts to account for the nature of a subject after it has occurred. To the pure scientist, an acceptable theory must be empirically verifiable. It should identify presumed key variables and hypotheses that predict a certain outcome. If certain combinations of factors are present, controlling for possible intervening factors, then certain results are expected to occur. If theorizing is done after the fact without any attempt to generate a testable proposition of some kind, it is generally regarded as anecdotal, or as a convenient interpretation of no particular scientific value.

The problem is that the working situations of pure and applied scientists are not the same. The pure scientist (one who researches subjects without any necessary concern to practical consequences), for example, may select a problem or subject to explore such as psychological maltreatment and design an experiment to test his or her ideas. Applied scientists, trained practitioners such as psychoanalysts and psychiatric social workers, must begin with problems and concerns presented to them by clients. Clients have individual problems that must be confronted by the means and knowledge available to the counselor, caseworker, or therapist. And of necessity, this entails seeking relevant bits of information from a variety of sources, including that supplied by the evidence of pure scientific research.

Simply put, solving the special problems of clients is quite different and certainly of no less importance than seeking generally relevant information by means of the methods of pure science. If the goal of all science is knowledge gathering about a generally recognized important subject, the findings and interest of applied science must be considered of no less importance than those of general science. Just as theory building may proceed from the particular to the general or vice versa, so too must it be considered to proceed from pure to applied theory and vice versa.

To date, a limited number of "pure" theoretical orientations have been of use to therapists and others who treat the psychologically maltreated. Primarily, these theories have been applied to illuminate the plight of the adult female victim with occasional application to an understanding of the male abuser. Feminist sensitivity is a dominant theme in this work. Also worthy of note is the absence of theoretical analyses of psychological maltreatment involving homosexual partners and the elderly.

Feminist Theory

For a number of reasons, particularly the rise of the women's movement and the fact that adult victims of family maltreatment tend to be disproportionately female, theorizing about adult psychological maltreatment has been heavily influenced by feminist views and assumptions. In the feminist perspective, a patriarchal tradition is the basic source of the problem. To Valerie Nash Chang, for example, "Physical and psychologial abuse can be explained as an extension of the patriarchical pattern of gender polarity that establishes dominance and control as central aspects of the masculine and as inappropriate in the feminine" (1996:15). Traditionally, the male has been assigned the dominant role in the family. He is expected to "rule the roost," to lead, initiate decision making in all essential matters, to discipline and control family members. And in accordance with the prevailing economic principle of private property, the male head of household is encouraged to think of his wife and children as his personal possessions to essentially dispose of as he sees fit. As Chang sees it, the greater power and authority vested in the male role make it easier for the female to become a victim of psychological abuse.

Chang regards psychological abuse as "emotional violence," a pattern of nonphysical behavior that systematically attacks the victim's self-concept and worth. Mary Susan Miller describes how this may occur as follows:

> A man may begin with a complaint and slide into constant criticizing and name-calling before she even senses a problem. . . . He may accuse her of having lovers and begin watching her every move, stalking her when she meets a friend. . . . He may throw accusations and curses at her parents and other relatives with whom she is close. He may forbid her to make decisions or offer an opinion in family matters and even in her own affairs. (1995:25)

Instead of rebelling and challenging the dominating efforts of her partner, many females succumb by coming to regard themselves as unworthy individuals requiring a controlling influence.

Female therapist Marti Tamm Loring echoes Chang's and Miller's views. In her view, emotional abuse attacks the self-worth of the victim because the "essential ideas, feelings, perceptions, and personality characteristics of the victim are constantly belittled" (1994:1). Unlike most practitioners who have published works on the subject, Loring is unique for considering a variety of theoretical viewpoints to account for the uniqueness of psychological maltreatment. Child development theory, attachment theory, and social learning theory are accorded particular attention.

Attachment Theory

Loring regards emotional abuse as "an ongoing process in which one individual systematically diminishes and destroys the inner self of another" (1994:1). This is possible in the case of married partners, Loring feels, because of the dependent bonding of the female victim to her abuser. Toward the end of exercising power and control, "the typical abuser," she finds, is alternatively considerate and empathic and cold and indifferent. As she describes it, "Confused by the intermittent connection and struggling to regain it, the victim clings anxiously to the abuser" (1994:25). Attachment, which to Loring means the effort by one person to bond with another, may be a one-sided process. In the usual case, she says, victims seek to maintain attachment to their abusers, even those who have clearly withdrawn any affection for them.

To Loring, the uniqueness of emotional abuse lies in the noncompromising attitude and behavior of the abuser. "Driven by his fear of loss and need to control," she says, "the abuser ridicules and demeans the victim's style of attachment and other unique forms of relating" (1994:26). With reference to Bowlby's work, Loring finds the case of the female adult victim of psychological abuse analogous to that of the "anxiously attached" child. Anxiety over possible abandonment by a partner can be as anxiety provoking to an adult as feared abandonment by a parent or parents may be to a child. From the vantage point of the attachment theorist, the common element in both situations is insecurity over potential loss of what is felt to be a crucially important social bond. As to why an adult victim of psychological maltreatment might cling to her abuser, Loring turns to clues from social learning theory.

Social Learning Theory

Social learning theory is most associated with the work of psychologist Albert Bandura (1977). The basic premise of this perspective is that human behavior, although influenced by genetic and biological factors, is something acquired rather than inherited. As Bandura puts it, "Except for elementary reflexes, people are not equipped with inborn repertoires of behavior. They must learn them" (1977:16).

Learning how to behave, what to say and do in the variety of circumstances people encounter, is a lifelong process. Active people are continually required to make new adustments, to learn to adapt to the changing world of work and the new and diverse people inevitably encountered on and off the job. How one adapts to the new must be assumed to be heavily influenced, if not often determined, by past experience. What one brings to a situation, the particular people encountered, the nature of the situation itself (for example, home versus office) are all involved in influencing particular patterns of behavior. Thus, to the social learning theorist, behavior is not automatic or so predetermined as to be easily predictable. Different situations and people bring out different individual feelings, emotions, and reactions. One is often dismayed to learn that one can be influenced by others and events in ways that evoke emotions and behavior we thought we had learned to control. Often, we are quite unaware of the learned nature of how we behave toward and seek responsiveness from others. The perpetration and experience of psychological maltreatment is one such possibility.

Therapists and others who work with perpetrators and victims of psychological maltreatment (and other forms of family abuse as well) tell us that both roles are heavily influenced, if not determined, by learned behavior. To the social learning theorist, role models, particularly those responsible for initial socialization, are the source of a good deal of what we do and how we think and feel.

Particularly in our early years, how our parents relate to one another and us at different times and in different situations, powerfully influences our own behavior and feelings toward others. The evidence suggests that male perpetrators and female victims of psychological maltreatment are repeating what they have learned from their own family backgrounds, that the marriage situation evokes patterns of behavior and roles to play acquired in one's family of orientation. In this theoretical framework, some of us, particularly males, are predisposed by family background to become abusers, and others of us, particularly females, are similarly predisposed to become victims. The social learning theorist assumes that cultural norms and values, not simply particular people and circumstances, are behind the pattern. In our culture, males have been generally socialized to be more aggressive and controlling than females and females more passive and obedient than males. Our male cultural heroes tend to be aggressive and violent, and our female cultural heroines loving and forgiving. One should not be surprised to learn, then, that therapists often find that

> [m]ost men who abuse their partners believe that it is justifiable and appropriate. Women brought up in the same atmosphere share these beliefs. Societally and culturally, abuse of women has been condoned and sanctioned as men abuse their power to control what they believe is theirs. (Frank and Golden 1992:5–6)

Therapists also find that those who abuse tend to have abused before and that those who are victims of abuse tend to have been abused before. Some describe such a situation as one of "codependency." The abuser is dependent on his victim and the victim on her abuser for the maintenance, however unhealthy, of a presumed invaluable social bond. As irrational as it appears, victims of abuse frequently have a difficult time either being convinced or convincing themselves that they can voluntarily sever the relationship with their abusers. Relational theorists provide some valuable clues to explain this apparent anomaly.

Relational Theory

Relational theory is associated primarily with the work of a group of psychologists and psychiatrists associated with the Stone Center for Developmental Services and Studies at Wellesley College. Their theoretical slant is unique for providing under-standing of the vulnerability of the American female to emotional maltreatment.

At the heart of relational theory is the assumption that there has been a biased interpretation of the growth of self-awareness, a bias that emphasizes the impor-tance of male role socialization to the virtual disregard of the importance of female role socialization. The views of prominent theorists such as Erikson, Freud, and Mead stress self-awareness as progressing from a state of childhood dependence to a condition of adult independence. Socialization is aimed at creating an autono-mous person, one who controls rather than is controlled by others and events. The goal is separation from social bonding, the creation of a person who perceives of himself or herself apart from others—one who can stand alone and become completely self-sufficient. As Jean Baker Smith describes it, self-development "presumably is attained via a series of painful crises by which the individual accomplishes a sequence of allegedly essential separations from others, thereby achieving an inner sense of separated individualism" (1991:11). In fact, she says:

> Few men ever attain such self-sufficiency. . . . They are usually supported by wives, mistresses, mothers, nurses, and other women (as well as other men who are lower than they in the socioeconomic hierarchy). Thus, there is reason to question whether this model accurately reflects men's lives. Its goals, however, are held out for all, and are seen as the preconditions for mental health. (1991:11–12)

In the traditional view, males and females who lack self-confidence, the ability to thrive as self-centered individualists, are regarded as inadequate at best and mentally troubled at worst. Such individuals may be referred to as "mama's boys" or "clingers," as individuals who either cannot or will not "grow up." In addition to finding shortcomings in the ability of males to live up to the ideal image of the independent individual, relational theorists find even more problems with the premise that male and female self-development is essentially the same and, therefore, to be assessed against the same ideal standard. According to Miller, "Girls are encouraged to augment their abilities to 'feel as the other feels' and to practice 'learning about' the other(s). Boys are systematically diverted from it" (1991:14).

Girls, according to Miller and her Stone Center colleagues, are socialized to develop an interactive or "relational self." "Our conception of self-in-relation," says Janet L. Surrey, "involves the recognition that, for women, the primary experience of self is relational, that is, the self is organized and developed in the context of important relationships" (1991:52). The basic elements of women's self-concept, says Surrey, consist of an abiding interest in others and the ability to empathize with them, mutual empathy and the sharing of experiences so that sense of self and others is a simultaneously evolving process, and "the expectation of interaction and relationship as a process of mutual sensitivity and mutual responsibility that provides the stimulus for the growth of empowerment and self-knowledge" (1991:58–59).

As Stiver notes, the developmental process followed by women and men is quite asymmetrical. "Men try to move from attachment to separation, to individuation and autonomy, with the goal of independence. . . . Women move from attachment to continued connection, always developing in the context of relationships; they experience the goal of 'independence' as lonely and isolating" (1991:153).

Therapists such as Loring (1994) contend that a cultural bias regarding the superiority of the male and the inferiority of the female self-concept conditions many women to feel a sense of inferiority and unworthiness about themselves. As she sees it, cultural devaluation of women's relational sense of self leads some women "to tolerate the discounting and negation characteristic of emotionally abusive relationships; they simply fail to recognize these as abuse and assume that such treatment is deserved" (68).

Loring also believes that the mutual empathic element in females' self-concept emphasized by relational theorists accounts for the fear of abandonment expressed by emotionally maltreated women. Despite an abusive pattern, threatened abandonment is often perceived as possible loss of an invaluable source of empathy from a significant other. Some emotionally abused women, says Loring, "value the rare moments of connection with the abuser and suffer profound loneliness and 'empathy hunger' when it is withdrawn" (1994:68–69).

Relational theory is also relevant to an understanding of a certain type of abuser, the individual who cannot empathize with the emotional needs of his partner. If relational theorists are correct, men generally are taught virtually from birth to develop a strong sense of independence and invulnerability, are predisposed to restrict, if not reject the validity of emotional claims on their time and energy. Sympathetic concern with the plight of others would appear to conflict with the claims of self-centeredness. If emotional sensitivity is not encouraged and made an integral part of childhood socialization, an adult may simply not have the ability to properly identify with and respond to an empathic appeal. Undoubtedly, many emotionally abusive men have themselves been emotionally abused or the products of a socialization process that has systematically ignored, neglected, or rejected the value and need for emotional expression and understanding.

Summary

The aim of this chapter is to identify and assess the available theoretical interpretations of psychological maltreatment. The initial problem of theory building is the creation of an operational definition of the subject, an agreed upon statement that guides and unifies research. Although concerted attempts have been made, the goal has yet to be achieved. Among the many reasons for the problem is the complexity of the subject.

One can look at psychological maltreatment as either a dependent or independent variable. Some regard it as primarily the effect of other types of abuse. Others regard it as a unique phenomenon with unique causal antecedents.

Additionally, one can conceive of psychological maltreatment as a term of general applicability regardless of age or gender considerations, or a term primarily relevant to a particular age group or victim category. The bulk of the theoretical work to date has been developed by those whose focus of attention has been the child. Ecological theory, child needs theory, and attachment theory are prime examples. The three have in common a concern with the effects of abuse on child development, how it may negatively influence the ability of an individual to become a basically untroubled adult capable of becoming a contributing member of society.

An equivalent concerted aim to develop a general theory to account for adult psychological maltreatment has not been undertaken. Those concerned to account for the nature and prevalence of adult psychological maltreatment have leaned heavily on the theories used to account for child psychological maltreatment—particularly attachment and social learning theory. The exception is feminist theory, which focuses on the female victim of a patriarchal society, a traditional societal institution in which a disproportionate amount of power and authority is assigned to the male head of household. A promising outgrowth of feminist oriented theorizing is relational theory, a viewpoint that seeks to account for the disproportionate vulnerability of females to psychological maltreatment in the traditionally different self-concepts imposed on males and females.

Yet to be contemplated is a general theory, one as relevant to the analysis of child as adult psychological treatment, regardless of age or gender of either victim or perpetrator. Whether or not a general theory can or should be constructed before more restricted theories are developed is, of course, debatable. To some, theory is something that must evolve inductively, from the gradual accumulation of empirical knowledge. To others, empirical knowledge cannot accumulate unless it is guided by a consistent theory.

Whatever one's position, answers to unresolved questions such as the following would do much to clarify a rather confusing situation: Can and should a general theory be developed to account for both the perpetration and the consequences of psychological maltreatment? Are separate theories needed to account for child and adult psychological maltreatment? Are separate theories needed to account for the perpetration and consequences of psychological maltreatment? Should psychological maltreatment theory, regardless of whether or not the subject is the cause of perpetration or the consequence of victimization, be gender free or gender specific? Should the elderly and gay and lesbian partners be the subject of special theories or included in theorizing about adult psychological maltreatment?

Study Questions

1. Why has it been difficult to construct a generally acceptable operational definition of psychological maltreatment?

2. What is the relevance of Maslow's concept of needs deficiency to an understanding of the nature of child psychological maltreatment?

3. How does attachment theory contribute to an understanding of the causes of child psychological maltreatment?

4. How does social learning theory add to the understanding of adult psychological maltreatment?

5. What are the strengths and weaknesses of feminist theories of adult psychological maltreatment?

6. Is there a need for special theories of child and adult psychological maltreatment?

7. Is a general theory of psychological maltreatment necessary? If yes, why? If not, why not?

REFERENCES

Ainsworth, Mary D. 1967. *Infancy in Uganda: Infant Care and the Growth of Love.* Baltimore: Johns Hopkins Press.

———. 1978. *Patterns of Attachment: A Psychological Study of the Strange Situation.* NY: Halsted Press.

Allen, Joseph P., Stuart T. Hauser, and Emily Borman-Spurrell 1996. "Attachment Theory as a Framework for Understanding Sequelae of Severe Adolescent Psychopathology: An 11-Year Follow-Up Study." *Journal of Consulting and Clinical Psychology.* 64:254–63.

Bandura, Albert. 1977. *Social Learning Theory.* Englewood Cliffs, NJ: Prentice-Hall, Inc.

Barnett, Douglas, Jody Todd Manly, and Dante Cicchetti. 1991. "Continuing Toward an Operational Definition of Psychological Maltreatment." *Development and Psychopathology.* 3:19–30.

Belsky, Jay. 1980. "Child Maltreatment: An Ecological Integration." *American Psychologist.* 35:320–35.

———. 1991. "Psychological Maltreatment: Definitional Limitations and Unstated Assumptions." *Development and Psychopathology.* 3:31–36.

Bowlby, John. 1969. *Attachment and Loss, Volume I, Attachment.* NY: Basic Books, Inc.

———. 1973. *Attachment and Loss, Volume II, Separation, Anxiety, and Anger.* NY: Basic Books, Inc.

———. 1980. *Attachment and Loss, Volume III, Loss, Sadness, and Depression.* NY: Basic Books, Inc.

Brassard, Marla B., Robert Germain, and Stuart N. Hart. 1987. *Psychological Maltreatment of Children and Youth.* NY: Pergamon Press.

Bronfenbrenner, Urie. 1977. "Toward an Experimental Ecology of Human Development." *American Psychologist.* 32:513–31.

———. 1979. *The Ecology of Human Development.* Cambridge, MA: Harvard University Press.

Carlson, Vicki, Dante Cicchetti, Douglas Barnett, and Karen G. Braunwald. 1990. "Finding Order in Disorganization: Lessons from Research on Maltreated Infants' Attachments to Their Caregivers." Pp. 494-528 in *Child Maltreatment: Theory and Research on the Causes and Consequences of Child Abuse and Neglect,* Dante Cicchetti and Vicki Carlson, eds. NY: Cambridge University Press.

Chang, Valerie Nash. 1996. *I Just Lost Myself: Psychological Abuse of Women in Marriage.* Westport, CT: Praeger Publishers.

Crittenden, Patricia M. 1988. "Distorted Patterns of Relationship in Maltreating Families: The Role of Internal Representational Models." *Journal of Reproductive and Infant Psychology.* 6:183–99.

Frank, P. and G. Golden. 1992. "Blaming by Naming: Battered Women and the Epidemic of Co-Dependence." *Social Work.* 37:5–6.

Garbarino, James and John Eckenrode. 1997. *Understanding Abusive Families.* San Francisco, CA: Jossey-Bass Publishers.

Garbarino, James, John Eckenrode, and Kerry Bolger. 1997. "The Elusive Crime of Psychological Maltreatment." Pp. 101–13 in *Understanding Abusive Families,* by James Gabarino and John Eckenrode. San Francisco, CA: Jossey-Bass Publishers.

Hart, Stuart N., Robert B. Germain, and Marla R. Brassard. 1987. "The Challenge: To Better Understand and Combat Psychological Maltreatment of Children and Youth." Pp. 3–24 in *Psychological Maltreatment of Children and Youth,* by Marla B. Brassard, Robert Germain, and Stuart N. Hart. NY: Pergamon Press.

Hirschi, Travis. 1969. *Causes of Delinquency.* Berkeley, CA: University of California Press.

Loring, Marti Tamm. 1994. *Emotional Abuse.* NY: Lexington Books.

Maslow, Abraham H. 1968. *Toward a Psychology of Being.* NY: D. Van Nostrand Company.

———. 1987. *Motivation and Personality,* 3rd ed. NY: Harper Collins Publishers.

McGee, Robin A. and David A Wolfe. 1991. "Psychological Maltreatment: Toward an Operational Definition." *Development and Psychopathology.* 3:3–18.

Miller, Jean Baker. 1991. "The Development of Women's Sense of Self." Pp. 11–26 in *Women's Growth in Connection: Writings from the Stone Center,* by Judith V. Jordan, Alexandra G. Kaplan, Jean Baker Miller, Irene P. Stiver, and Janet L. Surrey. NY: The Guilford Press.

Miller, Mary Susan. 1995. *No Visible Wounds: Identifying Nonphysical Abuse of Women by Their Men.* Chicago, IL: Contemporary Books, Inc.

Park, Robert E. and Ernest W. Burgess, eds. 1925. *The City.* Chicago, IL: University of Chicago Press.

Preston, Geoff. 1986. "The Post-Separation Family and the Emotional Abuse of Children." *Australian Journal of Sex, Marriage & Family.* 7:40–9.

Smith, Jean Baker. 1991. "The Development of Women's Sense of Self." Pp. 11–26 in *Women's Growth in Connection: Writings from the Stone Center,* by Judith V. Jordan, Alexandra G. Kaplan, Jean Baker Miller, Irene P. Striver, and Janet L. Surrey. NY: The Guilford Press.

Stiver, Irene P. 1991. "The Meanings of 'Dependency' in Female-Male Relationships." Pp. 143–61 in *Women's Growth in Connection: Writings from the Stone Center,* by Judith V. Jordan, Alexandra G. Kaplan, Jean Baker Smith, Irene P. Stiver, and Janet L. Surrey. NY: The Guilford Press.

Surrey, Janet L. 1991. "The 'Self-in-Relation': A Theory of Women's Development." Pp. 51–66 in *Women's Growth in Connection: Writings from the Stone Center,* by Judith V. Jordan, Alexandra G. Kaplan, Jean Baker Miller, Irene P. Stiver, and Janet L. Surrey. NY: The Guilford Press.

Tzeng, Oliver C. S., Jay W. Jackman, and H. C. Karlson. 1991. *Theories of Child Abuse and Neglect.* NY: Praeger.

7 The Status of Theory on Family Abuse and Its Consequences: Problems and Issues

The preceding chapters have detailed the range and types of theoretical orientations that have been developed to account for various aspects of family abuse and its consequences. The question is, how well do these theories illuminate the problem? Has theorizing reached a level where it can be said to be guiding significant research, investigations revealing the essential dynamics and major effects of family abuse? If not, why not? Is the field of family abuse marked more by theoretical fragmentation than unity? Why is theoretical unity important? Are separate theories needed to account for the alleged different types of family abuse? Is a general theory of family abuse possible let alone desirable? Has the concept of family abuse been sufficiently defined to permit solid and confidently informed theorizing? What, if any, body of theory has been developed to account for the connection between family abuse and deviancy? Are the consequences of family abuse so diverse as to require a variety of theoretical interpretations? These are some of the questions requiring careful consideration and which guide the following discussion. The goal is to identify problems and issues to be confronted if some answers to the above questions are to be found.

Operational Definition or Definitions?

As noted earlier, an agreed upon operational definition of family abuse or maltreatment is yet to be identified. There are many reasons for this fact, most of which are not accorded the attention they deserve. The basic problem is conceptual, deciding what is to be the unit of analysis or the phenomenon to be explained. Generally, the aim is to account for the maltreatment of family members by other family members. But what exactly is a family and what constitutes maltreatment or abuse in such a context? By family, one usually makes reference to a heterosexual couple with at least one dependent child. By abuse or maltreatment, one thinks of treatment (physical or psychological) that exceeds standards of common decency and fairness. The problem is that conceptions of what is a family and what is maltreatment are subject to interpretation due to changing customs and practices and cultural differences that permeate a complex society such as the United States. Thus, investigators must clearly state exactly what they mean by such terms so as to relate to the world as it is rather than as they or anyone else thinks it either should or might be and in ways that colleagues respect by using them in the conduct of their research. When investigators agree on what it is they are studying, research can proceed from a common focal point.

Equally in need of clarification are the referents of a useful operational definition. To date, and whether the subjects have been adults or children, the referent, the thing to explain, has been what acts constitute abuse. This has led to the identification of the different types of abuse, in particular, physical, sexual, and emotional abuse. Even so, no effort has been made to develop a complete and generally accepted typology, one that contains mutually exclusive types. Examples of the problem come readily to mind. Thus, sexual abuse is commonly regarded as a distinct type, but isn't it really a subtype of physical abuse? Further, emotional abuse is regarded by some as a distinct type of abuse and by others as the general effect of all types. Part of the problem is the failure to distinguish between the manner in which abuse is perpetrated from abusive consequences. That psychological abuse may be both a method of abuse and an effect of other methods as well seems readily apparent. The blurring of the distinction between cause and effect is too often at the root of the conceptual confusion as to the different types of family abuse.

Adding to the confusion is the failure to distinguish abusive methods from their targets. That is, child abuse, adult abuse, and elder abuse are said to be types of abuse, but these are obviously most often used to specify victims, not the manner in which abuse may be expressed. What is needed is an effort to specify the methods of abuse and comparatively analyze their different effects on different types of victims—children versus adults, women versus men, younger people versus elderly people.

A related problem is the failure to recognize the need to develop separate perpetrator and victim typologies. As it is, current type definitions are essentially descriptions of types of acts that indicate what authors have in mind. If research is to advance, however, there must be a clear sense of not only what abusive acts are, but the variety of ways their participants, perpetrators and victims, causally influence particular events. The focus of attention must at some point shift from concern with what family abuse is to how and why it occurs between different possible types of perpetrators and victims. As the causes of family abuse perpetration and victimization may be quite independent, each requires operational definition and unique theoretical interpretation. What next requires careful thought is whether the required separate lines of theoretical inquiry should be encouraged to be independent of one another or guided by a general perspective. Each position has advantages and disadvantages. The proliferation of subjects and theories may simply add to the current fragmented state of the field. Under the guidance of a general orienting theoretical framework, piecemeal work may be integrated and interrelated to permit systematic knowledge accumulation. On the other hand, unless certain lines of inquiry are freely pursued, important knowledge may never be acquired.

A General Theory or Particular Theories?

At present, a range of theories is used to account for adult and child physical abuse, child sexual abuse, child and adult emotional abuse, child neglect, and elder abuse and neglect. Mostly, these theories take the form of frames of reference and conceptual schemes, the majority of which are borrowed from those developed for analysis of subjects other than family abuse (for example, psychoanalysis, child development theory, and social control theory). Frames of reference are essentially slants, angles, perspectives, ways of "looking at" a subject. To some social control theorists, for example, the proper way to view the impact of child socialization is to focus on what parents don't do rather than on what they do do. In this view, deviancy is not so much learned as allowed. As Hirschi states, to the social control theorist, "Deviance is taken for granted; conformity must be explained" (1969:10). In feminist theory, the proper slant to take to make sense of the conflict and violence that occurs between married partners is to view it as a power struggle, something involving the quest for dominance and control on one side and equality and self-respect on the other.

Noticeably absent is theory in the sense of testable hypotheses derived from basic propositions and stated assumptions involving key variables aimed at explaining the causes of a defined act of family abuse or a problem such as a rate or a data trend in regard to a type of abuse. In place of this kind of specificity, we have many viewpoints and terms used to illuminate not particularly well-defined topics. Some feel that the way to reduce the confusion is to develop a general theory to structure research and facilitate knowledge accumulation. Such a theory would be analogous to a highway map with all relevant subjects identified and possible links between them specified. The equivalent "map" of family abuse and violence would have to contain a compelling frame of reference, a slant from which to observe and interpret relevant phenomena and activity, specified units of analysis or variables, specification of the variables antecedent to the perpetration of maltreatment, and stated testable hypotheses that interrelate the specified variables involved in victimization, and the perpetration and negative consequences of maltreatment.

To date, the most thoroughly developed general theory is based on an ecological perspective, a viewpoint that conceives of objects in a spatial universe. The idea is to identify all the relevant factors in a given environment that significantly influence the subject in question, in this case factors such as local, state, and national institutions and values that influence interaction among family members leading to abusive maltreatment by one or more of its members against another or other members.

Slightly modifying Bronfenbrenner's theory of child development (1977, 1979), Belsky (1980), as discussed in Chapter 6, has proposed an ecological perspective for the study of child maltreatment. Belsky's scheme calls for taking into account four possible environmental contributing factors: parental background (ontogenic development); family setting (the microsystem); the neighborhood, community, workplace (the exosystem); and cultural values and belief systems (the macrosystem). Belsky provides some research evidence and insights concerning what is known and what needs examining about the influence of factors from each of the four environmental sources on child maltreatment. Chief among these is the finding that those who abuse tend to be those who themselves have been abused. Unfortunately, neither Belsky nor anyone else has advanced his theory by cataloging and interrelating the variables behind the perpetration and effects of the different types of child maltreatment.

Belsky proposed a multivariate theory because of the lack of evidence for any single factor explanation of child maltreatment. From the available evidence, he identified four likely contributing sources and then discussed the explanatory strengths and limitations of each. He hoped that others would examine empirically how they may interrelate to precipitate child maltreatment. In particular, for example, which family settings provoke or prevent parental violence toward children in those who have and have not themselves been abused as children or adults? If only a certain proportion of parents from abusive backgrounds become abusers themselves, how precisely is parental background influenced by family setting, neighborhood, and cultural variables? These are the kinds of questions Belsky hoped would be explored within his proposed ecological perspective. While it has been accorded a good deal of recognition, it has not commanded widespread systematic attention. Empirical research on child maltreatment continues to be influenced by a variety of theoretical perspectives and conceptual devices. Knowledge accumulation, a more accurate understanding of the dynamics of child maltreatment, cannot be claimed to have advanced much, if anything, beyond what it was when Belsky published his views.

There are several possible reasons for the inability of Belsky's general theory to command a loyal and devoted following. One is its problem focus, namely, child maltreatment. It is not clear, for example, that many in the field feel the time is ripe to seek an explanation of child maltreatment generally as opposed to seeking a closer understanding of the factors behind the expression of its different types. To focus on child maltreatment generally would seem to require greater confidence in acquired knowledge about the details of its different manifestations than appears to be the case. While physical, sexual, and emotional abuse may be closely interrelated—that is, components of a general pattern of family abuse—current evidence suggests they are as likely as not to be separately expressed. Similarly, while the consequences of the different types of abuse may be interrelated, they may be also quite distinct.

Another contributing factor is Belsky's concern with child maltreatment rather than family abuse generally. He does not state why adult maltreatment is excluded from his theoretical concerns or how the subject might be integrated into the scheme. If it is believed that separate general theories of child and adult maltreatment are to be sought, some explanation is called for but none is provided. Of course, Belsky was most likely responding to circumstances as he found them, the two fields then and now are not marked by empirical and theoretical unity. They are separately studied by those with different concerns and agendas, from different substantive interests to radically held ideological convictions. But what requires consideration is the interrelation of child and adult maltreatment. Their underlying similarities and differences, causal antecedents and behavioral consequences, deviant and otherwise, require identification and analysis. This neglected avenue of study is as important as any other. Indeed, it may be the essential prerequisite behind the identification of a commanding general theory of family maltreatment.

Lastly, Belsky's focus is problematic from another angle, the absence of clarity about the related but also quite different subjects of maltreatment perpetration and maltreatment consequences. To discuss the two subjects simultaneously without discussing their basic differences, causal and otherwise, is to promote confusion rather than clarity.

A general problem one encounters in reading the literature on family abuse is whether or not the subject is exactly what it is and why and how it occurs, or how it affects victims. It is difficult not to get the impression that most writers think of family maltreatment in the sense of what it does to its victims. Much of the reason for this impression can be traced to the fact that so many writing and researching the subject are psychologists, those concerned with factors that influence the mind. The behavioral and psychological consequences of being maltreated are extremely important subjects, and it is important to connect them to the nature and kind of abuse experienced. The problem is that little attention has been paid to the possibly different causal antecedents (cultural, situational, sociological, and so on) behind family maltreatment perpetration and victimization. Particularly in the case of adults, we know that some adult partner victims of maltreatment have a background of family abuse. What is not understood is how some victims contribute to their own abuse, both because of what people bring to a relationship and how they have learned to interact with a partner. As noted in earlier chapters, research findings suggest that some adult victims expect to be maltreated to one degree or another because of their experiences in their family of origin or even a previous adult relationship. Parents, after all, are both positive and negative role models, and children often come to realize the difference between the two years after leaving the home. Thus, if, as a child, one witnesses a consistent form of interaction, whether it is within socially acceptable normative bounds or not, it may become ingrained as something normal. Further, apparently some adults learn to expect abuse as something normal in a relationship, a manifestation of an integral part of marriage or partner bonding. Victims, in other words, may to some degree contribute or even provoke their own abuse, and exactly why and with whom this occurs are dimly understood subjects.

Family background, cultural differences, relational experiences, are some of the factors that must be taken into account in the analysis of this important subject.

What this points to is the need to consider the value of separate theoretical accounts of family maltreatment victimization and perpetration. To consider them simultaneously before and without knowledge of their possibly quite different dynamics may generate premature if not erroneous inferences about their causal relationship.

As noted above, what is currently available is a jumble of theories of the so-called major types of child or adult abuse. The problem is that the subject to be explained is not unambiguously specified. From the applied side (that is, from the point of view of those who treat family abuse victims such as psychologists and social workers) the tendency is to take a problem as presented by a victim and then to account for it as best as possible from the available store of theories and explanations that seem to fit. As should be expected, given the current condition of the field and the need of practitioners to help people deal with their immediate problems, ideas and concepts are freely adapted to meet the needs of the situation.

So-called "pure researchers," nonpractitioners such as university scholars are, of course, free to pursue a subject in any direction they see fit and regardless of practical considerations. Notwithstanding this fact, those in the field of family abuse have been heavily oriented toward generating practical, useful knowledge. Their tendency has been to approach the problem by means of data and conceptions supplied by others, private and public agencies concerned with tabulating its extent and developing treatment strategies. This has had both positive and negative consequences.

On the positive side, academic researchers have aided practitioners by conducting carefully structured studies that have yielded some important, immediately useful information justifying the need for interventionist programs and strategies. (For example, Widom's National Institute of Justice sponsored studies demonstrating the deviant behavioral consequences of child abuse.)

On the negative side, by orienting themselves to obtaining immediately relevant practical information, investigators neglect the open-ended pursuit of knowledge, the theoretical examination of subjects worthy of close analysis from a variety of perspectives without the constraint of yielding immediately useful findings. We know from Widom's (1992, 1996) work and that of others that there is solid evidence indicating a meaningful correlation between family abuse and deviancy, including serious criminality such as serial homicide.

Nonetheless, it cannot be said that the cause-and-effect variables behind the connection have been isolated. Doubtless, this is in good measure due to concern with developing and implementing immediately effective intervention strategies and programs. But, if knowledge is to advance and intervention strategies are to be guided by more than expediency, more attention must be given to developing theory guided research aimed at identifying and interpreting presumed connections between measurable causes and effects. Family abuse and its deviant consequences are complex subjects requiring analysis from different perspectives and with different ends in view. Only by broadening and expanding our knowledge of the two can we improve our understanding of what can and cannot be done to mitigate its prevalence and costly consequences.

One way to proceed is by closely examining the role of key variables involved in family abuse. These include age, gender, race, and ethnicity. Perhaps only by amassing knowledge of the influence and interplay of such factors in the expression of family abuse can the ground be prepared to identify patterns preliminary to the derivation of a compelling general theory of family abuse, its causes and consequences. The intermediate step may well be the development of particular theories to account for the different types of child and adult family abuse that in time give rise to their synthesis by an astute observer or observers. This cannot be predicted to be something inevitable because of the different theoretical and practical interests of those in the field of family abuse. On one side are the practitioners (family therapists, counselors, social workers), and on the other the academics. The one seeks immediately useful knowledge, the other causal understanding by means of the scientific method. The theoretical interests and slants of the one are not necessarily compatible with those of the other. It may be, therefore, that the two must go their separate ways to properly develop to the point where representatives of each side see the need and find a way to combine forces toward the end of developing a common general theoretical approach.

Whether the goal is to identify particular patterns in limited spheres toward the end of building generalizations, or to first create a general scheme from which to locate and organize the study of particulars, certain common elements are involved. First of all, the subject, whether it be a basic concept such as family abuse, or a particular problem such as parental child sexual abuse, must be clearly defined and operationally measurable. Second, we must identify a clear slant, a frame of reference, from which to study and analyze the subject. As one cannot look at anything from all possible angles at once, one must choose the one most likely to provide fruitful observations of key phenomena. As human science frames of reference come at various levels, from quite general (psychological, sociological, and biological) to quite specific (a given family, or restricted type of family abuse), one must decide and be able to justify which variety is best under the circumstance of concern. As frames of reference are useful only insofar as they permit closer examination of objects and events that occur within its confines, one must have a sense of the objects and variables to be observed.

For example, in observing a family from a general sociological perspective, one would be inclined to delineate family statuses (father, mother, children, border, and so on) and what roles occupants play vis-à-vis one another. Before examining interaction patterns among the role players, it would be wise to control for a number of their social attributes (age, gender, race, education, employment status, family income).

Also to be considered is what those involved bring to the situation on the basis of past experience. In particular, has either or both parents a documented history of child abuse? Other possibly intrusive variables may also be involved, and the more one can control for them the greater the likelihood of obtaining solid, empirically defensible data.

After controlling for everything we can think of, we can proceed with the close examination of the interaction patterns of family members. We can observe them directly by means of participant observation or by some indirect means such as a close-ended questionnaire or an open-ended interview schedule, the number and timing of either to be decided.

These, then, are the ingredients of a systematic approach to the analysis of a subject such as child abuse. The problem is that they remain to be approximated to a desired degree by coordinated investigations concerned to amass longitudinal data. As to why, most would probably allude to some combination of the newness of concerted family abuse research, the need for more basic research, and the need for more research funding money and sources. Whatever the truth of the matter, systematic theoretical analysis of family abuse (from either a well-defined general or particular theoretical base) is lacking and much in need.

Family Abuse and Deviancy Theory

If theoretical interpretations of the genesis of family abuse are noteworthy for their limitations, theoretical interpretations of the connection between family abuse and deviancy are noteworthy for their absence. There is no shortage of deviancy theory (Merton 1938; Lefton, Skipper, and McCaghy 1968; Lemert 1972; Tittle 1995), or theories linking family background to types of deviancy such as juvenile delinquency and adult criminality (Hirschi 1969; Sampson and Laub 1993). What is missing are theoretical accounts of the reasons for measured correlations between types of family abuse and certain types of deviancy. In earlier chapters, it has been noted that investigators have found an association between child physical family abuse, males most of all, and propensity to engage in adult violent criminal offending. Despite the association, most physically abused male children were not found to subsequently become violent criminal offenders. Further, different types of family abuse may have the same or equivalent effect.

In fact, and contrary to what might be expected, Widom (1992:1) found childhood family neglect to have a higher association with future adult violent criminality than childhood family physical abuse. Why or how the two quite different forms of abuse have the same outcome has not been theoretically interpreted. The variables behind the measured effects, deviant and nondeviant, are yet to be delineated and subjected to close empirical scrutiny.

Questions to pursue toward these ends include the following: What are the different deviant effects of given forms of family abuse? If a given form of family abuse can have multiple consequences, deviant and nondeviant, what accounts for the variation? If different forms of family abuse can have the same consequences, whether deviant or not, what accounts for the variation? What are the key intervening variables that must be controlled to account for a given effect of a given form of family abuse? Solid answers to such questions hinge on first developing a much more precise, empirically measurable conception of family abuse, its nature and varieties.

The next part examines what is known about a topic greatly in need of attention by those concerned to more precisely understand the dynamics of family abuse and its effects, namely, what is known about its perpetrators and victims. Different analyses of the two may well lead to the uncovering of the key variables necessary to bring greater precision to what is known and remains to be known about the general subject. That the causes and effects of each require separate consideration appear not generally acknowledged. Thus, and as will become evident, we actually know very little about the separate dynamics of each and precisely how they interrelate. The chapter titles reflect the influence of key variables involved in the study of each, namely, age, gender, race, ethnicity, and family income.

Study Questions

1. What are some of the basic reasons for the failure to develop an acceptable operational definition of family abuse?

2. What is behind the typological confusion in the study of family abuse?

3. What is ambiguous about the subject of family abuse theory and research?

4. Is there a justifiable need for the development of particular theories of types of family abuse?

5. Is theory-guided research prerequisite to identifying the key variables behind the causes and effects of family abuse?

6. Why hasn't Belsky's general theory of child maltreatment attracted greater attention than it has?

7. How have practical considerations aided and hindered knowledge of the causes and effects of family abuse?

8. What must be done to develop sound theories on the relationship between family abuse and deviancy?

9. What is the value of developing separate theories of family abuse perpetration and victimization?

REFERENCES

Belsky, Jay. 1980. "Child Maltreatment: An Ecological Integration." *American Psychologist.* 35:320–35.

Bronfenbrenner, Urie. 1977. "Toward an Experimental Ecology of Human Development." *American Psychologist.* 32:513–31.

———. 1979. *The Ecology of Human Development.* Cambridge, MA: Harvard University Press.

Hirschi, Travis. 1969. *Causes of Delinquency.* Berkeley, CA: University of California Press.

Lefton, Mark, James K. Skipper, Jr., and Charles H. McCaghy, eds. 1968. *Approaches to Deviance: Theories, Concepts, and Research Findings.* NY: Appleton-Century-Crofts.

Lemert, Edwin M. 1972. *Human Deviance, Social Problems, and Social Control.* Englewood Cliffs, NJ: Prentice-Hall, Inc.

Merton, Robert K. 1938. "Social Structure and Anomie." *American Sociological Review.* 3:672–82.

Sampson, Robert J. and John H. Laub. 1993. *Crime in the Making: Pathways and Turning Points Through Life.* Cambridge, MA: Harvard University Press.

Tittle, Charles R. 1995. *Control Balance: Toward a General Theory of Deviance.* Boulder, CO: Westview Press.

Widom, Cathy Spatz. 1992. "The Cycle of Violence." Washington, DC: National Institute of Justice.

———. 1996. "The Cycle of Violence Revisited." Washington, DC: National Institute of Justice.

CHAPTER

8 Violence across the Life Course

Both family and community violence occur throughout the life course. While some types of violent activity are more likely to take place at certain times in the victim's or perpetrator's life, age in itself does not grant immunity from either crime or abuse. As we will see, the age of both the victim and the perpetrator is a factor governing whether family abuse will be perpetrated, especially in the cases of child physical, sexual, and emotional abuse. Further, the age of the perpetrator also relates to violent behavior within the community. The National Research Council Panel on the Understanding and Control of Violent Behavior concluded, "Age is one of the most important single predictors of violent victimization" (Reiss and Roth 1993:68).

The purpose of this chapter is to examine the types of family and community violence experienced by children, adolescents, adults, and the elderly across time. It examines the effect of age on victimization throughout the life span and explores the developmental events that may facilitate abuse of various kinds. The chapter also explores the significance of age in the perpetration of abuse.

Age of the victim and the perpetrator is significant because developmental changes and age-linked life experiences occur throughout the lifespan of individuals (Featherman 1981; Passuth and Bengston 1996). Developmental changes such as moving from childhood into adolescence directly affect the risk of victimization and abuse (Newberger and DeVos 1988; Seegmiller 1995).

Developmental changes arise from biological, psychological, social, and economic events that occur at different times in people's lives. The life course perspective examines how people respond to these age-related events and norms. The effects of developmental influences can also accumulate across time to intensify or, in some cases, reduce the occurrence of family abuse (Newberger and DeVos 1988). Some of the more common age-related events that can effect family abuse are described in Box 8.1.

The ability of people to effect their own developmental experiences is an important aspect of the life course perspective. How people perceive the experience of abuse intervenes between acts of abuse and how people respond (Newberger and DeVos 1988). It assumes that we can choose alternative perceptions of and responses to abusive events—even though at times the choices may be quite limited or repugnant.

BOX **8.1**

Age-Related Events that May Effect Family Abuse

The following events may occur at various ages for different people. However, public opinion tends to think they occur at a certain time in one's life. Consequently, societal norms say that people should do those things over which they have control when they are expected to. Failure to do those things may result in labeling the person as a deviant, even a baby who is slow to walk. Being labeled a deviant may attract abuse by other family members. For events beyond one's control, norms say we should respond in expected ways when they do occur. Failure to meet others' expectations may result in abuse. It should be noted, however, that perpetrators of abuse may themselves have deviant norms for these events and punish others who try to meet society's norms that conflict with those of the abuser.

- Walking
- Talking
- Toilet training
- Entering preschool, kindergarten, elementary, middle, high school, and college
- Wearing a particular type of clothing style
- Learning to use public transportation or to drive
- Learning about sexual behavior
- Onset of puberty
- Experimenting with drugs
- Reaching age of legal independence
- Getting a job
- Becoming unemployed
- Establishing a career
- Getting married
- Having children
- Divorce
- Reaching peak achievement in one's career
- Realizing not all one's life goals will be achieved
- Having grandchildren
- Death of a parent
- Onset of serious medical illness
- Disability resulting from substance abuse
- Death of a spouse
- Retirement
- Permanent disability

Source: Bernice L. Neugarten, Joan W. Moore, and John C. Lowe, 1996. "Age Norms, Age Constraints, and Adult Socialization." Pp. 194–203 in *Aging for the Twenty-First Century: Readings in Social Gerontology,* Jill Quadagno and Debra Street, eds. NY: St. Martin's Press.

The occurrence of historical events also affects developmental growth and changes. Each birth cohort experiences unique historical events, opportunities, and challenges to which it must respond. Responses to abuse become part of each individual's development (or lack of) across time, whether the individual is the perpetrator or the victim or abuse.

It has long been known by criminologists that the vast majority of street or community crime is committed by young men in their late teens and early twenties. In 1996, FBI statistics showed that those under age 18 were arrested for 19 percent of all crimes and 19 percent of all violent crimes (Snyder 1997). The relationship between age and crime is so strong it led Hirschi and Gottfredson to observe that "there is reason to believe that age could replace social class as the master variable of sociological theories of crime" (1983:553). Hirschi and Gottfredson state that most theories of crime focus on the adolescent and late teenage years, the period in life when one is at greatest risk for committing crime. It is one of the basic assumptions of criminology that the tendency to commit crime diminishes as people age.

The ability to understand our own experiences changes over time and changes dramatically from infancy through adolescence (Feiring, Taska, and Lewis 1999). It is certainly understandable that the age at which one is victimized can have bearing on the immediate response to victimization and subsequent recovery. Although many studies do not consider age as a critical issue, studies that do consider age at victimization show inconsistent results. For example, some research shows that onset of abuse and age of discovery do not have much relationship to the impact of sexual abuse. Other research shows that the older the victim of sexual abuse, the more extensive the effects. Still other research shows that the period before puberty is a more difficult time for sexual abuse than the earlier years or adolescence. See Feiring et al. (1999) for a discussion of the impact of age on sexual abuse victimization.

Age is also important to a discussion of victimization because age-related events and experiences may precipitate or create opportunities for family abuse. When children enter new levels of education, they typically try out new roles and behaviors. This tests established family relationships, the strain from which may lead to abuse. A spouse changing jobs may leave children alone with a partner who previously had little time alone with the children. A grandparent who becomes frail and moves in with a family member is more available for abuse than previously. If people respond to life's challenges with new coping skills and see these challenges as opportunities for personal growth, family abuse is less likely to result. If people remain rigid in the face of their changing lives, the risk of violence or abuse may increase.

The lives of the perpetrators and victims are intertwined in these life events. No simple relation exists between the abusive events and what happens as a result. A child's altered behavior may create more stress. A parent's insecurity over loss of power and control from the change may result in greater abuse, even if the child doesn't change his or her behavior. Despite the complex relationship between life events and family abuse, however, certain issues are more prominent at different stages of one's life.

Child Victimization and Deviance

Infants are at highest risk of maltreatment because they have no way to defend themselves from abuse or neglect. Garbarino puts it this way: "The infant can do virtually nothing to protect itself from abuse and is totally defenseless against neglect" (1989:694). Its immature development makes it impossible for it to defend itself or even avoid behaviors the parent finds aggravating. Since young children require constant monitoring from adults, they are vulnerable to abuse. Parents or other adults who have little knowledge of child development may misperceive the behavior of children as defiance, rather than lack of ability, which can provoke an abusive response from the adult (Jackson et al. 1999). The fact that children are perceived as defenseless accounts for strong public support for punishment for those who are child abusers (Johnson and Sigler 1995).

The line between discipline of a child and child maltreatment can be a fine one. The well-known National Family Violence Surveys of 1975 and 1985 found that over 90 percent of parents spank their toddlers or use another form of corporal punishment. The rate of corporal punishment declines after the age of five; however, for many it can still be an issue (Straus and Kaufman Kantor 1994). Corporal punishment declines further, as we will discuss, when children reach adolescence.

The relationship between child victimization and deviant behavior is very complex and it must be remembered that situations of maltreatment arise from a complex web of social problems, and can be very difficult to sort out the contributing factors. Shure points out:

> It is widely accepted that increases in delinquency and violence over the past decade are rooted in a number of interrelated social problems—child abuse and neglect, alcohol and drug abuse, youth conflict and aggression, and early sexual involvement—that may originate within the family structure. (1999:1)

Childhood Perpetration of Abuse

Victimization as well as perpetration of family abuse can begin at an early age. A national survey of women and sexual abuse found that approximately one-third of women reported sexual abuse before the age of nine, with more than half reporting their first sexual abuse experience before the age of 12 (Vogeltanz et al. 1999). While it can be hard to believe, there are also cases of children becoming sexually assaultive at a very young age. See Box 8.2 for a case of rape perpetrated by a nine-year-old boy.

Some evidence points to the perspective that it is never too early to prevent abuse and deviant behavior. In one study, prenatal and infant home visits from

BOX **8.2**

Rape of a Nine-Year-Old by a Nine-Year-Old

In Charlestown, Massachusetts, a 9-year-old boy was charged with raping a 9-year-old girl with whom he had been friends. The boy was accused of forcibly raping the girl in her bedroom. While the boy's attorney denied the charges, Assistant Suffolk District Attorney David Deakin, chief of the child abuse unit, said there was "very credible information from the 9-year-old victim that this boy had forced himself on her, sexually assaulted and raped her" (B5). The boy's attorney said that if convicted he would have had to register with the state and local police as a sex offender for a 20-year period. Prior to the decision to prosecute the 9-year-old boy, the prosecution offered to provide social services to the boy and his family. Services were refused by the family and the boy's attorney. A jury had been chosen for the trial in Boston Juvenile Court; however, the charges were dropped when the girl's parents asked that she not have to testify. Assistant District Attorney Deakin stated: "We didn't feel it was in her best interest to compel her to testify."

Source: John Ellement. 1999. "Case Accusing Boy, 9, of Rape Dropped." *The Boston Globe*, June 29:B5.

nurses were made to unmarried women and those of low socioeconomic status. A 15-year follow-up found these adolescents had fewer convictions and violations of probation, fewer episodes of running away, fewer lifetime sex partners, fewer cigarettes smoked each day, fewer alcohol-consuming days in the last six months, and fewer behavior problems related to the use of drugs and alcohol than the control group (Olds et al. 1998).

There is general agreement in the literature that adults exhibiting deviant sexual practices began their behavior before the age of 18 (Abel and Rouleau 1990; Becker et al. 1989). One study found that approximately half of adult sex offenders committed their first sexual assaults before the age of 18 (Groth, Longo, and McFadin 1982). FBI data from 1995 show that of arrests for forcible rape, 15.8 percent were younger than 18 years and 17 percent of other sexual offenses were committed by those younger than 18 (Sipe, Jensen, and Everett 1998). FBI data from 1997 show that for male arrests for rape, 6.36 percent were under the age of 15 and 17 percent were under the age of 18 at the time of arrest. For other sexual offenses in 1997, 9.2 percent were under the age of 15 and 18.3 percent were under the age of 18. While arrests for juveniles (ages 10–17) charged with forcible rape increased 44 percent between 1980 and 1991 the rate declined in 1999 to the 1980 rate of 16 arrests per 100,000 juveniles (Snyder 2000).

While it is true today that much more concern is expressed for violent juvenile crime, and there has been a strong trend by legislatures to "get tough" on juvenile crime, the proportion of juveniles in the juvenile justice system who first enter the system before the age of 14 has changed little between 1980 and 1995 high school graduates. There is some encouraging news as the juvenile crime rate is on the decline. In 1997, for every 1,000 juveniles, 31 serious crimes were committed, a reduction from 52 per 1,000 in 1993. Although these figures are the lowest since 1986, there were still 706,000 violent juvenile crimes nationally in 1997 (Meckler 1999). Since 1997 juvenile arrest rates have continued to decline—the arrest rate for murder by juveniles fell 68 percent between 1993 and 1999, the lowest juvenile murder rate since the 1960s (Snyder 2000).

In general, loneliness and isolation during childhood can have a strong impact on the perpetration of abuse. Tingle et al. (1986) found that approximately 80 percent of sampled sex offenders reported having no or very few friends as children. Lisak (1994) found that male survivors of sexual abuse experienced strong feelings of isolation and that a damaged sense of self can continue throughout the life course. One of the factors noted in the Columbine, Colorado, high school tragedy of 1999 is that before the murders the two boys responsible were ostracized by their peers.

Emotional distance from the father is another characteristic often found among abused boys. This can create an at-risk situation of sexual abuse if the boy pursues a relationship with a father substitute (Graham 1996). For example, a boy who has a poor relationship with his father can be vulnerable to abuse from an older male who shows interest in him.

One of the clues that may be missed in predicting future violent behavior is cruelty toward animals. See Box 8.3 for a description of some notorious murderers and their behavior toward animals during childhood.

Problems stemming from childhood maltreatment may take time to emerge. For example, some research shows that childhood maltreatment does not raise the risk of substance abuse during adolescence; however, it does increase the risk of

---

B O X **8.3**

Animal Cruelty and Murder: A Curious Relationship

A number of notorious murderers were known to have shown cruelty to animals. These murderers include David Berkowitz, known as the "Son of Sam," Charles Manson, Henry Lee Lucas, and Ted Bundy. A pattern of cruelty to animals—especially torture, dissection, burning, and killing—is thought to be a warning sign of dangerous behavior to follow. It has been suggested that in the torture and killing of animals, the animals are symbolic representations of people. Therefore, the killing of animals may actually serve as practice for the killing of humans.

Jeffrey Dahmer killed 17 people, and in some cases cannibalized his victims; Dahmer was himself murdered in prison in 1994. During his childhood, Dahmer was known to strangle cats and dogs. He nailed frogs to trees. Because he wanted to see their insides, he cut open live fish. He also was fascinated by animal dissections in school classes as well as his own animal road-kill dissections.

Source: Neal D. Barnard and A. R. Hogan. 1999. "The Animal Abuse-Violence Connection." *The Patriot Ledger,* Scripps Howard News Service, June 21:10.

substance abuse among adults (Ireland and Widom 1994). The same may be true for mental health problems—they may manifest in adulthood rather than during childhood or adolescence (Green 1993).

Adolescent Victimization and Deviance

It is generally the case that more attention is given to adolescent behavior problems than childhood problems. This is mainly because adolescent deviancy is typically more dangerous, including assaultive and sexually assaultive behavior. In the past 10 years more attention has been focused on adolescent sexual offenses and offenders, although there continues to be little actual research (Hagan and Cho 1996; Ryan and Lane 1991; Sipe et al. 1998). The focus on treating juvenile sexual offenders is considered by some to be "the most substantial shift in treatment in recent years" (Marshall 1996:189).

There is evidence that parental discipline techniques change as children grow (Jackson et al. 1999). Parents might stop hitting their children when they become adolescents because the children are physically bigger and can in turn inflict harm on the parent. Jackson et al. (1999) found that while parents of younger children said they had negative attitudes toward physical discipline, the younger the child, the greater the likelihood of using physical discipline. Nonphysical discipline was more often reserved for older children. Jackson et al. (1999) explain the difference between attitudes and actions by calling attention to the considerable amount of supervision required by younger children that can leave them at greater risk of abuse. The authors conclude: "While we found age was a predictor of parental attitudes and discipline practices, there is a need for a broader understanding of how a child's age and developmental characteristics mediate parental child-rearing attitudes and child-management practices" (1999:27). They also point out that having several children of varying ages can complicate parental attitudes and disciplinary practices. It is also the case that parents bring their own issues and problems to their parenting. See Box 8.4 for some parenting issues experienced by mothers who were victims of childhood sexual abuse.

For some, adolescent maltreatment is a continuation of the abuse suffered as a child. For others, the abuse begins during adolescence, as parents have difficulty adjusting to what may be new demands placed on them by their growing children. Adolescence is often depicted as a time of turmoil where changing bodies and raging hormones contribute to a confused identity. The developmental tasks are challenging and include establishing a stable personal and sexual identity and learning about intimate relationships (Green 1993). Other tasks for adolescents include development of skills in long-term planning, abstract reasoning, complex problem solving, attention concentration, and controlling short-term behavior to achieve long-term goals (S'guin et al. 1995). Abuse victimization can disrupt these developmental tasks. In families where abuse is common, there may be no role models for positive identities, intimate relationships, complex problem solving, delayed gratification, or other important developmental behaviors.

BOX **8.4**

Parenting by Women Who Endured Childhood Sexual Abuse

The relationship between parenting ability and maltreatment as a child is not thoroughly understood. Some parents who have experienced maltreatment themselves can become even more strongly committed to raising their children in a healthier environment than they had. Other parents can struggle in their parenting.

A review of research on parents who were sexually abused as children focuses on mothers, rather than fathers, and does show some negative effects. The following are some of the findings of research on the parenting skills of victims of childhood sexual abuse:

- Mothers focus more on themselves than their children.
- They tend to belittle and blame their children for problems.
- They are less affirming and understanding of their children.
- They are more likely to treat the child as a friend who will fulfill their emotional needs.
- They are more likely to perceive themselves as inadequate parents.
- They have unrealistic expectations of their children.

Source: Susan J. Zuravin and Cynthia Fontanella. 1999. "Parenting Behaviors and Perceived Parenting Competence of Child Sexual Abuse Survivors." *Child Abuse and Neglect.* 23:623–32.

It is important to stress that adolescence does not have to be filled with turmoil and, in most families, is not. However, Garbarino (1989) pointed out that negative stereotypes of adolescence can "contribute to the problems of troubled youth in troubled families" (690). Garbarino addressed the issue that parenting the adolescent is very different from parenting a younger child and that additional stresses can be brought to bear. An adolescent has greater power than a younger child, which means the adolescent can influence conflict in the family more than a younger child can. An adolescent has the power to physically defend himself against abuse. The social relationships of adolescents can be independent of involvement with parents and at this time there may be some involvement in sexual relationships. Adolescents gain more understanding of sexual behavior and the meaning attached to it and can examine their sexual experiences (and sexual abuse) in a different and more sophisticated light (Spaccarelli 1994).

Since the cognitive abilities of adolescents are more sophisticated than a child's, the task of parenting becomes more complex. Adolescents, if maltreated, are more capable and more likely to bring maltreatment to the attention of adults outside the family. Garbarino (1989) also points out that meeting the needs of adolescents is significantly more expensive than meeting the financial needs of a child, which can add further stress to the family.

Adolescents, whether male or female, as well as women generally, are less likely to elicit public sympathy than young children and the elderly who are victimized, as children and the elderly are perceived as more defenseless. Adolescents are more likely to be seen as contributing to the abuse through their own difficult behavior. While adolescents may be victims of all types of child maltreatment, they are more likely to be victims of sexual and psychological abuse (Garbarino 1989).

Green (1993) credits the work of Gomes-Schwartz, Horowitz, and Sauzier (1985) as "the first major study of the impact of child sexual abuse using a standardized instrument" (892). Their work lends support to the importance of a developmental perspective and that response to abuse is related to the age of the victim. The Louisville Behavior Checklist was administered to a sample of 156 sexually abused children evaluated in an outpatient clinic. Seventy-eight percent of the sample was female and 22 percent was male. Of the sexually abused preschool children (ages 4–6), 17 percent experienced "clinically significant psychopathology" (892). Forty percent of the school-age children (7–13) and 24 percent of the adolescents (14–18) had significant social and intellectual problems, including anxiety, depression, physical delays, and aggressive behavior. The relatively high rate of problems among the school-age children was attributed to their being more aware than the younger children of what constitutes deviant sexual behavior. Only about one-fourth of the adolescents experienced significant problems relating to sexual abuse, which may be related to what is called "sampling bias." In this context, this means that the more severely disturbed adolescents were probably not part of the clinic sample but were in psychiatric or correctional facilities or had run away.

Feiring et al. (1999) examined age and gender differences in children and adolescents and how they adapt to sexual abuse. They related the age when the abuse was discovered to psychological distress. Their research confirms the importance of age as having a bearing on response to the abusive events. Participants were interviewed within 8 weeks of the time sexual abuse was reported. A total of 169 were included in the sample, 96 children and 73 adolescents. Adolescents were more likely to be victimized by a "parental figure" than children (42 percent vs. 29 percent). Adolescents were also more likely to have been abused on 10 or more occasions (40 percent vs. 26 percent). Adolescents were more likely to experience the use of force than children (38 percent vs. 15 percent). Adolescents were also found to experience more depression and lower levels of self-esteem and social support than children. The higher levels of psychological distress of the adolescents may be related to the developmental tasks of adolescence and may continue into adulthood. In the words of Feiring et al., "A confluence of factors, including the stress of the abuse discovery, the normative increases in self-consciousness and negative self-evaluations, poor self-esteem and limited social support may contribute to adolescents being at higher risk for adopting an enduring negative self-view" (1999:122).

Kendall-Tackett, Williams, and Finkelhor (1993) reviewed 45 research studies showing that children who had been sexually abused experienced more problems than children who had not been sexually abused. Inappropriate sexual behavior or "sexualized behavior" was the symptom sexually abused children were most likely to manifest. Other behaviors that occurred most frequently among the sexually abused children were depression, withdrawal, anxiety, physical complaints, aggressive behavior, and school/learning problems. Overall, Kendall-Tackett et al. (1993) found that "for almost every symptom examined, including self-esteem, in most studies sexually abused children were found to be more symptomatic than their non-abused counterparts" (165).

Kelley, Thornberry, and Smith (1997) found that adolescents who had endured childhood maltreatment were far more likely to engage in problem behaviors such as drug use, academic problems, teen pregnancy, and violent and delinquent behaviors. In a sample of 1,000 adolescents, 14 percent had a history of childhood maltreatment and 86 percent did not. Researchers in this study did not separate the different types of childhood maltreatment. Twenty percent who grew up in poor families were victims of maltreatment. Only 8 percent of the nondisadvantaged were maltreated. Forty-five percent of maltreated children had official records of delinquency, while 32 percent of the nonmaltreated did. Adolescents who were maltreated as children had a higher rate of serious delinquency (42 percent) compared with the nonmaltreated (33 percent). They also had higher rates of violence (70 percent) than the nonmaltreated.

In Kelley et al.'s study, girls who had a history of maltreatment had a pregnancy rate of 52 percent as compared with 34 percent for the nonmaltreated girls. Girls who endured several types of maltreatment such as sexual and physical abuse were more likely to become pregnant than those who endured one type of maltreatment.

Of those with a history of childhood maltreatment, Kelley et al. (1997) found that 43 percent used drugs, while 32 percent of the nonmaltreated did. Poor grades in school were a problem for 33 percent of the maltreated group and 23 percent of the nonmaltreated. Twenty-six percent of the maltreated adolescents experienced mental health problems as compared with 15 percent of the nonmaltreated. In sum, for the problem areas of serious delinquency, violence, pregnancy, drug use, academic problems, and mental health problems, those who were maltreated were higher on each of these measures.

Research shows a link between sexual abuse in childhood and revictimization during adolescence. Krahe et al. (1999) found that 8.9 percent of 281 female adolescents (ages 17–20) in Germany reported childhood sexual abuse. (Interestingly, an additional 8.5 percent said they were not sure whether they were victims of childhood sexual abuse.) Abuse victims scored higher on all the items in the Sexual Experiences Survey than did the nonabused young women. Forty-eight percent of female adolescents with a history of sexual abuse acknowledged attempted intercourse through force, compared with 29.2 percent of the women who were unsure of their childhood abuse status, and 5.6 percent of women who had not experienced childhood sexual abuse. Forty percent of women with a history of childhood sexual abuse experienced completed intercourse through force, compared with 20.8 percent of those unsure of childhood victimization, and 1.7 percent of those who had not been sexually victimized as a child. Those women who were unsure of their victimization status were the most likely to have engaged in intercourse while using drugs or alcohol (25 percent), compared with the victimized women (20 percent) and those who had not been childhood victims (6.9 percent).

The work of Krahe et al. (1999) supports previous research that females who have been sexually abused as children are at risk for later sexual victimization. Importantly, the women who endured childhood sexual abuse had significantly higher numbers of sexual partners than the nonabused. Since there is a higher level of consensual sexual activity this can put females at higher risk for nonconsensual sex. Krahe et al. also found that feelings of worthlessness were associated with a greater likelihood of sexual victimization during adolescence.

As discussed in the theory chapters, there is evidence that those victimized are disproportionately likely to become perpetrators. In his sample of 286 sex offenders in treatment, Graham (1996) found 70 percent reported sexual abuse and 50 percent reported physical abuse in childhood. In the words of Graham, "There is a reenactment quality to the acting out" (1996:193). The need to reenact earlier abuse or acting out in response to the abuse indicates the offenders have not progressed beyond the earlier events. Their psychological and social development has been at least partially blocked. For all the concern for victimization and subsequent perpetration, however, this does not mean it is destined to occur (Straus and Gelles 1988). An encouraging finding from Kelley et al. (1997) was that 28 percent of the maltreated had no apparent problems in the designated problem areas: serious delinquency, violence, pregnancy, academic problems, drug use, and mental health problems. They concluded that "long-term developmental damage does not appear to be inevitable" (13). However, while not inevitable, the fact that almost three-quarters did experience some difficulty speaks to the potential for far-reaching effects of maltreatment.

Kendall-Tackett et al. (1993) examined the assumption that some victims of sexual abuse appear not to suffer negative effects from the abuse. They reviewed several studies that found that between 21 percent and 49 percent of sexual abuse victims suffered no symptoms. They offer three possible explanations for these findings. First, researchers may not be using appropriate problem lists or the tools used were not sufficiently sensitive to pick up problems. Second, children may have a delayed response to the abuse. It may be that the abused children are still in denial about the abuse or that the trauma of abuse will become evident later when they are better able to grasp the meaning of being a victim of abuse. We have already indicated some support for this explanation, especially in the development of mental health problems and substance abuse in adulthood. Third, some children may be genuinely unaffected by the abuse experience. Perhaps they were victimized over a shorter period of time and may have been victims of less intrusive abuse (fondling versus intercourse). Some children could simply be more "resilient" than others, or have better resources to cope with abuse. Kendall-Tackett et al. (1993) acknowledge that all three explanations may be correct at the same time. They call for research specifically on children who appear to be free of symptoms related to abuse.

A number of studies focus on the relationship between child maltreatment and subsequent violent behavior. In their review of the literature, Rivera and

Widom found "the relationship . . . to be consistent but modest" (1990:20). As indicated previously, this subject has had methodological problems and studies have often relied on unsubstantiated retrospective reports of child maltreatment. This means that adults typically are asked to remember whether they were maltreated as children. This can be problematic as faulty memory can create inaccuracies that can underestimate or overestimate abusive experiences. There are more of these retrospective studies of juveniles because they are easier to conduct than following a group of children who have been abused over time (Lewis, Mallouh, and Webb 1989). Rivera and Widom (1990) also point out that the cause-and-effect relationship between maltreatment and deviant behavior can be unclear. Does child maltreatment cause delinquency or does delinquency cause child maltreatment?

Malinosky-Rummell and Hansen (1993), in their review of the literature on the consequences of physical abuse, note the strong relationship between being a victim of physical abuse and adolescent aggressive behavior. In general, adolescents who engage in violent and aggressive behavior have higher rates of maltreatment than the nonmaltreated. Among males in residential care, those who have been violent have higher rates of physical abuse than nonviolent boys. Juveniles who are clients of mental health facilities and have been physically abused engage in more aggressive behavior than peers who were not abused.

Lewis et al. (1989) state that while approximately 20 percent of abused children become delinquent, studies indicate that high percentages of delinquents have a history of child maltreatment. Lewis and her colleagues are well known for studying the relationship between family violence, child abuse, and criminality. In general, they have found that abuse alone, while a critical factor, does not tell the whole story:

> Severe physical abuse is most likely to be associated with violent delinquency and criminality when one or more of the following factors is present: the child suffers from some sort of central nervous system dysfunction that impairs his ability to modulate his emotions and control his responses; the child suffers from some form of psychiatric disturbance that impairs his reality testing at times so that he misperceives his environment and feels needlessly and excessively threatened; the child is exposed to extraordinary household violence between parent or caretakers. (1989:717)

Rivera and Widom (1990) found that maltreated juvenile boys were not more likely to commit a violent crime than the males in the control group. Females who were maltreated did have higher risk for violence than females who were not maltreated. Race was an important issue here. Maltreated whites did not have significantly higher rates of arrest for violent crimes than the control group. However, African Americans who were maltreated as children had higher arrest rates for violence as juveniles and adults than those who were not maltreated.

It has long been held by criminologists that the age at which illegal activity begins has bearing on the likelihood of continuing to offend. Rivera and Widom (1990) found that maltreated children began delinquent behaviors at an earlier point than nonmaltreated children. Although there were differences in age in beginning violent behaviors and the extent of violence, overall nonmaltreated children were just as likely as the maltreated to continue with a pattern of violent offenses once they had begun.

Adolescent Perpetration of Abuse

The line between victimization and perpetration of abuse is not always as clear as we would like. The relationship between victimization and perpetration has been the subject of much research and controversy, as discussed in the section on the intergenerational transmission of abuse in Chapter 5. These issues are evident in the research that links childhood victimization to adolescent perpetration and recidivism.

In a comparison of a sample of adjudicated adolescent sexual offenders with nonoffenders, adolescent sex offenders reported significantly more sexual and physical abuse perpetrated against them by an adult. There was a greater likelihood of looking at pornography: 41 percent of adolescent sexual offenders reported frequent viewing of pornographic magazines as compared with 16 percent of nonoffenders (Zgourides, Monto, and Harris 1997).

A critical concern is that once sexual offending has begun, it is likely to continue. This speaks to the importance of examining the likelihood of reoffending. Recidivism rates among studies can vary due to methodological differences including reliance on official statistics such as arrests and convictions or being limited to only offender self-reports of sexual offending. The type of offense and the length of time offenders are monitored are also critical to research outcomes (Sipe et al. 1998). Of course, the longer the follow-up period the greater the likelihood of recidivism. In general, juvenile sexual offenders have a high rate of recidivism in sexual assaults, a point that speaks to the critical importance of treatment and prevention.

Groth et al. found that rapists and child molesters "admitted to having committed two to five times as many sex crimes for which they were not apprehended" (1982:450). Awad and Saunders (1991) found that 40 percent of child molesters had previously molested. In the majority of cases, it was with the same victim. Their work supports that juvenile sexual offenders are at high risk for repeating offenses with children and speaks to the need for long-term close monitoring.

Fehrenbach et al. (1986) found in their study of adolescent males in a juvenile sexual offender program that recidivism was high, particularly for sexual offenses. Fifty-eight percent of offenders (171) had committed at least one sexual offense before entering the treatment program.

Sipe et al. (1998) compared the recidivism rates of juveniles who were sexual offenders with other juvenile offenders. Sexual offenses in young adulthood were low in both groups. However, those who had committed sexual offenses as juveniles had a significantly higher rate of recidivism as young adults: 9.7 percent of juvenile sexual offenders were arrested as adults for sexual offenses compared with 3 percent of the nonsexual juvenile offenders. Those who were nonsexual juvenile offenders had higher rates of recidivism for all other types of offenses. According to Sipe et al., "The high rates of recidivism found in these studies have been a factor underlying an increasingly punitive and incarceration-based response to juvenile offenders" (1998:111).

These studies of recidivism show that adolescents are at great risk of repeating their sex offenses. However, the studies show also that there is a significant percentage (more than half) of offenders who do not (Smith and Monastersky 1986). In the Sipe et al. (1998) study, fewer than 10 percent of the adolescent sex offenders had been rearrested for sex offenses as adults. These findings should not minimize the risk of offenders repeating their sex crimes, but they do point to the fact that there are factors such as treatment that can reduce sexually abusive behavior.

Groth et al. (1982) found that sex offenders generally begin their perpetration during adolescence. In their study of rapists and child molesters, Groth et al. found that the modal age (the most frequently occurring age) of offenders at the time of their first sexual assault was 16. The authors discuss the importance of taking adolescent sexual offenses very seriously:

> Unfortunately, all too frequently sexual offenses by juveniles are dismissed as merely adolescent sexual curiosity or experimentation. Since such offenses go unrecognized by the criminal justice and mental health systems, they are not addressed. No intervention occurs until the offender is an adult; by then, many sexual assaults and victimizations may have occurred which might otherwise have been prevented. (1982:457)

The relationship of age to victimization and perpetration of maltreatment among children and adolescents is complex. As we will see, the relationship of age to victimization and perpetration among adults and the elderly is no less complicated.

Adult and Midlife Victimization and Perpetration

As adolescents enter adulthood they are faced with a number of developmental issues. How they respond to these issues affects the likelihood that adolescent abusers may continue their abuse into adulthood, that adolescent victims may become abusers. Resolving psychological conflicts about past abuse can help victims and perpetrators to develop skills to overcome a pattern of abuse or victimization. If the developmental issues of early adulthood are not successfully resolved, offenders are likely to continue to abuse. Victims who do not meet their developmental challenges may continue to expect victimization or may even develop into abusers themselves. When perpetrators recognize their adolescent victims now have adult roles and follow adult norms, this may lessen their abuse. When victims take on adult roles and follow adult norms they are also better able to move on with their lives. One of the important skills adults need to develop that will reduce family abuse is how to resolve interpersonal conflicts in a productive manner. Box 8.5 summarizes elements of this skill.

Developing appropriate adult role behaviors is difficult for both youthful abusers and victims. Stermac, Davidson, and Sheridan (1995) found that a large percentage of incest offenders and nonsexual offenders exhibit violence toward children and wives. Fifty-five percent of incest offenders engaged in physical violence in the home. This is a reminder that incest should not be dealt with as the only problem. Treatment should include addressing the problem of nonsexual violence in the home. When adolescent victims subsequently take on mature adult roles, the risk of victimization can be reduced. In particular, graduating from school, moving away from home, and marriage reduce the risk of continued family abuse, deviancy, and criminal behavior (Reiss and Roth 1993).

Rivera and Widom (1990) found a link between juvenile and adult violence. While this is a complex relationship involving many factors, they found that 63 percent of violent juvenile offenders became violent as adults. Of those adults who were arrested for violent crimes, 17 percent had been arrested for violent crimes as juveniles. Juveniles who abuse other family members as adolescents are at risk of continuing abusive behavior as adults. In general, those who were abused as adolescents have a greater risk of family abuse as adults.

BOX 8.5

Developing Techniques for Resolving Conflicts

The following is a list of techniques to help develop one's skill at resolving interpersonal conflicts in a productive manner. Not all will apply to a specific conflict, but they all can help achieve solutions that are constructive, rather than destructive and abusive.

- Attack the problem, not the people involved.
- Express your feelings without blaming others.
- Take ownership for your part in the problem.
- Listen to the other side and seek to understand their point of view before giving advice or defending your own view.
- Look at the needs of the individuals behind their stated positions or solutions.
- Don't rush in solving someone else's problem. Take time out from it when needed.
- Encourage different points of view and honest dialogue; and respect those different ideas.
- Focus on what can be done about the problem, not on what cannot be done.
- Work toward solving the problem and building a relationship.
- Use objective criteria when making decisions.

Source: Colorado School Mediation Project. 1999. "Resolving Conflicts Productively." (WWW http:www.csmp.org/handouts/tips.htm).

Women sexually abused as children are more likely to be victims of sexual and other types of abuse in adulthood. Russell (1986) compared female rape victims who had been sexually abused as children with female rape victims with no sexual abuse history. Rape was experienced by fewer than 20 percent of women with no history while from one- to two-thirds of women with a sexual abuse history were subsequently raped.

As adults approach midlife, further developmental challenges arise that can affect family abuse. This group is sometimes referred to as the "Sandwich Generation" because it comes between young adults and elders (Kennen 1997). This is the group for which the term *midlife crisis* may apply. This period often requires adults to develop skills to deal with such issues as understanding changes in their own life; dealing with family crises, marital disillusionment, divorce; caring for aging parents; helping one's own teens to mature; career changes and unemployment; grandparenting; making blended families work; geographic movement; and maintaining friendships into adulthood. In addition, adults may be faced with the process of healing from a dysfunctional childhood, coming to terms with their life goals and expectations, and dealing with the growing consequences from earlier family abuse and failure to meet earlier developmental challenges. Is it any wonder that adults may have a midlife crisis? What is problematic is how people respond to these events. If they deal with them in constructive ways, they develop better life skills, overcome or reduce earlier problems, and decrease the risk of abusive or other deviant behavior.

Divorce and remarriage may both play a role in precipitating or aggravating abuse. Offenders often threaten the victims with death or other dire consequences if the victim tries to break away from the abusive relationship. Separation and divorce are two occasions when abusers are more likely to kill their victims. Remarriage of the victim can play a role both for the former partner and for the new. The former abuser may see it as a reminder of his or her rejection. The new spouse, if an abuser, may see stepchildren as threatening to control the family. Stepchildren are much more likely to be targets of abuse than are one's biological children.

If family abuse begins when the perpetrator or victim is in middle age, it may result from previous life events. It may produce physical, sexual, or emotional violence against one's children, one's spouse or partner, or one's parents or elder relatives. From the viewpoint of adult victims, the added stress of coping with these events may make them more vulnerable to abuse by other family members. Sorting out the developmental issues in this case is complicated by the fact that middle age perpetrators and victims may be simultaneously dealing with children coping with adolescence, their own midlife crisis, and older parents coping with aging. Middle-age victims may also have to deal with these issues at the same time they are still recovering from prior abuse. It should be noted that abusive behavior is far less likely to begin in midlife and much more commonly develops earlier in life.

Midlife also begins to see the consequences of other developmental processes in which the abusers are involved. With substance abuse, health problems increase—creating stress with family members, employers, and medical providers. If involved in crime, treatment by the criminal justice system becomes harsher for career criminals. Prior employment disruptions and marginal occupations may be perceived by employers as "poor work history," making it increasingly difficult to be hired and more likely to be fired during recessions and downsizing. These events add to the family stress and may contribute to further abuse.

Elder Abuse

Earlier chapters have noted the extent and severity of elderly abuse. The occurrence of elderly abuse, however, is related to the life course of victims and perpetrators. Abuse by one's adult children or younger relatives is different from abuse by one's spouses or siblings. Spouse or sibling abuse in old age tends to be a continuation of earlier domestic violence, unless it can be traced to growing dementia and paranoia of the abuser. It may be a continuation of abuse of a parent by an offspring who was abusive as a child or it may reflect failure of the younger adults to deal with developmental challenges of their own entrance into adulthood or their elder's entrance into older age. Abusive behavior by adult children or younger relatives may reflect retaliation against a formerly abusive parent or caretaker or a desire to take control of their economic assets (Reinharz 1986). Economic exploitation is one of the more common forms of elder abuse and is discussed in Box 8.6.

Abuse may also represent a reactivation of an unresolved earlier conflict. Parent-child conflict tends to be highest when the children are in their early twenties (Hudson 1986). The conflict may abate as the children move out of the parent's home, however, this does not mean that the problems have been resolved. When, in old age, the parent becomes more dependent on the offspring and the children again become more involved in their parent's lives, these unresolved conflicts and abusive patterns may resurface.

Retaliatory abuse by a parent indicates that deviant behavior of an abusive parent may have been passed along to a child. When these children become adults, they may gain the upper hand physically and economically and use that power to retaliate against their former abusers. Whether seen as revenge or retribution for their former abuse, the assaultive behavior (physical, sexual, or emotional) involves them in deviance. Indeed, having justified assaulting those who treated them that way, they may then see justification in assaulting others who were not their persecutors. The psychological concept of projection, in which others may be blamed for actions not their own, and the mistrust that results from victimization can lead these former victims to become perpetrators themselves. Retaliatory abusers who start by abusing their former tormenters may continue by abusing others not involved in the original abuse.

While research attention has focused on a cycle of violence that perpetuates abuse within generations of a family, more research is also needed on why those who have been abused do not become abusers themselves.

Continuation of earlier abuse into old age indicates there has been no effective intervention in halting the earlier abuse of a parent by a child. A parent may have been assaulted for many years by a child. The parent may have intermittent respite from the abuse when her offspring is incarcerated or temporarily moved away; but

BOX **8.6**

Ripping off Nana

Abuse of a parent that begins when the parent becomes older is often associated with economic exploitation. It may be a struggle over a Social Security check, the family business, or the desire to pay bills from the parent's bank account. The motivations for controlling their parent's assets are many. The children may come to feel that they can better manage their parent's affairs than the parent. They may believe their parent is incompetent or untrustworthy. They may feel they deserve some of the parent's assets for having put up with, helped, or cared for the parent. They can also feel it is their "right" as an heir to prevent dissipation of their parent's estate.

Financial exploitation is difficult to recognize. There may be disagreement over how competent the parent is and how her assets should be spent. The offspring may have multiple motives. Some use of the assets may be quite legitimate. Other uses may be perfectly legal choices that also benefit the offspring. Siblings may disagree over appropriate or reasonable expenditures. There are, however, three signs that, taken together, indicate a high risk of exploitation: (1) expenditures of large sums for expenses not directly related to the health and care of the elder, (2) fear of the offspring by the elder or refusal to comment on the child's expenditures, and (3) neglect of medical or personal needs or wishes of the elder. When these three occur together, exploitation is very likely and there is a need to bring in outside professionals to evaluate the situation more closely.

However, as long as the older person has not been declared incompetent in a legal proceeding, there may be little that can be done to stop the exploitation. Adults can spend their money as they wish, however inadvisably. If an elder chooses to spend all his money on an adult child and leave nothing for his own medical care, he can do so. Until the elder seeks help for the financial exploitation or is convinced to cooperate with concerned parties, there may be little that can be done. The complexity of intervening in these cases is discussed further in the chapter on intervention and treatment (Chapter 11).

---

then it begins again. The parent lives a lifetime of terror at the hands of her own children.

Summary

This chapter examines how family abuse varies among the lives of individuals. At each stage of life there are different events, roles, norms, and perceptions with which we are faced. How we respond to and what we learn from these age-related issues affect our risk of victimization and the likelihood we will abuse family members. Failure to deal with developmental challenges can bring negative consequences across the life course.

Four periods of our lives have special significance for abuse, victimization, and deviance: childhood, adolescence, early and middle adulthood, and older adulthood. Each of these periods has life events and developmental challenges unique to those periods. The legal status and normative acceptability of behaviors in the family also change as we age. Actions perfectly acceptable for a person at one age may be deviant for someone who is much older or younger.

Childhood begins with dependency and helplessness. Every developmental milestone changes behavior and places new demands on the caretaker, the child, and the siblings. Those who have inadequate knowledge of child development may abuse the children because they perceive the child's behavior as challenging their authority or presenting unwanted changes in their lives. The deviant consequences for children may include nightmares, shyness, fear of adults, bed-wetting, aggression toward peers, obsessive behavior, fire-starting, animal torture, and sexual acting out.

Adolescence begins with teens seeking independence, autonomy, new identities. All of these are a challenge to the abuser, who wishes to maintain the status quo. The physical and intellectual development of teens begins to challenge the abuser. Adolescents are also more involved in the community than younger children and have a better basis for judging whether abusive behavior is normative for the community or deviant. This may intensify conflict with the abuser. Deviant consequences may include substance abuse, aggressive behavior, delinquency, animal killings, sexual acting out, and mental disorders (such as anxiety; depression; social, intellectual, and physical delays; self-mutilation; and suicide).

Adulthood presents additional developmental issues for victims and perpetrators. Learning what it means to be an adult and take on adult roles, giving up childish behavior, accepting responsibility for one's behavior and life situation are some of the issues raised. Victims have greater opportunity to separate from the abusive family through employment, legal independence, and adult peer support. Abusers may intensify their abuse and impose social isolation to prevent victims from breaking away from their domination. The deviant consequences for adults may build on earlier deviance. Substance abuse, psychopathology, and aggressive behavior may intensify. Control by the abuser might have prevented the victim from developing the skills necessary for holding an adequate full-time job. Difficulty in establishing positive social relationships may create isolation, fear of rejection, and cause the victim to drift into a deviant subculture. Earlier deviance may involve the victim in the criminal justice system, leading to stigmatization and ostracization by peers who could have been positive role models. Heightened sexuality and lack of skills or social supports may lead to prostitution, and intermittent delinquency may lead to systematic and more serious crime.

Study Questions

1. Why does corporal punishment by parents tend to decline when children reach adolescence?

2. Why are young children and the elderly who have been victims of maltreatment more likely to elicit sympathy than adolescents and adult women?

3. What are the reasons some children may not show effects of their maltreatment?

4. What is the relationship between childhood maltreatment and subsequent revictimization?

5. What is the relationship between childhood maltreatment and subsequent offending?

6. What are some of the major role transitions that impact abusive or deviant behavior?

7. How does deviant behavior by an adolescent tend to affect his or her deviance as an adult?

REFERENCES

Abel, G. G. and J. L. Rouleau. 1990. "The Nature and Extent of Sexual Assault." Pp. 9–20 in *Handbook of Sexual Assault: Issues, Theories, and Treatment of the Offender,* W. L. Marshall, D. R. Laws, and H. E. Barbaree, eds. NY: Plenum.

Awad, G. and E. Saunders. (1991). "Male Adolescent Sexual Assaulters, Clinical Observations." *Journal of Interpersonal Violence.* 6:446–60.

Becker, J., J. Hunter, R. Stein, and M. Kaplan. 1989. "Factors Associated with Erection in Adolescent Sex Offenders." *Journal of Psychopathology and Behavioral Assessment.* 2:355–63.

Colorado School Mediation Project. 1999. "Resolving Conflicts Productively." (WWW http://www.csmp.org/handouts/tips.htm).

Ellement, John. 1999. "Case Accusing Boy, 9, of Rape Dropped." *The Boston Globe.* June 29:B5.

Featherman, David L. 1981. "The Life-Span Perspective in Social Science Research." Washington, DC: Social Science Research Council.

Federal Bureau of Investigation. 1997. *Crime in the United States, Uniform Crime Reports.* Clarksburg, WV: U.S. Department of Justice.

Fehrenbach, P., W. Smith, C. Monastersky, and R. Deisher. 1986. "Adolescent Sexual Offenders: Offender and Offense Characteristics." *American Journal of Orthopsychiatry.* 56:225–33.

Feiring, Candice, Lynn Taska, and Michael Lewis. 1999. "Age and Gender Differences in Children's and Adolescents' Adaptation to Sexual Abuse." *Child Abuse and Neglect.* 23:115–28.

Garbarino, James. 1989. "Troubled Youth, Troubled Families: The Dynamics of Adolescent Maltreatment." Pp. 685–706 in *Child Maltreatment: Theory and Research on the Causes and Consequences of Child Abuse and Neglect,* Dante Cicchetti and Vicki Carlson, eds. Cambridge, Eng.: Cambridge University Press.

Gomes-Schwartz, B., J. Horowitz, and M. Sauzier. 1985. "Severity of Emotional Distress Among Sexually Abused Preschool, School Age and Adolescent Children. *Hospital and Community Psychiatry.* 36:503–08.

Graham, Kevin R. 1996. "The Childhood Victimization of Sex Offenders: An Underestimated Issue." *International Journal of Offender Therapy and Comparative Criminology.* 40:192–203.

Green, Arthur H. 1993. "Child Sexual Abuse: Immediate and Long-Term Effects and Intervention." *Journal of the American Academy of Child and Adolescent Psychiatry.* 32:890–902.

Groth, A., R. Longo, and B. McFadin. 1982. "Undetected Recidivism Among Rapists and Child Molesters." *Crime and Delinquency.* 28:450–58.

Hagan, Michael P. and Meg E. Cho. 1996. "A Comparison of Treatment Outcomes Between Adolescent Rapists and Child Sexual Offenders." *International Journal of Offender Therapy and Comparative Criminology.* 40:113–22.

Hirschi, Travis and Michael Gottfredson. 1983. "Age and the Explanation of Crime." *American Journal of Sociology.* 89:552–84.

Hudson, M. F. 1986. "Elder Mistreatment: Current Research." Pp. 125–66 in *Elder Abuse: Conflict in the Family*, K. A. Pillemer and R. S. Wolf, eds. Dover, MA: Auburn House.

Ireland, Timothy and Cathy Spatz Widom. 1994. "Childhood Victimization and Risk for Alcohol and Drug Arrests." *The International Journal of the Addictions*. 29:235–74.

Jackson, Shelly, Ross A. Thompson, Elaine H. Christiansen, Rebecca A. Coleman, Jennifer Wyatt, Chad. W. Buckendahl, Brian L. Wilcox, and Reece Peterson. 1999. "Predicting Abuse-Prone Parental Attitudes and Discipline Practices in a Nationally Representative Sample." *Child Abuse and Neglect*. 23:15–29.

Johnson, Ida M. and Robert T. Sigler. 1995. "Community Attitudes: A Study of Definitions and Punishment of Spouse Abusers and Child Abusers." *Journal of Criminal Justice*. 23:477–87.

Kelley, Barbara Tatem, Terrence P. Thornberry, and Carolyn A. Smith. 1997. "In the Wake of Childhood Maltreatment." *Juvenile Justice Bulletin*, August. Washington, DC: Office of Juvenile Justice and Delinquency Prevention.

Kendall-Tackett, Kathleen A., Linda Meyer Williams, and David Finkelhor. 1993. "Impact of Sexual Abuse on Children: A Review and Synthesis of Recent Empirical Studies." *Psychological Bulletin*. 113:164–80.

Kennen, Rita. 1997. "The Sandwich Generation." (WWW http://www.midlifemommies.com/the-sandwichgeneration.html).

Krahe, Barbara, Renate Scheinberger-Olwig, Eva Waizenhofer, and Susanne Koplin. 1999. "Childhood Sexual Abuse and Revictimization in Adolesence." *Child Abuse and Neglect*. 23:383–94.

Lewis, Dorothy Otnow, Catherine Mallouh, and Victoria Webb. 1989. "Child Abuse, Delinquency, and Violent Criminality." Pp. 707–21 in *Child Maltreatment: Theory and Research on the Causes and Consequences of Child Abuse and Neglect*. Cambridge, Eng.: Cambridge University Press.

Lisak, David. 1994. "The Psychological Impact of Sexual Abuse—Content Analysis with Male Survivors." *Journal of Traumatic Stress*. 7:525–48.

Malinosky-Rummell, Robin and David J. Hansen. 1993. "Long-Term Consequences of Childhood Physical Abuse." *Psychological Bulletin*. 114:68–79.

Marshall, W. L. 1996. "Assessment, Treatment, and Theorizing about Sex Offenders: Developments During the Past Twenty Years and Future Directions." *Criminal Justice and Behavior*. 23:162–99.

Meckler, Laura. 1999. "Drop in Teen Crime Found." *The Boston Globe*, July 9:A3.

Neugarten, Bernice L., Joan W. Moore, and John C. Lowe. 1996. "Age Norms, Age Constraints, and Adult Socialization." Pp. 194–203 in *Aging for the Twenty-First Century: Readings in Social Gerontology*, Jill Quadagno and Debra Street, eds. NY: St. Martin's Press.

Newberger, Carolyn M. and Edward DeVos. 1988. "Abuse and Victimization: A Life-Span Developmental Perspective." *American Journal of Orthopsychiatry*. 58:505–11.

Olds, David, Charles R. Henderson, Jr., Robert Cole, John Eckenrode, Harriet Kitzman, Dennis Luckey, Lisa Pettitt, Kimberly Sidora, Pamela Morris, and Jane Powers. 1998. "Long-term Effects of Nurse Home Visitation on Children's Criminal and Antisocial Behavior: 15-Year Follow-up of a Randomized Controlled Trial." *JAMA: Journal of the American Medical Association*. 280:1238–44.

Passuth, Patricia M. and Vern L. Bengston. 1996. "Sociological Theories of Aging: Current Perspectives and Future Directions." Pp. 12–30 in *Aging for the Twenty-First Century*, Jill Quadagno and Debra Street, eds. NY: St. Martin's Press.

Reinharz, Shulamit. 1986. "Loving and Hating One's Elders: Twin Themes in Legend and Literature." Pp. 25–48 in *Elder Abuse: Conflict in the Family*, Karl Pillemer and Rosalie Wolf, eds. Dover, MA: Auburn House.

Reiss, Albert J. and Jeffrey A. Roth, eds. 1993. *Understanding and Preventing Violence: Panel on the Understanding and Control of Violent Behavior*. Washington, DC: National Academy Press.

Rivera, Beverly and Cathy Spatz Widom. 1990. "Childhood Victimization and Violent Offending." *Violence and Victims*. 5:19–35.

Russell, D. E. 1986. *The Secret Trauma: Incest in the Lives of Girls and Women*. NY: Basic Books.

Ryan, G. D. and S. L. Lane, eds. 1991. *Juvenile Sexual Offending: Causes, Consequences, and Correction.* Lexington, MA: Lexington Books.

Seegmiller, Bonnie R. 1995. "Teaching an Undergraduate Course on Intrafamily Abuse Across the Life Span." *Teaching of Psychology.* 22:108–18.

S'guin, Jean R., Robert O. Pihl, Philip W. Harden, Richard E. Tremblay, and Bernard Boulerice. 1995. "Cognitive and Neuropsychological Characteristics of Physically Aggressive Boys." *Journal of Abnormal Psychology.* 4:614–24.

Shure, Myra B. 1999. "Preventing Violence the Problem-Solving Way." *Juvenile Justice Bulletin,* April. Washington, DC: Office of Juvenile Justice and Delinquency Prevention.

Sipe, Ron, Eric L. Jensen, and Ronald S. Everett. 1998. "Adolescent Sexual Offenders Grown Up: Recidivism in Young Adulthood." *Criminal Justice and Behavior.* 25:109–24.

Smith, W. and C. Monastersky. 1986. "Assessing Juvenile Sex Offenders' Risk for Reoffending." *Criminal Justice and Behavior.* 13:115–40.

Snyder, Howard N. 1997. "Juvenile Arrests 1996." Office of Juvenile Justice and Delinquency Prevention. *Juvenile Justice Bulletin,* November. Washington, DC: U.S. Department of Justice.

———. 2000. "Juvenile Arrests 1999." *Juvenile Justice Bulletin,* December. Washington, DC: U.S. Department of Justice. Office of Juvenile Justice and Delinquency Prevention.

Spaccarelli, Steve. 1994. "Stress, Appraisal, and Coping in Child Sexual Abuse: A Theoretical and Empirical Review." *Psychological Bulletin.* 116:340–62.

Stermac, Lana, Alison Davidson, and Peter M. Sheridan. 1995. "Incidence of Nonsexual Violence in Incest Offenders." *International Journal of Offender Therapy and Comparative Criminology.* 39:167–78.

Straus, Murray and Richard Gelles. 1998. *Intimate Violence.* NY: Simon and Schuster.

Straus, Murray A. and Glenda Kaufman Kantor. 1994. "Corporal Punishment of Adolescents by Parents: A Risk Factor in the Epidemiology of Depression, Suicide, Alcohol Abuse, and Wife Beating." *Adolescence.* 29:543–61.

Tingle, D., G. Barnard, L. Robbins, G. Newman, and D. Hutchinson. 1986. "Childhood and Adolescent Characteristics of Pedophiles and Rapists." *International Journal of Law and Psychiatry.* 9:103–16.

Vogeltanz, Nancy D., Sharon C. Wilsnack, T. Robert Harris, Richard W. Wilsnack, Stephen A. Wonderlich, and Arlinda F. Kristjanson. 1999. "Prevalence and Risk Factors for Childhood Sexual Abuse in Women: National Survey Findings." *Child Abuse and Neglect.* 23:579–92.

Zgourides, George, Martin Monto, and Richard Harris. 1997. "Correlates of Adolescent Male Sexual Contact, Sexual Attitudes, and Use of Sexually Explicit Materials." *International Journal of Offender Therapy and Comparative Criminology* 41:272–83.

Zuravin, Susan J. and Cynthia Fontanella. 1999. "Parenting Behaviors and Perceived Parenting Competence of Child Sexual Abuse Survivors." *Child Abuse and Neglect.* 23:623–32.

9 Victims and Perpetrators: Family Abuse by Gender, Race, Ethnicity, and Other Correlates

As pointed out earlier, the victims of family abuse are disproportionately those with the least ability to defend themselves. These include those of less or diminished physical power, the aged (discussed in Chapter 8), children, and women (discussed in this chapter). Also to be considered are those with limited economic means of defense. Such individuals may be of either gender or any racial or ethnic group, but especially certain racial or ethnic minorities.

Lacking to date are data from sufficiently large samples of the population to enable close examination of the bearing of variables such as gender, family income, race, and ethnicity on family abuse victimization and perpetration. The available evidence, limited as it may be, is suggestive of connections between the variables greatly in need of further study. The aim of this chapter, then, is to review and assess what is known and what remains to be determined about the influence of certain important sociocultural variables on family abuse.

The Victims of Family Abuse by Gender, Race, Ethnicity, and Family Income

Adult Victims by Gender

Data from the National Crime Victimization Survey (NCVS) indicate that each year approximately 1 million adults are victims of violent crimes (murder, rape, robbery, and assault) committed by intimates (current or former spouses, boyfriends, and girlfriends). Table 9.1 reports basic evidence by crime and gender. Clearly evident is the fact that while one is most likely to be violently victimized by an acquaintance

TABLE 9.1 Annual Average Number of Violent Crime Victimization by Lone Offenders*, 1992–93

	Victims	
	Female	Male
Known	2,715,000	2,019,400
Intimate	1,008,000	143,400
Relative	304,500	122,000
Acquaintance/friend	1,402,500	1,754,000
Stranger	802,300	1,933,100

*Excludes homicides.

Source: Bureau of Justice Statistics, *Female Victims of Violent Crime*, Washington, DC: U.S. Department of Justice, December 1996. Pp. 3–4.

or a friend rather than an intimate or relative, females are much more likely than males to be victimized by an intimate.

Considering the years for which recent data are available (1993–98), one notes a steady decrease in the rate of violence by intimate adult partners between 1993 and 1997, but an increase between 1997 and 1998 (see Table 9.2). Worthy of note is that the number and rate of increase from 1997 to 1998 were much greater for males (+49,480 and +0.5) than females (+27,860 and +0.2).

Interestingly, the homicide rates for both male and female victims of intimate violence have declined, but the decline has been noticeably less for females than males. Thus, between 1976 and 1998, the number of males victimized by intimate partner homicide decreased an average of 4 percent per year and females 1 percent per year.

TABLE 9.2 Violence by Intimate Partners by Gender, 1993–98

	Female Victims		Male Victims	
Year	Number	Rate per 1,000	Number	1,000
1993	1,072,090	9.8	163,570	1.6
1994	1,003,180	9.1	176,180	1.7
1995	953,700	8.6	115,490	1.1
1996	879,290	7.8	150,730	1.4
1997	848,480	7.5	107,850	1.0
1998	876,340	7.7	157,330	1.5

Source: Marie Rennison and Sarah Welchans. May 2000. *Intimate Partner Violence.* Bureau of Justice Statistics, Special Report. Washington, DC: U.S. Government Printing Office. Table 2, P. 3.

Whatever the type of physical violence, then, females are much more likely than males to be victimized by an intimate. Box 9.1 highlights important details concerning both lethal and nonlethal intimate partner violence.

BOX 9.1

Intimate Partner Violence Trends

Intimate partners: current or former spouses, boyfriends, and girlfriends
Violent crimes include lethal (homicide) and nonlethal (rape, sexual assault, robbery, aggravated assault, and simple assault) offenses.

Lethal

- Intimate partners committed fewer murders in each of the 3 years 1996, 1997, and 1998 than in any other years since 1976
- Between 1976 and 1998, the number of homicides fell an average 4 percent per year and the number of female victims fell an average 1 percent.
- In 1998 women were nearly 3 out of 4 victims of the 1,830 murders attributed to intimate partners. In 1976 women were just over half the approximate 3,000 victims.
- The percentage of female murder victims killed by intimate partners has remained at about 30 percent since 1976.

Nonlethal

- The number of female victims of intimate violence declined from 1993 to 1998. In 1998 women experienced about 900,000 violent offenses at the hand of an intimate, down from 1.1 million in 1993.
- In both 1993 and 1998, men were victims of about 160,000 violent crimes by an intimate partner.
- Between 1993 and 1998 women ages 16 to 24 experienced the highest per capita rates of intimate violence (19.6 per 1,000 women).
- About half the intimate partner violence against women, 1993–98, was reported to the police; black women were more likely than other women to report such violence.
- About 4 of 10 female victims of intimate partner violence lived in households with children under age 12. Population estimates suggest that 27 percent of U.S. households were home to children under 12.
- Half of female victims of intimate partner violence reported a physical injury. About 4 in 10 of these victims sought professional medical treatment.

Source: Callie Marie Rennison and Sarah Welchans. May 2000. *Intimate Partner Violence.* Bureau of Justice Statistics, Special Report. Washington, DC: U.S. Government Printing Office. P. 1.

Child Victims by Gender

When child victims of family abuse are considered, national data indicate a more equitable gender pattern than in the case of adults. In the most recent compilation by NCANDS (the National Child Abuse and Neglect Data System 1998), about 48 percent of child abuse victims were male and 52 percent female. Table 9.3 contains data on type of child maltreatment by victim gender. One notes an essentially reverse trend from the general pattern in the case of physical abuse, neglect, and medical neglect where males outnumber females (roughly 52 percent to 48 percent). Girls, however, outnumber boys in frequency of emotional abuse (53 percent to 47 percent) and far outnumber boys in frequency of sexual abuse (77 percent to 23 percent).

More male than female children are the victims of homicide by a family member. A survey of homicides in the nation's largest urban counties (Dawson and Langan 1994) identified a total of 285 children slain by a parent (160 males and 125 females). Box 9.2 contains identified parental reasons for the murder of their offspring under age 12 as well as the methods used.

Adult Victims by Race, Ethnicity, and Family Income

For years, the number of black victims of homicide by intimates, male and female, greatly exceeded that for whites. And while the difference continues, the gap between the two races has steadily declined. In 1976, for example, the per capita intimate homicide rate for blacks was eleven times higher than that for whites. By 1996, the rate for blacks was four times higher than that for whites (U.S. Department of Justice 1998).

The decline in the intimate homicide rate has been highest for black males. The per capita rate for black males in 1976 was 19 times higher than that for white males. Also in 1976, the per capita rate for black females was seven times higher than for white females. By 1996, the rate for black males had shrunk to seven times

TABLE 9.3 Type of Child Maltreatment by Victim Gender

Type of Maltreatment	Gender		
	Male	Female	Totals
Physical Abuse	31,316 (51.6%)	29,367 (48.4%)	60,683 (100.0%)
Neglect	76,955 (51.2%)	73,426 (48.8%)	150,381 (100.0%)
Medical Neglect	5,386 (52.0%)	4,975 (48.0%)	10,361 (100.0%)
Sexual Abuse	6,454 (22.8%)	21,867 (77.2%)	28,321 (100.0%)
Emotional Maltreatment	4,989 (47.0%)	5,622 (53.0%)	10,611 (100.0%)
Totals	125,100 (48.0%)	135,257 (52.0%)	260,357 (100.0%)

Source: U.S. Department of Health and Human Services, Children's Bureau. 1998. *Child Maltreatment 1996: Reports from the States to the National Child Abuse and Neglect Data System.* Washington, DC: U.S. Government Printing Office. Slightly modified Table 2–4, P. 2–10.

BOX **9.2**

Parental Murder of Offspring under Age 12

Prosecutors' files contained information on reasons why a parent murdered an offspring under age 12. One or more reasons were given for 62 of the total 84 offspring murder victims under age 12. The following presents reasons and the number of victims:

- Unspecified forms of child abuse (18)
- Victim's behavior, such as crying or misbehavior (15)
- Parent's emotional instability or retardation (9)
- Unwanted newborn baby (8)
- Unintended consequence of the commission of another crime (lethal conflict between the parents) (6)
- Neglect (5)
- Difficulty handling the responsibility of child rearing (3)
- Child held hostage (1).

Examination of the details concerning the method of killing covered all but 3 of the victims. By far the most frequent method of murder was beating: punching with fists, kicking, throwing, pushing, slapping, hitting (with belts, hammers, or wooden brushes), and striking body against furniture (shower head or walls). With five of the victims counted under two or three methods of murder, specific methods and the number of victims were as follows:

- Beating (35)
- "Shaken baby syndrome" (10)
- Arson (6)
- Newborn disposed of in toilet or trash can (6)
- Drowning in bathtub (6)
- Firearm (5)
- Suffocation/strangulation (5)
- Neglect (dehydration, starvation, and failure to use infant heart monitor) (4)
- Stabbing (3)
- Starvation (2)
- Other methods, including poisoning with carbon monoxide, lethal doses of drugs, running over with a car, boiling, and putting in freezer (5).

Of the 5 victims who were shot to death, 3 died because the assailant accidentally fired a gun while committing another crime; therefore, two offspring victims under age 12 were intentionally killed with a firearm.

Source: John M. Dawson and Patrick A. Langer. July 1994. "Murder in Families," U.S. Department of Justice, Bureau of Justice Statistics Special Report. Washington, DC: U.S. Government Printing Office. P. 6.

higher for white males, and the rate for black females three times that for white females. Over the two decades from 1976 to 1996, the average annual decline in the intimate homicide rate per capita for black males was 8 percent, 5 percent for black females, 4 percent for white males, and 1 percent for white females. As one notes in Box 9.3, only one victim category of intimate homicide registered an increase between 1976 and 1996, that for white girlfriends.

When the subject is nonlethal violence among intimates, black women suffer higher rates of victimization than white women. Between 1993 and 1998, black women averaged about 12 violent victimizations a year by an intimate per 1,000 females in the population and white women about 8. Over these years, there was

---

BOX **9.3**

Trends in the Rate of Intimate Homicide by Gender and Race between 1976 and 1996

- The decline in the rate of intimate murder among black husbands/ex-husbands has been greater than for any other category of intimate murder victims.
- From 1976 to 1996 the per capita murder rate of black husbands and former husbands declined an average of 10 percent a year.
- Between 1976 and 1989 more black men were killed by their wives than black women were killed by their husbands. After 1990 the order was reversed, and the murder rate among black wives and ex-wives was higher than that among black husbands and ex-husbands.
- Only one category of intimate murder victims, white girlfriends, has increased over the past two decades.
- In 1976 there were 1.69 murders of white women (shown as girlfriends) killed by their boyfriends or other nonmarital intimates per 100,000 unmarried white women age 20–44 in the U.S. resident population. In 1996 the intimate murder rate for white girlfriends was 1.97 per 100,000.
- The average annual percentage changes in the rates of intimate murder between 1976 and 1996, classified by victim–offender relationship, were as follows:

	Victims	
	White	Black
Husbands/ex-husbands	−5%	−10%
Boyfriends	−3	−7
Wives/ex-wives	−2	−6
Girlfriends	+1	−3

Source: U.S. Department of Justice. March 1998. *Violence by Intimates.* Washington, DC: U.S. Government Printing Office. P. 8.

little difference in the intimate victimization rates for males. White men averaged about 1 per 1,000 males in the population and black men about 2.

The one broadly designated ethnic group for which there is some reported evidence on nonlethal violence between intimates is Hispanics. Between 1993 and 1998, there was little difference in the annual average recorded by Hispanics and non-Hispanics. Hispanic females (about 8 per 1,000 females in the population) had a slightly lower average annual intimate nonlethal violent victimization rate than non-Hispanics (about 7 per 1,000 non-Hispanic females). For males, there was no essential difference between Hispanics and non-Hispanics. Both groups recorded an annual average of about 1 per 1,000 males in each population.

Adult intimate victimization rates by household income reveal some important differences. From Table 9.4 one sees that for women there is an inverse relationship between household income and rate of nonlethal violence by an intimate. As household income increases, the rate of nonlethal violence by an intimate consistently and sharply decreases. For males, who noticeably suffer much lower rates of victimization than women, the rate trend is much less dramatic. Those lowest in household income have the highest and those highest in household income the lowest rate of victimization, but the rates for income categories between the extremes show little difference.

Child Victims by Race, Ethnicity, and Family Income

As mentioned in Chapter 1, The National Child Abuse and Neglect Data System (NCANDS) has two components—the Summary Data Component (SDC) and the

TABLE 9.4 Nonlethal Victimization Rates by Gender and Household Income, 1993–98

Household Income	Average Annual Rate of Nonlethal Intimate Violence per 1,000 Persons	
	Male	Female
Less than $7,500	2.6	20.3
$7,500–$14,999	1.3	12.3
$15,000–$24,999	2.0	10.1
$25,000–$34,999	1.7	7.8
$35,000–$49,999	1.0	6.3
$50,000–$74,999	1.2	4.5
$75,000 or more	0.9	3.3

Source: Callie Marie Rennison and Sarah Welchans. May 2000. *Intimate Partner Violence.* Bureau of Justice Statistics, Special Report. Washington, DC: U.S. Government Printing Office. P. 3.

Detailed Case Data Component (DCDC). The Summary Data Component contains alleged cases of child abuse and neglect, the results of investigations as to the authenticity of alleged instances, and victim and perpetrator characteristics. As described in a recent report, the Detailed Case Data Component (DCDC) "permits more detailed analysis of state child abuse and neglect data than is possible with the aggregate data in the SDC" (U.S. Department of Health 1996:1–2).

The case-level data compiled in the DCDC are provided by 11 states (Delaware, Florida, Illinois, Louisiana, Massachusetts, New Jersey, North Carolina, South Carolina, Texas, Vermont, and Washington). Table 9.5 reports type of child maltreatment in the 11 states by victim race and ethnicity. As can be seen, white victims are predominant in all types of maltreatment but one—medical neglect. The highest proportion of medical neglect victims are African Americans (44.0 percent) with whites second (41.3 percent). Also noteworthy is the high proportion of emotional maltreatment (nearly 69 percent) and sexual abuse (nearly 65 percent) victims accounted for by white children. The other racial and ethnic categories reveal rather even distributions across the maltreatment types.

Family income data reveal a strong influence on rates of child maltreatment. Box 9.4 contains summary statements published in the most recent *National Incidence Study of Child Abuse and Neglect* (NIS-3). It will be recalled that NIS-3 data are based on two measures of child maltreatment: the *Harm Standard* and the *Endangerment Standard*. Children who have experienced "demonstrable harm" by being abused or neglected meet the Harm Standard. Those who have been known to have been abused and neglected and judged by specified professionals (referred to in the NIS-3 report as "sentinels") to be in danger of harm meet the Endangerment Standard.

Those responsible for analyzing the NIS-3 data (Sedlak and Broadhurst 1996) emphasize that the strong correlation between family income and child maltreatment outlined in Box 9.4 is consistent with NIS-2 findings. Even more important,

TABLE 9.5 Type of Child Maltreatment by Victim Race/Ethnicity, 1996

Type of Maltreatment	Race/Ethnicity		
	White	African American	Hispanic
Physical Abuse	33,181 (56.1%)	16,406 (27.7%)	8,053 (13.6%)
Neglect	76,967 (52.3%)	50,401 (34.3%)	16,447 (11.2%)
Medical Neglect	4,224 (41.3%)	4,509 (44.0%)	1,229 (12.7%)
Sexual Abuse	17,978 (64.8%)	5,339 (19.2%)	3,901 (14.1%)
Emotional Maltreatment	7,130 (68.9%)	1,684 (16.3%)	1,265 (12.2%)
Totals	139,480 (54.8%)	78,339 (30.8%)	30,965 (12.2%)

Source: U.S. Department of Health and Human Services, Children's Bureau. 1998. *Child Maltreatment 1996: Reports from the States to the National Child Abuse and Neglect Data System.* Washington, DC: U.S. Government Printing Office. Table 2–5, P. 2–12.

they stress that the findings are not to be explained away by claims that children from low-income families are more visible to family professionals than those from other income classes. As they see it, because the NIS design includes only public schools, and because about 89 percent of school age children in the nation attend public schools, children in public schools represent a broad range of family income levels. Furthermore, and in their words, "If the income finding is interpreted as an artifact of selective observation of low-income families, then it would mean that there have to be enough undetected abused and neglected children in the middle- and upper-income brackets . . . to equalize the incidence rates across different income categories." Under the Harm Standard, this would amount to some 2,138,700 children who were maltreated but not identified, and under the Endangerment Standard some 4,500,700 maltreated children who did not come to the attention of community professionals. "Considering the implications of these alternatives," say Sedlak and Broadhurst (1996:15–16), "it appears more plausible to assume that the income-related differences in incidence found in the NIS reflect real differences in the extent to which children in different income levels are being abused or neglected."

Similarities and Differences between Adult and Child Victims of Family Violence

To summarize the above, the evidence is that in the case of adult victims of family violence by gender: (1) women are more likely to be victimized than men; (2) women are more likely than men to be the victims of both lethal and nonlethal violence by an intimate, relative, or friend; and (3) the rate of homicide by intimates has declined for both genders, but less for women than men.

Native American/ Alaskan Native	Asian/Pacific Islander	Totals
670 (1.1%)	842 (1.4%)	59,152 (100.0%)
2,018 (1.4%)	1,275 (0.9%)	147,108 (100.0%)
145 (1.4%)	61 (0.6%)	10,238 (100.0%)
349 (1.3%)	198 (0.7%)	27,765 (100.0%)
167 (1.6%)	104 (1.0%)	10,350 (100.0%)
3,349 (1.3%)	2,480 (1.0%)	254,613 (100.0%)

BOX **9.4**

Family Income and Incidence of Child Maltreatment

Despite the fact that only a rather gross index of family income was available, and despite a substantial percentage of cases with missing data on this factor, family income was significantly related to incidence rates in nearly every category of maltreatment. Compared to children whose families earned $30,000 per year or more, those in families with annual incomes below $15,000 per year were

- more than 22 times more likely to experience some form of maltreatment under the Harm Standard and over 25 times more likely to suffer maltreatment of some type using the Endangerment Standard;
- almost 14 times more likely to be harmed by some variety of abuse and nearly 15 times more likely to be abused using the Endangerment Standard criteria;
- more than 44 times more likely to be neglected, by either definitional standard;
- almost 16 times more likely to be a victim of physical abuse under the Harm Standard and nearly 12 times more likely to be a victim of physical abuse using the Endangerment Standard;
- almost 18 times more likely to be sexually abused by either definitional standard;
- thirteen times more likely to be emotionally abused under the Harm Standard criteria and more than 18 times more likely to be emotionally abused in a manner that fit Endangerment Standard requirements;
- forty times more likely to experience physical neglect under the Harm Standard and over 48 times more likely to be a victim of physical neglect using the Endangerment Standard;
- over 29 times more likely to be emotionally neglected under the Harm Standard definitions and over 27 times more likely to be emotionally neglected by Endangerment Standard criteria;
- nearly 56 times more likely to be educationally neglected, by either definitional standard;
- sixty times more likely to die from maltreatment of some type under the Harm Standard and over 22 times more likely to die from abuse or neglect using the Endangerment Standard;
- over 22 times more likely to be seriously injured by maltreatment under the Harm Standard and almost 22 times more likely to be seriously injured by maltreatment that fit the Endangerment Standard requirements;
- about 18 times more likely to be moderately injured by abuse or neglect under the Harm Standard and nearly 20 times more likely to have a moderate injury from maltreatment as defined by the Endangerment Standard;
- 57 times more likely to be classified as having an inferred injury under the Harm Standard and 39 times more likely to meet the criteria for inferred injury as defined by the Endangerment Standard; and
- over 31 times more likely to be considered endangered, although not yet injured, by some type of abusive or neglectful treatment.

Source: Andrea J. Sedlak and Diane D. Broadhurst. September 1996. *Executive Summary of the Third National Incidence Study of Child Abuse and Neglect.* Washington, DC: U.S. Department of Health and Human Services Administration on Children, Youth and Families, National Center on Child Abuse and Neglect. Pp. 14–15.

The general pattern for child victims of family violence is noticeably different than that for adults in that it is more equitable. Only a 4 percentage difference (52 percent to 48 percent) differentiates the overall rate for girls versus boys. Girls far outnumber boys in rates of sexual abuse, but boys outdistance girls in rates of physical abuse, neglect, and medical neglect.

The basic patterns for adult and child victims of family abuse by race, ethnicity, and family income also reveal some important differences. In the case of adults, and although the gap between the two has steadily declined, blacks have higher rates of lethal and nonlethal family violence victimization than whites. However, the difference is primarily due to a higher proportion of black to white female victims. Black males have only a slightly higher rate of nonlethal victimization at the hands of an intimate than white males. There is no essential difference in these rates for Hispanics versus non-Hispanics.

For adults, as family income increases, the rate of intimate victimization decreases. But women in low-income households have much higher rates of nonlethal victimization by an intimate than either women in higher income households or men at any household income category.

In contrast to adult victims, child victims of intimate violence are much more likely to be white than black. The exception is medical neglect, where black children have higher victimization rates than whites. The essential difference between the races is accounted for by two types of abuse—emotional abuse (where 69 percent of the victims are white) and sexual abuse (where nearly two-thirds of the victims are white children). As in the case of adults, rates of family child maltreatment, too, reveal an inverse connection to family income. As family income increases, rates of maltreatment decrease.

The Perpetrators of Family Abuse by Gender, Race, Ethnicity, and Family Income

Perpetrators of Adult Family Violence by Gender

Men are the chief perpetrators of family violence involving adult victims. Identifying the gender of the primary perpetrator in child maltreatment cases is a more complicated matter.

Between 1976 and 1996, 31,260 women were murdered by an intimate (64 percent by a husband, 5 percent by an ex-husband, and 32 percent by a boyfriend or other unmarried partner). Over the same period, 20,311 men were slain by an intimate (62 percent by wives, 4 percent by ex-wives, and 34 percent by a girlfriend or other unmarried partner). Some 30 percent of all the women and 6 percent of all the men murdered over the 2 decades were the victims of an intimate.

What is known and thought about male perpetrators of adult family violence comes from different sources: prison population data and from attempts by family clinicians, counselors, therapists, and scholars to identify types of offenders. U.S. Department of Justice surveys in 1991 and 1995 (1998) found that approximately 24 percent of convicted jail inmates and 7 percent of convicted violent offenders in state prisons victimized an intimate. More than half of each incarcerated population were under the influence of alcohol or other drugs at the time they committed the crime. The sentence imposed for those who victimized an intimate did not differ significantly from those who did not.

Among state prison inmates with intimate victims, about 42 percent killed the victim, about 21 percent raped or sexually assaulted the victim, about 3 percent robbed the victim, and about 30 percent assaulted the victim. The family background of state prisoners who victimized an intimate did not differ from those who victimized nonintimates. Of those who victimized an intimate,

- about half grew up living with both parents
- 12 percent had lived in a foster home at some time
- 22 percent reported some physical or sexual abuse
- 31 percent had parents who abused drugs or alcohol
- 35 percent had a family member who served time in prison or jail. (U.S. Department of Justice, *Violence between Intimates* 1994)

Clearly, not all with the above characteristics become family violence perpetrators. And perpetrators express their violence in different ways and degrees. Some assault but do not maime or kill. Others psychologically torment but do not physically violate the victim. Thus, clinicians and scholars have sought to identify types of perpetrators, male batterers most of all, and their causal antecedents.

After examining a host of proposed typologies, Munroe-Holtworth and Stuart (1994:481) identified three focal dimensions common to all: the frequency and severity of the expressed violence, the generality of the violence expressed, and psychopathology/personality disorder. They hypothesize that researchers oriented to these three dimensions will most likely derive three types of batterers: family only, generally violent/antisocial, and dysphoric/borderline. The dysphoric/borderline type is the in-between category, those who express violence mainly toward family members but on occasion toward others as well. Munroe-Holtzworth and Stuart (494) emphasize that they offer their typology not as revealed truth, but in the hope that they will "provide others with a theory-driven framework for future research."

Others seek less the identification of types of batterers than the factors that lead some men rather than others to become batterers. The major antecedents are generally traced to three primary sources: biological/genetic, societal/cultural, and psychological/personality factors.

Some seek to account for the disproportionate involvement of men in family battering in the different biological composition of men and women. For example, it is commonly assumed that men are inherently more aggressive than women due to the influence of the male hormone testosterone. The problem is, of course, not all men become batterers. But could it be that batterers have higher levels of testosterone than nonbatterers? The question remains unanswered for a number of reasons, chief among them is the difficulty of selecting scientifically representative samples of men in each category. Nonetheless, in a study conducted some years ago by Kreuz and Rose (1972) young incarcerated male violent offenders were found to have higher than average levels of circulating testosterone. In their view, higher than average levels of circulating testosterone in some males may predispose them, or make them more vulnerable, to becoming violent at certain times and under certain stressful conditions, as, for example, during adolescence. But no one to date has identified a one-to-one correspondence between a precise level of circulating testosterone and the expression of battering or any other act of social deviance. The tendency has been to identify other chemical imbalances that may be involved. One of these that has attracted some attention is *serotonin*.

Serotonin is both a hormone and a neurotransmitter. It has been determined to play a role in regulating aggression. Virkkunen et al. (1989) found lower than normal levels of serotonin among a sample of violent offenders. But here, too, the data were far from enabling the researchers to identify the exact threshold when the measurable level of serotonin triggers a given violent act. While attempts to isolate the biochemical bases of aggression and violence continue to be explored, those seeking inherited clues to violent behavior such as male battering have also explored other avenues such as identical twin studies.

Commonly, studies of male identical twins raised apart are cited to show that they are more likely to be influenced by behavioral traits more common to their biological than their adoptive parents. In the most famous of these studies involving a Danish population (Mednick, Gabrielli, and Hutchings 1987), boys were much more likely to become involved in crime if their biological rather than adoptive parent had a criminal record. However, not all twins with criminally involved biological parents became offenders, and some twins behaved more like their adoptive than biological parent.

Some have sought to trace the influence of other possible biologically influencing factors such as birth complications and head injuries. In a longitudinal study involving birth cohort populations, Kandel and Mednick (1991) found birth defects to predict higher involvement in violent (excluding property) crime. Further, Rosenbaum and Hoge (1989) found a high proportion of a sample of batterers to have a history of head injuries. But again, not all batterers had a history of birth defects or head injuries, and not all men with birth defects and head injuries became batterers.

Most of those interested in documenting the influence of biological and genetic factors in the expression of violence emphasize that they do not expect to find a violence or criminal gene or an exactly identifiable biological element that causes violent criminality (Wilson and Herrnstein 1985). Most also acknowledge the influence of a host of other contributing factors (individual, psychological, situational, and sociocultural factors).

Barnett, Miller-Perrin, and Perrin (1997:243–46) identify the following as possible individual differences in personality and psychopathology that may influence whether or not one becomes a batterer: anger and hostility, low self-esteem, jealousy and emotional dependence, deviations in "normal" personality traits (problems in regard to intimacy, impulsivity, and problem-solving skills), depression, "abnormal" personality traits (passive dependent/compulsive, narcissistic/antisocial, and schizoidal/borderline), and antisocial personality disorder. The last is traced to the influence of child socialization and family experiences in regard to both being abused and witnessing abuse.

Socialization, how a society practices child rearing and the attitudes, values, and behavioral attributes parents and caregivers instill in the young, is a primary focal point for students of human behavior, whatever the subject. Of particular interest to those wishing to account for battering and the disproportionate involvement of males in violent activity generally, is differential gender socialization. Traditionally, males have been reared to be the aggressors, the asserters, the dominant role players, the ones granted the most power and authority over family members. When physical punishment is to be meted out, it is the male who is traditionally expected to be the primary dispenser. Research aimed at exploring the relationship between patriarchal sex-role attitudes and values and propensity to become a batterer have yielded mixed results. Barnett and Ryska (1986) examined wife batterers and found that different test instruments produced different sex-role scores. Rosenbaum (1986) used tests to distinguish between masculine and feminine personality traits and found a significant difference between violent and nonviolent married men. More recently, Sugarman and Frankel (1993) used a continuous measure of masculinity and femininity and found no essential difference in the scores of known violent and nonviolent males.

A variety of situational factors have been thought to contribute to the likelihood of male battering. Barnett et al. (1997:241–43) list the following: marital dissatisfaction, lack of verbal skills resulting in poor communication, stress along with poor problem-solving skills, and a need for power and control.

At present, then, it is wise to assume that the antecedents of male family violence are a combination of factors—biogenetic, individual personality attributes and psychological status, social and cultural conditioning—and a variety of situational possibilities. Studies employing a theoretical perspective integrating these elements and conducted by means of a sophisticated research design based on lessons learned are much in order.

TABLE 9.6   Type of Child Maltreatment by Gender of Perpetrator

Gender	Maltreatment Type		
	Physical Abuse	Neglect	Medical Neglect
Male	17,590 (44.7%)	20,617 (28.1%)	1,893 (21.7%)
Female	21,757 (55.3%)	52,675 (71.9%)	6,818 (78.3%)
Total	39,347 (100.0%)	73,292 (100.0%)	8,711 (100.0%)

Source: U.S. Department of Health and Human Services, Children's Bureau. 1998. *Child Maltreatment 1996: Reports from the States to the National Child Abuse and Neglect Data System.* Washington, DC: U.S. Government Printing Office. Table 2–8, P. 2–15.

Perpetrators of Child Maltreatment by Gender

The most recent national incident study of child abuse and neglect in the United States (Sedlak and Broadhurst 1996) contains gender perpetrator data based on the Detailed Case Data Component (DCDC) described earlier. The data from 43 states reveal that parents were the perpetrators of child maltreatment in 77 percent of the documented cases and relatives of the victim in 11 percent of the cases. About 2 percent were other caretakers (foster parents, child care facility staff). The remaining 10 percent were cases where the identify of the perpetrator was unknown.

Verified cases of child maltreatment in the 43 states in 1996 totaled 150,384. Of the total, 91,250 (61 percent) were perpetrated by females and 59,134 by males (39 percent). Table 9.6 identifies type of child maltreatment by perpetrator gender.

To identify the gender of child maltreatment perpetrators by relationship to the victim, one must turn to the evidence supplied by NIS-3 (1996:16–22). In the case of birth parents, children were much more likely to be maltreated by their mothers than their fathers. Conversely, children abused by other relatives or nonrelatives were more likely to be maltreated by a male than a female.

Similar information is available for infanticide, generally defined as homicides of children under age 5. Although the number of children murdered under age 5 increased steadily over the past two decades, it has recently begun to decline. U.S. Department of Justice Statistics (1998) data show that for all children age 5 and under murdered from 1976 through 1997:

- 27 percent were killed by mothers
- 27 percent were killed by fathers
- 24 percent were killed by acquaintances
- 6 percent were killed by other relatives
- 3 percent were killed by strangers
- 12 percent were killed by perpetrators whose relationship was unknown.

Sexual Abuse	Emotional Maltreatment	Total
16,448 (71.5%)	2,586 (43.0%)	59,134 (39.3%)
6,571 (28.5%)	3,429 (57.0%)	91,250 (60.7%)
23,019 (100.0%)	6,015 (100.0%)	150,384 (100.0%)

TABLE 9.7 Number of Homicides of Children Under Age 5 by Gender of Victim/Perpetrator, 1976–96

Year	Male on Male	Female on Male	Male on Female	Female on Female
1976	153	120	124	87
1977	162	108	124	96
1978	183	112	130	91
1979	146	93	139	75
1980	182	96	122	90
1981	184	90	148	92
1982	192	98	153	106
1983	174	107	132	104
1984	175	86	134	95
1985	180	92	147	89
1986	200	138	153	109
1987	181	105	157	100
1988	205	96	165	104
1989	188	132	143	123
1990	199	124	158	86
1991	235	126	193	130
1992	247	94	164	94
1993	253	122	189	104
1994	261	128	161	119
1995	241	113	172	116
1996	244	105	193	133
1997	186	124	145	115

Source: U.S. Department of Justice, Bureau of Justice Statistics. 1999. *Homicide Trends in the U.S.: Infanticide.* Washington, DC: U.S. Government Printing Office.

Table 9.7 identifies the number of homicides of children under age 5 by the gender of the victim and perpetrator. Evident is the fact that most of the victims and perpetrators are males.

An important subject not reported in primary data sources are cases of maltreatment and infanticide perpetrated in single-parent families by gender. Unknown is whether or not mothers outnumber fathers as perpetrators of child maltreatment because data are not presented controlling for number of single-parent families headed by a female versus a male. It is known that child maltreatment is more likely to occur in single-parent families than in families with both parents present (NIS-3:12–3). Infanticide data are not similarly documented.

Perpetrators of Adult Family Violence by Race, Ethnicity, and Socioeconomic Factors

The earliest national surveys of family abuse controlling for race were conducted from 1975–85 by Straus and Gelles (1986). They employed measures of minor violence (throwing something, pushing, grabbing, shoving, slapping) and severe violence (kicking, hitting, beating, weapon threatening, weapon using). In both studies, husband-to-wife and wife-to-husband minor and severe violence was found to be higher in black than white families. Between the two decades, the gap between the races declined, but black families continued to evidence higher rates of family violence.

A recent study published by the U.S. Department of Justice (2000) on trends between 1993 and 1998, which used conventional definitions of intimate partner violence (murder, rape, assault, robbery), found a continuing wide gap between black and white intimate partner violence. The rate of intimate partner violence suffered by black females was 35 percent higher than that suffered by white females and 2.5 times the rate for females of other races. The rate for black males was 62 percent higher than the rate for white males and, as in the case of females, 2.5 times greater than the rate for males of other races. Between 1993 and 1998, and regardless of gender, no difference in the rate of intimate partner violence was found between Hispanic and non-Hispanic persons.

A consistent finding of the victimization surveys is that partner violence is the primary form of violence against women. With this fact in mind, the National Institute of Justice and the Centers for Disease Control and Prevention jointly sponsored a national telephone survey on violence against women, which was conducted from November 1995 to May 1996. A major finding (Tjaden and Thoennes 1998:2) was that 76 percent of the women who reported being raped or physically assaulted said they were victimized by a partner or former partner. African American women reported a slightly higher rate of rape (18.8 percent versus 17.7 percent) and physical assault (52.1 percent versus 51.3 percent) than white women.

Another major finding was the tendency of Native American/Alaska Native women to report significantly higher and Asian/Pacific Islander women to report significantly lower rates of violent victimization than respondents from other racial and ethnic groups. Caution in drawing conclusions was emphasized as the number of respondents in these categories was relatively small. However, the finding that Native American women are at greater risk of being violently victimized by a partner than other racial and ethnic groups was noted as being consistent with the results of a study conducted by Bachman (1992).

Lastly, the survey found that Hispanic women were not as likely to report rape victimization as non-Hispanic women. However, as Tjaden and Thoennes point out, as other studies report contradictory findings in regard to comparative rates of violence between Hispanic and non-Hispanic women, their findings must be interpreted as neither confirming nor contradicting earlier findings by others.

Socioeconomic differences are thought to account for differences in rates of partner violence among America's several racial and ethnic segments. Lockhart (1991) surveyed a "purposive sample" of African American women (n = 155) and European American (n = 152) women, controlling for their socioeconomic status (measures, of education, income, and occupation). Pointing out that the sampling frame did not permit drawing inferences about the general population, Lockhart found no appreciable difference between the African American and European American women who reported husband-to-wife violence. She did find a higher percentage of middle-class African American women than middle-class European women who said they had been violently victimized by a married partner.

Stets (1990) examined the influence of socioeconomic status on comparative black and white married partner differences in the expression of verbal and physical aggression. His working hypothesis was that verbal aggression was generally antecedent to physical aggression. His data base was the Second National Family Violence Re-Survey (Straus and Gelles 1986). Gross comparisons of black and white respondents in this study showed that black respondents (regardless of gender) were more prone to verbal and physical aggression toward a partner than white respondents. "Based on a nationally representative sample and examining male-to-female aggression as well as female-to-male aggression, the present study shows that race still has an effect, even when social class is controlled, for both men and women" (Stets 512). Controlling for the influence of indicators of being raised in a subculture of violence (for example, reports of having witnessed intra- and extra-family violence during childhood) did account for the difference between black and white males. That is, when controlling for exposure to a subculture of violence, the difference in reported aggression between black and white males disappeared.

A more recent study by Hutchison et al. (1994) found no difference in black and white rates of partner violence when controlling for the effects of socioeconomic status. Perhaps, then, it is wise to heed the words of Barnett et al. (1997), who after reviewing the research literature, observed that "studies exploring race and ethnicity prevalence rates should be taken as speculative."

Perpetrators of Child Family Violence by Race, Ethnicity, and Socioeconomic Factors

The amount of published research concerned with identifying basic social and economic characteristics of child abuse perpetrators is noteworthy for its spareness. A 1985 study (Hawkins and Duncan) on all known cases of child abuse and neglect in Missouri at the time of the study (n = 923) found male perpetrators of abuse (63 percent) and neglect (85 percent) to have been unemployed. This pattern was not supported by the evidence conveyed in the Executive Summary (Sedlak and Broadhurst 1996) of the Third National Incidence Study of Child Abuse and Neglect (NIS-3). In more than a third of the maltreated children identified in NIS-3, the perpetrator's employment status was unknown. However, among those for which this was known, about half were found to have been abused by an employed perpetrator. Unemployed perpetrators were a minority in all categories of child maltreatment. Whether or not the inconsistency between the findings of the Missouri and NIS-3 studies is due to the difference between a statewide as opposed to a national study, data collection differences, or a host of other possibilities, is unknown.

In the matter of race, the NIS-3 Executive Summary (Sedlak and Broadhurst) reports some differences between white and nonwhite victims. Among sexually abused victims, white children were most often victimized by their birth parents. Among physically abused children, white children were more often victimized by non–birth parents. Nonwhite children were a minority of victims in all maltreatment categories. As no mention is made of the proportionate representation of white and nonwhite children among those maltreated, it is not known whether or not either white or nonwhite children were disproportionately represented among the ranks of those maltreated. When physically or sexually abused, nonwhite children were most likely to be abused by someone other than a parent or a parent substitute. White children were the majority of those suffering serious injuries. Nonwhite children were more likely than white children to constitute a majority of those suffering moderate injury. This, then, is the extent of the information provided by the NIS-3 Executive Summary. Further information on perpetrator racial, ethnic, and socioeconomic characteristics must be sought from the few studies that have addressed these subjects and implications from other sources of evidence on child victimization.

It is commonly stated that although they occur across the socioeconomic spectrum, child abuse and neglect are disproportionately prevalent in the lower socioeconomic strata. Those with the least income evidence the highest rates. For example, in a recent (1997) Office of Juvenile Justice and Delinquency Prevention (OJJDP) publication based on data supplied by 4,000 participants in three sites (Rochester, New York; Denver, Colorado; and Pittsburgh, Pennsylvania), 20 percent of children raised in disadvantaged families as compared to 8 percent of children raised in nondisadvantaged families in Rochester were maltreated. A disadvantaged family was one in which the principal wage earner was unemployed, or family income was below the poverty level, or the family was on welfare.

A recent (1997) U.S. Department of Justice sponsored publication involving a national sample of 4,023 adolescents and their parents examined, in addition to other factors, the bearing of ethnicity, race, and household income on the prevalence and effects of child victimization. The sample studied was evenly divided by gender and selected to have demographic characteristics comparable to the country's general population. Some 70 percent of the sample were non-Hispanic whites, 14.7 percent African American, 7.8 percent Hispanic, and 3.8 percent other racial/ethnic groups. Some 16 percent of those interviewed were in families with reported incomes under $20,000, 44 percent in families with incomes between $20,000 and $50,000, and 33 percent with reported family incomes over $50,000. The remaining 7 percent withheld reporting family income. Rates of physical and sexual assault were highest in the lower income families. Additionally, "Native Americans, African Americans, and Hispanics had higher rates than Caucasians and other racial and ethnic groups in all categories of victimization" (1997:3).

In a study of all child homicides in Los Angeles between 1980 and 1989, Sorenson et al. (1997) identify certain characteristics of all suspected perpetrators. Over 85 percent of all suspects were victim family members. Homicides by family members totaled 112. The highest number of victims were in black families (59 or

53 percent), followed by Hispanic families (32 or 28 percent), and white families (21 or 19 percent). No information was provided on suspects' socioeconomic status.

Similarities and Differences between Adult and Child Perpetrators of Family Violence

By gender, males, by a wide margin, are the major perpetrators of adult family violence. The perpetrators of child maltreatment are largely female, but the male–female gap is not nearly as wide as that between male and female perpetrators of adult abuse. Adult victims of family violence are mostly women, and they are primarily victimized by their male partners. The primary abusers of children are their parents, mothers most of all.

When homicide is considered, the gender gap narrows for both adult-on-adult and adult-on-child victimization. Between 1976 and 1996, more women were murdered by a male intimate (31,260) than males by a female intimate (20,311). However, between these years a comparable percentage of wives murdered by an intimate were slain by their husbands (64 percent) and husbands murdered by an intimate were slain by their wives (62 percent). Considering children age 5 and under murdered from 1976 through 1997, an equal percentage were murdered by mothers and fathers (27 percent).

Reasons for the predominance of males as perpetrators of adult family violence on other adults or children have been traced to a variety of biogenetic, psychological, sociocultural, and situational factors. Whether or not there is an essential difference between some number of males who abuse either but not both adult family members or children is unknown as systematic comparisons of perpetrators of adult and child family violence remain to be conducted.

By race and ethnicity, major national surveys conducted in 1975 and 1985 by Straus and Gelles indicated that family violence generally was more pronounced in black than white families. More recent studies find parity between the races in terms of indicators of amount of adult family violence. The most recent NIS-3 report showed a greater number of white than black maltreated children. As children are victimized most of all by parents, the data indicate family differences. Black children were the second most often victimized followed by Hispanic children, Native American/Alaskan Native children, and Asian/Pacific Islander children.

Rather consistently, perpetration of family violence has been found to be greater in non-Hispanic than Hispanic families and lowest of all in Asian families. Differences in the willingness of victims of family violence in certain ethnic groups to report incidents have been found, which encourage caution in drawing conclusions about the relationship between perpetrator ethnicity and family abuse.

The perpetrators of both adult and child family violence have been mainly those in the lower socioeconomic strata. Some attribute this finding not primarily to basic differences among the several social classes but to the ability of more affluent groups to conceal family problems from public attention. But the NIS-3 data, as interpreted by Sedlak and Broadhurst, do not support such an assumption.

Some believe that differences among black and white families in terms of family violence is a function of socioeconomic status. However, studies comparing rates of black and white family violence perpetration after controlling for socioeconomic status have yielded conflicting and, therefore, inconclusive results.

Summary

To briefly and concisely summarize major patterns from the above, it was found, in regard to the victims of family abuse, that: (1) Adult victims of family violence are much more likely to be women than men, and child victims only slightly more likely to be girls rather than boys; (2) adult blacks experience higher rates of family abuse than whites, Hispanics, or members of other ethnic groups; (3) Hispanics experience lower rates of family abuse victimization than non-Hispanics; (4) Asians experience the lowest rates of family abuse victimization; (5) the different rates of family abuse victimization experienced by blacks and whites is due primarily to higher rates of victimization by black than white females; (6) as family income increases, rates of family abuse decrease; and (7) with the exception of medical neglect, child victims of family maltreatment are much more likely to be white than black.

In regard to the perpetrators of family abuse, major findings include: (1) Men are the primary perpetrators of adult family abuse; (2) females perpetrate a much higher overall amount of child maltreatment than men; (3) children raised by birth parents are more likely to be abused by their mothers than their fathers, but children raised by others are more likely to be abused by males than females; (4) of children murdered by a parent, an equal proportion is the victim of a mother or father; (5) black males appear to have higher rates of family violence perpetration than white males or members of other ethnic groups; and (6) the lower the socioeconomic status, the higher the proportion of family violence perpetrators.

Rigid conclusions concerning the summarized items should be strictly avoided. The evidence is abundantly clear that distinct patterns and trends revealed at one time are as likely as not to fade if not vanish at a later date. It must be said, however, that we know more about the victims than the perpetrators of family violence. Doubtlessly, this is in good measure the consequences of the fact that those investigating family violence have been professionals concerned with treating victims, such as clinicians, family therapists, and social workers. Much more needs to be known about the perpetrators. Why do some men, those with comparable individual and sociocultural characteristics, rather than others become family violence perpetrators? What accounts for the apparent decline in family violence generally? Which situational factors differentiate those who perpetrate family violence from those who do not? Do the same situational factors (single parent versus two parent households, employed versus unemployed head of household, and so on) determine whether or not a male or a female becomes a family abuse perpetrator? Do comparable situational factors influence men and women differently? These and a host of other possible questions are greatly in need of research and analysis.

Study Questions

1. What are the similarities and differences in the adult and child victims of family violence?

2. What are the similarities and differences in those who perpetrate adult as opposed to child family violence?

3. Are the victims of family violence differentiated by race, ethnicity, and socioeconomic status?

4. Are the perpetrators of family violence differentiated by race, ethnicity, and socio-economic status?

5. What are the gender differences in those victimized by adult and child family abuse?

6. What are the gender differences in those who perpetrate adult and child family abuse?

7. How solid is the evidence concerning exactly who are the victims and the perpetrators of family abuse?

8. Why is more known about the victims than the perpetrators of family abuse?

REFERENCES

Bachman, Ronet. 1992. *Death and Violence on the Reservation: Homicide, Family Violence, and Suicide in American Indian Populations.* Westport, CT: Auburn House.

Barnett, Ola W., Cindy L. Miller-Perrin, and Robin D. Perrin. 1997. *Violence Across the Lifespan: An Introduction.* Thousand Oaks, CA: Sage Publications.

Barnett, Ola W. and T. A. Ryska. 1986. "Masculinity and Femininity in Male Spouse Abusers." Symposium presented at the annual meeting of the American Society of Criminology, Toronto, Canada.

Dawson, John M. and Patrick A. Langan. 1994. "Murder in Families." U.S. Department of Justice, Bureau of Justice Statistics Special Report. Washington, DC: U.S. Government Printing Office.

Hawkins, Wesley E. and David F. Duncan. 1985. *Psychological Reports.* 56:407–10.

Hutchison, I. W., J. D. Hirschel, and C. E. Pesacks. 1994. "Family Violence and Police Utilization." *Violence and Victims.* 9:299–313.

Kandel, E. and S. A. Mednick. 1991. "Perinatal Complications Predict Violent Offending." *Criminology.* 29:519–29.

Kreuz, L. E. and R. M. Rose. 1972. "Assessment of Aggressive Behavior and Plasma Testosterone in a Young Criminal Population." *Psychosomatic Medicine.* 34:321–32.

Lockhart, Lettie L. 1991. "Spousal Violence: A Cross-Racial Perspective." Pp. 85–101 in *Black Family Violence,* Robert L. Hampton, ed. Lexington, MA: Lexington Books.

Mednick, S. A., W. F. Gabrielli, and B. Hutchings. 1987. "Genetic Factors in the Etiology of Criminal Behavior." Pp. 74–91 in *The Causes of Crime,* T. E. Moffit and S. S. Stack, eds. Cambridge, Eng.: Cambridge University Press.

Munroe-Holtzworth, Amy and Gregory L. Stuart. 1994. "Typologies of Male Batterers: Three Subtypes and the Differences Among Them." *Psychological Bulletin.* 116:476–97.

Pagelow, Mildred Daley. 1984. *Family Violence.* NY: Praeger.

Rennison, Callie Marie and Sarah Welchans. 2000. "Intimate Partner Violence." Bureau of Justice Statistics, Special Report. Washington, DC: U.S. Department of Justice.

Rosenbaum, A. 1986. "Of Men, Macho, and Marital Violence." *Journal of Family Violence.* 1:121–29.

Rosenbaum, A. and S. K. Hoge. 1989. "Head Injury and Marital Aggression." *American Journal of Psychiatry.* 146:1048–51.

Sedlak, Andrea J. and Diane D. Broadhurst. 1996. *Executive Summary of the Third National Incidence Study of Child Abuse and Neglect.* Washington, DC: U.S. Government Printing Office.

Sorenson, Susan B., Jule G. Peterson, and Barbra A. Richardson. 1997. "Child Homicide in the City of Los Angeles: An Epidemiologic Examination of a Decade of Deaths." Pp. 189–205 in *Violence and Sexual Abuse at Home,* Robert Geffner, Susan B. Sorenson, and Paula K. Lundberg-Love, eds. NY: The Haworth Press, Inc.

Stets, Jan E. 1990. "Verbal and Physical Aggression in Marriage." *Journal of Marriage and the Family.* 52:501–14.

Straus, Murray A. and Richard J. Gelles. 1986. "Societal Changes and Change in Family Violence from 1975 to 1985 as Revealed by Two National Surveys." *Journal of Marriage and the Family.* 48:465–79.

Sugarman, D. B. and S. L. Frankel. 1993. "A Meta-Analytic Study of Wife Assault and Patriarchal Beliefs." Paper presented at the annual meeting of the American Psychological Association, Toronto, Canada.

Tjaden, Patricia and Nancy Thoennes. 1998. *Prevalence, Incidence, and Consequences of Violence Against Women: Findings from the National Violence Against Women Survey,* National Institute of Justice Centers for Disease Control and Prevention. Washington, DC: U.S. Government Printing Office.

U.S. Department of Justice, Bureau of Justice Statistics. 1994. *Violence between Intimates.* Washington, DC: U.S. Government Printing Office.

U.S. Department of Health and Human Services, Children's Bureau. 1998. *Child Maltreatment 1996: Reports From the States to the National Child Abuse and Neglect Data System.* Washington, DC: U.S. Government Printing Office.

U.S. Department of Health and Human Services, Administration on Children, Youth, and Families. 2000. *Child Maltreatment 1998: Reports from the States to the National Child Abuse and Neglect Data System.* Washington, DC: U.S. Government Printing Office.

U.S. Department of Justice, Bureau of Justice Statistics. 1996. *Child Victimizers: Violent Offenders and Their Victims.* Washington, DC: U.S. Government Printing Office.

U.S. Department of Justice, Bureau of Justice Statistics. 1998. *Homicide Trends in the U.S.: Infanticide.* Washington, DC: U.S. Government Printing Office.

U.S. Department of Justice, Office of Justice Programs. 1997. *The Prevalence and Consequences of Child Victimization.* Washington, DC: U.S. Government Printing Office.

U.S. Department of Justice, Office of Juvenile Justice and Delinquency Prevention. 1997. *In the Wake of Childhood Maltreatment.* Washington, DC: U.S. Government Printing Office.

U.S. Department of Justice, Bureau of Justice Statistics. 2000. *Intimate Partner Violence.* Washington, DC: U.S. Government Printing Office.

Virkkunen, Matti, Judith DeJong, John Bartko, Frederick K. Goodwin, and Markkun Linnoila. 1989. "Relationship of Psychobiological Variables to Recidivism in Violent Offenders and Impulsive Fire Setters." *Archives of General Psychiatry.* 46:600–03.

Wilson, James Q. and Richard J. Herrnstein. 1985. *Crime and Human Nature.* NY: Simon and Schuster.

CHAPTER

10 Special Populations and Complicating Factors

Previous chapters have discussed the many complexities in trying to establish the causes and the consequences of family abuse, especially childhood maltreatment. In some cases the causes and consequences are so complex and have such unique aspects that they require special attention. Those having these unique complexities are often referred to as *special populations*. Major topics covered in this chapter include the relationship among family abuse and mental illness, substance abuse, and suicide. The chapter also examines the relationship between child maltreatment and prostitution and discusses the experience of perpetration of family abuse among prison inmates and sex offenders who are in the criminal justice system.

Mental Health Problems

Mental health problems bear a strong relationship to childhood maltreatment. Earlier chapters have identified some of the mental health problems associated with family abuse. This chapter examines the complexity of this association in more detail. The association is a complex web of influences, as mental illness can result from a variety of factors, including genetics. It is extremely difficult to sort out these complicating factors, and, therefore, it is difficult to say that childhood maltreatment is clearly the cause of someone's mental illness. In general, it is more appropriate to say that maltreatment and mental illness are associated rather than to state conclusively that childhood maltreatment is the cause of mental illness.

It was during the 1970s and 1980s especially that the link between childhood sexual abuse and adult psychiatric problems began to be investigated (Glod 1993). This section reviews some of the best documented mental health problems often associated with childhood maltreatment.

In looking at a history of psychiatric illness in families, Brown and Anderson (1991) found that women who were physically or sexually abused were far more likely to have psychiatric illness in their families. Women with no history of physical or sexual abuse reported psychiatric illness in their families in 51 percent of the cases. Nearly two-thirds (65 percent) of women who had been physically or sexually abused reported a psychiatric history in their families. More than three-fourths (78 percent) of women with both physical and sexual abuse reported a family history of psychiatric illness.

Palmer et al. (1993) compared British women who were under psychiatric care (both inpatient and outpatient) for a range of mental disorders with women who were patients of general practitioners. Nearly one-third (30 percent) of the psychiatric patients reported being victims of sexual abuse as compared with 11 percent of the general practice patients. No clear relationship was found between the childhood sexual abuse and the type of psychiatric disturbance.

In a sample of 437 adolescent girls treated in a psychiatric hospital, Husain and Chapel (1983) found 14 percent were victims of incest. In a study of 26 women who had extended hospitalizations for psychotic disorders, 46 percent (12) reported histories of incest. This group was more threatening and assaultive than patients without a history of incest (Beck and van der Kolk 1987).

There is some evidence that psychiatric problems among adults may be even more severe when the person has experienced more than one type of abuse; but multiple abuse is not always reported. It can be easier to discuss physical abuse, rather than sexual abuse; and it is therefore possible that some patients who admit only to physical abuse were also sexually abused (Bryer et al. 1987).

One of the important concepts in examining mental health effects of abuse is known as "cognitive appraisal." That is, victim perceptions of the abuse are an important factor that can have an effect on psychological functioning (Fondacaro, Holt, and Powell 1999). This means it is important to have knowledge of the victim's understanding of what has occurred and whether the victim of abuse defines the behavior as abuse or defines it as something else.

Lamb emphasizes the importance of not seeing all victims of abuse as having the same experiences and subsequent problems:

> One child may have been fondled one time by an uncle in a swimming pool; another may have experienced lifelong incestuous abuse from her father. They are both victims of abuse, but doesn't it make sense to acknowledge that in the first case the child may remember the incident only as something confusing and unpleasant while in the second, the girl may need long-term psychotherapy to deal with the issues of betrayal, exploitation, fear, and sexuality that such abuse often brings? (1999:E2)

Children are influenced by their own history, support systems, and internal resources and therefore respond differently to abuse. A child who has been fondled by her grandfather several times may consider the behavior a defining one in her life, causing her great emotional pain. In hindsight, another child who had a supportive family and the ability to tell her mother who then stopped the abuse might see the experience as unpleasant but not self-defining (Lamb 1999).

As mentioned previously, there is some evidence that males and females may react differently to childhood maltreatment. Rind, Tromovitch, and Bauserman (1998) found in their meta-analysis of 59 studies of college students that men reacted less negatively to childhood sexual abuse than women. Respondents said that at the time of the sexual abuse, 72 percent of females felt it was a negative experience compared with only 33 percent of the males. Thirty-seven percent of males reported thinking at the time of the experience that it was positive while only 11 percent of the females felt it was a positive experience. In looking back on their sexual abuse experiences from adulthood, 59 percent of females reported it as a negative experience compared with 26 percent of males. In their adult reflections, 42 percent of males thought it was a positive experience but only 16 percent of females reported experiences as positive. (Other research discussed later offers some possible explanations for these differences.)

Carmen et al. (1984) studied a group of 188 adult and adolescent males and females who were patients in a psychiatric hospital. Forty-three percent (80) of the patients had a history of physical or sexual abuse or both. Fifty-three percent (65) of the abused were female and 23 percent (15) were male. Abuse of females typically started in childhood and continued through adulthood. They were abused by parents, partners, and strangers. Males (primarily adolescents) were more frequently abused by parents during childhood and their teenage years. The characteristic that most distinguished abused males from abused females was that females became more passive and males became more aggressive.

Briere et al. (1988) studied 40 men and 40 women who were survivors of childhood sexual abuse and were clients at a crisis counseling center. The abuse began at approximately the same age for both groups (age 9), yet the females experienced more intense abuse over a longer period of time. The sexually abused men and women were equally high in their previous suicide attempts (55 percent) as compared with control groups of nonabused men (20 percent) and nonabused women (25 percent). Abused men and women were also equal in their scores on the Trauma Symptom Checklist (TSC-33). Briere et al. concluded, "It is possible that childhood sexual victimization has an equivalent impact on males and females regardless of any differences in its severity or duration between the sexes" (1988:460).

Since men had responses equal to women even though they endured less intense abuse over a shorter period of time, a possible explanation is that men may find sexual abuse even more traumatic than women. If the men had endured the same level of sexual abuse as women they may have had even more severe symptoms. Briere et al. acknowledge the difficulty of determining what would be considered equal amounts of abuse.

In a study of 125 male psychiatric outpatients, 48 percent reported a history of abuse (Swett, Surrey, and Cohen 1990). Forty-four percent of the maltreated reported physical abuse, 7 percent reported sexual abuse, and 6 percent reported both physical and sexual abuse.

Jacobson and Richardson (1987), in their study of 50 men and 50 women in psychiatric hospitals, found that 57 percent had experienced childhood physical or sexual abuse. Patients were asked directly about their abuse experiences rather than relying on reviews of medical records as do many other research studies. Of the 40 percent of the patients who said the abuse they endured as children and/or adults had "major effects on their current functioning, the majority of the effects were negative, such as decreased self-esteem and avoidance of sexual relationships. A few reported increased self-reliance or efforts not to abuse their own children" (1987:910).

There is considerable agreement among researchers and the general public that childhood maltreatment can have negative and far-reaching consequences. In the words of Bryer et al.: "Abuse has profound deleterious effects on psychological functioning" (1987:1429). However, there are exceptions. We have previously discussed the concept of resilience and that people may have the skills, resources, and support from others to overcome negative life events.

The notion that childhood sexual abuse causes intense harm has recently been challenged. Rind et al. (1998) in a meta-analysis of 59 studies of male and female college students found that those who were sexually abused were only slightly less well adjusted than the control group. They found that "lasting effects are not prevalent and when negative effects occur, they are often temporary, implying that they are frequently not intense" (1998:37). This work has raised considerable controversy: the House of Representatives voted in 1999 to condemn this work stating that it supported pedophilia. A letter from the American Psychological Association President, Raymond Fowler, to House majority leader, Tom DeLay, stated that the APA made a mistake in publishing the article (Lamb 1999).

In general, there appears to be a strong relationship between childhood maltreatment and subsequent mental illness; but this relationship depends on additional factors. As will be discussed further, gender issues in maltreatment and the consequences for males and females is in need of further investigation. Specific types of mental health problems often associated with childhood maltreatment are discussed in the following section. These include depression, personality disorders, and eating disorders.

Depression

There is considerable evidence of a relationship between child maltreatment and depression. Those suffering from depression are more likely to have been physically or sexually abused than those who have not (Lizardi et al. 1995). For some who experience depression, Lizardi et al. found that 10 was the average age of onset. Not surprisingly, adolescents who have been physically abused are more likely than nonabused adolescents to have depression (Becker et al. 1991; Farber and Joseph 1985).

There is evidence that those who are sexually abused are very likely to suffer from depression. As a matter of fact, depression is known to be the most common symptom of adults who have endured childhood sexual abuse (Finkelhor 1986). A study of 286 working-class mothers in England found that 9 percent (25) reported they had been sexually abused before the age of 17. Nearly two-thirds (64 percent) of the abused group were depressed during a 3-year period in comparison with 26 percent of the women who were not sexually abused. The highest rates of depression were found among those who endured the most severe forms of sexual abuse such as sexual intercourse. A childhood history of sexual abuse increased the risk for separation/divorce or for never cohabiting or marrying (Bifulco, Brown, and Adler 1991). These are considered indicators of difficulty with intimate relationships.

Brown and Moran (1994) found that problems in childhood, such as family violence, sexual abuse or parental indifference, play an important role in adult depression. Childhood problems along with the onset of adult problems such as difficulties in relationships (with partner or children) can predict whether a person will develop chronic depressive episodes. More than half the 404 women in the study developed chronic depression. One-third of the women with chronic depressive episodes had childhood problems but not adult onset interpersonal difficulties. Brown and Moran caution that "there is an uncomfortable gap here between past and present, with the process by which such a distant experience can affect current symptom duration left unexplained" (1994:455).

In her review of the literature, Sheerer (1997) concluded that the most consistent finding is that physical, sexual, and emotional abuse is associated with some form of depression.

Personality Disorders

Personality disorders refer to patterns of thinking and behaving that are different from what is expected of individuals within the culture. Personality disorders often begin in adolescence or young adulthood and are "pervasive and inflexible" and lead to "distress or impairment" (American Psychiatric Association 1994:629). The *Diagnostic and Statistical Manual* reviews 10 types of personality disorders, several of which are especially relevant to a discussion of childhood maltreatment. The most relevant ones include borderline personality disorder, antisocial personality disorder, and multiple personality disorder (also called dissociative identity disorder).

Borderline Personality Disorder

Research has shown that there is a relationship between childhood maltreatment and the development of *borderline personality disorder* (Brown and Anderson 1991; Bryer et al. 1987; Glod 1993; Herman, Perry, and van der Kolk 1989). Borderline personality disorder is characterized by unstable personal relationships, an unstable self-image, and impulsive behavior. See Box 10.1 for the DSM-IV criteria.

Brown and Anderson (1991) found in their sample of psychiatric inpatients that 3 percent of nonabused patients were diagnosed with borderline personality disorder. Thirteen percent of the sample who were either physically or sexually abused as children were diagnosed with borderline personality disorder.

Herman et al. (1989) found a strong relationship between childhood maltreatment and borderline personality disorder. Eighty-one percent of patients diagnosed with borderline personality disorder had suffered childhood maltreat-

B O X **10.1**

DSM-IV Criteria for Borderline Personality Disorder

A pervasive pattern of instability of interpersonal relationships, self-image, and affects, and marked impulsivity beginning by early adulthood and present in a variety of contexts, as indicated by five or more of the following:

1. frantic efforts to avoid real or imagined abandonment.
2. a pattern of unstable and intense interpersonal relationships, characterized by alternating between extremes of idealization and devaluation.
3. identity disturbance, markedly and persistently unstable self-image or sense of self.
4. impulsivity in at least two areas that are potentially self-damaging (e.g., spending, sex, substance abuse, reckless driving, binge eating).
5. recurrent suicidal behavior, gestures, or threats, or self-mutilating behavior.
6. affective instability due to a marked reactivity of mood (e.g., intense episodic dysphoria, irritability, or anxiety usually lasting a few hours and only rarely more than a few days).
7. chronic feelings of emptiness.
8. inappropriate, intense anger or difficulty controlling anger (e.g., frequent displays of temper, constant anger, recurrent physical fights).
9. transient, stress-related paranoid ideation or severe dissociative symptoms.

Source: Reprinted with permission from the *Diagnostic and Statistical Manual of Mental Disorders*, 4th ed. Copyright 1994 American Psychiatric Association. P. 654.

---

ment. Seventy-one percent had been physically abused, 67 percent had been sexually abused, and 62 percent had been a witness to family violence. Over half (57 percent) reported that abuse took place between infancy and age 6. See Box 10.2 for an example of borderline personality disorder.

While there is a strong association between abuse and borderline personality disorder, Herman et al. conclude that abuse is not sufficient by itself to cause borderline personality disorder. "It is possible that trauma is most pathogenic for children with vulnerable temperaments or for those most lacking protective factors, such as positive relationships with other caretakers or siblings" (1989:493). The relationship between family abuse and borderline personality disorder thus depends on both the presence of disposing factors of temperament and the absence or impairment of protective factors.

Borderline personality disorder is regarded as a mental disorder that is especially difficult to treat. Herman et al. put it this way:

> It is generally agreed that patients with borderline personality disorder are difficult to treat because of the intensity of their engagement with caregivers, the sometimes overwhelming nature of their demands for care, and the strong emotions and conflicts that they provoke in others. (1989:490)

BOX 10.2

Background of a Woman with Borderline Personality Disorder

Ms. A., a 35-year-old woman with borderline personality disorder, was the fourth of five siblings born to two alcoholic parents. After her father deserted the family when she was 3 years old, the household became increasingly chaotic; her mother enforced unclear and inconsistent rules by screaming, hair pulling, hitting on the head and face, and kicking in the knees and genital area. In Ms. A.'s words, "You never knew when to expect it. You could do something really wrong and she wouldn't notice, and then you could knock over your milk and she would fly off the handle." Her mother remarried when Ms. A. was 9 years old, and the level of violence in the home diminished. Shortly after entering the home, however, the stepfather began sexually molesting Ms. A. and her three sisters. The incestuous relationship, which proceeded to oral sex and intercourse, continued until she ran away from home at age 15. While on the road, Ms. A. frequented bars where she would pick up older men, offering sex in exchange for shelter. At age 17 she was brutally raped and beaten in one such encounter, requiring hospitalization for her injuries.

Source: Judith Lewis Herman, J. Christopher Perry, and Bessel A. van der Kolk. 1989. "Childhood Trauma in Borderline Personality Disorder." *American Journal of Psychiatry.* 146:490–95, P. 493.

Antisocial Personality Disorder

Antisocial personality disorder, formerly known as the psychopathic or sociopathic personality, is characterized by a lack of concern for and the violation of the rights of others (American Psychiatric Association 1994). Perhaps the best-known trait of those with antisocial personality disorder is the inability to feel guilt. If a person is unable to feel guilt, it is with relative ease that dangerous and harmful acts can be committed. It is much more common in men than women and it is of no surprise that the diagnosis of antisocial personality disorder tends to be more common among criminal justice clients and substance abusers than other groups. See Box 10.3 for the DSM-IV criteria for antisocial personality disorder.

There is some agreement that a history of childhood maltreatment is related to development of antisocial personality disorder, and the earlier the abuse, especially total neglect, the more likely antisocial personality will develop. Luntz and Widom (1994) found that 14 percent of those who endured childhood maltreatment met the criteria for antisocial personality disorder compared with 7 percent of a nonabused comparison group. Windle et al. (1995) found that a family history of alcoholism was associated with antisocial personality disorder in men.

Very recently it has been suggested that the development of antisocial personality disorder may be related to maternal lack of nutrition. In a study of wartime famine, it was found that "severe nutritional deficiency in the first or second trimester of intrauterine life is associated with risk for development of ASPD (antisocial personality disorder)" (Neugebauer, Hoek, and Susser 1999:460). The link between childhood maltreatment and antisocial personality disorder may, thus, depend on biological shocks to the system at particular developmental stages.

BOX **10.3**

DSM-IV Criteria for Antisocial Personality Disorder

    A. There is a pervasive pattern of disregard for and violation of the rights of others occurring since age 15 years, as indicated by 3 or more of the following:
        1. failure to conform to social norms with respect to lawful behaviors as indicated by repeatedly performing acts that are grounds for arrest.
        2. deceitfulness, as indicated by repeated lying, use of aliases, or conning others for personal profit or pleasure.
        3. impulsivity or failure to plan ahead.
        4. irritability and aggressiveness, as indicated by repeated physical fights or assaults.
        5. reckless disregard for safety of self or others.
        6. consistent irresponsibility, as indicated by repeated failure to sustain consistent work behavior or honor financial obligations.
        7. lack of remorse, as indicated by being indifferent to or rationalizing having hurt, mistreated, or stolen from another.
    B. The individual is at least 18 years old.
    C. There is evidence of conduct disorder with onset before age 15 years.
    D. The occurrence of antisocial behavior is not exclusively during the course of schizophrenia or a manic episode.

Source: Reprinted with permission from the *Diagnostic and Statistical Manual of Mental Disorders,* 4th ed. Copyright 1994 American Psychiatric Association. Pp. 649–50.

Multiple Personality Disorder/Dissociative Identity Disorder

Multiple personality disorder is among the most interesting of the major mental disorders due to its very unusual symptoms. Individuals take on different personalities—from as few as two or three to over 20. It has received considerable public attention through the popular books *Sybil* and *The Three Faces of Eve.* Multiple personality disorder is considered a dissociative disorder and is now called dissociative identity disorder by the American Psychiatric Association in the DSM-IV. *Dissociative disorders* are characterized by disruption in the "functions of consciousness, memory, identity or perception of the environment" (American Psychiatric Association 1994:477). Dissociative disorders can occur gradually or suddenly and can be chronic or can come and go. They are typically present when the person is subjected to overwhelming traumatic or abusive experiences. Extremely painful events are made less painful by withdrawing attention from them and focusing elsewhere. In dissociative identity disorder or multiple personality disorder events can be disowned by the victim to the point that the traumatic experiences are viewed as happening to someone else (Chu and Dill 1990). See Box 10.4 for the DSM-IV criteria for dissociative identity disorder.

    Glod's (1993) review of the literature found that of those with the diagnosis of multiple personality disorder, 60–90 percent had been victims of childhood

---

BOX **10.4**

DSM-IV Criteria for Dissociative Identity Disorder

A. The presence of two or more distinct identities or personality states (each with its own relatively enduring pattern or perceiving, relating to, and thinking about the environment and self).

B. At least two of these identities or personality states recurrently take control of the person's behavior.

C. Inability to recall important personal information that is too extensive to be explained by ordinary forgetfulness.

D. The disturbance is not due to the direct physiological effects of a substance (e.g., blackouts or chaotic behavior during alcohol intoxication) or a general medical condition (e.g., complex partial seizures).

Note: In children, the symptoms are not attributable to imaginary playmates or other fantasy play.

Source: Reprinted with permission from the *Diagnostic and Statistical Manual of Mental Disorders,* 4th ed. Copyright 1994 American Psychiatric Association. P. 487.

---

physical and/or sexual abuse. Putnam et al. (1986) found that out of 100 patients with multiple personality disorder, 97 percent were victims of child maltreatment. Chu and Dill (1990) studied 98 women during psychiatric hospitalizations. Sixty-three percent reported that they had endured childhood physical and/or sexual abuse. Chu and Dill found that childhood victims had a significantly higher level of dissociative symptoms in adulthood. Scores on the Dissociative Experiences Scale were higher when physical and sexual abuse was perpetrated by a family member than by a nonfamily member. Scores were highest in those women who endured both physical and sexual abuse in childhood. Chu and Dill emphasize that dissociative symptoms are underestimated and often overlooked in women who are in treatment. They recommend that treatment professionals consider posttraumatic stress and dissociative disorders as possible diagnoses. As noted above, the joint occurrence of multiple types of abuse may be more associated with some problems, rather than others. Dissociative identity disorder seems most likely when individuals experienced multiple forms of abuse.

Eating Disorders

Eating disorders, *bulimia nervosa* and *anorexia nervosa,* have emerged as a serious problem within the last 20 years. Although this area of research has commanded a fair amount of attention, the relationship between childhood maltreatment and eating disorders remains unclear (Sheerer 1997). Anorexia is characterized by the refusal to maintain a normal body weight, a persistent disturbance in views of body size and weight with a strong fear of gaining weight. Bulimia is characterized by recurrent uncontrolled episodes of binge eating with behaviors designed to prevent weight gain such as vomiting, misusing laxatives or enemas, or excessive exercise (American Psychiatric Association 1994).

In her review of the long-term consequences of childhood physical and sexual abuse, Glod noted that research "has shown a 7 percent to 50 percent association between childhood sexual abuse and the development of eating disorders" (1993:165). Glod reviewed the work of Root and Fallon (1988), who found that of 172 women who had bulimia, 28 percent reported sexual abuse as children or adults. Briere and Runtz (1987) reported that bulimia, but not anorexia, is associated with childhood sexual abuse.

Some researchers feel that methodological problems with these studies have led to results that are questionable (Connors and Morse 1993). The rates of sexual abuse for those with eating disorders reported above are not substantially higher than the rates noted in earlier chapters for the general population. Sheerer's (1997) review of the literature led her to conclude that the relationship between eating disorders and childhood maltreatment is "uncertain." In general, Sheerer concluded that anorexia does not appear to be associated with childhood maltreatment, while bulimia may be more related to childhood sexual abuse rather than physical abuse. Almost no research attention has been given to the relationship between emotional abuse and eating disorders. Glod's discussion of eating disorders concluded: "The role that childhood abuse plays in the pathogenesis of eating or other disorders remains controversial and unresolved" (1993:168). Further research on this subject is needed.

Substance Abuse Problems

Substance abuse is linked to family abuse on the part of the perpetrator and on the part of the victim, although the relationship is not a clear one and may be even more complex than researchers initially suggested (Brown and Anderson 1991; Ireland and Widom 1994; Kroll, Stock, and James 1985). There is general agreement that although family abuse and substance abuse are often correlated, it is inappropriate to assume that one is the cause of the other. It is the case, however, that adult substance abusers tend to report more physical abuse than the general population, with estimates between 13 and 35 percent (Malinosky-Rummell and Hansen 1993).

A discussion of the relationship between substance abuse problems and history of family abuse is complicated by their mutual association with mental illness. A person with substance abuse problems and mental illness is said to have a dual diagnosis. A thorough history taken on a client may shed some light on which occurred first. However, for clients with very long histories of substance abuse problems and mental illness it can be very difficult to determine which came first. It is even more difficult when the substance abuse and mental illness occur simultaneously with family abuse.

The intertwining of family abuse, depression, and substance abuse is a good example of how difficult it can be to understand the causes of these problems. A study by the National Institute of Mental Health found that 37 percent of alcoholics had co-existing mental disorders (Regier et al. 1994). The relationship of depression to substance abuse is very hard to sort out and presents difficult issues in diagnosis (Gallant 1994) although depression is common among alcoholics (Zimberg 1994). Most clinicians acknowledge that depression is both the cause and the effect of substance abuse (Van Wormer 1995). It can be very difficult to know whether alcohol causes the depression or if drinking is the individual's effort to self-medicate the depression (Gallant 1994). Either or both of these may result from family abuse or may act as precipitating factors in the occurrence of abusive episodes.

Some mental health professionals such as psychiatrists tend to see depression as an underlying cause of alcoholism (Van Wormer 1995). A review of research shows that 30 to 50 percent of alcoholics meet the diagnostic criteria for major depression according to the *Diagnostic and Statistical Manual of Mental Disorders* (1994). Since both depression and alcoholism may have predisposing genetic factors, there is much to be clarified regarding the underlying causes.

While some clients may be diagnosed as having both mental health and substance abuse problems, many clients are given a primary diagnosis according to the type of facility that is treating the client. In other words, psychiatric facilities are far more likely to give a primary diagnosis of mental disorder, while substance abuse facilities give a diagnosis of alcohol or drug addiction. These differing views are reflected in the research that gives greater credence to one problem over the other. In general, most studies of psychological consequences of childhood maltreatment focus more on psychiatric populations who may also have substance abuse problems (Glod 1993).

A number of explanations have been offered as to why substance abuse may be related to childhood maltreatment. In adults, it is possible substance abuse can be an attempt to ease painful memories of a history of maltreatment (Green 1993). Ireland and Widom (1994) offer other explanations gleaned from their review of the literature. For those children or adolescents who are still being maltreated, substance abuse may ease the physical and emotional pain. It can provide a respite from the abusive situation. Substance abuse can initially enhance self-esteem and may be an effort to self-medicate depression or other problems. Substance abuse can serve to reduce loneliness and isolation by giving the person access to a group of others who are substance abusers. Substance abuse can also be self-destructive behavior in the person with a poor self-image and feelings of worthlessness associated with the maltreatment.

In a study of 802 men and women in alcohol inpatient treatment programs, the overall prevalence for childhood maltreatment was 59 percent for women and 30 percent for men (Windle et al. 1995). Almost half the women had a history of childhood sexual abuse and almost half of this group also reported severe physical abuse. While women and men did not differ significantly in terms of rates of physical abuse, women were much more likely to be sexually abused (49 percent vs. 12 percent). A family history of alcoholism was associated with greater rates of sexual and physical abuse. Windle et al. found that "childhood abuse predicted coexisting major depression among male (but not female alcoholics), and generalized anxiety among female (but not male) alcoholics" (1995:1326).

Brown and Anderson (1991) found patients with a physical abuse history had a higher rate of alcohol problems than those who had not been physically abused (50 percent vs. 32 percent). They also had a higher rate of illegal substance use than the nonphysically abused (38 percent versus 24 percent). Interestingly, this relationship was not found for sexually abused respondents.

In a sample of alcoholic men who were physically abused as children, Kroll et al. (1985) found that the perpetrator was typically the biological father (90 percent), also an alcoholic (83 percent). The alcoholic men with a history of abuse were significantly more likely to have legal problems, to engage in violence, to have higher rates of anxiety and more serious suicide attempts.

In their study of 50 men and 50 women in a psychiatric hospital, Jacobson and Richardson (1987) found that 51 percent reported alcohol or drugs were used by the perpetrator, the victim, or both. Carmen, Rieker, and Mills (1984), in a study of males and females in psychiatric hospitals, found that in comparing abused patients with nonabused patients, diagnosis did not distinguish between the two groups. However, an important distinguishing characteristic was the high rate of alcoholism on the part of the parents of the abused group. Among the abused group, 30 percent had alcoholic fathers and 13 percent had alcoholic mothers. This compares with 13 percent of the nonabused group with alcoholic fathers and 5 percent of the nonabused group with alcoholic mothers.

Ireland and Widom (1994) found that childhood maltreatment was a significant predictor of adult substance-related offenses. Interestingly, in contrast to other research, the relationship did not hold true for juvenile offenders. Ireland and Widom offer a number of possible explanations for this—including differences in sample, such as whether the youths are institutionalized or not, and the reliance on official arrest data rather than self-reports. Ireland and Widom caution that the role of delinquent behavior must be addressed when examining later substance abuse. They conclude: "Abused and/or neglected youth are at greater risk than controls for adult arrests for alcohol and/or drug offenses, in part because they are at greater risk for an arrest as a juvenile" (1994:252).

In a sample of 77 clients in inpatient and outpatient substance abuse treatment facilities, 47 percent reported a history of incest (Janikowski and Glover 1994). Thirty-six percent reported that they had used alcohol or drugs during the sexual abuse and 53 percent reported that the incest perpetrator was using alcohol or drugs at the time. Janikowski and Glover offer the explanation: "The depression of normal social and sexual inhibitions people experience while under the influence of alcohol and some drugs may account for this finding" (1994:181). Thirty percent said they believed there was a causal relationship between their incest experiences and their later development of a substance abuse problem. While one-third indicated that their substance abuse counselors were aware of their history of incest, only 8 percent said they received counseling around their incest experiences.

In their later work, Glover, Janikowski, and Benshoff (1996) surveyed 732 clients in 35 substance abuse treatment programs. Overall, 36 percent of the respondents reported a history of incest, 55 percent of females and 29 percent of males.

It is clearly an important issue in substance abuse treatment if family abuse has occurred. Janikowski and Glover's recommendation that substance abuse professionals screen clients for a history of sexual trauma could be extended to screening clients for a history of any type of child maltreatment or adult abuse. Those in recovery from substance abuse whose issues of childhood maltreatment remain untreated have a greater potential for relapse (Janikowski and Glover 1994).

Suicide

A discussion of suicide and its causes is complicated by the fact that it is often associated with childhood maltreatment, depression, and/or substance abuse. It is known that alcoholics and other substance abusers are at high risk for suicide (Van Wormer 1995). Once again we see it can be hard to disentangle the causes or consequences of deviant behavior.

Fergusson and Mullen (1999) reviewed 12 studies published since 1990 on the long-term impact of childhood sexual abuse. Six of the studies found that childhood sexual abuse is associated with increased risk of suicide (Bagley, Wood, and Young 1994; Beautrais, Joyce, and Mulder 1994; Fergusson, Horwood, and Lynskey 1996; Gould et al. 1994; Mullen et al. 1993; and Silverman, Reinherz, and Giaconia 1996). In a study of 85 individuals who made serious suicide attempts, childhood sexual abuse was reported by 35.3 percent of respondents as compared with 4.4 percent of the nonabused control group (Beautrais et al. 1994).

Bryer et al. (1987) found more suicidal symptoms in a sexually abused group of women in a psychiatric hospital. Windle et al. (1995) found that among those receiving inpatient substance abuse treatment, physical abuse for men and physical and sexual abuse for women predicted higher lifetime suicide attempts. Those who were both physically and sexually abused were five times more likely to make a suicide attempt.

Brown and Anderson (1991) found that patients who were suicidal upon psychiatric hospitalization had significantly higher rates of childhood physical or sexual abuse. Suicidal thoughts or a recent suicidal gesture or attempt was present in 79 percent of patients who suffered both physical and sexual abuse. Of the men with sexual abuse histories, 88 percent were considered suicidal upon admission as compared with 57 percent of men who had not been sexually abused.

Prostitution

While little attention, in general, is paid to prostitution as a social problem, the debate exists whether prostitution really is a victimless crime and whether legalization of prostitution is desirable (Lentz and Stitt 1996). Little has been written on the relationship between childhood maltreatment and prostitution. The research that does exist focuses on whether prostitutes were sexually abused as children. While male prostitution exists, prostitution is still seen as a women's issue. The fact that official statistics report that prostitution is engaged in more often by women than men probably accounts for why little professional attention has been given to this social problem. However, there is not as big a difference in arrest rates for males and females for prostitution as one might think. The FBI Uniform Crime Reports show that in 1997 arrests for prostitution were 60 percent female and 40 percent male. Chesney-Lind and Shelden (1998) note in their review of the work of Cernkovich and Giordano (1979) that in a study of youths, boys were more likely to engage in prostitution than girls (5.3 percent of boys and 1.1 percent of girls).

Regarding prostitution among girls, figures vary widely (Chesney-Lind and Shelden 1998) making it difficult to determine the extent of youth prostitution. The FBI Uniform Crime Reports for 1997 show that 145 male and female arrestees (0.2 percent of all prostitution arrests) were under the age of 15 while 992 of the arrestees (1.4 percent) were under the age of 18. Among girls, Boyer and James (1982) state that 40–75 percent of teenage prostitutes have been victims of sexual and/or physical abuse.

International prostitution appears to be a burgeoning problem, especially in Asian countries. See Chesney-Lind and Shelden (1998) for an excellent discussion of international prostitution. For an example of young girls sold into prostitution, see Box 10.5.

In general, and not surprisingly, prostitutes have had more negative life experiences than women who are not prostitutes (James and Meyerding 1977; Silbert and Pines 1981). A woman's decision to prostitute does have some basis in

---

B O X **10.5**

Colombian Girls Kidnapped and Sold into Prostitution

In Bogotá, Colombia, at least 7 girls were abducted in a working class neighborhood during the span of 1 year. The girls ranged in age from 11 through 15. They were very likely to have been kidnapped and brought to Japan to become prostitutes. They had no passports or official papers to help in their return home.

CNN talked with several girls who had been able to escape the kidnap attempt. Their stories were very similar: A man drove by one day and photographed them. Several days later another man tried to abduct them.

Mothers of the missing girls are trying to find them, feeling that they get little help from the government. One mother said: "Our daughters are from poor but honorable families. Why when a rich person's child is kidnapped they're found? Because they have money and status and we don't."

Source: Cable News Network, CNN. "Colombian Girls Kidnapped, Believed Sold into Prostitution." April 1, 1996. (WWW http://www.cnn.com/).

her past experiences and her perceptions of her own sexuality (James and Meyerding 1977).

James and Meyerding (1977) conducted 2 studies in the early and mid-1970s
in which prostitutes self-reported on their backgrounds and experiences. A total of
228 women participated in their study. In comparing their results with other
research on adolescents and women who were not prostitutes, women who *became*
prostitutes had experienced sexual intercourse at an earlier age than others. In the
first study, four-fifths of adolescent prostitutes had sexual intercourse at or before
the age of 14. In the second study, 7 percent of the women had sexual intercourse
at age 12 or younger, 57 percent reported their first intercourse between the ages
of 15 and 19, with 92 percent of the prostitutes having had intercourse by age 18.
Twenty-three percent of the women said there was physical force used during their
first sexual intercourse experience and 7 percent said they felt emotionally coerced
into their first intercourse. In study two, 57 percent of the women reported having
been raped at least once. Thirty-six percent of this group had been raped more than
once while 7.5 percent had been raped multiple times.

James and Meyerding addressed the issue of childhood sexual abuse in this
sample by asking respondents: "Prior to your first intercourse, did any older person
(defined as more than ten years older) attempt sexual play or intercourse with
you?" (1977:1383). The answer was yes for 46 percent of the women in study two.
For the women who endured sexual abuse at the hands of their fathers or "father
figures," 37 percent answered yes.

In focusing exclusively on adolescent prostitutes in study 1, James and
Meyerding found that 13 of the 20 (65 percent) adolescent prostitutes reported a
"force/bad sexual experience" (1977:1383). Eleven of the 13 (85 percent) adolescents stated that they were 15 years old or younger at the time of the sexual abuse.
Fathers were responsible for 23 percent of the cases of sexual abuse while other
relatives perpetrated 15 percent of the sexual abuse.

More recent work underscores the fact that childhood maltreatment and
prostitution are associated. In a sample of 50 female street prostitutes (Norton-
Hawk 2001), 56 percent reported they were severely verbally abused as children.
Forty-six percent reported physical abuse, and 42 percent reported sexual abuse
before reaching the age of seventeen.

The work of James and Meyerding (1977) sheds some light on how and why
women become prostitutes. Because it is a common pattern for prostitutes to have
suffered some form of childhood maltreatment, they may find at an early age that
there can be rewards for the victim in giving sexual gratification to the abuser.
Rewards can include the victim appreciating the interest shown from an adult,
along with some form of affection, however inappropriate. "This type of positive
reinforcement for sexual behavior, particularly when coupled with the cultural
stereotype of women as primarily sexual beings, may cause some women to
perceive their sexuality as their primary means for gaining status" (1977:1384).
Chesney-Lind and Shelden (1998) offer another explanation by pointing out that
entry into prostitution may be a survival tactic on the part of young girls who may
not have other options. Citing Campagna and Poffenberger (1988), Chesney-Lind

and Shelden (1998) state a girl may be seduced, tricked, coerced, or blackmailed by a pimp. Of course, a girl coming from a disorganized family where maltreatment is the norm may have little self-esteem and, therefore, think she deserves to be a prostitute or has little alternative to being a prostitute.

Prostitutes were more likely to learn about sexual intercourse from friends or from personal experiences than from their parents. In agreeing with previous literature, James and Meyerding state:

> This lack of parental guidance in sexual matters is one aspect of the general weakness of the parent–child relationship that is typical of many prostitutes. Whether the parent–child relationship is marked by simple neglect by absence or by outright psychological or physical abuse, the result for the child is generally considered to be alienation from the parents and a consequent inability—the severity of which depends on the circumstances—to adequately socialize the conventional mores of "respectable" society. (1977:1382)

Silbert and Pines (1981) studied 200 juvenile and adult street prostitutes. The authors make the point that in contrast to other research on prostitutes, these girls and women were not referred by social service agencies and were not receiving services at the time they were interviewed. The average age was 22, with the oldest, age 46, and the youngest, age 10. Sixty percent of the sample was under age 16. Silbert and Pines found that 60 percent of the respondents had been sexually abused before the age of 16. Ten was the average age of the first sexual victimization. Sixty-seven percent were abused by a father figure: either the biological father (33 percent), stepfather or foster father (30 percent), or mother's common law husband (4 percent). For this sample, 16 was the average age at which girls started prostituting. Seventy-eight percent were under age 18 and 62 percent were under 16. Silbert and Pines note that several were under 10 years old.

Feelings of powerlessness were overwhelming: 91 percent said they felt there was nothing they could do about the abuse. Importantly, 70 percent stated that the sexual abuse they endured did have bearing on the decision to become a prostitute. One woman in the study said, "My brother could do it. Why not everybody else? Might as well make them pay for it." Another respondent had this to say, "My father bought me, so who cares who else does?" (Silbert and Pines 1981:410). Another factor, already discussed, is the lack of options for young girls as the reason for turning to prostitution. Ninety-six percent of the juveniles in the sample were runaways. In response to the question of why they started prostituting, 89 percent responded that they were hungry and needed money.

Most clients do not report childhood sexual abuse on their own and therapists may not ask about abuse (Beck and van der Kolk 1987; Briere and Runtz 1987; Bryer et al. 1987). Kroll et al. (1985) found in their study of alcoholic men who were survivors of childhood maltreatment that information on past abuse had to be specifically solicited by therapists. Swett et al. (1990) found that among patients who acknowledged abuse as part of their response to a questionnaire, 50 percent had discussed the abuse with their therapist. This, of course, means that half had not discussed their childhood maltreatment. Carmen et al. (1984) point out that victims of abuse may not reveal abuse in therapy because of their lack of trust in others and because it can be especially difficult for abuse victims to form a relationship with a therapist. Jacobson and Richardson (1987) stress the importance of obtaining a history of abuse from clients early in their therapy to avoid possible pitfalls such as incorrectly assuming that a client who is apprehensive or distrustful cannot establish a therapeutic relationship.

Sex Offenders

The chapters on physical and sexual abuse, as well as material in this chapter, note that sex offenders tend to have a history of abuse as a child. Although sexual abuse is frequently mentioned, physical and emotional abuse appear common as well. However, the same term of *sex offender* applied to many different types of perpetrators obscures the fact that there are many influences on sex offenders and many different ways in which they express their sexual abuse of others. Pedophiles, adult serial rapists, and exhibitionists are not all the same.

One action taken to deal with sex offenders in the community is to create a computerized list of offenders that is publicized in communities where the offenders live. Box 10.6 discusses controversies in sex offender registration.

Many states have also required sex offenders to have long-term probation, so that their living circumstances and life activities can be monitored for evidence that the offender is involved in situations that may pose a risk for potential victims. Courts have yet to provide a definitive ruling whether a "life sentence" of probation is constitutionally permitted as appropriate to the severity of the offense.

Recidivism of Sex Offenders

There has been much public discussion of whether sex offenders can ever be "cured" or made to stop abusing others. Some politicians, activists, and criminal justice officials have said that all sex offenders recidivate, that their behavior cannot change. Proponents of this view have many anecdotal stories of individuals who went through some treatment program or who served his or her time and then went out and sexually abused others again. This view has led many states to adopt "sexual predator laws," in which special penalties are applied for repeated sex crime offenses and which require long-term listing in a sex offender registry or even life imprisonment.

What are the facts? What is meant by recidivism of abuse? How often do sex offenders relapse? The use of the term *recidivism* is varied. It can mean repeating abusive behavior in any form toward anyone at any time in the future. This usage, however, is useless for policy or programmatic intervention because it says nothing about the severity, nature, or context of the repeated behavior and is open to highly subjective interpretation. It is more common to limit recidivism to a subsequent report of a offense for which a perpetrator has previously been reported, investigated, indicated, or convicted.

B O X **10.6**

Megan's Law: Sex Offender Registration

In every state offenders who commit any of a list of specified sex offenses are required to notify the local law enforcement agency of the community in which they reside upon their release from prison or jail. The law requires offenders to be classified into levels of risk—usually low, moderate, and high. Different actions result from an offender's risk classification. Low-risk offenders may be monitored by the law enforcement agency, but their identities may not be given out or publicized to the community. The presence of moderate to high-risk offenders may be publicized by the law enforcement agency, but strategies vary between communities. In some towns, names, addresses, and pictures are posted on an Internet web page or at police headquarters. In other locations, handbills and posters may be distributed. In some places, officers may go from door to door in the neighborhood of the offender warning residents to beware of this individual.

Sex offender registration has been found constitutional for those committing offenses after passage of the statute. Courts continue to disagree as to whether offenses prior to such law's passage can require registration and public notification. Some courts have held that it raises questions of an ex post facto punishment that was not legal when the offense was originally committed. The longer states have had these statutes, however, the more irrelevant that issue will become.

The biggest issue regarding these statutes has been the conflict between threats to public safety posed by the offenders versus threats posed by vigilante groups who threaten or assault the offenders who are trying to live peaceably. In some cases, local residents have noticed registered offenders hanging out near schools or playgrounds because of public notice about the offenders. In other cases, offenders have been assaulted, near riots have occurred, and homes have been burned down by community residents when they received notice of the offenders in their neighborhoods.

How much notification for which offenses will continue to be debated. The appropriate means for notifying the public without inciting public disturbances continues to be discussed. Except for those designated "habitual sexual offenders," these statutes usually allow removing a name from being required to register after a period of time of no further arrests; but they don't remove it from the memory of the community in which they reside. For "habitual offenders" the registration requirement is for the rest of their lives.

Sources: Office of the New York State Attorney General. 1999. "Megan's Law." (WWW http://www. oag.state.ny.us/consumer/tips/megans_law.html). Oklahoma Department of Corrections. 1999. "Sex Offender Registration." (WWW http://www.doc.state.ok.us/offtech/op020307.htm).

While this usage leaves out unreported, hidden behavior, such behavior isn't amenable to intervention because it isn't known who is doing what to whom, where, or when. Recidivism is difficult to research (Doren 1998; Furby, Weinrott, and Blackshaw 1989). Studies produce widely varied estimates of the recidivism rates. Anywhere from 40 to 80 percent of offenders will commit another sex offense within 5 years of release from prison (Doren 1998). Among juveniles who commit sex offenses, between 40 and 60 percent are subsequently arrested as adults for a sex crime (Furby, Weinrott, and Blackshaw 1989). This means that about half of sex offenders are not known to recidivate upon release. These estimates are not substantially higher than those for other violent career criminals. Indeed, if even an average of 60 percent of offenders recidivate after release, then by the time they've been incarcerated three times, only about 20 percent of the original group is still actively offending.

No credible study has found that *every* offender recidivates (Doren 1998; Furby, Weinrott, and Blackshaw 1989; Marquis, Day, and Nelson 1994). As noted above, estimates of the extent of recidivism vary widely. However, this range in recidivism rates may be more a result of variation in risk factors in different populations than a result of differences in research designs (Witt, DelRusso, and Ferguson 1996). Serial rapists, for example, generally have higher recidivism rates than those arrested for "lewd and lascivious behavior." Factors that predict recidivism have been identified (Marquis et al. 1994; Witt et al. 1996), which may lead to intervention strategies that reduce recidivism. These factors are discussed in the next chapter on treatment.

Family Implications

Recidivism of those who commit sexual abuse is of particular concern to family members. First, some family members may side with the abuser, denying the actions or blaming the victim. Second, it is extremely difficult to repair broken family ties when some members have been labeled "sex offenders." Nor is it clear that ties with the offender should always be repaired. Family bonds of trust and support may be irreparably broken. When offenders assault former victims, those victims are most likely to be family members. The offenders may find it easier to locate family victims from other family members, neighbors, or former friends than to track down acquaintances who may have moved away. Even if the offender doesn't recidivate, family victims may continue to live in fear of repeated sexual assault.

Sex offenders also pose a medical risk for family members. Perpetrators tend to have multiple partners in consensual sex and multiple victims. They may also abuse drugs. If incarcerated, they are at high risk of exposure to the human immunodeficiency virus (HIV) ("Prisoner's with AIDS" 1999).

Prison Inmates

Prison inmates report higher levels of family abuse than the general population and a higher prevalence of mental health problems. The previous discussion of serial killers in Chapter 2 also notes that for mass murderers who are imprisoned, they report very high levels of abuse, violence, and degradation that occurred to them.

In their study of male jail and prison inmates, Fondacaro et al. (1999) found that 40 percent (86) of inmates in the sample met standard criteria for childhood sexual abuse. However, 41 percent of these 86 men (35) did *not* define themselves as having been sexually abused. Those inmates who considered themselves as sexually abused in childhood reported higher rates of posttraumatic stress and obsessive-compulsive disorders. The inmates who did not consider themselves as sexually abused, despite having met the criteria on a questionnaire, had higher rates of substance abuse. Fondacaro et al. (1999) speculate that those who were abused, yet do not consider themselves abused, may be in denial or emotionally disengaged and may be more likely to abuse alcohol. Those who consider themselves as having been abused are more aware of the abuse and its impact and may experience greater anxiety disorders.

Reports of child abuse of prison inmates must be evaluated carefully. They could be lying to gain sympathy or manipulate others. However, the few studies that have checked actual child abuse report records or have interviewed neighbors or family members of those alleging abuse have found that the majority of such reports are independently confirmed. Most of the reports of child abuse by prisoners are true. Nevertheless, as part of a larger study of substance-abusing female offenders, Hardy-Fanta and Mignon (2000) found in interviews with incarcerated substance abusers that 12 of 16 reported they were sexually abused as children. This information was not part of the interview protocol and therefore the women offered this information on their own. It is very likely that even more of this small sample were abused yet it was not revealed in the interview process.

Family abuse aggravates the abuse of prisoners—whether physically, sexually, or emotionally. As noted, prisons contain both former victims as well as abuse perpetrators. Prisons and jails have traditionally tolerated abuse of inmates by other inmates, so the victims may continue to be abused by other prisoners, and the offenders may find new victims among weaker inmates. Whether abuser or victim, abuse may continue in a context of coercion and exploitation ("Abuse of Prisoners" 1999). Continued experience with abuse in such facilities may well reinforce prior patterns of abuse and potential deviant consequences.

The experiences that prisoners have behind bars tend to aggravate subsequent family abuse. It reinforces the use of power and coercion for controlling interaction and obtaining compliance. It may reinforce the deviant identity of the perpetrator and the victim. Abused children who are removed from home while their cases are being investigated or their parent-offenders are incarcerated are also at high risk for re-victimization in foster care ("Abused Again" 1996).

Controversies exist as to what treatment programs should be used for prisoners to reduce the negative consequences of imprisonment and whether treatment should be provided at all. Those who see abusers as incorrigible certainly see little need for treatment. However, a mental health assessment of those who are incarcerated should include a trauma assessment (Fondacaro et al. 1999). The issue of treatment is discussed in the next chapter.

Summary

This chapter reviews special problems associated with family abuse. It reviews the relationship between family abuse and mental illness, substance abuse, and suicide. The presence of depression, personality disorders, and eating disorders poses particular mental health complications in their relationship with family abuse.

Substance abuse can be both a result of abuse as well as an aggravating factor. The risk of suicide is significantly increased when abuse is combined with mental illness or substance abuse.

The chapter documents a strong relationship between child maltreatment and prostitution. It discusses the experience of victimization and perpetration of childhood maltreatment among prison inmates and sex offenders who are in the criminal justice system. It notes how victim and perpetrator involvement in the criminal justice system often creates circumstances that complicate the abuse as well as its consequences.

The association of family abuse with these special problems often depends on the presence of additional factors that are likely to reinforce the effects of abuse. Many times it is difficult to say whether the family abuse produced the other deviant behavior or whether the abuse is itself influenced by the complicating factors. It is clear, however, that there is a significant association among these factors and that interventions designed to deal with any one of these problems must consider the likelihood that the other problems will also be present. Implications of these issues for treatment programs are discussed in the next chapter.

Study Questions

1. What are some of the mental health problems associated with childhood maltreatment?

2. Discuss the gender differences in adults who have been maltreated as children. Are men or women more affected by childhood maltreatment?

3. In what ways are child maltreatment and substance abuse related?

4. What is the relationship of prostitution to childhood maltreatment?

5. To what extent do you think persons in sex offender registries should be publically identified in their local communities? In what ways could this create potential problems of public safety?

6. In what ways does the prison experience encourage abusive behavior by offenders?

REFERENCES

"Abuse of Prisoners." 1999. *The CQ Researcher.* 9:368–76.

"Abused Again: Competing Constitutional Standards for the State's Duty to Protect Foster Children." *Columbia Journal of Law and Social Problems.* 29:385–401.

American Psychiatric Association. 1994. *Diagnostic and Statistical Manual of Mental Disorders,* 4th ed. Washington, DC: Author.

Bagley, C., M. Wood, and L. Young. 1994. "Victim to Abuser: Mental Health and Behavioral Sequels of Child Sexual Abuse in a Community Survey of Young Adult Males." *Child Abuse and Neglect.* 18:683–97.

Beautris, A., P. R. Joyce, and R. T. Mulder. 1994. "Child Sexual Abuse and Risks of Suicidal Behavior." Pp. 141–48 in *Development, Personality, and Psychopathology,* P. R. Joyce, R. T. Mulder, A. Oakley-Browne, J. D. Sellman, and W. G. A. Watkins, eds. Christchurch, NZ: Christchurch School of Medicine.

Beck, James C. and Bessel van der Kolk. 1987. "Reports of Childhood Incest and Current Behavior of Chronically Hospitalized Psychotic Women." *American Journal of Psychiatry.* 144:1474–76.

Becker, J. V., M. S. Kaplan, C. E. Tencke, and A. Tartaglini. 1991. "The Incidence of Depressive Symptomology in Juvenile Sex Offenders with a History of Abuse." *Child Abuse and Neglect.* 15:531–36.

Bifulco, A., G. W. Brown, and Z. Adler. 1991. "Early Sexual Abuse and Clinical Depression in Adult Life." *British Journal of Psychiatry.* 159:115–22.

Boyer, Debra and Jennifer James. 1982. "Easy Money: Adolescent Involvement in Prostitution. In *Justice for Young Women,* S. Davidson, ed. Seattle: New Directions for Young Women.

Briere, John, Diane Evans, Marsha Runtz, and Timothy Wall. 1988. "Symptomatology in Men Who Were Molested as Children: A Comparison Study." *American Journal of Orthopsychiatry.* 58:457–61.

Briere, John and Marsha Runtz. 1987. "Post-Sexual Abuse Trauma: Data and Implications for Clinical Practice." *Journal of Interpersonal Violence.* 2:367–79.

Brown, George R. and Bradley Anderson. 1991. "Psychiatric Morbidity in Adult Inpatients with Childhood Histories of Sexual and Physical Abuse." *American Journal of Psychiatry.* 148:55–61.

Brown, George W. and Patricia Moran. 1994. "Clinical and Psychosocial Origins of Chronic Depressive Episodes I: A Community Survey." *British Journal of Psychiatry.* 165:447–56.

Bryer, Jeffrey B., Bernadette A. Nelson, Jean Baker Miller, and Pamela A. Krol. 1987. "Childhood Sexual and Physical Abuse as Factors in Adult Psychiatric Illness." *American Journal of Psychiatry.* 144:1426–30.

Cable News Network, CNN. 1996. "Colombian Girls Kidnaped, Believed Sold into Prostitution." April 1, 1996. (WWW http://www.cnn.com/).

Campagna, D. S. and D. L. Poffenberger. 1988. *The Sexual Trafficking in Children.* Dover, MA: Auburn House.

Carmen, Elaine Hilberman, Patricia Perri Rieker, and Trudy Mills. 1984. "Victims of Violence and Psychiatric Illness." *American Journal of Psychiatry.* 141:378–83.

Cernkovich, S. and P. Giordano. 1979. "A Comparative Analysis of Male and Female Delinquency." *Sociological Quarterly.* 20:131–45.

Chesney-Lind, Meda and Randall G. Shelden. 1998. *Girls, Delinquency and Juvenile Justice,* 2nd ed. Belmont, CA: West/Wadsworth.

Chu, James A. and Diana L. Dill. 1990. "Dissociative Symptoms in Relation to Childhood Physical and Sexual Abuse." *American Journal of Psychiatry.* 147:887–91.

Connors, M. E. and W. Morse 1993. "Sexual Abuse and Eating Disorders: A Review." *International Journal of Eating Disorders.* 13:1–11.

Doren, Denis M. 1998. "Recidivism Base Rates: Prediction of Sex Offender Recidivism, and the 'Sexual Predator' Commitment Laws." *Behavioral Sciences & the Law.* 16:97–106.

Farber, E. D. and J. A. Joseph. 1985. "The Maltreated Adolescent: Patterns of Physicial Abuse." *Child Abuse and Neglect.* 9:201–06.

Federal Bureau of Investigation. 1997. *Uniform Crime Reports.* Washington, DC: U.S. Department of Justice.

Fergusson, D. M., L. J. Horwood, and M. T. Lynskey. 1996. "Childhood Sexual Abuse and Psychiatric Disorders in Young Adulthood. Part II. Psychiatric Outcomes of Sexual Abuse." *Journal of the American Academy of Child and Adolescent Psychiatry.* 35:1365–74.

Fergusson, D. N. and P. E. Mullen. 1999. "Childhood Sexual Abuse: An Evidence Based Perspective," 40.

Finkelhor, David. 1986. *A Sourcebook on Child Sexual Abuse: New Theory and Research.* Beverly Hills, CA: Sage Publications.

Fondacaro, Karen M., John C. Holt, and Thomas A Powell. 1999. "Psychological Impact of Childhood Sexual Abuse on Male Inmates: The Importance of Perception." *Child Abuse and Neglect.* 23:361–69.

Furby, Lita, Mark R. Weinrott, and Lyn Blackshaw. 1989. "Sex Offender Recidivism: a Review." *Psychological Bulletin.* 105:3–18.

Gallant, Don. 1994. "Treatment of Patients for Specific Drugs of Abuse: Alcohol." Pp. 67–89 in *Textbook of Substance Abuse Treatment,* Marc Galanter and Herbert D. Kleber, eds. Washington, DC: American Psychiatric Press, Inc.

Glod, Carol A. 1993. "Long-Term Consequences of Childhood Physical and Sexual Abuse." *Archives of Psychiatric Nursing.* VII:163–73.

Glover, Noreen M., Timothy P. Janikowski, and J. J. Benshoff. 1996. "Substance Abuse and Past Incest Contact: A National Perspective." *Journal of Substance Abuse Treatment.* 13:185–93.

Gould, D. A., N. G. Stevens, N. G. Ward, A. S. Carlin, H. E. Sowell, and B. Gustafson. 1994. "Self-Reported Childhood Abuse in an Adult Population in a Primary Care Setting. Prevalence, Correlates and Associated Suicide Attempts." *Archives of Family Medicine.* 3:252–56.

Green, Arthur H. 1993. "Child Sexual Abuse: Immediate and Long-Term Effects and Intervention." *Journal of the American Academy of Child and Adolescent Psychiatry.* 32:890–902.

Hardy-Fanta, Carol and Sylvia Mignon. 2000. *Alternatives to Incarceration for Substance Abusing Female Offenders in Massachusetts.* Boston, MA: University of Massachusetts.

Herman, Judith Lewis, J. Christopher Perry, and Bessel A. van der Kolk. 1989. "Childhood Trauma in Borderline Personality Disorder." *American Journal of Psychiatry.* 146:490–95.

Husain, Arshad and James L. Chapel. 1983. "History of Incest in Girls Admitted to a Psychiatric Hospital." *American Journal of Psychiatry.* 140:591–93.

Ireland, Timothy and Cathy Spatz Widom. 1994. "Childhood Victimization and Risk for Alcohol and Drug Arrests." *The International Journal of the Addictions.* 29:235–74.

Jacobson, Andrea and Bonnie Richardson. 1987. "Assault Experiences of 100 Psychiatric Inpatients: Evidence of the Need for Routine Inquiry." *American Journal of Psychiatry.* 144:908–13.

James, Jennifer and Jane Meyerding. 1977. "Early Sexual Experience and Prostitution." *American Journal of Psychiatry.* 134:1381–85.

Janikowski, Timothy P. and Noreen M. Glover. 1994. "Incest and Substance Abuse: Implications for Treatment Professionals." *Journal of Substance Abuse Treatment.* 11:177–83.

Kroll, Philip D., Dorothy F. Stock, and Mary E. James. 1985. "The Behavior of Adult Alcoholic Men Abused as Children." *The Journal of Nervous and Mental Disease.* 173:689–93.

Lamb, Sharon. 1999. "Some Victims Don't Need Pity." *The Boston Globe,* August 1:E1, E2.

Lentz, Susan A. and B. Grant Stitt. 1996. "Women as Victims in 'Victimless Crimes': The Case of Prostitution." *Journal of Contemporary Criminal Justice.* 12:173–86.

Lizardi, Humberto, Daniel N. Klein, Paige Crosby Ouimette, Lawrence P. Riso, Rochelle L. Anderson, and Shauna K. Donaldson. 1995. "Reports of the Childhood Home Environment in Early-Onset Dysthymia and Episodic Depression." *Journal of Abnormal Psychology.* 104:132–39.

Luntz, Barbara K. and Cathy Spatz Widom. 1994. "Antisocial Personality Disorder in Abused and Neglected Children Grown Up." *American Journal of Psychiatry.* 151:670–74.

Malinosky-Rummell, Robin and David J. Hansen. 1993. "Long-Term Consequences of Childhood Physical Abuse." *Psychological Bulletin.* 114:68–79.

Marquis, Janice K., David M. Day, and Craig Nelson. 1994. "Effects of Cognitive-Behavioral Treatment on Sex Offender Recidivism: Preliminary Results of a Longitudinal Study." *Criminal Justice and Behavior.* 21:28–42.

Mullen, P. E., J. L. Martin, J. C. Anderson, S. E. Romans, and G. P. Herbison. 1993. "Childhood Sexual Abuse and Mental Health in Adult Life." *British Journal of Psychiatry.* 163:721–32.

Neugebauer, Richard, Hans Wijbrand Hoek, and Ezra Susser. 1999. "Prenatal Exposure to Wartime Famine and Development of Antisocial Personality Disorder in Early Adulthood." *JAMA: The Journal of the American Medical Association.* 282, August 4:455–62.

Norton-Hawk, Maureen. 2001. "The Counter-Productivity of Incarcerating Female Street Prostitutes." *Deviant Behavior,* forthcoming.

Office of the New York State Attorney General. 1999. "Megan's Law." (WWW http://www.oag. state.ny.us/consumer/tips/megans_law.html).

Oklahoma Department of Correction. 1999. "Sex Offender Registration." (WWW http://www. doc.state.ok.us/offtech/op020307.htm).

Palmer, R. L., L. Coleman, D. Chaloner, R. Oppenheimer, and J. Smith. 1993. "Childhood Sexual Experiences with Adults: A Comparison of Reports by Women Psychiatric Patients and General-Practice Attenders." *British Journal of Psychiatry.* 163:499–504.

"Prisoner's with AIDS: Constitutional and Family Rights Implicating in Family Visitation Programs." *Boston College Law Review.* 31:967–79.

Putnam, F. W., J. J. Guroff, E. K. Silberman et al. 1986. "The Clinical Phenomenology of Multiple Personality Disorder: Review of 100 Cases." *Journal of Clinical Psychiatry.* 47:285–93.

Regier, D. A., M. E. Farmer, D. S. Rae. 1990. "Comorbidity of Mental Disorders with Alcohol and Other Drug Abuse." *JAMA: Journal of the American Medical Association.* 264:2511–18.

Rind, Bruce, Philip Tromovitch, and Robert Bauserman. 1998. "A Meta-Analytic Examination of Assumed Properties of Child Sexual Abuse Using College Samples." *Psychological Bulletin.* 124:22–53.

Root, M. P. P. and P. Fallon. 1988. "The Incidence of Victimization Experiences in a Bulimic Sample." *Journal of Interpersonal Violence.* 3:161–73.

Sheerer, Laurie. 1997. "Childhood Maltreatment and Adult Psychosocial Functioning." *Perspective: A Mental Health Magazine,* September-October. (WWW http://www.cmhc.com/perspectives/articles/art09974.htm [September 26]).

Silbert, Mimi H. and Ayala M. Pines. 1981. "Sexual Child Abuse as an Antecedent to Prostitution." *Child Abuse and Neglect.* 5:407–11.

Silverman, A. B., H. Z. Reinherz, and R. M. Giaconia. 1966. "The Long–Term Sequelae of Child and Adolescent Abuse: A Longitudinal Community Study." *Child Abuse and Neglect.* 20:709–23.

Swett, Chester, Jr., Janet Surrey, and Caryn Cohen. 1990. "Sexual and Physical Abuse Histories and Psychiatric Symptoms Among Male Psychiatric Outpatients." *American Journal of Psychiatry.* 147:632–36.

Van Wormer, Katherine. 1995. *Alcoholism Treatment: A Social Work Perspective.* Chicago, IL: Nelson-Hall Publishers.

Windle, Michael, Rebecca C. Windle, Douglas M. Scheidt, and Gregory B. Miller. 1995. "Physical and Sexual Abuse and Associated Mental Disorders Among Alcoholic Inpatients." *American Journal of Psychiatry.* 152:1322–28.

Witt, Philip H., Joseph DelRusso, and Glenn Ferguson. 1996. "Sex Offender Risk Assessment and the Law." *The Journal of Psychiatry & Law.* 24:343–55.

Zimberg, Sheldon. 1994. "Individual Psychotherapy: Alcohol." Pp. 253–73 in *Textbook of Substance Abuse Treatment,* Marc Galanter and Herbert D. Kleber, eds. Washington, DC: American Psychiatric Press, Inc.

11 Treatment and Prevention of Family Abuse

Treatment and prevention are clearly among the most important issues to examine when studying family abuse and its consequences. The masses of data that have been compiled on family abuse in recent years have the most meaning when they are used to provide guidance for treatment and prevention programs.

This chapter provides an overview of treatment of victims/survivors of family abuse and treatment of sex offenders. It reviews federal, state, and local efforts to provide treatment. The chapter also examines family abuse prevention strategies and federal, state, and local prevention efforts.

Treatment of Victims and Survivors of Family Abuse

Treatment of victims of family abuse refers to a number of options and can occur in a number of ways. It includes treatment of victims while they are still children and recently victimized or adults who have just remembered a history of abuse. Treatment can take the form of inpatient treatment, typically in a psychiatric facility. It can mean individual and/or group psychotherapy on an outpatient basis. Treatment can begin with crisis intervention in which a woman and her children enter a shelter for battered women. Basically, treatment of family abuse tends to fall into four general categories: individual therapy, group therapy, family therapy, and community-based services such as child welfare, medical, legal, and emergency shelter agencies (Howing et al. 1989).

Since there are many kinds of problems victims of family abuse are likely to endure, it is not realistic to think generalizations can be made about the best or most effective type of treatment. Treatment effectiveness involves too many factors: the willingness of the individual to enter treatment, the age at which the abuse took place, the type of abuse and the length of time over which it occurred, the age at which treatment begins, and the type of treatment offered. It can also be the case that a person enters treatment for a different problem such as substance abuse or depression and then a history of childhood maltreatment is discovered. Professionals who specialize in the treatment of victims/survivors of childhood maltreatment agree that counseling or some form of therapeutic intervention can be helpful.

Professionals who specialize in the treatment of some type of family abuse are often social workers, psychologists, and social service agencies who employ a variety of types of counselors. Since there are so many types of family abuse, the following is necessarily a general review of ideas about the treatment of family abuse. Treatment efforts, because they focus on individuals and families, typically have a psychological rather than a sociological orientation.

Safety, of course, is the first consideration. Children who have been victimized at times may need to be immediately removed from the home by child protective services. At times, it is the perpetrator of the abuse who will be removed from the home. When the crisis situation has passed, psychotherapy can be helpful in dealing with the emotional consequences and can help victims or survivors to be more fully functioning. In psychotherapy with victims it is critical to develop an appropriate treatment plan and to assess the pace at which therapy can proceed with each client (Patten et al. 1989). Briere (1997) addresses the importance of having the correct level of intervention. An insufficient intervention avoids dealing with the abuse itself and focuses only on providing support despite the fact that the client would be able to process the trauma and its effects. Briere notes that this approach is "rarely dangerous" (186); however, it is not a very effective intervention and can waste time and resources.

The opposite problem is to provide services that are more intense than can be appropriately tolerated by the client. This means the client is expected to confront feelings about the past abuse that were much too painful at the time. If a client is pressured to deal with the feelings stemming from the abuse before he or she is psychologically ready, the therapy can actually become harmful to the client. The client may engage in behaviors such as trying to distract the therapist from the abuse, becoming argumentative, or using other strategies to avoid the issue, even terminating treatment. According to Briere, effective therapy achieves a middle ground by providing safety for the client and creating an environment in which the client can process the difficult material related to the maltreatment without risk of psychological injury.

According to Briere (1997), there are three major treatment steps for those who have been victimized. Initially, there must be an *acknowledgment* that abuse took place. Second, there needs to be a *gradual exposure to memories* of the abuse. Third, there needs to be *emotional processing* of the abuse. The type of treatment needed will depend on the nature and severity of the abuse. For children whose trauma from sexual abuse is considered mild and who have a strong support network, therapy lasting six months to one year is likely to be appropriate. For those who are very traumatized by sexual abuse, therapy of two or more years may be needed (Schneider 1997).

Although there is very little information on the treatment of male victims, there appears to be reason to believe that male victims of sexual assault react in ways similar to women (Mezey 1993). The differences that have been noted are that male victims of child sexual abuse focus their anger externally and therefore are more prone to aggressive behavior. Women are more likely to direct anger toward themselves, which can manifest as low self-esteem and depression. These differences may be related to the socialization process in which men are discouraged from expressing their feelings and encouraged to be assertive and aggressive.

Recovered Memories of Abuse

One of the hottest issues in recent years regarding childhood maltreatment, especially sexual abuse, is the notion of *recovered memories.* In psychological terms, a victim of abuse may experience psychogenic amnesia; that is, he or she may "forget" or repress extremely painful memories. There is some evidence that traumatic memory may be different from ordinary memory. While earlier it was thought that traumatic memories retained their original force, more recent evidence suggests that memories of traumatic events can be inaccurate (Chu 1999). There is evidence that both victims and perpetrators can have distorted memories of abuse (Stillwell and Baumeister 1997). In their review of the literature, Herman and Harvey (1997) found that most studies reported that 20 to 50 percent of patients reported a period of complete amnesia. In their own study, Herman and Harvey found that those who had periods of complete amnesia were more likely to report one type of abuse, mostly sexual abuse.

This issue of recovered memories of childhood sexual abuse has become extremely controversial. It has been suggested that psychotherapists have gone so far as to plant false memories in the minds of their clients. Perhaps the most famous case involved the Freyd family. Jennifer Freyd, a psychologist, remembered sexual abuse perpetrated by her father, Peter Freyd, a mathematics professor (Lein 1999). In response to what were considered false accusations of abuse, the mother, Pamela Freyd, founded the False Memory Syndrome Foundation in 1992, which now boasts a membership of 18,000. The False Memory Syndrome Foundation website lists Pamela Freyd, Ph.D., as Executive Director. The website states that the purpose of the foundation is to seek reasons for the spread of the syndrome, to prevent new cases from surfacing, and to aid the victims of false memory syndrome.

The American Psychological Association acknowledges that false memories may be induced in children and adults. Telling the difference between a recovered memory and a false memory can be difficult in the absence of other evidence. Sometimes the only evidence is circumstantial, such as proof that a person was at the time or place when the alleged event took place. Other times, there might be no external evidence at all. It could rest entirely on the credibility of the alleged victim and the alleged perpetrator. Further complicating the issue is the fact that there might be simultaneous legal cases pending before civil and criminal courts. Since the criminal trial requires evidence beyond a reasonable doubt and the civil case might only require a preponderance of evidence, it is possible for the criminal adjudication to find the alleged perpetrator not guilty (a victim of false memories) and the civil trial to find the perpetrator guilty (an offender revealed by recovered memories).

In general, it does not appear that psychotherapy opens the door to delayed recall of maltreatment, rather it is the delayed recall of trauma that results in people seeking psychotherapy. The work of Herman and Harvey also suggests that delayed recall "is often a process that unfolds over time rather than a single event, and that it occurs most commonly in the context of a life crisis or developmental milestone. . . ." (1997:567).

In response to intense controversy over the ethical and legal dilemmas this topic engenders, some professional organizations have developed policies and standards regarding the clinical and ethical issues in treating survivors of childhood sexual abuse. One such effort is a set of principles and standards of the NASW (National Association of Social Workers) National Council on the Practice of Clinical Social Work, titled the "Evaluation and Treatment of Adults with the Possibility of Recovered Memories of Childhood Sexual Abuse" (1997). See Pope and Brown (1996) for a review of the research, including false memory syndrome, and a discussion of the difficulties facing therapists who treat clients with recovered memories of childhood sexual abuse.

Treatment Programs for Victims and Survivors of Family Abuse

Treatment programs operate on federal, state, and local levels and in recent years more efforts have been made to coordinate these interventions. On the federal level there are a number of important initiatives to treat and prevent child maltreatment and family abuse. An example of a federal initiative is the Violence Against Women Act, which will be discussed in detail in the section on prevention.

Another example of a federal initiative involved 23 law enforcement training projects that operated from 1986 to 1992 ("Evaluation of Family Violence Training Programs" 1995). Funded by the Office for Victims of Crime, 16,000 police officers, court personnel including judges and prosecutors, and community service providers received training in the effort to improve the criminal justice response to family abuse. These efforts were successful in bringing about more uniform and progressive policies about the treatment of family violence. More positive attitudes toward victims of family abuse were noted. The training projects also resulted in better cooperation between police and community service agencies. Areas for further work included continued training of law enforcement and training of other professionals such as child welfare workers, health care providers, and the clergy.

Each state has an agency designated to provide child protective services. These state agencies respond to reports that have been filed that allege abuse or neglect of a child. Child protective agencies are very likely to make interventions in multiproblem families, such as those with low income, low educational attainment, substance abuse problems, and involvement with the criminal justice system. They have access to a range of services to assist families including counseling, parenting skills programs, and day care. In cases where children are unable to remain in the home for reasons of abuse or neglect, placement is arranged in foster care or in a residential program. Some states have recently paid more attention to addressing the needs of maltreated children. For example, in Massachusetts, during the summer of 1999, the state child protective agency (the Department of Social Services) committed $630,000 for services for children who are impacted by family abuse, estimated at 60 percent of their client population (Hart 1999).

Olsen, Capoverde, Holmes, and Mumm (1996) evaluated a child abuse intervention program for families with substantiated abuse or neglect reports and at high risk of re-abuse. The program included substantial elements of parent education and multiple service supports for the families. The researchers found that subsequent reports of child abuse for these families were substantially lower than for a matched comparison group of cases from a state Department of Children and Families. Even more poignantly, several of the children in the comparison group subsequently died from abuse, but none died of those who received services from the intervention program. Whipple and Welser (1996) have found similar benefits from other parent education programs. Such programs tend to not only reduce negative behaviors but also encourage more positive relationships among family members (Fennell and Fishel 1998).

Another example of a statewide effort to reduce family abuse is a new effort by the state of New Hampshire to have medical professionals routinely screen patients for violence in the home ("Doctors to Screen" 2000). As part of a standardized form, patients are asked if there is violence in the home. Those who answer "yes" to the question will receive referrals to community professionals. Also as part of this program, Dartmouth Medical School, Notre Dame College, and New Hampshire's schools of nursing will include family violence in their curricula. The licensing boards of medical professions are also encouraged to mandate that family violence be a part of required continuing education programs.

In Massachusetts there is a new initiative to involve employers in the fight against family abuse (Bombardieri 2000). A group called Employers Against Domestic Violence (EADV) has 62 companies as members throughout the state and the group is considered a model for other developing programs across the country. A major premise of this initiative is that the job offers perhaps the only place where a woman is not controlled by her abuser. Services include referrals for counseling, legal assistance, and arrangements for flexible work hours.

Local efforts to provide treatment for family abuse are also of critical importance. An example of a local initiative is The Child Witness to Violence Project at Boston Medical Center in Boston, Massachusetts. The project began in 1992 to deal with street violence but changed its emphasis as a response to the types of referrals made to the program. Children who have witnessed family abuse are provided with age-appropriate interventions that might include play therapy or individual psychotherapy.

The treatment of perpetrators of maltreatment is especially complex and is the subject of the next section.

Treatment of Abuse Offenders

The attitudes we hold about the perpetrators of abuse very much determine whether we feel they are in need of punishment or treatment. Increasingly we hear of sex offenders referred to as *predators*. This term is demeaning and connotes that offenders are less than human. It does not appear to add anything positive to the debate over how sex offenders should be handled. A study of attitudes toward incest perpetrators found that police were more likely to view perpetrators as criminals while mental health practitioners were more likely to see perpetrators as mentally disturbed (Trute, Adkins, and MacDonald 1996). This illustrates the distinction that is often made between seeing offenders as "bad" people in need of punishment or "sick" people in need of treatment.

For all the concern about sex offenders, the majority do not receive treatment (Barbaree and Marshall 1998). Those that do are most likely to be treated in a prison or in a mental hospital. Less often, sex offenders receive treatment in a community setting while on probation or parole. While there has been much attention paid to treatment of adult sex offenders, there is far less known about the relatively new and complicated treatment of adolescent sex offenders (Hagan and Cho 1996). It is known that most adult sex offenders begin their offending during adolescence and therefore more attention to sexual offending among this age group is needed.

The effectiveness of sex offender treatment is very controversial and the general public seems to be under the impression that it does not work. Assessing the risk of sex offenders is a very new area of research and has not yet incorporated the effects of treatment (Marshall 1996). Of course, the purpose of treatment is to reduce the likelihood that the perpetrator will reoffend. The methodological problems in research have been reviewed in previous chapters and these concerns are clearly present in studying sex offender recidivism. It is known that official records of reoffense underestimate recidivism and it has been estimated for sex offenses that the recidivism rate is likely to be up to 2.5 times higher than official records indicate.

The measurement of treatment effectiveness certainly can be difficult for a number of reasons. In terms of evaluating the effectiveness of sex offender treatment, the vast majority of studies do not compare the treated group with an untreated group. It is important that studies match offender characteristics so that the two groups are as equal as possible except for treatment (Barbaree and Marshall 1998). Of course, ethical issues are raised by assigning a dangerous offender who may benefit from treatment to a control group within which no treatment will be provided. Some programs reject offenders who are unable or unwilling to accept responsibility for their sexually abusive behavior (Marshall 1996). Barbaree and Marshall (1998) give an example of a research study in which only 30 percent of incarcerated offenders were considered appropriate candidates and only 66 percent of these were finally accepted into a treatment program. Another important factor in evaluating sex offender treatment programs is the dropout rate with some research reporting a dropout rate of 35 percent. Thus, the concern is that many offenders are refused treatment and a large minority are not able or willing to complete treatment programs.

Surprisingly, there is some professional consensus that the majority of sex offenders do not suffer from significant mental illness. According to Barbaree and Marshall (1998), Abel, Mittleman, and Becker (1985) reported that fewer than 25 percent of sex offenders treated in an outpatient setting had serious mental disorders. They cite Knopp (1984) as reporting that in a sample of incarcerated sex offenders, no more than 10 percent had significant mental disorder. This is hard for the general public to understand and most people are far more comfortable seeing offenders as "bad" or "sick" but definitely not normal. Sex offenders occupy the lowest status in general society and the same low status even within the prison hierarchy. Recent laws requiring sex offenders to register with the local police department and giving the information to members of the community reinforce the perception that sex offenders will continue to be a threat to the community.

There is also some evidence that a relatively small number of sex offenders account for a significant proportion of sex offenses. A study completed by the Massachusetts Department of Probation followed 3,211 sex offenders from 1988 to 1998 (Ellement 2000). It found that in 1988 approximately 9 percent of sex offenders arrested made up 33 percent of sexual offense court arraignments. In 1998, 8.5 percent of sex offenders accounted for 37 percent of sexual offense court arraignments.

Graham (1993) compared 42 sex offenders with 26 non–sex offenders, and 42 men from a community control group. The sex offenders had more dissociative experiences than the other two groups. This refers to feelings that the sex offenders had no control over their abusive behavior, that they were powerless over the abuse. Since dissociation is known to occur among sexual abuse victims, that sex offenders were more dissociative than the other groups supports the idea that the offenders themselves were victims of abuse. This finding suggests that treatment providers can use certain techniques to deal with the amnesia around dissociated memories. These techniques include hypnotherapy, active imagination exercises, and dream work. Graham discusses the two reasons it is important for the treatment of sex offenders to make the connection between the offender's own victimization and subsequent perpetration. First, the working through of the offender's own victimization experiences encourages a healthier level of functioning. Second, if the offender is successful in dealing with his own abusive background, a greater empathy for the victim is likely to develop.

Graham (1993) found that sex offenders were more external on the locus of control issue than the non–sex offender group, but not the community control group. Locus of control refers to the degree offenders felt they had control over their own behavior or felt that their instincts are external and beyond their ability to control. There is considerable shame in acknowledging responsibility for sexually abusive behavior. Seeing the causes as external rather than internal allows the sex offender to avoid the shame and other negative feelings associated with being a perpetrator of sexual abuse. This finding of the tendency to have an external locus of control has important ramifications for treatment. It confirms that the treatment environment should focus on helping the offender to learn the limits of the expression of feelings and that the offender needs to learn to accept responsibility for his behavior.

Graham found that sex offenders were more alienated than the other two groups, alienated from self and from others. This means that the offender may not be able to experience feelings or a sense of personal identity. Sex offenders can lack a connection to others, feel uncomfortable in social situations, and in general be withdrawn and isolated from others. From a treatment perspective, this finding speaks to the importance of group therapy and social skills training as ways to learn to trust others and to decrease the feelings of social isolation.

Denial has long been considered the cornerstone of sex offenders. Sex crimes are so abhorrent that offenders do not or cannot take responsibility for their behavior and search for explanations that minimize their responsibility. Some sex offenders may use their own background of abuse as justification or excuse (Graham 1993). Barbaree (1991) examined denial in rapists and child molesters. He found that 54 percent of rapists exhibited complete denial and an additional 42 percent minimized their behavior. Sixty-six percent of child molesters were in denial and 33 percent minimized their behavior. Offenders minimized the extent or severity of their offenses or even claimed that there was no harm to the victim. Treatment providers must deal with denial early on in the treatment process as the acceptance of responsibility is crucial. Offenders need to see that they are responsible for their own actions rather than see their sexually abusive behavior as an inevitable outcome of their own abuse histories.

The particular methods of treatment rest on assumptions about the causes and nature of sexual crimes (Barbaree and Marshall 1998). Abel is credited with playing a critical role in developing treatment approaches, especially cognitive–behavioral programs (Marshall 1996). Again, it is noted that sex offender treatment is typically based on psychological or biological explanations rather than sociological explanations. Abel called attention to the distortions in thinking processes offenders can have about themselves and their victims. This encouraged more work with offenders on trying to elicit empathy for their victims, a component that has existed in sex offender treatment since the mid-1980s. An emphasis on relapse prevention strategies for sex offenders also developed in the 1980s. The treatments—biological, nonbehavioral psychotherapy, and cognitive–behavioral therapy—are reviewed in the next sections.

Biological Treatments

The purpose of biological or organic treatments is to prevent further offending by reducing the sexual or violent urges of the offender. This in itself is controversial.

Critics of these approaches, such as physical castration and chemical castration, point out that the underlying assumption is that offenders commit these crimes because their biological drives are excessive. Offenders that have temporal lobe lesions or tumors may also exhibit violent outbursts and be subject to biological intervention.

Physical castration is the surgical removal of the testicles. Chemical castration can be accomplished through the administration of medroxyprogesterone acetate (MPA), cyproterone acetate (CPA), or triptrelin. While the biology of how these drugs work cannot be discussed here, the purpose is to reduce sexual drive, which will lead to a reduction in deviant sexual behavior. The long-term effects of these hormonal treatments are not yet known. Barbaree and Marshall's review of the literature found dropout rates from 30 to 100 percent. They also point out that sex offenders may need to be permanently treated this way.

Barbaree and Marshall (1998) are critical of the biological treatments, finding that there is very little evidence to support the notion that a too strong sex drive is responsible for sex offenses. Overall, Barbaree and Marshall's assessment is that biological treatments have not shown clear evidence of effectiveness. Rösler and Witztum (1998), however, report much higher success rates than Barbaree and Marshall, which means the debate over chemical castration will continue until there is more consensus on research findings.

One of the many concerns about biological treatments involves the notion of informed consent and whether sex offenders are truly in a position to "volunteer" for biological treatments or whether there is some form of coercion. The long-term consequences of using such chemicals are largely unknown, which raises additional issues about whether there really can be informed consent. Long-term medical monitoring of offenders receiving such treatment is necessary in addition to the criminal justice monitoring (Lisko 1999). This is highly controversial work and will continue to be so in the future.

For those who have organic brain dysfunction associated with their violence, surgical or chemical treatment may lessen or terminate the violence. However, this problem accounts for only a very small percentage of the cases of family abuse. The public tends to regard it with skepticism, as it may be regarded as a convenient excuse. To what extent are individuals with organic brain problems truly able to control their behavior? To what extent should medical treatment of such problems be used? To what extent should biological treatments substitute for the more accepted criminal justice punishments?

Nonbehavioral Psychotherapy

Nonbehavioral approaches are of such a wide variety that Barbaree and Marshall (1998) remind us that it is very difficult to make generalizations. Included here are sex offender treatment programs that are based on psychological models that maintain offenses are committed in response to unconscious and unresolved conflicts over castration anxiety. Since these programs do not clearly define the nature of sexual offenses, it is especially difficult for them to be effective. Some approaches focus on the perspective that sexual offending results from a build-up of stress and that group therapy focusing on dealing with stress will reduce the chances of reoffending. Other approaches focus on the importance of peer treatment. Overall, Barbaree and Marshall (1998) conclude that nonbehavioral psychotherapy approaches have failed to define goals within the course of treatment and have not been especially effective.

Cognitive–Behavioral Therapy

Cognitive–behavioral approaches are currently considered the most effective and also provide a model for relapse prevention (Barbaree and Marshall 1998; Kear-Colwell and Pollock 1997). The cognitive–behavioral model assumes that sexual crimes do not result from a single cause, but that there are many sociological and psychological variables that come into play in sexual offenses. In contrast to the biological treatments that locate the source of sexual offenses in biology, and the nonbehavioral psychotherapy which locates the source of sexual offenses in the psychoanalytic model, the cognitive–behavioral model is a form of the social learning model. The model acknowledges the importance of the offender's background, including family situation. A chaotic or abusive background can lead to psychological disturbances, which may or may not be considered major mental disorders. The model acknowledges the widely held view that sex offenders and other family abusers are deficient in social skills and that training in this area is a worthwhile part of offender treatment.

The cognitive–behavioral model is considered preferable to the other models because (1) it offers a framework for understanding the individual offender, (2) it provides an assessment of behavioral issues that contribute to the offense, and (3) it focuses on treating behavior that will reduce the likelihood of future offending (Barbaree and Marshall 1998).

Other treatment programs are not so easily categorized and can have as a focus the healing of the victim, the perpetrator, and the community. The Ojibway, of Manitoba, Canada, offer one such alternative as discussed in Box 11.1.

Even though a sex offender treatment program has an appropriate mission statement, treatment objectives, and qualified staff, that is no guarantee of integrity in the provision of services. Pithers (1997) documents examples of how treatment can go awry and how intrusive measures offered under the guise of being therapeutic can serve to demean and humiliate sex offenders. Pithers describes cases of sex offenders having to endure drama therapy, which was supposed to reenact the sexual abuse the offender experienced as a child but which was found to be even more abusive than the original events.

Sex offender treatment is typically provided for those who are convicted of crimes associated with rape or sexual assault with children or adults. Treatment is also provided for those who are convicted of spousal battering and has become a frequent court requirement for those who have violated a restraining order or are

BOX **11.1**

Sexual Abuse Treatment among the Ojibway

An unusual treatment approach to sex offenders is found among an aboriginal group in Manitoba, Canada—the Ojibway. This very different approach focuses on "sacred justice" for the sex offender, which is based on the premise that community dysfunction is at the root of sexual offending. Incarceration is discouraged as abusers are encouraged to stay within the community and endure the shame that results from their sexually abusive behavior. The Ojibway feel they must work to eliminate the abuser's disconnectedness to his community; spiritual treatment rather than psychological treatment is what is needed. Frequently efforts are made to reconcile with the victim. Restitution can happen in the form of community service work. The guiding principle is to provide support to sex offenders in order to help them reconnect to the community, not to seek punishment and vengeance. Evaluation research has not been completed; however, anecdotal evidence appears to support the healing of sex offenders and the community.

Source: Geral Blanchard. 1997. "Aboriginal Canadian Innovations in the Treatment of Sexual Violence." *The Carnes Update: Sexual Disorder at The Meadows,* Summer.

---

convicted of assault and battery on a partner. As we have seen, legal interventions and treatment often go hand in hand.

Group Treatment

Group treatment is frequently used in treating batterers (Williams 1994). One of the difficulties with this approach is that minorities tend to be underrepresented in such programs. Research suggests this is partly because those responsible for running these programs tend not to be sensitive to the fact that minorities who are batterers are often victims of racism and need to also deal with their own victimization (Williams 1994). If those running the programs also have prejudice against minorities, this discourages participation even further.

A good example of combining legal and treatment interventions is a group treatment program for male batterers who are incarcerated. Known as the Relating Without Violence Program (RWV), treatment is designed to help batterers process their own traumatic life experiences, to help improve their self-esteem, and to better understand and respect the emotions of others (Wolfus and Bierman 1996). Another goal is to develop and strengthen conflict resolution skills among this group. The evaluation of the Relating Without Violence Program concluded that it was effective in meeting treatment goals and that participants were determined to have reduced anger, irritability, and defensiveness. A significant limitation of this research is that there was no follow-up after the offenders returned to the community.

Brown and Brown's (1997) review of the incest literature found that group therapy is an appropriate treatment for incest offenders. The group offers a place where offenders can deal with a wide range of issues relating to their own childhoods and current role expectations in the family. Some groups have offenders write their autobiography, a detailed accounting of their incest offenses, and a journal of their sexual fantasies.

Treatment of Incest Offenders

The treatment of the incest offender can be especially complex because there may be the expectation that the offender, at the very least, maintains contact with the daughter or son who has been victimized as well as other family members. At times, the treatment goal is to reunite the family. Initially, either the offender or the victim may be removed from the home. In both cases, this is a major crisis for all family members once the incest has been acknowledged. As many as two-thirds of incest families may choose to reunite, as is the experience of participants in Parents United, a peer support program (Roundy and Horton 1990).

The treatment of incest offenders is still developing and no one type of treatment is known to be more effective than others (Brown and Brown 1997). The types of treatment that are offered to incest offenders depend on the orientation of therapists regarding the causes of incest. If the belief is that offenders misinterpret the victim's reaction to the incest, treatment will focus on increasing the awareness of harm to the victim. If the belief is that family dysfunction is the cause of incest, intervention will focus on greater awareness of family dynamics and providing services to family members (Brown and Brown 1990). The following is a brief discussion of two programs that are part of the family dynamics model.

One example of incest treatment is the Child Sexual Abuse Treatment Program (CSATP) in San Jose, California (Giarretto and Giarretto 1990). The goal is for the victim to return to her family by working with all family members to create a nurturing family environment. The CSATP also emphasizes the importance of collaboration among police, court personnel, social service workers, therapists, and family members, including participation in the self-help groups, Parents United and Daughters and Sons United.

A systems model for the treatment of child sexual abuse was developed by therapists at the Family Resource Institute in Chicago (Barrett, Sykes, and Byrnes 1986). The program is divided into three stages. The first stage, *Creating a Context for Change*, focuses on assessment of the problem and the coordination of legal and therapeutic services. Perhaps the most difficult part of treatment is known as the apology session in which the perpetrator apologizes to his child-victim. The apology session takes many weeks of planning and includes all family members (Trepper 1986). To be considered successful, the apology must be genuine, both parents must give the message to the children that the problems are the responsibility of both parents, and that each family member needs to be involved in making things better. At the end of the session the family receives the message from the therapist that the worst is now over and the remainder of treatment will be an easier process.

The second stage of the systems approach is *Challenging Patterns and Expanding Alternatives* (Barrett et al. 1986). At this point the therapist works with the family to break dysfunctional patterns of communication and behavior and replace them with healthy alternatives. This includes individual treatment sessions with the offender, the child, and the nonabusing parent. Also included are marital sessions, sibling therapy sessions, and group sessions with other victims and perpetrators of incest. In the third stage, *consolidation*, gains have been made in therapy and attention is paid to problem-solving in the future. This 3-stage therapy process takes between 12 and 18 months (Barrett et al. 1986).

The treatment of incest can be especially difficult for therapists who must examine their own professional and personal biases in doing this challenging work (Roundy and Horton 1990). Treatment of incest perpetrators is difficult to evaluate and more empirical data are needed on offenders and different treatment approaches (Brown and Brown 1997).

While there is much controversy over the effectiveness of offender treatment, Barbaree and Marshall (1998) point out that the majority of treatment programs have not been subject to a formal evaluation. Clearly, further efforts are needed in improving the effectiveness of programs and providing quality evaluations of the treatments provided. Additionally, more innovative approaches to the treatment of family abuse perpetrators are needed. See Box 11.2 for a description of a new response to family violence offenses by police officers.

BOX **11.2**

New Sanctions for Police Officers Convicted of Family Abuse Offenses

An example of a relatively new intervention is the penalty for police officers convicted of domestic violence offenses. At the request of the United States Department of Justice, the International Association of Chiefs of Police drafted a model policy that states that officers convicted of a misdemeanor or felony domestic violence crime should be "removed from their enforcement position, and either reassigned or terminated" (1). This policy follows the 1996 federal law that bars anyone with a conviction for domestic violence from owning a gun. The model policy does emphasize prevention and early intervention as law enforcement agencies are encouraged to screen police recruits for a history of perpetrating family abuse and to notify police chiefs of any aggressive behaviors. The policy recommends that the police department's internal affairs division conduct the domestic violence investigation.

Source: "An Ounce of Prevention, a Pound of Penalty Urged for Spouse-Beating Cops." 1998. *Law Enforcement News*, XXIV, April 30:1, 9.

Prevention of Family Abuse

The topic of prevention is one of the most complex issues in family abuse. As with treatment, in prevention we must grapple with how effective prevention efforts have been. Proving the effectiveness or ineffectiveness of any prevention program is very difficult. For example, effectiveness can be defined in a number of ways. Is effectiveness of a prevention program proven by simply providing education to children or is it the children using the information that proves the effectiveness of a prevention program (Plummer 1993)? Are prevention efforts successful if the number of reports of abuse decrease or are prevention efforts more effective if abuse reports increase as people have learned to identify and take action against abuse (Plummer 1993)? Programs for the prevention of sexual abuse of children are still in the process of being developed (Schneider 1997) and Reppucci and Haugaard (1993) have argued that the current state of knowledge is such that it simply is not known whether child sexual abuse programs are effective.

The topic of prevention and measuring its effectiveness is further complicated when one considers the array of sociological factors that are correlated with family abuse. While gender socialization issues and low socioeconomic status are correlates of family abuse, these issues are so broad and intricate that it is too complex to specifically measure their impact on family abuse.

In the wake of the Columbine High School massacre of 1999 and a number of other traumatic school shootings, a closer tie has been drawn between family abuse prevention and community violence prevention. Increasingly there is recognition that prevention of violence must be a coordinated effort by individuals, parents, schools, and communities. Suggestions for the prevention of school violence are reviewed in Box 11.3.

In general, programs that aim at preventing or reducing childhood maltreatment have some common components. Often they include education for children, parents, and teachers. The goals of sexual abuse prevention programs are reviewed in Box 11.4. Prevention discussions often focus on three types: *primary, secondary,* and *tertiary prevention.* Primary prevention seeks to prevent abuse from occurring at all. Primary prevention programs focus on promoting healthy parent–child relationships. These programs are often not implemented due to lack of financial resources and resistance to such services. Those programs that do exist tend to focus on educational efforts with high school students and teaching young adults about child development and parenting skills (Wolfe et al. 1997). Of course, by definition, primary prevention occurs prior to the development of the problem and proving that an intervention prevented the problem is impossible as the problem may not have developed anyway (Plummer 1993). This makes evaluation of primary prevention programs exceedingly difficult. Reppucci and Haugaard go so far as to state: "No evidence exists that primary prevention has ever been achieved by the existing prevention programs" (1993:318). However, there are descriptive studies showing that levels of violence in schools and families tend to

---

B O X **11.3**

What Schools Can Do to Prevent Violence

1. Administrators and teachers cannot accept the social stratification and ostracism that exist in schools. The importance of social acceptance and the effects of rejection need to be part of a school curriculum.
2. Respect for teachers, staff, and students must be a priority of administrators. This means that students observe school professionals treating one another with respect, and the expectation is that they will do the same.
3. Schools need to create projects that encourage students from different ethnic and racial groups to mix with one another. These projects will require close monitoring to ensure cooperation.
4. All administrators, teachers, and students need training to recognize the symptoms of social alienation so that they can be brought to the attention of the appropriate authorities.
5. Clear boundaries need to be set for appropriate student behavior. Those who act inappropriately should receive a professional intervention.

Source: Eva Skolnick-Acker. 1999. "Why Do Children Kill and Can We Stop Them?" *Focus,* Publication of the Massachusetts Chapter of the National Association of Social Workers, 26, July:1, 8.

---

decline after violence prevention programs have been introduced into schools (Wolfe et al. 1997).

The criminalization of family abuse has primary prevention as one of its aims to the extent it provides deterrence against others initiating abuse. Arresting offenders is intended not only to incapacitate the specific offender so he or she cannot reoffend; it is also a message to the community that family abuse is taken seriously and that those who are considering abusive behavior need to realize the potential for punishment.

Secondary prevention seeks to identify those at high risk of offending or becoming a victim and tries to intervene at an early point in abusive situations. These secondary prevention efforts appear to be very promising especially if efforts are made to closely match the needs of the family with the appropriate community resources (Wolfe et al. 1997). These interventions are typically aimed at parents or expectant parents whose risk factors may include being a low-income or a single parent. Programs offering early intervention home nursing services or other professionals who visit families in their homes are good examples (Wolfe et al. 1997). Straus and colleagues (1998) have tested the Conflict Tactics Scale as a screening tool to identify those at high risk of abuse. Using this or similar scales that measure emotional or sexual abuse may identify those at high risk so they may be targeted for secondary prevention programs.

Secondary prevention efforts often include having victims at risk of re-abuse develop a safety plan. This requires the victim and her or his family to plan what they are going to do in the event the abuser returns. How are they going to escape?

BOX **11.4**

Typical Goals of Sexual Abuse Prevention Programs

1. Raise awareness of sexual abuse among the general public.
2. Educate parents about abuse prevention and early intervention.
3. Train professionals, including teachers, about the dynamics of abuse, and to identify symptoms of abuse and acknowledge and act on their legal responsibilities to report abuse.
4. Teach children factual information about sexual abuse.
5. Help children develop the skills that can assist them in avoiding abuse.
6. Work toward eliminating child sexual abuse within the community.

Source: Carol A. Plummer. 1993. "Prevention Is Appropriate, Prevention Is Successful." Pp. 288–305 in *Current Controversies on Family Violence*, Richard J. Gelles and Donileen R. Loseke, eds. Newbury Park, CA: Sage Publications. P. 295.

What are they going to need if they flee their homes? Do they know where they can go and how they will get there? Who is available to help them and what kind of help will be offered? These are some of the questions that victims must address if they want to plan for prevention of re-abuse. A list of recommendations for a safety plan is provided in Box 11.5.

Mandatory arrest programs for family abusers also have a secondary prevention element. They are intended to deter those who have been arrested for abuse from doing so in the future. Although mandatory arrest programs have not been highly successful for those with long criminal histories of violent crimes, there is evidence that they do reduce the risk of repeating the abuse for many offenders; especially those who are older, employed, or who do not have prior criminal records (Holmes 1993; Mignon and Holmes 1995; Sherman 1995).

Tertiary prevention refers to efforts to treat offenders and prevent relapse (Schneider 1997). According to Wolfe et al., tertiary prevention studies "have reported some degree of success at improving child-rearing skills and knowledge of child development, although limited follow-up data, evidence of recidivism, and high cost of delivery reveal the inadequacy of delivering prevention or treatment services only after maltreatment has occurred and been identified" (1997:104).

The education of children, as potential victims of maltreatment, has consistently been part of prevention programs. Children need to be taught in age-appropriate ways about sexual abuse. They need to learn to say "no" and need encouragement to talk about abuse that may have already occurred. Teaching children about sexual abuse is an important part of prevention strategies; however, it should not be the only strategy (Plummer 1993). In Plummer's words: "Children were never meant to accomplish prevention singlehanded" (1993:296). Reppucci and Haugaard (1993) point out the difficulty in relying on the child to bring an end to abuse. The child first must recognize that she is being abused; the child must feel she can or should do something about it; and finally the child must acquire and use

BOX **11.5**

Suggestions for a Safety Plan

- Have a phone easily accessible and teach young children how to dial 911. Some family violence programs have loaner cell phones available.
- Tell trusted family, friends, and neighbors about the risk.
- Identify and arrange for a safe place to escape to.
- Prepare a bag of clothing, medication, and essentials. Hide it where it can be obtained quickly.
- Make copies of important papers. Keep one with the emergency bag.
- If you have a car, make an extra set of keys and hide them.
- If an incident occurs and you can leave, do so.
- If you cannot leave, call for help and avoid the kitchen, bathroom, garage, or other rooms where weapons may be kept.
- If the abuser leaves, change the locks and phone numbers. Reinforce locks on the doors and windows.
- Learn phone numbers and locations of agencies helping domestic violence victims, including the National Domestic Violence Hotline (1-800-799-SAFE; TDD for the Hearing Impaired: 1-800-787-3224).

Source: King County, Washington. 1998. "Love Shouldn't Hurt: King County Domestic Violence Home Page." (WWW http://www.metrokc.gov/dvinfo/dv1_0.htm).

---

her skills in bringing this to the attention of an adult who can put a stop to it. This, of course, is a tall order and Reppucci and Haugaard (1993) argue that all three skills must be imparted to children or the effectiveness of prevention efforts is seriously reduced. In discussing sexual abuse prevention, Plummer makes the point that a comprehensive approach is needed. The critical components of a sexual abuse prevention strategy must include parent, child, and teacher education, a multidisciplinary community task force, and ongoing updates and evaluation.

Most sexual abuse prevention programs are provided for preschool and elementary school children and less often for junior and senior high school students (Reppucci and Haugaard 1993). Reppucci and Haugaard raise the question of the developmental readiness of young children to understand and use the information they receive on prevention. Their review of the work of Gilbert et al. (1989) and Berrick and Gilbert (1991) shows some small knowledge gains for first and third graders but little evidence that preschoolers respond.

Family Abuse Prevention Programs

Prevention, like treatment, is offered on the federal, state, and local levels. The Office for Victims of Crime (OVC) with other programs for the Office of Justice Programs (OJP) administers funds for the development of strategies and recommendations to combat and prevent child abuse and domestic violence. Funding comes from fines and penalties paid by criminal offenders in the federal system. In

1997, $363 million was given to states to assist in funding victim assistance and compensation programs. The Office for Victims of Crime provides funds to almost 3,000 local victim services nationally, which are used for crisis counseling, shelter, and advocacy in the criminal justice system.

The Center for the Study and Prevention of Violence at the University of Colorado at Boulder instituted a project in 1996 that focused on identifying programs that have been shown to be effective in reducing adolescent aggressive behavior, substance abuse, and criminal activity ("Blueprints: A Violence Prevention Initiative" 1999). The Office of Juvenile Justice and Delinquency Prevention joined these efforts to provide training within community organizations interested in implementing 1 of 10 programs. The programs include a prenatal and infancy home visitation program, a school-based bullying prevention program, the Big Brothers/Big Sisters of America mentoring program, a program designed to improve basic high school academic skills known as Quantum Opportunities, a family therapy model known as Functional Family Therapy, two substance abuse prevention programs known as The Midwestern Prevention Project and Life Skills Training for middle and junior high school students, Multisystemic Therapy, which addresses family and community factors that contribute to delinquent behavior, and Multidimensional Treatment Foster Care as an alternative to residential treatment for chronic delinquents.

An example of one program—Safe Kids/Safe Streets: Community-Based Approaches to Intervening in Child Abuse and Neglect—received support from the Bureau of Justice Assistance, the Bureau of Justice Statistics, and the National Institute of Justice. The goal is to develop a federal, state, and local partnership to provide a comprehensive intervention and prevention programs for victims and their families. Included are efforts to provide training to clinicians treating abuse victims and efforts to work toward a continuum of services including public information, assessment, and prevention education.

School-based prevention programs tend to focus on problem-solving strategies and improved interpersonal skills so that violence can be avoided. While these programs have grown in the last few years, there have been few efforts to evaluate their effectiveness (Grossman et al. 1997). An example of one effort was a school-based violence prevention program in elementary schools in Washington state. The *Second Step: A Violence Prevention Curriculum, Grades 1–3*, second edition, was used (Seattle: Committee for Children 1992). Teachers and parents rated the behavior of the children as part of the effort to evaluate the effectiveness of the curriculum. Trained observers were placed in the classroom, cafeteria, and playground. There was no significant difference in observed behavior according to teachers and parents. According to the trained observers of the children's behavior at school, there was a decrease in physical aggression and an increase in neutral/prosocial behavior two weeks after the curriculum ended. Grossman et al. (1997) conclude that there was a "moderate observed decrease" (1605) in physical aggression and an increase in neutral or more social behaviors.

A state initiative in California consists of two statewide centers, one in the northern part of the state and one in the south, to train service providers in the area of child sexual abuse prevention (Child Sexual Abuse Prevention Training

Centers 1999). Training is provided for social service, medical, mental health providers, and criminal justice agencies. Once trained in interventions with victims of child sexual abuse and their families, these professionals train others in the field. Specifically, the curriculum focuses on identifying and treating victims of child sexual abuse, responsibility for reporting such abuse, and interviewing victims and their families. These training centers also focus on meeting the needs of special groups such as preschoolers, the developmentally disabled, and minorities.

A statewide family abuse prevention policy recommendation aimed specifically at child abuse and neglect has been put forward by the Massachusetts Chapter of the National Association of Social Workers (Brill and Stein 1999). In addition to recommendations for early intervention and protection of children, the report deems prevention as the first component of an organized effort. The cornerstone is the recommendation for community-based "Family Centers" that would be available to all families in Massachusetts. The Family Centers would provide a complete range of social, health, and mental health services, including financial and housing assistance, day care, parenting skills training, and crisis intervention.

Family abuse and violence prevention do not fall just within the fields of criminal justice and human services. Increasingly the medical field has been willing to acknowledge that violence poses significant risks to health. The Massachusetts Medical Society Committee on Violence developed a series of *parent education tip cards* that focus on violence prevention for children and youth (Massachusetts Medical Society 1997). Each card is designed to be short and easy to understand. Parents are given tips on raising their toddlers with praise and how to appropriately use time-outs as a disciplinary measure. For preschool and school-age children, parents can read about the consequences of children witnessing real violence, television violence, and bullying. For adolescents, information is given on teen dating violence. Physicians are encouraged to give the cards to their patients or to leave them in waiting areas so that patients will have easy access. An example of a large hospital's efforts is the Beth Israel Deaconess Medical Center's (Boston) Center for Violence Prevention and Recovery, which started in 1997. The program provides outreach to victims of childhood maltreatment, partner violence, sexual assault, and elder abuse ("Taking a Broader Look" 1998).

Although adolescents have received little attention in violence prevention until recently, "Adolescence represents a crucial link in the prevention of violence in relationships because it is both an important time for relationship formation and a period in which the scars of childhood can impair normal adjustment" (Wolfe et al. 1997:112). Wolfe et al. focus on educational efforts aimed toward adolescents in the 14- to 16-year-old age group who have experienced childhood maltreatment. The Youth Relationships Project has 2 cofacilitators, one male and one female. Eight to 12 participants meet for 2 hours each week for an 18-week period. The first 3 sessions focus on issues of power and how they are part of violence in relationships. The next 3 sessions focus on recognizing and dealing with abuse in their own relationships and learning the skills to create healthy relationships. The next 5 sessions place relationship violence within a broader context in the effort to understand societal issues that have bearing on abuse such as gender socialization, sexism, and peer pressure. The final sessions assist the adolescents to become knowledgeable about community resources and active in community efforts to educate others on family and dating violence. Early efforts to evaluate this program are encouraging as the adolescents reported a decrease in abusive behavior and victimization and the development of healthier relationships.

Violence Against Women Act

An important new element in efforts against family abuse is the federal Violence Against Women Act of 1994 (VAWA) (42 U.S.C. 13981). This legislation provides funds for treatment and prevention programs for a range of strategies. It funds programs against child abuse; sexual assault; domestic violence; and violence against women in the military, workplace, educational institutions, and women in underserved communities. It also funds research on violence against women.

The principal funding program under VAWA is the S.T.O.P. Violence Against Women formula grant program. S.T.O.P describes areas funded by this program— Services, Training, Officers, and Prosecutors. These programs have funded programs for the training of prosecutors, police, judges, and victim advocates in dealing with victims of family violence. Each state is granted funds to develop a plan to deal with violence against women in the state and funds projects to carry out that plan.

Distribution of sexual assault evidence kits to hospital emergency rooms and outpatient clinics is one of the programs funded by VAWA. Many sexual abuse incidents went unprosecuted because evidence that would meet legal standards for admission to court was often unavailable. Most states now provide training for medical personnel on what evidence they need to collect when they treat the victim to assist in prosecution efforts. These kits also protect the quality of the evidence and establish a chain of custody. The rate of successful prosecutions for sexual assault has increased in states where the kits have been used.

There are two important legal changes resulting from VAWA. States must give full faith and credit to court protection orders from other states and victims of violence are granted power to sue for injury, loss, or damages, including punitive damages when the abuse is gender related. The former change was necessary because victims who visited other states were not usually covered in the new state by the civil protection order of their state of origin. Even when a state would honor an out-of-state restraining order, it was often difficult for the other state to verify the existence of the order in a way that would allow arresting the violator. Arrests for violation in some states require written verification of the order, rather than affirmation by a phone call. To facilitate this process and improve their criminal history records systems, most states are developing a computerized database of offenders having domestic violence restraining orders active against them. This will allow much easier verification of restraining orders and their enforcement in other states. This change that allows enforcement of civil orders across state lines has not been significantly challenged in court.

The second legal change allows family members to sue for damages, which was difficult or impossible in some states, and to also ask for punitive damages, which was usually not allowed previously. The suit may be under a claim of civil rights violation for a gender motivated crime. The legal change has been challenged on the claim that the federal government is regulating family life and does not have the constitutional authority to do so. These challenges have been rejected by the courts. The rationale for the latter change was found under the interstate commerce clause of the Constitution because domestic violence significantly disrupts employment and business activity, not because the federal government asserts authority over family life. Indeed, the claim that "It's just a family matter" has always been used as an excuse to avoid community involvement in family abuse.

The Violence Against Women Act encourages states to enact mandatory arrest and pro-arrest policies for domestic violence offenders. A majority of states already have statutes that mandate arrest for violating restraining orders. There is more variability between states on mandating arrest without a restraining order. This is partly because states differ on what evidence is needed to establish probable cause that the violence occurred. Traditionally, the abuse had to occur practically in front of the officers before they were deemed to have had probable cause for arrest. More recently, states are beginning to accept such evidence as injuries, damage to the residence, witness statements, and "spontaneous utterances" by the perpetrator or victim as establishing probable cause for arrest.

Reluctance to arrest also occurred because officers were not always sure whether the relationship between the parties constituted a "domestic" relationship that met statutory requirements. Certainly, those who were married or related by a close blood tie and who lived together were regarded as having a domestic relationship. There was less certainty about same-sex individuals living together or persons who have dated a few times. A pro-arrest policy would encourage officers to err on the side of calling it a domestic relationship and making the arrest. The judge at the arraignment could then make a legal determination as to whether the relationship was domestic or not. Even if the relationship turns out not to have met the legal requirements of being a domestic relationship, there would still have been probable cause evidence of a crime. The arrest would not have been a false or unwarranted arrest.

In 2000 the Violence Against Women Act was dealt a severe blow. The case began when a Virginia Tech freshman was reportedly raped by two men in 1994 (Masters 2000). Neither man was ever charged with a crime. One produced a witness who offered an alibi, the other man stated he had engaged in consensual sex with the woman. The woman was stunned to find that both men were allowed to remain at Virginia Tech and play on the football team. She became the first woman under the Violence Against Women Act to sue her attackers in federal court for sexual violence. In a five to four U.S. Supreme Court ruling the Violence Against Women Act was declared unconstitutional: The case was thrown out on the grounds that "the federal government has no right to regulate a private act, such as rape, that is neither part of interstate commerce nor caused by state officials" (Savage 2000:A3). Chief Justice William H. Rehnquist stated: "The Constitution requires a distinction between what is truly national and what is truly local" (A3). The effects of this important U.S. Supreme Court decision remain to be seen.

Treatment, Incapacitation, and Punishment

Prevention can occur through treatment, incapacitation, or punishment. Treatment helps to prevent family violence by rehabilitating offenders. Incapacitation prevents family abuse by keeping offenders in prisons or jails so they aren't available to abuse others. Punishment contributes to prevention if it is done in a way that deters others from abuse. Not all punishment results in deterrence, just as not all treatment results in rehabilitation.

The various strategies for preventing family abuse often face a conflict between the desire to preserve families, on the one hand, and the desire to do what maximizes public safety, on the other. The former tends to use educational programs for primary prevention and treatment programs for rehabilitation. The latter tends to use incapacitation and punishment. This conflict can be especially severe where child abuse may result in the children being placed in foster care and questions are raised about terminating the parental rights if treatment is seen as not successful. Courts have always been reluctant to terminate parental rights. State laws require that reasonable efforts to preserve the family and return the child must be made before parental rights can be terminated. Additional treatment may even allow eventual reunification. In the meantime, children may linger in foster placement without a situation of family permanency. In domestic assault cases there may be a conflict between the desire to prosecute and jail the offender and the desire to change his or her behavior so that the domestic relationship might be restored. The ambivalence in society regarding family preservation versus punishment of family abusers is likely to continue. This conflict will challenge lawmakers to address these competing issues.

Efforts to prevent family abuse must take into consideration a wide variety of social forces that affect the family and the offender and can contribute to family violence. While socioeconomic status tends to be overlooked in research on family violence, this is an important factor (Moore 1997). A national conference on reducing family violence sponsored by the National Institute of Justice and the American Medical Association reaffirmed the importance of societal factors in the prevention of family abuse:

> Prevention of family violence should be viewed in terms of social justice and affirmation of basic human rights, rather than retributive criminal justice. We support the shift of social, economic, and political resources toward strengthening communities and families in their many forms. This means ensuring equitable access to employment, education, housing, and health care. (Witwer and Crawford 1995:25)

In addition, more research on the effectiveness of treatment and prevention programs is needed. Toth and Cicchetti (1993) made recommendations for future research in the area of child maltreatment, reviewed in Box 11.6.

BOX **11.6**

Recommendations for Future Research in Child Maltreatment

1. *Research on the sequelae of child maltreatment must be expanded, and these investigations must become increasingly theoretically guided and longitudinal in nature.*

   This recommendation emphasizes the need to examine the consequences of child maltreatment across the lifespan—from the very early years into adulthood. It is difficult to examine the effects of childhood maltreatment when relying only on the recollections of adults; this speaks to the need to have long-term investigations that follow the maltreated child through adulthood.

2. *Efforts to specify the experience of maltreatment and to operationalize all associated variables must be expanded.*

   Research often investigates one subtype of maltreatment such as sexual abuse or neglect. The study of more than one type of maltreatment allows for a more comprehensive approach.

3. *Creative efforts to evaluate child therapy within the very real context of a maltreating home environment must be developed.*

   Efforts to treat the child must exist within the broad array of human service organizations, including child protection agencies and the court system. Family treatment must be considered in addition to individual treatment of the child.

4. *The importance of incorporating developmental considerations into the design and evaluation of treatment programs for maltreated children must be emphasized.*

   Therapists must consider the developmental impact of the abuse on the victim. Therapy with an adult abused as a young child who has little memory of the abuse is different from therapy with an adolescent who is still living in the home of the perpetrator. Thus, therapeutic interventions and research must be tied to the appropriate developmental period.

5. *Investigators of child therapy outcome in the area of child abuse and neglect must clearly define their criteria for success.*

   It is difficult to determine the success of treatment for those who have been abused. Outcome measures must be linked to the specific areas in which the client is experiencing problems in functioning while the therapy addresses the appropriate developmental period of the client.

6. *Despite the difficulties inherent in implementing and evaluating therapy for child victims of maltreatment, it is of the utmost importance that work be conducted in this area.*

   Clinicians and researchers face many obstacles in this challenging field. Efforts need to be made to overcome important obstacles such as methodological problems, difficulty in obtaining research grants, and the suspicion clients may have toward the organizations providing services.

Source: Sherre L. Toth and Dante Cicchetti. 1993. "Child Maltreatment: Where Do We Go From Here in Our Treatment of Victims?" Pp. 399–437 in *Child Abuse, Child Development, and Social Policy*, D. Cicchetti and S. L. Toth, eds. Norwood, NJ: Ablex Publishing Corporation. Pp. 421–24.

Summary

This chapter examines a wide variety of issues in the treatment and prevention of family abuse, an area in which more programs are needed. It describes programs designed to help the victims, their families, and their communities. It discusses treatment of the offenders and issues involved in their rehabilitation and risk of recidivism.

Prevention programs are identified that address primary, secondary, and tertiary prevention. These include education programs and services to families, victims, and offenders. Cognitive–behavioral and group therapy programs for offenders seem especially promising. The chapter discusses the role of criminal justice programs in assisting victims, promoting prosecution, and dealing with incarceration and punishment in their role of helping to prevent subsequent family abuse.

The importance of the Violence Against Women Act is discussed as a coordinated national strategy for dealing with family abuse. It funds many of the treatment and prevention programs mentioned in this chapter. It also makes legal changes that allow victims to more easily sue abusers for loss and punitive damages, to obtain enforcement of protection orders across state lines, and it encourages mandatory and pro-arrest policies.

The tension between treatment and punishment programs is also noted. Both treatment and punishment can contribute to prevention of family abuse, but they also conflict with each other. An ongoing issue is deciding on an appropriate balance between these two approaches for dealing with family abuse.

Study Questions

1. What are the three main types of treatments available for sex offenders?

2. Why are "recovered memories" of childhood maltreatment considered so controversial?

3. Why is castration of sex offenders such a controversial topic?

4. What are some of the factors that make it difficult to determine the effectiveness of specific treatment programs?

5. How do primary, secondary, and tertiary prevention programs for dealing with family abuse differ in their approach to dealing with their problem?

6. What is the Violence Against Women Act and how does it affect family abuse programs?

7. How should society decide on a balance between preserving the family and punishing the offenders? Under what circumstances, if any, should punishment be reduced or diverted for the sake of rehabilitating the family relationship?

REFERENCES

Abel, G. G., M. S. Mittleman, and J. V. Becker. 1985. "Sex Offenders: Results of Assessment and Recommendation for Treatment." Pp. 207–20 in *Clinical Criminology: The Assessment and Treatment of Criminal Behavior,* M. H. Ben-Aron, S. J. Hucker, and C. D. Webster, eds. Toronto, Canada: M & M Graphics.

"An Ounce of Prevention, a Pound of Penalty Urged for Spouse-Beating Cops." 1998. *Law Enforcement News,* XXIV, April 30:1,9.

Barbaree, Howard E. and William M. Marshall. 1998. "Treatment of the Sexual Offender." Pp. 265–328 in *Treatment of Offenders with Mental Disorders,* Robert M. Wettstein, ed. NY: Guilford Press.

Barrett, Mary Jo, Cece Sykes, and William Byrnes. 1986. "A Systemic Model for the Treatment of Intrafamily Child Sexual Abuse." Pp. 67–82 in *Treating Incest: A Multiple Systems Perspective,* Terry S. Trepper and Mary Jo Barrett, eds. NY: The Haworth Press.

Berrick, J. D. and N. Gilbert. 1991. *With the Best of Intentions: The Child Sexual Abuse Prevention Movement.* NY: Guilford.

Blanchard, Geral. 1997. "Aboriginal Canadian Innovations in the Treatment of Sexual Violence." *The Carnes Update: Sexual Disorder Services at The Meadows.* Summer.

"Blueprints: A Violence Prevention Initiative." 1999. *OJJDP Fact Sheet.* Washington, DC: Office of Juvenile Justice and Delinquency Prevention, June, #110.

Bombardieri, Marcella. 2000. "Abused Women Find Aid at Work." *The Boston Globe,* April 16:B1, B2.

Briere, John. 1997. "Treating Adults Severely Abused as Children: The Self-Trauma Model." Pp. 177–204 in *Child Abuse: New Directions in Prevention and Treatment Across the Lifespan,* David A. Wolfe, Robert J. McMahon, and Ray DeV. Peters, eds. Thousand Oaks, CA: Sage Publications.

Brill, Carol and Miriam Stein. 1999. *Our Children and Families: A Social Work Statement Addressing Child Abuse and Neglect.* Boston, MA: National Association of Social Workers, Massachusetts Chapter.

Brown, Joanne L. and George S. Brown. 1997. "Characterstics and Treatment of Incest Offenders: A Review." Pp. 335–54 in *Violence and Sexual Abuse at Home: Current Issues in Spousal Battering and Child Maltreatment,* Robert Geffner, Susan B. Sorenson, and Paula K. Lundberg-Love, eds. NY: Haworth Press.

Child Sexual Abuse Prevention Training Centers. 1999. "Child Sexual Abuse Prevention Training Centers" (WWW http:www.ocjp.ca.gov/sxabstrning.html).

Chu, James. 1999. "The Nature of Traumatic Memories of Childhood Abuse." *McLean Hospital Psychiatric Update.* 1:5. Belmont, MA: McLean Hospital.

"Doctors to Screen for Home Violence." 2000. *The Boston Globe,* July 13:A11.

Ellement, John. 2000. "State Study Eyes Repeat Sex Offenders." *The Boston Globe,* May 3:B3.

"Evaluation of Family Violence Training Programs." November 1995. *Research Preview.* Washington, DC: National Institute of Justice.

False Memory Syndrome Foundation. 1998. (WWW http//advicom.net/~fitz/fmsf/).

Fennell, Dana C. and Anne H. Fishel. 1998. "Parent Education: An Evaluation of STEP on Abusive Parents." *Journal of Child and Adolescent Psychiatric Nursing.* 11:107–15.

Giarretto, Henry and Anna Einfeld-Giarretto. 1990. "Integrated Treatment: The Self-Help Factor. Pp. 219–26 in *The Incest Perpetrator: A Family Member No One Wants to Treat,* Anne L. Horton, Barry L. Johnson, Lynn M. Roundy, and Doran Williams, eds. Newbury Park, CA: Sage Publications.

Gilbert, N., J. Berrick, N. LeProhn, and N. Nyman. 1989. *Protecting Young Children from Sexual Abuse: Does Preschool Training Work?* Lexington, MA: Lexington.

Graham, Kevin R. 1993. "Toward a Better Understanding and Treatment of Sex Offenders." *International Journal of Offender Therapy and Comparative Criminology.* 37:41–57.

Grossman, David C., Holly J. Neckerman, Thomas D. Koepsell, Pin-Yu Liu, Kenneth N. Asher, Kathy Beland, Karin Frey, and Frederick Pivara. 1997. "Effectiveness of a Violence Prevention Curriculum Among Children in Elementary School." *JAMA: Journal of the American Medical Association.* 277:1605–11.

Hagan, Michael P. and Meg E. Cho. 1996. "A Comparison of Treatment Outcomes Between Adolescent Rapists and Child Sexual Offenders." *International Journal of Offender Therapy and Comparative Criminology.* 40:113–22.

Hart, Jordana. 1999. "Children Affected by Domestic Violence." *The Boston Globe,* April 20:B1, B5.

Herman, Judith L. and Mary R. Harvey. 1997. "Adult Memories of Childhood Trauma: A Naturalistic Clinical Study." *Journal of Traumatic Stress.* 10:557–71.

Holmes, William M. 1993. "Police Arrests for Domestic Violence." *American Journal of Police.* 12,4:101–25.

Howing, Phyllis, John S. Wodarski, James M. Gaudin, Jr., and P. David Kurtz. 1989. "Effective Interventions to Ameliorate the Incidence of Child Maltreatment: The Empirical Base." *Social Work.* 34:330–38.

Kear-Colwell, Jon and Philip Pollock. 1997. "Motivation or Confrontation: Which Approach to the Child Sexual Offender." *Criminal Justice and Behavior.* 24:20-33.

Knopp, F. H. 1984. *Retraining Adult Sex Offenders: Methods and Models.* Syracuse, NY: Safer Society Press.

Lein, James. 1999. "Recovered Memories: Context and Controversy." *Social Work.* 44:481–84.

Lisko, Elaine. 1999. "Recently Reported Chemical Castration of Sex Offenders." (WWW http://www.law.uh.edu/LawCenter/Programs/Health/LLPIHELP/Biology/980225Pedophile.htm).

Marshall, W. L. 1996. "Assessment, Treatment, and Theorizing About Sex Offenders: Developments During the Past Twenty Years and Future Directions." *Criminal Justice and Behavior.* 23:162–99.

Massachusetts Medical Society Committee on Violence. 1997. *Violence Prevention for Children and Youth.* Waltham, MA: Author.

Masters, Brooke A. 2000. "Rape Case, Court Fight End in Disappointment, Shattered Dreams." Washington Post. *The Boston Globe,* May 28:A20.

Mezey, Gillian C. 1993. "Treatment for Male Victims of Rape." Pp. 130–44 in *Male Victims of Sexual Assault,* Gillian C. Mezey and Michael B. King, eds. Oxford, Eng.: Oxford University Press.

Mignon, Sylvia and William Holmes. 1995. "Police Response to Mandatory Arrest Laws." *Crime and Delinquency.* 41:430–42.

Moore, Angela. 1997. "Intimate Violence: Does Socioeconomic Status Matter?" Pp. 90–100 in *Violence Between Intimate Partners: Patterns, Causes, and Effects,* Albert P. Cardarelli, ed. Boston, MA: Allyn and Bacon.

NASW National Council on the Practice of Clinical Social Work. 1997. "Evaluation and Treatment of Adults with the Possibility of Recovered Memories of Childhood Sexual Abuse." *Focus, Newsletter of the National Association of Social Workers, Massachusetts Chapter,* 24:5. Boston, MA: NASW.

Olsen, Lenore, Karen Capoverde, William Holmes, and Mimi Mumm. 1996. *Project Connect: Project Evaluation.* Providence, RI: Children's Friend and Service.

Patten, Sylvia B., Yvonne K. Gatz, Berlin Jones, and Deborah L. Thomas. 1989. "Posttraumatic Stress Disorder and the Treatment of Sexual Abuse." *Social Work.* 34:197–203.

Pithers, William D. 1997. "Maintaining Treatment Integrity with Sexual Abusers." *Criminal Justice and Behavior.* 24:34–51.

Plummer, Carol A. 1993. "Prevention Is Appropriate, Prevention Is Successful." Pp. 288–305 in *Current Controversies on Family Violence,* Richard J. Gelles and Donileen R. Loseke, eds. Newbury Park, CA: Sage Publications.

Pope, Kenneth S. and Laura S. Brown. 1996. *Recovered Memories of Abuse: Assessment, Therapy and Forensics.* Washington, DC: American Psychological Association.

Reppucci, N. Dickon and Jeffrey J. Haugaard. 1993. "Problems with Child Sexual Abuse Prevention Programs." Pp. 306–22 in *Current Controversies on Family Violence,* Richard J. Gelles and Donileen R. Loseke, eds. Newbury Park, CA: Sage Publications.

Rösler, Ariel and Eliezer Witztum. 1998. "Treatment of Men with Paraphilia with a Long-Acting Analogue of Gondotropin-Releasing Hormone." *New England Journal of Medicine.* 338: 416–34.

Roundy, Lynn M. and Anne L. Horton. 1990. "Professional and Treatment Issues for Clinicians Who Intervene with Incest Perpetrators." Pp. 164–89 in *The Incest Perpetrator: The Family Member No One Wants to Treat,* Anne L. Horton, Barry L. Johnson, Lynn M. Roundy, and Doran Williams, eds. Newbury Park, CA: Sage Publications.

Savage, David G. 2000. "U.S. Supreme Court Bars Rape Case." Los Angeles Times. *The Boston Globe,* May 16:A3.

Schneider, Hans Joachim. 1997. "Sexual Abuse of Children: Strengths and Weaknesses of Current Criminology." *International Journal of Offender Therapy and Comparative Criminology.* 41:310–24.

Skolnick-Aker, Eva. 1999. "Who Do Children Kill and Can We Stop Them?" *Focus,* Publication of the Massachusetts Chapter of the National Association of Social Workers, 26, July:1, 8.

Sherman, Lawrence. 1995. *Family Violence.* Washington, DC: National Academy of Science.

Stillwell, Arlene M. and Roy F. Baumeister. 1997. "The Construction of Victim and Perpetrator Memories: Accuracy and Distortion in Role-Based Accounts." *Personality and Social Psychology Bulletin.* 23:1157–72.

Strauss, Murray A., Sherry L. Homey, and Desmond Runyon. 1998. "Identification of Child Maltreatment with the Parent Child Conflict Tactics Scales: Developmental and Psychometric Data for a National Sample of American Parents." *Child Abuse & Neglect.* 22:249–66.

"Taking a Broader Look: Center for Violence Prevention and Recovery." June 1998. *Our News: A Publication for Beth Israel Deaconess Medical Center Staff and Employees.* Boston, MA.

Toth, Sheree L. and Dante Cicchetti. 1993. "Child Maltreatment: Where Do We Go From Here in Our Treatment of Victims?" Pp. 399–437 in *Child Abuse, Child Development, and Social Policy,* vol. 8, D. Cicchetti and S. L. Toth, eds. Norwood, NJ: Ablex Publishing Corporation.

Trepper, Terry S. 1986. "The Apology Session." Pp. 93–101 in *Treating Incest: A Multiple Systems Perspective,* Terry S. Trepper and Mary Jo Barrett, eds. NY: The Haworth Press.

Trute, Barry, Elizabeth Adkins, and George MacDonald. 1996. "Professional Attitudes Regarding Treatment and Punishment of Incest: Comparing Police, Child Welfare, and Community Mental Health." *Journal of Family Violence.* 11:237–49.

Whipple, Ellen E. and Steven R. Welser. 1996. "Evaluation of a Parent Education and Support Program for Families at Risk of Physical Child Abuse." *Families in Society.* 77:227–35.

Williams, Oliver J. 1994. "Group Work with African American Men Who Batter: Toward More Ethnically Sensitive Practice." *Journal of Comparative Family Studies.* 25:91–104.

Witwer, Martha B. and Cheryl A. Crawford. 1995. *A Coordinated Approach to Reducing Family Violence: Conference Highlights.* Washington, DC: Department of Justice and the American Medical Association.

Wolfe, David A., Christine Wekerle, Deborah Reitzer-Jaffe, Carolyn Grasley, Anna-Lee Pittman, and Andrea MacEachran. 1997. "Interrupting the Cycle of Violence: Empowering Youth to Promote Healthy Relationships." Pp. 102–29 in *Child Abuse: New Directions in Treatment and Prevention Across the Lifespan,* David A. Wolfe, Robert J. McMahon, and Ray DeV. Peters, eds. Thousand Oaks, CA: Sage Publications.

Wolfus, Beverly and Ralph Bierman. 1996. "An Evaluation of a Group Treatment Program for Incarcerated Male Batterers." *International Journal of Offender Therapy and Comparative Criminology.* 40:318–33.

CHAPTER

12 What Do We Know?
What Is To Be Done?

The aim of this book has been to document the nature and extent of family abuse and its consequences. The available evidence on the identified varieties of child and adult abuse has been presented and assessed. Also identified and discussed are the major theoretical explanations for particular types of family abuse. Particular attention has been devoted to identifying the victims and perpetrators of family violence across the lifespan and by gender, race, ethnicity, and socioeconomic factors such as education and family income. Particular and continuous attention has been given to the deviant behavioral effects of family abuse (from mental health problems to juvenile and adult criminality). Various intervention approaches and strategies have been examined, and special populations (for example, sex offenders, prostitutes, substance abusers) have been identified as complicating the difficult task of developing and implementing effective ways of deterring, if not preventing, family violence. What does the analysis of these subjects tell us? What precisely do we know and not know? What are the policy and programmatic implications of what we know and don't know? These are some of the questions behind the subjects discussed in this concluding chapter.

Family Abuse Research: Facts, Trends, Weaknesses

As brought out in Chapter 7, two major interrelated problems in the family violence field are being able to specify what is and is not family abuse and the difficulty this brings to an exact measurement of its nature and extent. Most students of the subject conceive of family abuse as a series of types based on the means used as well as their behavioral consequences. Four major types of family abuse are commonly identified: neglect, physical, sexual, and emotional. Some analysts specialize in one particular type. Others consider all four as aspects of a single problem and structure their analyses accordingly: some emphasize the act of abuse, how it is perpetrated, by whom, why, and with what effects; others focus their analytical gaze on the diverse independent effects of abuse, regardless of its manner of perpetration.

On the one hand, these and other possible slants on the subject are important and provide a more rounded sense of the problem than might otherwise be the case. On the other, they point to the absence of a generally agreed on and sustained viewpoint, the effect of which is to hinder systematic data collection. Exactly what is and is not family abuse depends on how it is conceived and defined not only by students of the subject but also by state and federal law makers. Conceptual ambiguity among scholars and practitioners is matched by different views as to what legally constitutes family abuse by lawmakers in the states and the federal government. Because exactly what does and does not constitute family abuse varies from one jurisdiction to another, the evidence provided by those responsible for reporting its occurrence must be cautiously interpreted. Thus, the fact is that we have only some idea of the nature and extent of family abuse in the United States. Whether what we know over- or understates reality is unknown.

Facts

The fact is, the true extent of family violence and its consequences is not accurately measurable. Because of its personal and social sensitivity and possible criminal ramifications, one should expect it to be an underinvestigated and underreported phenomenon. One cannot simply draw a random sample of families in the United States and closely observe the daily interaction patterns of their members toward the end of empirically verifying exactly when and under what circumstances the various types of family abuse occur. Short of round-the-clock observance of interaction patterns in a representative sample of American families, information brought to the attention of a variety of private (counseling services, medical clinics) and public concerns (school and law enforcement personnel, social workers, battered women's centers) by disparate sources (victims, witnesses, friends, relatives) must be relied on—in addition to what is known by the prevalence surveys on child abuse, family violence, and elder abuse. Confirming the accuracy of such "after-the-fact" evidence is, at best, difficult and challenging and, at worst, impossible. The available evidence suggests that the problem is extensive.

With these limitations in mind, the best estimates of family violence (for example, Witmer & Crawford 1995) suggest that approximately 4 million women, 1 to 2 million older adults, and some 2 to 4 million children are abused annually by a family member or members. Data on how many perpetrators account for these estimated victimizations and whether the estimated number of known perpetrators has increased or decreased is unavailable.

Trends

Trends in regard to family abuse remain somewhat unclear not only for the above stated reasons, but also because of changes in the data collection procedures by available authoritative sources, such as the annual National Crime Victimization Survey (NCVS) and the Uniform Crime Reports (UCRs). The best available information on violence against intimates indicates a slightly declining trend for female and a relatively stable trend for male victims. Thus, from 1993 to 1998, intimate partner violence decreased 21 percent. Over these years the victimization rate declined from 9.8 to 7.5 per 1,000 females in the population. For males, the rates for these years show only a 0.1 percent decline (from 1.6 to 1.5 per 1,000 males in the population).

Homicide data are particularly valuable because homicide is the most accurately documented of the major crimes. In Table 12.1, Bureau of Justice Statistics show a moderately declining trend in the number of females murdered by an intimate (husband, ex-husband, common-law husband, same-sex partner, or boyfriend) over the years from 1976 to 1997, but an upturn from 1997 to 1998.

Between 1976 and 1998, the average number of females murdered by an intimate declined by 1 percent a year and male victims by 4 percent a year. The decline is traced to the drop in the number of murders of an intimate by means of a firearm (an average decline of 3 percent a year). The number of intimate murders by other means has remained virtually unchanged. No explanation is provided for the decrease in the number of intimate murders by means of a handgun.

Reports from the states to the U.S. Children's Bureau indicate declining rates of child abuse. As can be seen in Figure 12.1, substantiated cases of emotional maltreatment declined from 6.8 to 5.9 percent, sexual abuse cases declined from 14.9 to 12.3 percent, physical abuse cases declined from 23.6 to 22.2 percent. The exception is cases of neglect which increased from 54.9 to 57.7 percent. The declining rates of substantiated cases, however, must be interpreted with caution because protective service agencies that have cutbacks in resources may find the decline is due to reduced ability to investigate.

Elderly abuse data also indicate a rising trend. In 1990, a report issued by the U.S. House of Representatives stated that elder abuse had increased 50 percent since

TABLE 12.1 The Number of Murders by an Intimate,* 1976–1998

Year	Male Victims	Female Victims	Year	Male Victims	Female Victims
1976	1357	1600	1988	854	1582
1977	1294	1437	1989	903	1415
1978	1202	1482	1990	859	1501
1979	1262	1506	1991	779	1518
1980	1221	1549	1992	722	1455
1981	1278	1572	1993	708	1581
1982	1141	1481	1994	692	1405
1983	1113	1462	1995	547	1321
1984	989	1442	1996	515	1324
1985	957	1546	1997	451	1217
1986	985	1586	1998	512	1317
1987	933	1494			

*Note: Intimates include spouses, ex-spouses, common-law spouses, same sex partners, boyfriends, and girlfriends.

Source: U.S. Department of Justice, Bureau of Justice Statistics, *Violence by Intimates*. Washington, DC: U.S. Government Printing Office. March 2000, P. 10.

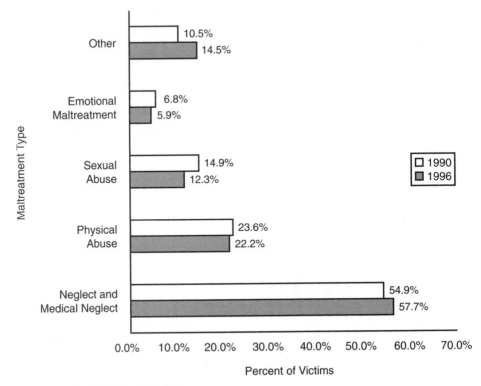

1990: N = 558,234 victims in 31 States.
1996: N = 572,943 victims in 31 States.

FIGURE 12.1 Trends in Violence Against Intimates

Source: U.S. Department of Justice, Bureau of Justice Statistics, *Violence by Intimates*, Washington, DC: March, 1998, Pp. 3–4.

1980 (Skabronski 1995/1996). More recently (O'Hanlon 1997), cases of domestic abuse involving elderly victims reportedly increased 150 percent from 1986 to 1996 (from some 117,000 to 293,000 cases). These figures include only those who said they were the victims of physical abuse, neglect, or financial exploitation.

Weaknesses

How much factors such as data collection approaches and changing attitudes in regard to public sensitivity and willingness to report incidents influence knowledge is unknown. Research of the problem would be greatly enhanced by a national agency assigned the task of collecting and disseminating information about cases involving both children and adults, victims and perpetrators. One of the requirements of the Violence Against Women Act specified development of domestic violence data systems in the states. This process is ongoing. Therefore, as the matter stands, we do not know how much the trends noted reflect data collection

limitations or the influence of other considerations, from nationwide family intervention programs of different kinds to changing attitudes and values.

Just as the actual number of family violence perpetrators and victims is
uncertain so, too, are its behavioral consequences, deviant and otherwise. From
the research reports and anecdotal evidence provided by mental health research
professionals and therapists (for example, Gross and Keller 1992; Iwaniec 1995;
Jantz 1995), it is evident that the abused suffer a variety of psychological and
behavioral problems. Incapacitating mental illness, prostitution, propensity to
self-abuse by means of drugs and alcohol, juvenile delinquency, violent and
nonviolent adult criminality all have been associated with abuse by a family
member or members. Some evidence indicates support for cycles of violence (see,
in particular, Widom 1992, 1996), that a disproportionate number of those victimized by abuse and violence today become the abusers of family members and
acquaintances tomorrow. Nonetheless, most victims have not been found to
become victimizers. What differentiates those who perpetuate their abuse from
those who do not remains to be determined.

In spite of its limitations, the available evidence is more than sufficient to
warrant recognition of family violence as a major medical, psychological, and social
problem. While national and local public policy and programs designed to treat the
problem are clearly in order, greater specification of the nature of the problem (how
it is expressed, by whom, under what circumstances) and its causes is necessary if
proposed solutions are to have a reasonable chance of succeeding. This task includes
development of an agreed on operational definition of family abuse, clearer
differentiation of the different types of family abuse, and deciding whether or not
to develop a general theory of family abuse or separate theories to account for the
different types of family abuse. Research funded by the Violence Against Women
Act will address some of these issues. Longitudinal studies of family abuse that are
in progress will also help to sort out how abuse, deviance, and crime are related.

Victims and Perpetrators: Problems and Issues

Prerequisite to these chores is the need to examine certain relatively unexamined
subjects, particularly the need to clarify assumptions regarding the causes of family
abuse victimization and perpetration. Greatly in need of attention are the causal
paths leading to perpetration and victimization and how the two interrelate. The
two undoubtedly causally interact, but exactly how, when, and why remains to be
determined.

Information Issues

We have much more information on victims than perpetrators of family abuse. The
available information indicates that victims are disproportionately those at the
mercy of other family members because of lower or weakened physical or mental
abilities or fewer economic resources—children, women, older adults. Thus, perpetrators tend to be parents vis-à-vis children, males vis-à-vis female partners, and

the children of elderly parents. Because frequency of perpetration is undoubtedly effectively concealed, its actual extent is a dark figure, something to be ferreted out in future research and investigation. Prerequisite to this endeavor is supportive public demand, a popular call to identify and take to task those responsible for family abuse. Intrusion into family life on the scale and frequency required is much too sensitive an act to be expected to be allowed without widespread support and thoroughly developed and approved methods.

Consequently, although much in order, and whatever its perceived need by scholars and practitioners, the creation of something analogous to the National Crime Victimization Survey to clarify the extent, frequency, and varieties of family victimization would at present appear to be too controversial to be taken seriously by the federal authorities. The national surveys on child maltreatment, violence against women, family violence, and elder abuse provide a useful beginning in this process.

How many victims are repeat or new victims each year is not generally available. Also unavailable is documented evidence of frequency of abuse by victim type and perpetrator, and frequency of perpetration by various perpetrator characteristics. Some people stop being victims and perpetrators for any number of possible reasons, the range of reasons for which are unknown.

While it is important to collect annual information on the prevalence of family abuse and to identify its victims and perpetrators, it is no less important to collect longitudinal data. Complicating the long-term trend are changing social and cultural conceptions of what is and is not family abuse. Needed is not only a precise and generally accepted conception of family abuse that can be applied to data collection at a given time, but also a conception that can be modified to take into account changing sociocultural norms and values. One generation's sense of proper child discipline may come to be regarded as abusive to another. Trends in family abuse prevalence and among the different types remain much too elusive and unspecified. This problem must certainly be confronted and effectively dealt with if we are to be able to confidently determine what the problem is and how effectively it is being identified and treated.

Policy Issues

Lacking an objective and nationally approved official means of gauging the nature and extent of family abuse means that plans and strategies to correct the problem must be developed from limited after-the-fact information supplied primarily by those who come forward to report incidents. The problem is that far too many victims cannot be expected to report their victimization because they either fear the consequences or are deterred or prevented from coming forward by threats to their well-being, physical, financial, and so on. Therefore, questions to consider involving indirect preventative measures include the following: Should we consider passing laws requiring all prospective parents to take courses in parenting, included in which are discussions of child rights and adult responsibilities, and the difference between abusive and nonabusive disciplinary measures? Should prospective adult partners in some way be required to demonstrate awareness of their legal responsibilities to one another and be alerted to the factors, individual and situational, associated with battering and other forms of abuse? Parent education and premarital counseling programs provide such information. To what extent should they be required?

It must be assumed that many become abusers for reasons unclear to themselves but which they may well be able to be alerted to by becoming acquainted with the lessons gained from known cases. Similarly, it must be assumed that many become victims for unclear reasons that they may be alerted to before the fact from knowledge of victimization. Therefore, should such knowledge be required at some point or level in the public educational process, or at the very least made directly available to prospective parents? England and other countries have home visitation programs for families with neonatal children to provide such parent education and check for medical and other family needs. Could a program like that help reduce family abuse in America?

There is an ongoing conflict between policies designed to preserve, restore, and rehabilitate abusive families and those intending to criminalize abusive behavior, punish offenders, and blame victims. How is our society going to resolve these conflicts? When do they conflict? Which policies shall have priority? How many resources should be committed to implementing these policies? When there are not enough resources to fully implement competing policies, how shall we determine who gets what? To what extent can research information help resolve these issues?

Programmatic and Intervention Strategies

Chapter 11 contains a thorough review of the variety of programs and intervention strategies that have been devised and implemented to treat the victims and perpetrators of different types of family abuse and criminality, such as offenders with a history of physical or sexual abuse victimization. Treatment and prevention efforts are evident at the federal, state, and local levels. Lacking is a carefully designed nationally coordinated plan to systematically identify and treat both the victims and perpetrators of family violence. Piecemeal efforts are the order of the day, and as useful and important as they may be, they are clearly minimal to the need. With all the talk about the importance of family values, there continues to be little progress toward acknowledging the extent of the problem of family abuse and its personal and societal consequences. This, notwithstanding the fact that the available evidence as contained in this work and several others, clearly points to the need for a national public policy to confront the problem by concerted programmatic means of prevention and intervention.

Education

Much in need are educational programs, beginning at least as early as the grammar school level, designed to show what family abuse is, what its various forms are and how it may be perpetrated with what effects, and how victims may seek help without endangering themselves. Simultaneously required is parent and guardian education about the subject. They, too, need to understand what does and does not constitute child abuse. Many, after all, are from different cultures with different standards of child discipline, some of which may be contrary to American norms and laws. And they, too, need to be alerted to available treatment for those wishing to confront their own problems.

As noted throughout this book, many parents can be expected to have a background of family abuse victimization. It must be assumed, therefore, that many discover they have a problem only after having their own children, a problem of repeating a pattern of abuse that they come to realize and recognize as requiring specialized treatment. Admitting the need for help is difficult for most adults. Admitting that one is an actual or potentially abusive parent in need of treatment must be assumed to be among the most difficult forms of public confession. How to facilitate such admissions, and the programs needed to respond to them, should be seriously and thoughtfully integrated into any effective educational or treatment plan.

General adult education about the problem of family abuse is an obvious deficiency requiring remediation. To be considered are ways of educating young adults prior to marriage or before having children. Educating immigrants about the problem, at least by providing a lecture on child abuse and what it is, is one place to begin. Another is at the point of marriage application. At present, premarriage counseling is voluntary. Making it a legal requirement, part of the licensing process, and including instruction about family abuse is well worth considering (see, for example, Westman 1996).

Treatment and Prevention

The greatest need is for prevention of abuse and treatment for adult perpetrators and victims of family abuse. Once reaching adulthood, it is difficult to treat problems; behavioral attitudes and problems are inclined to become deeply embedded and difficult to uproot and correct. Yet, the mere fact of willingness to confront the problem, to admit the need to deal with it as best one can must be encouraged and widely supported. We are much more willing to chastise, punish, and isolate adults with serious problems than to respond to them in caring and thoughtful ways. Clearly in order is sympathetic responsiveness to the problem of the abusive adult. The dominant mode is to escalate the punitive consequences of child or wife battering without simultaneous recognition of the need to treat the batterer sympathetically. The batterer is seen as the enemy, not the patient. Notwithstanding justification for this judgment, it alone may serve more to worsen than alleviate the problem. For too many, violence after court ordered restraint seems to escalate rather than decline. Restraining orders are a necessity to protect victims, but efforts to temper punishment of perpetrators by regarding them, too, as victims requiring public assistance must be considered. Admittedly, it is difficult to empathize with those who do serious violence to others; but unless we learn to respond to abusers with more sympathetic understanding than is presently the case, to regard them as essential to prevention and treatment efforts, we are likely to contribute more toward the perpetuation than the reduction of the problem. Punishment and isolation are needed to protect the innocent; but unless they lead to positive and sympathetic treatment efforts, they may provoke the very problem they are intended to prevent. Punishment without treatment may reinforce the belief that force and violence are the ways to control others. Primary deviation may lead to secondary deviation. Societal reactions to deviancy may not only discourage, but also encourage, if not causally influence, future deviancy. According to Edwin Lemert: "When a person begins to employ his deviant behavior or a role based upon it as a means of defense, attack, or adjustment to the overt and covert problems created by the consequent societal reaction to him, his deviation is secondary" (1994:262). As a labeling theorist would advise us, societal conceptions and reactions to deviancy are to be viewed as causes of the problem (see, for example, Becker 1963). Programs are needed to aid both the victims and perpetrators of family abuse.

Future Issues in Child Maltreatment

Several issues emerge regarding child maltreatment: its relationship with poverty reduction, child welfare efforts, and community efforts. While treatment efforts must continue within the psychological realm, we think our best hope for reducing family abuse lies within the sociological realm; that is, treatment must continue for both victims and perpetrators of maltreatment while at the same time attention must be given to the prevention and treatment of family abuse by addressing the related problems of poverty, lack of education, substance abuse, and other social factors. We now turn to a discussion of sociological factors we expect will aid in the prevention of family abuse.

Poverty and Child Maltreatment

It is not the position of these authors that poverty causes child maltreatment. If anything, the reverse is true. Abusers use economic deprivation as a tool to control family members. The offenders disrupt efforts of family members to gain employment or other economic resources. They want the members to be dependent on them as their sole source of economic support. When victims leave this relationship, they typically suffer even greater economic hardship. Even after they leave, abusers may harass the departing parent at work, or they may stalk the child at school (in an effort to force the other parent to leave work to deal with the situation). The negative economic consequences of the abusers' actions is so great that Congress included in the Violence Against Women Act a clause that allows victims to sue the offenders for economic loss on the grounds of gender discrimination.

Overall, we have to conclude that the economic status of children has not been and is not a high priority in our society. Children in poverty are at greater risk of abuse and exploitation. Andrews and Ben-Arieh (1999) express concern that children's interests have been subordinated to issues of economic wealth:

> Sophisticated data systems permit monitoring of trends and forecasts for everything from pork bellies to airline tickets, but the capacity to portray children's needs and resources is limited. The combination of silent voices and insufficient information in their interests has contributed to the relatively powerless position of children in society. (106)

One of the obvious indicators of the overall status of children in our country is the economic conditions in which children live. Ozawa (1999) puts forth an indictment of a system where children have lost and will continue to lose economic ground: "In the eyes of policymakers, income security for children has not been a high political priority. Thus no income support program addresses the income needs of all poor children" (14). Ozawa points to a U.S. House of Representatives report (1994) that showed the median payment to poor families from the AFDC program (Aid to Families with Dependent Children) "declined 47 percent in real terms from 1970 to 1994" (1999:15). With recent "welfare reforms" of Congress, AFDC has been effectively abolished, which undermines the efforts of abused families to leave the abuser. Ozawa recommends income security for children, which would be independent of social programs for parents. These programs could include free medical care and equal access to quality education.

Social welfare policies do not ensure that children have enough food. According to the U.S. Department of Agriculture, 10 percent of households nationally were considered "food insecure" (insufficient food or the threat of insufficient food) for the years 1996 to 1998 (Brasher 1999). The highest rate of hunger or the threat of hunger was found in New Mexico (15 percent of the population) followed by Mississippi, Texas, Arizona, Louisiana, Arkansas, and Oregon (all at 12.6 percent or above). The lack of concern for adequate nutrition for children calls to mind the efforts in the 1980s by former President Ronald Reagan to have ketchup designated as a "vegetable" in school lunch programs. School programs are required to provide a balanced meal, and making ketchup a "vegetable" was a clear effort to save money by denying children a real vegetable. The willingness to remove food from the mouths of children is a sad commentary.

From an even broader perspective, malnutrition is a major international social problem. The World Health Organization (1998) found that malnutrition contributed to the death of almost half of the over 10 million children under the age of 5 in developing countries (Seipel 1999). Mental and physical abilities are impaired by malnourishment, which increases the risk of abuse and exploitation by making it more difficult for victims to defend themselves against abusers. Basic food itself becomes a tool abusers use to mistreat others. The fact that millions of children are starving today should serve as a strong call to action on behalf of all the world's children.

Another reminder of how poorly we are doing in providing for our country's children can be seen in the burgeoning problem of adolescent homelessness. Youth who live on the streets are at extreme risk of further abuse and exploitation. They are also at great risk of exposure to developing a variety of deviant and criminal behaviors. The National Coalition for the Homeless estimates that 300,000 youths under age 18 are homeless each year (Lambert 1999). Adolescents now comprise the fastest-growing population in shelters. According to the Massachusetts Housing and Shelter Alliance, two-thirds of the state's adolescents in shelters have been at some time in the custody of the state. Forty percent have spent time in foster care through the Department of Social Services. One in four adolescent shelter residents has been a juvenile offender, having spent time in a Department of Youth Services juvenile correctional facility (Lambert 1999).

Child Welfare Efforts

While our country has a long history of providing social services for children, we should acknowledge that these efforts have not been consistent. Addressing abuse and neglect issues is even more difficult when a child's basic needs for food, clothing, shelter, and emotional support are not being met. Unfortunately, child protective services have long been overburdened and incapable of providing services to all families in need. The media at times report on disquieting cases when a child welfare agency has inappropriately intervened in a family and false accusations of abuse or neglect have been made. These cases may involve parents who briefly leave young children unattended in a car while running into the store for two minutes to buy a loaf of bread. While certainly this is not exercising good parental judgment, some may argue that this kind of incident is not an appropriate use of the limited resources of child protective agencies, which should focus on the more severe cases of abuse and neglect.

Unfortunately, public perceptions of child welfare agencies tend to be negative and support the view of unfair and inappropriate interventions with families, which often include fears that agencies are ripping children away from their parents. A recent case in Massachusetts highlights the belief that the state child protective agency is lurking around the corner waiting to interfere in private family matters. The case involved a 12-year-old handicapped boy whose father, a minister, spanked him with a belt (Ellement 1999). This was brought to the attention of the child protective agency by the boy's teacher in 1997. The child protective agency, the Department of Social Services, found that the spanking constituted abuse and offered no further intervention if the father agreed to stop spanking (Finucane 1999). The father refused. This case made its way to the Massachusetts Supreme Judicial Court, which ruled in November 1999 that there was not sufficient evidence that the minister had abused his son. The Supreme Judicial Court chastised the Department of Social Services stating that they should do a better job of distinguishing "permissible physical discipline" from child abuse (Finucane 1999). This case received considerable media attention and clearly reflects societal ambivalence about corporal punishment. Unfortunately, to many who approve of physical discipline of children, it appears that an overzealous Department of Social Services falsely accused parents of abuse, which, in turn, engenders mistrust of child protective services.

On the other hand, the media also report cases of children living in situations of squalor and extreme neglect. Great attention is given to children who die from abuse. Here child protective agencies are rapped for not intervening at an early point. Child protective workers can easily feel between "a rock and a hard place" in carrying out their considerable responsibilities. The dilemma of too much intervention or too little continues to challenge the child welfare system.

It is disconcerting that through many years of child protective interventions the same issues continue to haunt child welfare efforts. These include high caseloads, low salaries, staff turnover, and burnout in dealing with extremely complex and disturbing cases of family abuse (Beaucar 1999). A number of states including Connecticut, Massachusetts, Missouri, New York, and Kansas have been challenged through the courts with providing inadequate child protection services and ordered to improve. While a national standard recommends a caseload of no more than 15 families in child protection, the norm is far higher. Maryland data show a caseload of 30 or more in each month per worker (Beaucar 1999). The U.S. Department of Health and Human Services (2000) reported an average annual workload in 1998 for child protective investigative workers to be 94 investigations. The Massachusetts Chapter of the National Association of Social Workers in publishing *Our Children and Families: A Social Work Statement Addressing Child Abuse and Neglect* (Brill and Stein 1999) strongly recommends lower caseloads and professional training for social workers.

Sadly lacking in family abuse treatment and prevention efforts is a genuine effort to place the needs of children in the forefront. While our system has long paid lip service to the notion of the "best interests of the child," child welfare professionals are aware that there are many people with their own agendas within child maltreatment cases—parents, perpetrators, attorneys, and child protective workers. Observers of the child welfare system often note that the system does not operate for the benefit of the children in their care; for example, stays in multiple foster homes can exacerbate a child's problems.

This negative view needs to be changed so that child welfare agencies are seen as providing services that are appropriate and helpful to children and their parents. Of course, the onus falls to child protective agencies themselves to change their image, but they must be given the fiscal resources to do so. Higher salaries could go a long way in attracting professional child protective workers who might make fewer mistakes in intervention decisions. All could benefit from an increase in status accorded to child protective work.

The fact that the United States has no national policy on children is further evidence of the lack of concern for the interests of children. Ozawa writes: "A nation that fails to nurture its offspring can only anticipate a bleak future. The United States seems to be heading to such a future" (17). A national policy on children needs to explore ways to encourage the healthy functioning of children and their families through both prevention and treatment efforts. Box 12.1 reviews some recommendations for the treatment of maltreated children, which could be part of a national policy.

Andrews and Ben-Arieh (1999) take a very broad view of children's needs by supporting an international initiative to measure and monitor the status of children.

B O X 12.1

Recommendations for Inclusion in a National Policy for the Prevention and Treatment of Maltreated Children

1. *Our educational efforts in preparing professionals to meet the needs of maltreated children must be improved.*
   Child protective workers need to be educated about the short- and long-term effects of maltreatment. Therapists need to explore more innovative treatment approaches including extensive outreach efforts aimed toward clients. Improved communication and cooperation are needed among mental health, child protective, welfare, and legal organizations.

2. *The integration of developmental principles into the training of researchers and clinicians interested in maltreated children is needed.*
   Educational institutions need to revise curricula to include the effects of maltreatment from a developmental perspective.

3. *Mechanisms to allow for the continuity of services to maltreated children must be developed.*
   Abused clients may be more likely to need long-term rather than short-term therapy. In reality, health care costs can reduce the availability of treatment services to the maltreated and reduce the length of time that treatment is available.

4. *Data on the effectiveness of therapy for maltreated children are essential.*
   More evidence of the effectiveness of treatment, especially psychotherapy, is needed.

5. *In the provision of therapy to maltreated children, sensitivity toward the ethnic, racial, and cultural milieu must be maintained.*
   Clinicians who specialize in child maltreatment and family abuse should have expertise in ethnic, racial, and cultural differences.

6. *Tertiary prevention efforts directed at decreasing the emergence of psychopathology in maltreated children must be intensified.*
   While primary and secondary prevention is critical, it is also critical to provide services that can reduce the consequences of the maltreatment.

7. *We must become increasingly sophisticated at providing legislators and policy advocates with information gained from research investigations.*
   The gap between research findings and implementing recommendations needs to be closed. Researchers on child maltreatment and family abuse need to see that their findings and policy recommendations are disseminated to policy makers.

Source: Sheree L. Toth and Dante Cicchetti. 1993. "Child Maltreatment: Where Do We Go From Here in Our Treatment of Victims?" Pp. 399–437 in *Child Abuse, Child Development, and Social Policy,* D. Cicchetti and S. L. Toth, eds. Norwood, NJ: Ablex Publishing Corporation, 426–29.

The authors are part of a group seeking standards that will foster equal living conditions for all the world's children. The international study group has reached a consensus that indicators of the status of children should include the following: social connectedness, civil life skills, personal life skills, safety and physical status, and an examination of a children's subculture as separate from adult activities. See Box 12.2 for variables correlated with appropriate child development.

⟍ Community Efforts

One promising effort in the prevention of child maltreatment is targeted at the neighborhood level and focuses on both families and communities at the same time (Mulroy and Shay 1997). This work is based on ecological theory as developed by Bronfenbrenner (1979) and is known as the CARES model. The underlying issue is to deal with childhood maltreatment associated with poverty by shoring up supports available to the family from the community. The CARES model is based on the premise that the parents' ability to care for their children is bolstered by strengthening informal and formal supports and reducing social isolation. Closest to the family are *informal supports* available through friends and neighbors brought together by a center for neighborhood families. Programs here include educational and social activities, child care, advocacy, and support groups. The next level provides *interagency prevention services,* which has as its base more formal programs and more clearly targets families at high risk for child maltreatment. These services include home health visits, parent education, and therapeutic services. The final level of *community systems* is the connection to systems beyond the neighborhood

---

BOX **12.2**

Variables Associated with Positive Child Development

- Adequate nourishment
- Good health and access to health services when needed
- Dependable attachments to parents or other adult caregivers
- More than one consistently involved adult who provides economic resources, interaction, support, regulation, and positive role modeling to the child
- Firm, consistent, flexible discipline strategies
- Social support and guidance when faced with adversity
- Protection from physical and psychological harm
- Cognitively stimulating physical and social environments
- Play activities and opportunities to explore
- Meaningful participation in community life appropriate for age and ability
- Access to resources for special needs

Source: Arlene Bowers Andrews and Asher Ben-Arieh. 1999. "Measuring and Monitoring Children's Well-Being Across the World." *Social Work.* 44:105–15.

level and include law enforcement, legal services, welfare services, school departments, and employment and training programs. This integrated effort is a welcome improvement over the traditionally fragmented public child welfare system (Mulroy and Shay 1997).

Other promising child welfare efforts stem from the Adoption and Safe Families Act of 1997, which requires the U.S. Department of Health and Human Services to assess the services provided by state child welfare agencies (Marble 1999). A number of national organizations, including the National Association of Public Child Welfare Administrators and the American Humane Association, are developing policies and trainings related to outcome measures in rating the performance of child welfare agencies. The Child Welfare League of America is involved in several projects that follow youths who have been in residential treatment, foster care, and group care. An assessment of the effectiveness of child welfare agencies is crucial to a revamping and strengthening of the system.

Community-oriented policing and problem-oriented policing can both add to community efforts to deal with child maltreatment. It is more common that community involvement efforts of police include cooperation with domestic violence service agencies and battered women shelters. Law enforcement officers are mandated reporters of child abuse and neglect. The closer ties between police and social service agencies resulting from these programs may alert the officers to be more watchful and more willing to report. Some suggestions for community efforts are summarized in Box 12.3.

Domestic violence response training can also improve reporting of child maltreatment. It was previously noted that when there is abuse between domestic partners, there is a high risk of child abuse as well. Officers who receive domestic violence response training are alerted to the possibility that if children are in the home, they should be considered as possible abuse victims as well.

We have discussed the importance of focusing prevention efforts on national, state, and local levels. While these efforts are challenging at best, it is also the case that individuals and small groups can make a very real difference in the prevention of child maltreatment. A local effort can consist of three phases of implementing a prevention program. See Box 12.4 for a recipe for how to start a child abuse prevention program in your community.

Future Issues in Adult Family Abuse

While tremendous strides have been made in social services, law enforcement, and courts in the treatment of battered women over the last 30 years, much remains to be done. A study of state agencies and coalitions to combat the battering of women found that there was considerable agreement concerning four critical gaps in services for battered women: unstable funding for shelter programs, insufficient shelter beds to meet the need, lack of accessible shelters available to all state residents, and lack of adequate transitional housing (Davis, Hagan, and Early 1994). Clearly the increased public attention given to battering will be diminished if

---

B O X   **12.3**

Suggestions for Community Response Efforts

- Develop an inventory of community resources available to abused families.
- Have persons mandated for reporting child abuse and elder abuse receive training in responding to domestic violence incidents.
- Hold periodic meetings with law enforcement, social services, and advocacy groups dealing with domestic violence, elder abuse, and child abuse.
- If a community's law enforcement agency is large enough, create a domestic violence or crisis response team.
- Have law enforcement and victim's assistance units do periodic checks on the status of the victims and inform the victims of the status of any legal proceedings regarding the abuser.
- Introduce violence prevention programs in the schools that include coverage of child abuse, sibling abuse, and date rape.
- Publicly post information about abusers for whom arrest warrants have been issued and about sex offenders, according to the procedures of the "Megan's Law" in your state. Many law enforcement agencies now post such information on World Wide Web pages.
- Publicly post information about resources in your community for dealing with family abuse and include the National Domestic Violence Hotline number.

---

treatment options are not provided to women in need. In the words of Davis et al., "Services for abused women remain on the fringe of the social services delivery system" (1994:703). Indeed, family abuse victims who also have substance abuse or mental health problems resulting from the abuse are commonly refused access to shelters or granted access under more limited conditions than families without these problems. Thus, much more needs to be done to integrate services for battered women into the human services system.

Federal Coordination

Mills recommends a federally-funded Domestic Violence Commission that could be locally administered and would "oversee and monitor, legally, fiscally, and programmatically, services for battered women" (1998:217). The Domestic Violence Commission would serve as a clearinghouse for services for battered women. This coordinated effort would include restraining orders, financial assistance, and child care. The Office of Violence Against Women in the U.S. Department of Justice, created by the Violence Against Women Act, currently coordinates and funds many of these efforts. Further coordination is necessary. Domestic violence courts, modeled after the Unified Court in Hawaii, would have judges with special training

BOX 12.4

Developing a Community Child Abuse Prevention Program

Phase One: Planning

1. *Mobilize community support* by contacting law enforcement, educators, human service agencies, business and community leaders, and the clergy.
2. *Assess community resources* by gathering information on services that are available and services that are needed but unavailable.
3. *Determine the prevention program design* by examining different approaches such as parenting programs, home visitation programs, and family resource centers.
4. *Secure funding* through the federal or state governments, foundations, corporations, or the local community.
5. *Establish the mechanisms to evaluate the program,* acknowledging that determining its effectiveness is a critical part of any prevention program. Local colleges and universities can provide evaluation expertise.

Phase Two: Implementation

1. *Recruit and train staff,* searching for the best-qualified individuals, some of whom have ties within the community.
2. *Ensure access* by locating the program in an area convenient to public transportation. This also includes advertising in local papers and on local television, as well as contacting potential sources of referrals.
3. *Obtain feedback to improve services* by seeking the input of staff, clients, and the community.

Phase Three: Continuation

1. *Solidify relationships with sources of funding* to ensure continuity of services.
2. *Generate and publicize data* that will show the effectiveness of the program and, in turn, will make the community want to continue the prevention program.

Source: "How to Start a Child Abuse Prevention Program in Your Community." 2000. National Clearinghouse on Child Abuse and Neglect Information. (WWW http:www.calib.com/nccarch/).

in family abuse, and would be a critical element in coordinated service delivery to battered women (Mills 1998).

Mills (1996) extends the discussion of future needs of battered women to looking at the international picture as battering is a major social problem around the world. Brazil is the first country in the world whose constitution addresses the problem of family violence (Mills 1996). This political and legal stance has been translated into effective social policy. For example, the state of São Paulo developed 41 police stations staffed by women officers whose job it is to focus on crimes against women. In addition to police officers who investigate reports of assaults and sex crimes, social workers assist women with other needs. Since these programs have been put into place, abuse complaints have increased dramatically, a sign that women view these programs as helpful and effective. Much can be learned from other countries' strategies to reduce family abuse.

Discrimination and Family Abuse

Many victims of family abuse are also subject to prejudice and discrimination. That is why gender, for example, is part of many hate crime statutes and specifically mentioned as a basis for a civil rights lawsuit under the Violence Against Women Act. In some states hate crime prosecution of domestic violence offenders has been initiated when there is a pattern of serial abuse against multiple victims. Prejudice against the very young and very old also leads to discounting their complaints of abuse as fantasy or senility.

Minority victims tend to be doubly victimized; first by age or gender, then by race or ethnicity. Treatment programs and victim services need to improve their ability to work with minority family abuse victims. The race of victim and race of perpetrator have also been shown to affect prosecution and sentencing in the criminal justice system. Closer monitoring of how family abuse cases are handled by the criminal justice system is needed to prevent such double victimization.

Summary

This final chapter reviews the importance of future research, which can give a clearer picture of the types and amount of family abuse. It also considers the murky picture of family abuse theories. While continued theoretical work tied to the practical efforts to treat victims and offenders is still very much needed, a broader perspective is needed as well. Research and treatment efforts must also take a broader view to examine the social, economic, and political factors that contribute to family abuse.

In the future, regardless of the types of treatment and prevention efforts, money will continue to be a critical issue. More advocacy on behalf of victims and perpetrators of family abuse is needed. It is especially difficult to do clinical work in the family abuse field and still be responsible for obtaining the financial resources to provide the services. Unfortunately, the growth of managed health care has and will continue to decrease the length of treatment for both victims and perpetrators of family abuse (Wallace 1996).

It is generally acknowledged that social problems are never solved through treatment alone and that prevention is the key to reduction of family abuse. At this state of our knowledge it is critical that both prevention and treatment efforts receive political and economic support. Caseworkers have long known the importance of coordinated efforts by social services, child protective services, and the juvenile and criminal justice systems. There also needs to be a stronger acknowledgment of the relationship between family abuse and community violence (Cardarelli 1997). Improved communication and stronger working relationships among all facets of human service delivery systems that deal with family abuse will go a long way in ensuring appropriate treatment interventions.

Study Questions

1. What are some of the major factors that hinder the accurate measurement of the nature and extent of family abuse?

2. Why is the true extent of family abuse not accurately measurable?

3. What are the best estimates of the extent of family abuse in the United States?

4. What inhibits the collection of trend data on family abuse?

5. Why is it important to consider ways of educating prospective parents about family abuse?

6. What are the strengths and weaknesses of existing intervention strategies to combat family abuse?

7. Is there a need for a national public policy and program to deal with the problem of family abuse?

8. Why is it important to evaluate existing child welfare programs?

9. What are some of the promising efforts to combat childhood maltreatment?

REFERENCES

Amuwo, Shaffdeen A. and Jacqueline B. Hill. 1998. "Child Neglect." Pp. 57–81 in *Violence in Intimate Relationships: Examining Sociological and Psychological Issues*, Nicky Ali Jackson and Gisele Casanova Oates, eds. Boston: Butterworth-Heinemann.

Andrews, Arlene Bowers and Asher Ben-Arieh. 1999. "Measuring and Monitoring Children's Well-Being Across the World." *Social Work.* 44:105–15.

Beaucar, Kelley O. 1999. "Child Welfare Workers Cry Out for Reform: Case Overload Compounds Children's Peril." *NASW News (Newsletter of the National Association of Social Workers)*, May 3.

Becker, Howard S. 1963. *Outsiders.* NY: The Free Press.

Brandon, Karen. 1999. "Stopping Crime Before It Starts." *The Boston Globe*, August 8:A10.

Brasher, Philip. 1999. "Study Finds Hunger Widespread in U.S." *The Patriot Ledger*, October 14:11.

Brill, Carol and Miriam Stein. 1999. *Our Children and Families: A Social Work Statement Addressing Child Abuse and Neglect.* Boston, MA: National Association of Social Workers, Massachusetts Chapter.

Bronfenbrenner, Uri. 1979. *The Ecology of Human Development.* Cambridge, MA: Harvard University Press.

Cardarelli, Albert P. 1997. "Confronting Intimate Violence: Looking toward the Twenty-First Century." Pp. 178–85 in *Violence Between Intimate Partners: Patterns, Causes, and Effects*, Albert P. Cardarelli, ed. Boston, MA: Allyn and Bacon.

Davis, Liane V., Jan L. Hagen, and Theresa J. Early. 1994. "Social Services for Battered Women: Are They Adequate, Accessible, and Appropriate?" *Social Work.* 39:695–704.

Ellement, John. 1999. "Minister Cleared of Child Abuse in Spanking of Son." *The Boston Globe*, November 18:A1, A36.

Finucane, Martin. 1999. "Spanking Minister Cleared: State Justice Reject Finding of Child Abuse." *The Patriot Ledger,* November 18:9.

Gross, Amy B. and Harold R. Keller. 1992. "Long-Term Consequences of Childhood Physical and Psychological Maltreatment." *The Journal of Aggressive Behavior.* 18:171–85.

Iwaniec, Dorota. 1995. *The Emotionally Abused and Neglected Child: Identification, Assessment and Intervention.* NY: John Wiley & Sons.

Jantz, Gregory L. 1995. *Healing the Scars of Emotional Abuse.* Grand Rapids, MI: Fleming H. Revell.

Lambert, Lane. 1999. "Young and Homeless: Teenagers Seeking Shelter in Greater Numbers." *The Patriot Ledger,* 1:2.

Lemert, Edwin. 1994. "Primary and Secondary Deviation." Pp. 261–63 in *Classics of Criminology,* Joseph E. Jacoby, ed. Prospect Heights, IL: Waveland Press, Inc.

Marble, Lynn. 1999. "Initiatives to Improve Child Welfare Outcomes." Office of Juvenile Justice and Delinquency Prevention. *OJJDP Fact Sheet,* October. Washington, DC: U.S. Department of Justice.

Mills, Linda. 1996. "Empowering Battered Women Transnationally: The Case for Postmodern Interventions." *Social Work.* 41:261–68.

———. 1998. *The Heart of Intimate Abuse: New Interventions in Child Welfare, Criminal Justice, and Health Settings.* NY: Springer Publishing Company.

Mulroy, Elizabeth A. and Sharon Shay. 1997. "Nonprofit Organization and Innovation: A Model of Neighborhood-Based Collaboration to Prevent Child Maltreatment." *Social Work.* 42:515–24.

O'Hanlon, Kevin. 1997. "Reports of Elder Abuse Rose 150% Since 1986." Associated Press Bulletin Online, November 16, 1997.

Ozawa, Martha N. 1999. "The Economic Well-Being of Elderly People and Children in a Changing Society." *Social Work.* 44:9–19.

Seipel, Michael M. O. 1999. "Social Consequences of Malnutrition." *Social Work.* 44:416–25.

Skabronski, Jill C. 1995/1996. "Elder Abuse: Washington's Response to a Growing Epidemic." *Gonzaga Law Review.* 31, 3:627–43.

U.S. Department of Health and Human Services. 2000. *Child Maltreatment 1998: Reports from the States to the National Child Abuse and Neglect Data System.* Washington, DC: U.S. Government Printing Office.

U.S. House of Representatives, Committee on Ways and Means. 1994. *Overview of Entitlement Programs: 1994 Green Book.* Washington, DC: U.S. Government Printing Office.

Wallace, Harvey. 1996. *Family Violence: Legal, Medical, and Social Perspectives.* Boston, MA: Allyn and Bacon.

Westman, Jack C. 1996. "The Rationale and Feasibility of Licensing Parents." *Society.* 34:1. Pp. 46–52.

Widom, Cathy Spatz. 1992. "The Cycle of Violence." Washington, DC: National Institute of Justice.

———. 1996. "The Cycle of Violence Revisited." Washington, DC: National Institute of Justice.

Witmer, Martha B. and Cheryl A. Crawford. 1995. "A Coordinated Approach to Reducing Family Violence: Conference Highlights." Washington, DC: National Institute of Justice.

World Health Organization. 1998. *Nutrition Program.* Washington, DC: Author.

Family Abuse, Deviance, and Crime Web Resources

Resource sites for topics in family abuse, deviance, and crime. Updated links are available at: **http://omega.cc.umb.edu/~holmes/fadlinks.htm**

General Sites

General Bibliography ABA Publications: Addressing Domestic Violence in Communities: A Program Guide. Special Alliance Against Violence. The Young Lawyers Division. Domestic Violence: The Brutal Truth About the American Family. http://www.abanet.org/domviol/biblio.html

IGC: Violence against Women: Internet-Resources Collection Violence Against Women Links IGC Discussion Groups IGC Members: Read Violence Against Women discussion groups via the Web on the IGC Discussion Groups Page. http://www.igc.org/igc/issues/violencewn/

Abuse Characteristics Nashville Police Abuse Web Site info http://nashville. net/~police/abuse/characteristics.htm

Open Directory—Society: Women: Domestic Violence Netscape Open Directory > Society > Women > Domestic Violence and Legal & Privacy Notices http://directory. netscape.com/Society/Women/Domestic_Violence

To Be Equal: Dedication to the Fight Against Violence Done to Women Welcomes men and women. This is dedicated to the fight against violence done to women. It's time that we open our eyes to a major overlooked problem in our society. http://members.tripod.com/~marcnoel/tobequal. html

YWCA. Research and Training Institute Domestic Violence Institute. The YWCA Division of Domestic Violence announced the opening of the Domestic Violence Research & Training Institute in 1995. http://www.wycasandiego. org/inst.html

NNFR National Network for Family Resiliency http://www.nnfr.org/

PAVNET Partnership against Violence Network http://www.pavnet.org/

Domestic Violence—Gayscape Domestic Violence http://www.webcom. com/jwpub/ gayscape/domvio.html

Child Abuse

American Academy of Pediatrics Web Site (AAP)   American Academy of Pediatrics website: the AAP is an organization of over 55,000 pediatricians. AAP: information on child health, baby, infant, kids, pediatrics, family, teen, SIDS, safety, injury, and much more.   http://www.aap.org//

Child Abuse, Domestic Violence Survivors Chat Room: YesICAN offers Facilitated Chat Room for survivors of Child Abuse, Domestic Violence . . . www.yesican.org/chat.html

International Society for Prevention of Child Abuse and Neglect   ISPCAN New Zealand International Congress, September 6–9, 1998   http://child.cornell.edu/ispcan/ispcan.html

National Data Archive on Child Abuse and Neglect   A U.S. child abuse and neglect data archive serving researchers performing secondary analysis with statistical software such as SPSS (TM) or SAS . . .   www.ndacan.cornell.edu/

Child Abuse Information Resource Links   Miscellaneous Child Advocacy Resources on the Internet   www.angelfire.com/mi/oaxamaxao/index.html

B.A.C.A. "Bikers Against Child Abuse"   BACA. Bikers against Child Abuse. www.enol.com/~jyeoman/baca.html

HHS Reports New Child Abuse and Neglect Statistics   U.S. Department of Health and Human Services Administration for Children and Families. Recent News. News Archive. Fact Sheets. Statistics. ACF. HHS Press.   www.acf.dhhs.gov/news/abuse.htm

Prevent Child Abuse America: Teaching Children Discipline   www.childabuse.org/discpln.html

Prevent Child Abuse America: Child Abuse Prevention Research   In 1986, Prevent Child Abuse America recognized the need for a systematic effort to document the effectiveness of specific child abuse prevention programs. www.childabuse.org/research.html

Prevent Child Abuse America: Child Abuse Hotline Numbers   Need Help? Here are some important 24-hour toll-free numbers to know for help any day, any time . . . Boys Town National Hotline—Call if you have any questions. www.childabuse.org/phone.html

Prevent Child Abuse America Parenting Tips   www.childabuse.org/parentin.html

Child Abuse in School   Superintendent of Public Instruction Delaine Eastin's legacy—child abuse in school. Web site chronicles one family's five year struggle.   www.aisforabuse.com/

Prevent Child Abuse Carolina—Greenville, SC   Prevent Child Abuse Carolina—Greenville, South Carolina. A nonprofit organization for the prevention of child abuse serving upstate South Carolina.   www.kidsyoucantbeatem.org/

C.A.P.A.—The Child Abuse Prevention Association   CAPA is a nonprofit organization that seeks to prevent child abuse.   www.childabuseprevention.org/main.html

Connecticut Center for Prevention of Child Abuse—Home Page CCPCA: Fostering healthy family relationships, a program of Wheeler Clinic. The Connecticut Center for Prevention of Child Abuse (CCPCA) is a statewide organization. www.wheelerclinic.org/ccpca1.htm

Child Abuse and Neglect in California—Part II Legislative Analyst's Office, January 1996. Child Abuse and Neglect in California Part II. The Child Welfare Services System. www.lao.ca.gov/cw11096b.html

Child Abuse Prevention Month CHILD ABUSE PREVENTION AWARENESS MONTH. Conservation & Production Research Laboratory, Bushland, Texas, USA. April is Child Abuse Prevention month. www.cprl.ars.usda.gov/capm.htm

Cornell News: Child Abuse Policy www.news.cornell.edu/releases/April99/

Child Abuse & Trauma Recovery Project Did you experience abuse or trauma in your childhood? Please help . . . with a research project designed to study the recovery of adults who have experienced. www.rebrown.com/rebrown/phillips.htm

Preventing Child Abuse and Neglect through Parent Education (Reppucci, Britner et al.) Preventing Child Abuse and Neglect Through Parent Education. www.pbrookes.com/catalog/books/reppucci.htm

Child Abuse and Neglect Clearinghouse: Conference Calendar—Call for Papers, Conference Calendar. Calls for Papers. Head Start's Fifth National Research Conference: Developmental and Contextual Transitions of Children and Families. www.calib.com/nccanch/calendar/index.htm

Elder Abuse

Elders at Risk SECTION I. Selected References to Journal Articles Focused Specifically on the Abuse, Victimization, and Suicide of the Elderly. Elder Abuse Family/Domestic Violence. http://www.apa.org/books/eldriskt.html

BWA Summary http://members.home.net/dwoodhouse/bwa/dv.html

National Center on Elder Abuse The Resource Directory for Older People. A Cooperative Effort of the National Institute on Aging and the Administration on Aging. National Center on Elder Abuse. www.aoa.dhhs.gov/aoa/dir/143.html

Nursing Home Malpractice—Identify, prevent, and report elder abuse Our member Attorneys are experienced and ready to assist you and your family. What Nursing Home Abuse & Malpractice may include: www.nursinghomemalpractice.com/

Elder Abuse or Abuse of Senior Citizens Abuse of Senior Citizens or Crimes against Seniors. Here we offer individuals the opportunity to post information on abuse perpetrated on senior citizens. http://seniors-site.com/fraud/abuse.html

CCAAA, Inc. Stop Elder Abuse www.aginginfo.org/abuse.htm

CTF Structured Abstract: Secondary prevention of elder abuse Canadian Task Force on Preventive Health Care. Structured Abstract. Secondary Prevention of Elder Abuse. Prepared by Christopher Patterson, MD, FRCPC, . . . www.ctfphc.org/Abstracts/Ch77abs.htm

Elder Abuse   General information about Elder Abuse along with a list of websites. www.calregistry.com/resources/eldabpag.htm

CTF Summary Table: Secondary prevention of elder abuse   Canadian Task Force on Preventive Health Care. Summary Table. Secondary Prevention of Elder Abuse.   www.ctfphc.org/Tables/Ch77tab.htm

Elder Abuse   Muskoka-Parry Sound Health Unit. Elder Abuse—The Hidden Crime.   www.mpshu.on.ca/SeniorsIssues/elder.htm

Elder Abuse FAQ   Frequently Asked Questions about Elder Abuse. Q. I think my client may be the victim of elder abuse. What should I do? A. Ask questions. www.ianet.org/nyeac/ea_faq.htm

Elder Abuse   Elder Abuse. What You Need to Know. Recent studies suggest that 4 percent of seniors—perhaps as many as 1.2 million Americans 65 years of age and older—may be abused.   www.elderserve.org/elderabuse.htm

Elder Abuse   It provides information about elder abuse and suggestions. http://courts.co.calhoun.mi.us/book004.htm

Seniors Scene—Elder Abuse   Elder abuse is any violent or abusive harm done to an older person. Physical abuse includes pushing, hitting, or confining a senior.   http://info.london.on.ca/seniors/abuse.html

Elder Abuse   Elder abuse is harm done to persons over the age of 65, by a person in a position of trust, by doing or not doing something.   www.ci.punta-gorda.fl.us/ElderAbuse.htm

Understanding Elder Abuse in Minority Populations   Understanding Elder Abuse in Minority Populations. Toshio Tatara, Ph.D., National Center on Elder Abuse, Washington, DC.   www.bmpub.com/0876309201.htm

Elder Abuse   Chemung County Office for the Aging. It Shouldn't Hurt to be Old. Elder Abuse Mistreatment and Neglect.   www.chemungcounty.com/new-page3.html

Elder Abuse Discussion Group Search Form   Elder Abuse Discussion Group. Find articles posted to this discussion containing matching words.   www.lawrmw.com/disc1_srch.htm

Elder Abuse Discussion Group TOC   Elder Abuse Discussion Group.   www.lawrmw.com/disc1_toc.htm

The National Elder Abuse Incidence Study   The National Elder Abuse Incidence Study; Final report September 1998. . . .   www.aoa.gov/abuse/report/main-pdf.htm

San Francisco Police Officers' Association.   Elder Abuse. A MAJOR ISSUE. www.sfpoa.org/Elder_Abuse.html

Elder Abuse Prevention   Preventing elder abuse   www.oaktrees.org/elder/

Elder Abuse   Elder Abuse. Counseling/Protective Services. Bucks County Area Agency on Aging 30 East Oakland Avenue, Doylestown, PA 18901. 215-348-0510 24-HOUR HOTLINE: www.buckscounty.org/vp-elder_abuse.htm

People's Green Book: Elder Abuse and Crime   Crime and Abuse. Crime and abuse are tragic realities that some seniors must face. If you are a crime or elder abuse survivor, there are several places to go for help. www. pubadvo-cate.nyc.gov/~advocate/

Elder Abuse/Financial Exploitation Daddysang. Hits to Page: Welcome to my Web Page! I am creating this site in memory of my father who was a victim of this horrible crime known as Elder Abuse. http://members.theglobe.com/daddysang/

Library: Elder Abuse Alzheimer's Association, Northern Virginia Chapter provides programs/services for families/caregivers, funds research, and educates the general public . . . www.alz-nova.org/libelder.htm

Elder Abuse FAQ Toll free outside Toronto: 1-800-665-9092 Toronto local calls: (416) 482-4359 TTY: (416) 482-1254. http://128.100.250.10/infoability/re-sources/elder_abuse_faq.html

Elder Abuse resources Elder Abuse resources. Elder Abuse includes physical and mental mistreatment, neglect, financial exploitation and abandonment. www.nas.com/nwrc/ELDERABU.HTM

Domestic Violence Statistics—Elder Abuse Elder Abuse. According to a national survey of the health of women conducted for the Commonwealth Fund in 1992, an estimated 1.4 million women were victims of elder abuse. http://home.cybergrrl.com/dv/stat/stateld.html

Understanding Elder Abuse Online Course—Registration Form Marquette University Continuing Education Wisconsin Geriatric Education Center Enrollment Form: Understanding Elder Abuse Online Course Course Fee: $68. . . . www.marquette.edu/wgec/elderabuse/reg-form.htm

Gay, Lesbian, Bisexual Family Violence

Rainbow Query: Search the Queer Internet for Domestic Abuse Look here for support and answers! Violence and abuse in the home, between partners and cross-generational. http://www.rainbowquery.com/categories/Domes-tic_Abuse.html

Domestic Violence—Gayscape Domestic Violence. We are performing a MA-JOR reorganization of our listings to make it easier to find what you want. New subcategories may be incomplete as listings are added. http://www.webcom.com/jwpub/gayscape/domvio.html

Men Who Beat the Men Who Love Them Myth One: Only Straight Women Get Battered; Gay Men Are Never Victims of Domestic Violence. This is not true. The Gay Men's Domestic Violence Project at the Community United Against Violence (CUAV) in San Francisco estimates that for every police incident report on gay men's domestic violence that CUAV receives, there are between 10 and 20 incidents that go unreported. http://www.sdc.uwo.ca/psych/glbt/gayman.html

Second Closet Title: The Second Closet: Domestic Violence in Lesbian and : Gay Relationships: A Western Australian Perspective Author : Lee Vickers Organ-isation : Keywords : domestic violence; same-sex relationships; : "battered wife syndrome"; provocation; Western Australia Abstract : This article focuses on the little discussed problem of : domestic violence in same sex relationships, and the : silence . . . http://www.murdoch.edu.au/elaw/issues/v3n4/vickers.txt

Anti-Violence Project Anti-Violence Project Crisis Hotline Number 303-852-5094 (in Denver) 888-557-4441 (statewide outside Denver area) The Anti-Violence Project of Equality Colorado is dedicated to ending violence against gay, lesbian, bisexual, and transgender victims. http://members.tde.com/equality/avp/index.html

Interventions

(CASA) Center Against Spouse Abuse (St. Petersburg, FL) CASA, located in St. Petersburg, FL, offers information about Domestic Violence, legal advocacy, public awareness and education, crisis and safety planning, and related links. http://www.casa-stpete.org/

Victim Services: Largest Victim Assistance Organization Domestic violence, rape, crime victims, and survivors helped here. Research and materials on victimization and victim assistance. We're the largest victim assistance organization. We're New York City based. http://www.victimservices.org/

Domestic Violence Project AAFPRS IS TAKING A FIRM STAND . . . The American Academy of Facial Plastic and Reconstructive Surgery (AAFPRS) is the first surgical group to take a firm stand and become involved in helping individuals of Domestic Violence break out of the cycle of violence, enhance their self-esteem, and rebuild their lives. http://www.facial-plastic-surgery.org/about/dvproject.html

Domestic Violence Resources

Houston Area Women's Center The Houston Area Women's Center is a non-profit, United Way agency that is celebrating its 20th year serving Houston. We provide a wide range of services to the community, including counseling and a shelter for battered women and their children, a hotline offering counseling and referral services for abused women, a rape crisis hotline, education programs, and the Second-to-None Resale Shop. http://www.hawc.org/

Domestic Violence—Professional Resources Professional resources for the treatment of domestic violence. Resources for working with those recovering from domestic violence, and working with victims of domestic violence in learning to break the cycle of violence in their lives. http://hawk-systems.com/web_pages/garson/ domesticP.htm

Domestic Violence Resources THE AIMS OF JCDVPP. To raise awareness and inform the church community as to causes, extent, nature, and consequences of Domestic Violence. To urge church communities to speak out against domestic violence. http://www.home.gil.com.au/~stillerk/DV.html

Links and Referrals: Sacramento Sheriff's Dept, Police Dept, Ambulance . . . 911 Sacramento Sheriff's Office . . . 440-5115 Sacramento Police Dept . . . 264-5471 Kaiser Emergency Room . . . 973-6600 Mercy San Juan Emergency Room . . . 537-5120 Methodist Emergency Room . . . 423-6020 Sutter General Emergency Room . . . 733-8900 Sutter Memorial Emergency Room . . . 733-1000 UCD Medical Center Emergency Room . . . 734-2455 . . . http://www.weaveinc.org/links.html

SAFE: Resources and Information These essays are written by individuals like you. If you would like to submit something here, write to jade@cs.utoronto.ca. Please make sure your submission is well edited and in text, HTML, or RTF format. http://www.dgp.utoronto.ca/~jade/safe/resources.html

Immigration and Family Violence: Oregon Taking the first step towards the American Dream for immigrants in Oregon and the Pacific Northwest Immigration counseling services (ICS) is a private, nonprofit organization that provides full legal representation to low income immigrants and their families in immigration-related matters. http://www.immigrationcounseling.org/

Hispanics: History of WEAVE 1975—A community action group comprised of Hispanic battered women established WEAVE to address the issues of domestic violence in their community. 1978—The first WEAVE shelter opened with funding from the County of Sacramento; the abuser treatment program known as Positive Anger Control (PAC) was established. 1979—Federal funding allowed WEAVE to expand services. http://www.weaveinc.org/history.html

Family Violence Prevention Fund (FUND) LAST UPDATED: December 1996 Contact: Esta Soler Executive Director Family Violence Prevention Fund 383 Rhode Island Street, Suite 304 San Francisco, CA 94103-5133 Tel: 415-252-8900 Fax: 415-252-8991 E-mail: fund@fvpf.org URL: http://www.fvpf.org/ http://www.reeusda.gov/pavnet/cf/cffamvio.htm

The Health Care Response to Domestic Violence Domestic Violence: The actual or threatened physical, sexual, psychological or economic abuse of an individual by someone with whom they have or have had an intimate relationship. http://eng.hss.cmu.edu/feminism/domestic-violence.html

NDVH National Domestic Violence Hotline: 1-800-799-SAFE TDD for the Hearing Impaired: 1-800-787-3224 Edt Saturday, October 14, 1995. http://www.usdoj.gov/vawo/radio.htm

Lighthouse Training Center Mi Casa is a transitional safe home and therapeutic community for women with and without children who struggle with Post-Traumatic Stress Disorder (PTSD) resulting from childhood trauma and/or adult domestic violence, and who are also chemically dependent. Mi Casa is a state-of-the-art model program using creative approaches in the treatment of unresolved victimization/PTSD and substance . . . http://lighthouse.aculink.net/

Domestic Violence Program Domestic Violence Program INTRODUCTION Welcome to the Domestic Violence Program developed by Team's Health's

InPhyNet Medical Management Institute. Team Health is dedicated to the highest quality of medical education, while offering convenience, quality service and support in a cost-effective manner. http://www.team-health. com/physiciansonly/July1998/domvol/

Anti-Violence Project Anti-Violence Project Crisis Hotline Number 303-852-5094 (in Denver) 888-557-4441 (statewide outside Denver area). The Anti-Violence Project of Equality Colorado is dedicated to ending violence against gay, lesbian, bisexual, and transgender victims. http://members.tde.com/ equality/avp/index.html

Iris Counseling Center, Family Violence Intervention Agency Family violence program intervention in SC for counseling services, intervention family violence agency, volunteer site by Kathy Belew a social worker for family preservation and child welfare services in the family violence program. http://hadm.sph.sc.edu/students/KBelew/iris.htm

Cleveland, Ohio, Domestic Violence Resources Some Facts. Battering occurs at similar rates among different ethnic groups. Battering occurs among all religions. Marriage does not end abusive behavior; marrying the batterer will not protect the victim. http://www.en.com/users/allison/dvpage.html

Domestic Violence Identification and Management of Battered Women in the Primary Care Setting: Information compiled by K. Snyder, MS4 Oregon Health Sciences University August 1997. http://cybermed.ucsd.edu/curricu-lar_resources/Primary_Care/

Advocates for Battered Women ADVOCATES FOR BATTERED WOMEN P.O. Box 1954 Little Rock, AR 72203 (501) 376-3219 (phone) (501) 376-4720 (fax) For help or more information: acadv18@arkansas.net To communicate with the director: abw989@aristotle.net http://www.aristotle.net/~abw/in-dexabw.htm

Nature and Extent of Family Violence

Domestic Violence Information Manual: "Contents" Domestic Violence Information Manual containing informative articles, resources and web links designed to: increase public awareness of the nature and extent of domestic violence, to provide information on how anyone interested in the issue of domestic violence can overcome this serious social problem. http://www.in-foxchange.net.au/wise/DVIM/

Abuse Characteristics Nashville Police Abuse web site info http://nashville. net/~police/abuse/characteristics.htm

The Facts Bills Effective 10/1/97 AB170 AN ACT relating to domestic violence; creating the repository for information concerning orders for protection against domestic violence within the central repository for Nevada records of criminal history; requiring certain persons to transmit certain information regarding orders for protection against domestic violence to the central repository for Nevada . . . http://www.state.nv.us/ndvpc/bills. html

Statistics on Domestic Violence While exact numbers on domestic violence incidents differ, because this is such an underreported crime and a relatively new area of study, there are statistics on which most experts agree. http://www.libertynet.org/waasafe/stats.html

On Domestic Violence On Domestic Violence. There are many definitions of Domestic Violence, and there's much that is true in all of them. At the same time, there's something that's usually left out. http://www.jmahoney.com/domviol.html

Children and Domestic Violence In a national survey of over 6,000 American families, 50 percent of the men who frequently assaulted their wives also frequently abused their children. Child abuse is 15 times more likely to occur in families where domestic violence is present. http://www.fvpf.org/the_facts/children.html

Statistics on Domestic Violence While exact numbers on domestic violence incidents differ, because this is such an underreported crime and a relatively new area of study, there are statistics on which most experts agree. http://www.libertynet.org/waasafe/stats.htm

Symptoms Domestic Violence Net Symptom List http://www.domestic-violence.net/dv/women/symptom.htm

On Domestic Violence On Domestic Violence. There are many definitions of Domestic Violence, and there's much that is true in all of them. At the same time, there's something that's usually left out. http://www.jmahoney.com/domviol.html

Children and Domestic Violence In a national survey of over 6,000 American families, 50 percent of the men who frequently assaulted their wives also frequently abused their children. Child abuse is 15 times more likely to occur in families where domestic violence is present. http://www.fvpf.org/the_facts/children.html

Educating to End Domestic Violence—Intro Domestic violence is a societal problem of epidemic proportions. Experts estimate that 2 to 4 million American women are battered every year, (1) and that between 3.3 and 10 million children witness violence in their homes. (2) Battering affects families across America in all socioeconomic, racial, and ethnic groups. http://www.ojp.usdoj.gov/ovc/infores/etedv/intro.htm

Men Who Beat the Men Who Love Them MYTH ONE: Only Straight Women Get Battered; Gay Men Are Never Victims of Domestic Violence. This is not true. The Gay Men's Domestic Violence Project at the Community United Against Violence (CUAV) in San Francisco estimates that for every police incident report on gay men's domestic violence that CUAV receives, there are between 10 and 20 incidents that go unreported. http://www.sdc.uwo.ca/psych/glbt/gayman.html

Apna Ghar—Domestic Violence Facts Facts about domestic violence http://www.apnaghar.org/dv/dv-facts.htm

Facts & Info The United States Surgeon General reports that domestic violence is the greatest single cause of injury among U.S. women, accounting for more emergency room visits than auto accidents, mugging, and rape combined. http://www.weaveinc.org/facts.html

UM SSW—NIMH Center: Domestic Violence and Mental Health Problems This University of Michigan study assesses the prevalence and co-morbidity of psychiatric disorders, physical disabilities, and domestic violence among low-income single mothers . . . http://www.ssw.umich.edu/nimhcenter/Domestic.html

Myths about Domestic Violence Myths about domestic violence. There are many popular myths and prejudices about domestic violence. Not only do these myths lead to many women feeling unable to seek or feel unworthy of seeking help, but they can cause unnecessary suffering. http://www.gn.apc.org/www.womensaid.org.uk/helpline/

Statistics on Domestic Violence PREVALENCE. Domestic violence crosses ethnic, racial, age, national origin, sexual orientation, religious and socioeconomic lines. By the most conservative estimate, each year 1 million women suffer nonfatal violence by an intimate partner. http://kimberleyc.mswin.net/statistics.htm

Corporate and Personal Security/Intelligence/Violence against Women/ Figures found on this page are from Canadian and American government statistics and private studies. The Consequence on the Justice System. The government of Nova Scotia responded to the serious issue of Domestic Violence by establishing a Zero Tolerance Policy and a responsible agency called the Nova Scotia Family Violence Prevention Initiative. http://www3.ns.sympatico.ca/defender.group/domestic.html

The Health Care Response to Domestic Violence Domestic Violence: The actual or threatened physical, sexual, psychological, or economic abuse of an individual by someone with whom they have or have had an intimate relationship. http://eng.hss.cmu.edu/feminism/domestic-violence.html

Violence and Criminal Justice Violence and Criminal Justice RTI has a long history of conducting research that examines violent behavior, the risk factors for such behavior, and approaches used by the criminal justice system to address violent criminal behavior. http://www.rti.org/units/shsp/factsheets/E008.cfm

The Psychological Impact of Domestic Violence GOVERNOR'S OFFICE OF CHILD ABUSE AND DOMESTIC VIOLENCE SERVICES. The Psychological Impact of Domestic Violence on Domestic Violence Victims and Child Witnesses. http://www.state.ky.us/agencies/gov/domviol/impact.htm

DV Info Domestic Violence Information. What Is Domestic Violence? Socially Based Causes of Domestic Violence Domestic Violence is not caused by Necessary Aspects of Battering Development of Domestic Violence Theory History of Domestic Violence Treatment success rates The Effects of Battery on Women Why do battered women stay with the batterer Examples of ways in which Batterers use Collusion, . . . http://www.compbhs.com/ dvinfo.htm

Reflections of Monday Mornings at the Domestic Violence Clinic by Daniel Gordon Le Vine, Esq. I know that Monday morning will be interesting and busy—for some time now I volunteer on Monday mornings at the Domestic Violence Clinic at the downtown Family Law Building. http://www.sdcba.org/reflections.html

MenWeb—Battered Men Official Policy: Blame the Victim Official WA policy: the perpetrator is not to blame the victim, unless the perpetrator is a woman. The program must give special consideration to her prior domestic violence victimization. WA http://www.vix.com/pub/menmag/gjdvblam.htm

Cleveland, Ohio, Domestic Violence Resources Some Facts. Battering occurs at similar rates among different ethnic groups. Battering occurs among all religions. Marriage does not end abusive behavior; marrying the batterer will not protect the victim. http://www.en.com/users/allison/dvpage.html

The Profile of Domestic Violence Offenders Governor's Office of Child Abuse and Domestic Violence Services. The Profile of Domestic Violence Offenders Introduction Studies related to perpetrators of domestic violence have, for the most part, documented small percentages of a major mental illness among this population, but nonetheless indicate predominate dysfunctioning in the affective, cognitive, and interpersonal spheres of their lives. http://www.state.ky.us/agencies/gov/domviol/profile.htm

Stoneham Police Domestic Violence THE FACTS: "Abuse is behavior that physically harms, arouses fear, or prevents a victim from doing what he/she wishes. It is the intent of abusive behavior to undermine the will of the victim and substitute the will of perpetrator for the will of the victim. http://www.stonehampolice.com/domestic.html

Myths, Facts, Stats—DV Domestic violence does not affect many people. A woman is beaten every 15 seconds. (Bureau of Justice Statistics, Report to the nation on Crime and Justice.) http://www.biddeford.com/~sanpd/domest6.html

Domestic Violence—Everybody's Business Domestic violence is everybody's business. It is cruel and costly. It decreases productivity, increases medical costs, and increases the burden on our police, our courts, and criminal justice system. http://www.pdxcityclub.org/report/domvio.htm

Policy, Statutes, Legislation, Regulations

Domestic Violence Accomplishments of Rep. Louise Slaughter Fighting to Protect the Vulnerable. As Chair of the Congressional Caucus on Women's Issues Health Care Task Force, sponsored the Women's Health Equity Act, a comprehensive package of women's health research and services initiatives, many of which would assist victims of domestic violence. http://www.house.gov/slaughter/leg-record/dv.htm

Public Sees Domestic Violence as a Major Problem: but Unwilling to Pay . . . Public Sees Domestic Violence as a Major Problem: but Unwilling to Pay Added Costs for Insurance contact: Mr. Terrie E. Nearly three-fourths of the public say domestic violence is a major problem; similarly, three out of four say it occurs frequently. http://www.ircweb.org/news/997dome.htm

Families without fear: Women's Aid agenda for action on domestic violence . . . Families without fear: Women's Aid agenda for action on domestic violence: Recommendations for a national strategy. Domestic violence is not a new problem.   http://www.gn.apc.org/www.womensaid.org.uk/nofear/

Arizona Governor's Commission on Violence against Women Commission News. The Governor's Commission on Violence against Women continues to focus on promoting and coordinating effective programs addressing violence against women in Arizona.   http://www.governor.state.az.us/dvp/index.html

Public Affairs: Testimony on Domestic Violence October 5, 1994 Testimony of the American College of Emergency Physicians before the House Government Operations Committee Subcommittee on Human Resources and Intergovernmental Relations.   http://www.acep.org/policy/pa001300.htm

BILL INFO—1996 Regular Session—SB 424 1996 Regular Session bill information current as of January 23, 1997—15:59 File Code: Domestic Abuse Crossfiled with: HOUSE BILL 489 Divorce Actions—Additional Filing Fee for Domestic Violence Programs.   http://mlis.state.md.us/1996rs/billfile/SB0424.htm

Corporate and Personal Security/Intelligence/Violence against Women/ Figures found on this page are from Canadian and American government statistics and private studies. The Consequence on the Justice System. The government of Nova Scotia responded to the serious issue of Domestic Violence by establishing a Zero Tolerance Policy and a responsible agency called the Nova Scotia Family Violence Prevention Initiative.   http://www3.ns.sympatico.ca/defender.group/domestic.html

Joint U.S.–Russian Conference on Family Violence against Women Joint U.S.–Russian Conference on Family Violence against Women. Ambassador James F. Collins Moscow, Russia, October 28, 1998. Deputy Minister Karelova, Deputy Minister Stukolova, distinguished guests and participants.   http://www.usia.gov/usa/womenusa/famvio.htm

Guidelines on Police Response Procedures in Domestic Violence Cases Domestic Violence. Guidelines on Police Response Procedures in Domestic Violence Cases Issued October 1991. Revised November 1994 Introduction. These general guidelines consolidate the police response procedures for domestic violence cases, including abuse and neglect of the elderly and disabled, based on State law, Court Rules, and the Domestic Violence Procedures Manual which was jointly . . .   http://www.state.nj.us/lps/dcj/ag-guide/dvpolrsp.htm

Violence Against Women Act of 1994 Last Updated: 24 July 1996 National Domestic Violence Hotline: 1-800-799-SAFE TDD for the Hearing Impaired: 1-800-787-3224 Violence Against Women Act of 1994.   http://www.usdoj.gov/vawo/vawa/vawa.htm

domviolarch Under the new law, the Personal Responsibility and Work Opportunity Reconciliation Act of 1996 (P.L. 104-193)(PRWORA), states have the option to waive TANF requirements if these requirements would unfairly penalize families or their special circumstances, e.g., presence of domestic violence, would make it difficult or impossible to comply with the provisions of the law. http://carbon.cudenver.edu/public/cwr/issues/domviolarch.htm

TDCAA Family Violence Book Outline Texas District & County Attorneys Association (TDCAA) Publications: Family Violence Manual for Prosecutors—Book Outline. http://www.tsgweb.com/tdcaa/fvoutln.htm

Families without Fear: Women's Aid Agenda for Action on Domestic Violence Families without fear. Women's Aid agenda for action on domestic violence Divorce and court proceedings. The implementation of Parts 1, 2 and 3 of the Family Law Act 1996 should be monitored and evaluated to assess whether new arrangements for divorce and mediation are putting women at risk of domestic violence. http://www.gn.apc. org/www.womensaid.org.uk/nofear

Checklist: Steps to End Violence Against Women ". . . what can we do about it?" On July 13, 1995 we created the Advisory Council on Violence Against Women to help promote greater awareness of the problem of violence against women and its victims, to help devise solutions to the problem, and to advise the federal government on implementing the 1994 Violence Against Women Act. http://www.usdoj.gov/vawo/checklist.htm

Violence Against Women Office National Domestic Hotline: 1-800-799-SAFE TDD for the Hearing Impaired: 1-888-787-3224 In March of 1995, President Clinton named Bonnie Campbell, former Attorney General of Iowa, to be Director of the Violence Against Women Office at the Department of Justice. http://www.usdoj.gov/vawo/vawofct.htm

Racial and Ethnic Groups

Statistics on Domestic Violence PREVALENCE. Domestic violence crosses ethnic, racial, age, national origin, sexual orientation, religious and socioeconomic lines. By the most conservative estimate, each year 1 million women suffer nonfatal violence by an intimate partner. http://kimberleyc.mswin.net/statistics.htm

History of WEAVE 1975—A community action group comprised of Hispanic battered women established WEAVE to address the issues of domestic violence in their community. 1978—The first WEAVE shelter opened with funding from the County of Sacramento; the abuser treatment program known as Positive Anger Control(PAC) was established. 1979—Federal funding allowed WEAVE to expand services. http://www.weaveinc.org/history.html

Joint U.S.–Russian Conference on Family Violence against Women Joint U.S.–Russian Conference on Family Violence against Women. Ambassador James F. Collins Moscow, Russia, October 28, 1998. Deputy Minister Karelova, Deputy Minister Stukolova, distinguished guests and participants. http://www.usia.gov/usa/womenusa/famvio.htm

CONF: The Color of Violence: Violence Against Women of Color Date: 18 Mar 1999 01:27:01 From: Electronic Drum Subject: CONF: The Color of Violence: Violence Against Women of Color, April 14-15, 2000-PART I

Electronic Drum Save the Date! http://theafrican.com/Magazine/Bulletin/19990320c.htm

Lighthouse Training Center   Mi Casa is a transitional safe home and therapeutic community (TC) for women with and without children who struggle with Post-Tramatic Stress Disorder (PTSD) resulting from childhood trauma and/or adult domestic violence, and who are also chemically dependent. Mi Casa is a state-of-the-art model program using creative approaches in the treatment of unresolved victimization/PTSD and substance . . . http://lighthouse.aculink.net/

Sibling Abuse

NNCC Child Abuse links   Child Abuse Links. Note: These links lead out of the National Network for Child Care web site and are not associated with NNCC. www.exnet.iastate.edu/Pages/families/

CSPP News Items and Press Releases http://w3.cspp.edu/news/news.htm

Washingtonpost.com: Juvenile Murders www.washingtonpost.com/wp-srv/national/

Conference Information   Conference. APTA is pleased to announce the following information regarding the 1998 annual conference. Presenter: Eliana Gil. Date: April 17–18, 1998. . . . www.cadvision.com/apta/conferen.htm

FAMILYPROG   Selections. What's Hot What's New Work–Life Phone Numbers Newsletter Wellness Bulletins Scholarships List Staff Roster. www.uscg.mil/hq/hsc/worklife/familypr.htm

Healthy Life Style   Reference. Healthy Life Style. Resource Information. Document Title: Self Care: Taking Better Care of Your Health Author: Linda Patterson, RN, MSN . . . www.oznet.ksu.edu/ndhn/Products/liferef.htm

Saddleback College Sports Medicine Program   Saddleback College features a sports medicine program to prepare you for your educational career as an athletic trainer, exercise physiologist. http://iserver.saddleback.cc.ca.us/div/sportsmed/health1ch9.html

Violence and Drugs

MA-DV   A Cyber-based Organization Sponsored by: The Paladin Group Men and Women Against Domestic Violence is an Internet-based coalition of men and women working to address the issue of domestic violence. http:// www.sil-com.com/~paladin/madv//

Prevention Primer: Violence   Alcohol and other drug use is associated with approximately 50 percent of spouse abuse cases, 49 percent of homicides, 38 percent of child abuse cases, and 52 percent of rapes. http://www.health.org/pubs/PRIMER/violence.htm

Drug Use Is Life Abuse—Home Page   Mission to create an attitude that will eliminate drug abuse, gangs, and violence by focusing on youth, family, and the workplace through awareness, enforcement, and education. http://www.duila.org//

Engler Announces Drug and Violence Prevention Program Funding Available . . . FOR IMMEDIATE RELEASE CONTACT: John Truscott Engler Announces Drug and Violence Prevention Program Funding Available. Governor John Engler today announced that drug and violence prevention programs targeting high-risk and out-of-school youth, law enforcement partnerships and other drug and violence prevention initiatives can apply for program funding. http://www.migov.state.mi.us/prs/9803/drugandv.html

Perry Innovations, Inc. We provide antidrug and antiviolence education in the form of assemblies and literature. http://www.perryinc.qpg.com//

D.A.R.E. commitment Hi, my name is Kristi and this is my D.A.R.E. commitment to be a drug and violence free person. These are my feelings about the program D.A.R.E. I feel a lot more comfortable knowing about the harmful effect drugs has on you. http://www.bir.bham.wednet.edu/DARE/STANDS/Kristi.htm

Virginians Against Drug Violence Virginians Against Drug Violence is a real grassroots organization working for drug peace. We go to the root of the drug war, namely the state house to demand representation for the often unheard voice of reason in these troubled McCarthy/Orwell days we live in. New materials are constantly being added, so check back often. http://www.drug-sense.org/dpfva//

MINCAVA: Alcohol, Other Drugs, and Violence Alcohol, Other Drugs and Violence: (We are not responsible for the quality of the sites listed below. They are provided as a reference only.) Alcohol, Tobacco, and Other Drugs: A Resource Guide gives information about the connection between alcohol and drugs and violent crime as well as listing resources available on preventive measures that people can take. http://www.mincava.umn.edu/alcoviol.asp

D.A.R.E. commitment Hello, my name is Naomi and this is my commitment to be a drug- and violence-free person. These are my feelings about the D.A.R.E. program. I feel that D.A.R.E. gave me more information about drugs and the harmful effects of them. http://www.bir.bham.wednet.edu/DARE/STANDS/NAOMI.htm.

Talking with Kids about Tough Issues: Home Page Talking with Kids about Tough Issues: sex, sexuality, AIDS, violence, drugs, alcohol. http://www.talkingwithkids.org//

Young Line "Drug Free" Welcome to: Young-Line "Drug Free" Associations, Inc. (Growing Up Drug, Violence, Gang, Alcohol, and Suicide Free) USA/ African Multicultural Exchange Programs, Inc (Accepting Each Other's Cultural Heritage). http://www.younglinedrugfree.com//

Suppression of Drug Abuse in Schools Suppression of Drug Abuse in Schools Program Ending illegal drug use among youth means stopping the flow of drugs in and around schools. To combat this growing problem, the Suppression of Drug Abuse in Schools Program provides financial and technical assistance to law enforcement agencies and school districts. http://www.ocjp.ca.gov/drgabschl.html.

Federal Title IV Safe and Drug-Free School Program In 1994, the president signed into law the Improving America's Schools Act. The primary purpose is to improve the teaching and learning of all children, and in particular those in high-poverty schools, to enable them to meet challenging academic content and performance standards. http://www.sde.state.id.us/instruct/safe/federal.htm.

Safe and Drug-Free Schools and Communities/Communities Federal Activity . . . Safe and Drug-Free Schools and Communities/Communities Federal Activities Grants U.S. Department of Education Office of Elementary and Secondary Education Safe and Drug-Free Schools Program Portals Building 600 Independence Avenue S.W., Room 604 Portals Washington, DC 20202 Tel: 202-260-3954. http://www.reeusda.gov/pavnet/ff/ffdrugfr.htm

D.A.R.E., Drugs, Drug Education Hi, my name is Nathan. This is my commitment to be a drug and violence-free person. This is how I feel about the D.A.R.E. program. D.A.R.E. was fun and we learned new things. http://www.bir.bham.wednet.edu/DARE/STANDS/97/nat.htm

Dauphin County Radar—Publications—Violence The RADAR Network Centers gather, share, and exchange information responding to both the immediate and long-term substance abuse prevention needs of their communities. http://dcradar.org/Vi.html

Child.net Main Page Everything for children, youth, parents, teachers, and youth workers. Resources from Streetcats Foundation for Youth and National Children's Coalition. http://www.child.net//

Research Digest—Risk Behavior HIV Risk Behavior/Violence/Crack Use. The relationship between crack use and HIV risk behavior has been well established. Crack use has also been linked to violence. http://www. rgs.uky.edu/ca/digest/hiv-aids/risk.html

D.A.R.E. commitment Hi my name is Jacki and this my commitment to stay a drug- and violence-free person for the rest of my life. These are my feelings about D.A.R.E. program. http://www.bir.bham.wednet.edu/DARE/STANDS/Jacki.htm

Utah Federation for Youth The Utah Federation for Youth, Inc. . . . promoting safe, healthy youth and communities through the prevention of substance abuse and violence. Great Programs & Related Sites: . . . http:// www.ufyi.org//

Bogus War on Drugs The Bogus War on Drugs has increased violence and repression in communities, victimized small time users and has been sabotaged by CIA operations. The War on Drugs should end and the Political Prisoners should be released. The CIA should be prosecuted for fueling the Crack Cocaine epidemic. http://www.boguswarondrugs.org//

Office of Elementary and Secondary Education: William Modzeleski Mr. Modzeleski currently is serving as the Director of the U.S. Department of Education's Safe and Drug Free Schools Program. The program provides funds and assistance to Governors, State Education Agencies, and local school districts to develop strategies and programs to meet the seventh National Education Goal: That by the Year 2000, all schools will be safe, disciplined, and drug-free. http://www.ed.gov/offices/OESE/modzeleski.html

About SDFS Safe & Drug-Free Schools Program. The Safe and Drug-Free Schools Program is the Federal government's primary vehicle for reducing drug, alcohol, and tobacco use, and violence, through education and prevention activities in our nation's schools. http://www.ed.gov/offices/OESE/SDFS/aboutsdf.html

Gang Expert and Consultant: Lisa Taylor-Austin, MS Ed. Lisa Taylor-Austin is a Gang Consultant, Counselor, Educator, and an expert on gangs and gang behavior. http://www.gangcolors.com//

Justice Information Center (NCJRS): Drug Policy Information Documents Research and Evaluation "Boot Camp" Drug Treatment and Aftercare Interventions: An Evaluation Review Case Management Reduces Drug Use and Criminality Among Drug-Involved Arrestees: http://www.ncjrs.org/drgsres.htm

I Can Make a Difference I Can Make a Difference is a service project for the Teen Law students at Wood MS. Every year the students work at making a difference in their lives and their community. http://www.teenlaw.org/difference.htm

D.A.R.E. commitment Hi my name is James Pearson and this is my commitment to be a drug- and violence-free person. These are my feelings about the D.A.R.E. program. I felt that it was good to have D.A.R.E. because it teaches kids to stay away from drugs and how harmful they are to your body and, of course, you. http://www.bir.bham.wednet.edu/DARE/STANDS/james.htm

DEA—Publications—Press Releases—February 23, 1999 Department of Justice Drug Enforcement Administration. DEA ANNOUNCES NATIONAL PLAN OF ACTION TO ADDRESS DRUG PROBLEMS IN AMERICA'S MID-SIZED COMMUNITIES. http://www.usdoj.gov/dea/pubs/pressrel/pr022399.htm

D.A.R.E., Drugs, Drug Education Hi my name is Cory. This is my commitment to stay a drug- and violence-free person. This is how I feel about the D.A.R.E. program. I like D.A.R.E. a lot. http://www.bir.bham.wednet.edu/DARE/STANDS/97/COR.Htm

Criminal Law Links—Crimes Assault Prevention Information Network. National Center for Missing and Exploited Children Missing Persons Resources. http://dpa.state.ky.us/~rwheeler/crimes.htm

Meddling Abroad (DRCNet Activist Guide 1/96) A recent study by University of Missouri professor Scott Decker has added yet more evidence to the well-established relationship between prohibition and violence. http://mir.drugtext.org/drcnet/guide1-96/guns.html

Mayor worried about new violence Publication Date: Friday Dec 12, 1997. Current gang problem is similar to the city's pre-1992 troubles. http://www.paweekly.com/PAW/ morgue/news/1997_Dec_12.MAYOR.htm

2/12/97—News: ED Solicits Advice on Combating Youth Drug Use Read the remarks of U.S. Secretary of Education Richard Riley to the Safe and Drug-Free Schools Press Conference of Feb. 9, 1997. ED Solicits Advice On Combating Youth Drug Use. http://www.edweek.com/ew/vol-16/20drug.h16

Welcome to Michigan's Safe and Drug Free Schools Web Site Welcome to Michigan's Safe and Drug-Free Schools and Communities web site. Here you'll find information and resources to support local school coordinators who are administering drug and violence prevention programs with funds available under the federal Safe and Drug-Free Schools and Communities Act (SDFSCA) of 1994. http://www.mdch.state.mi.us/odcp/safe/index.htm

D.A.R.E. commitment Hi my name is Danielle and this is my commitment to stay drug- and violence-free. These are my feelings about the D.A.R.E. program. I like the D.A.R.E. program because it makes me feel more comfortable saying NO. http://www.bir.bham.wednet.edu/DARE/STANDS/Danielle.htm

Michigan SDFSCA: Q & A, Public School Academies May Public School Acadamies (PSAs) apply for federal funds and state grants directly? Yes. Each PSA is allocated funding based on their student enrollment. http://www.mdch.state.mi.us/odcp/safe/qa_psas.htm

National Educational Goal SEC. 4003. PURPOSE. The purpose of this title is to support programs to meet the seventh National Education Goal by preventing violence in and around schools and by strengthening programs that prevent the illegal use of alcohol, tobacco, and drugs, involve parents, and are coordinated with related Federal, State, and community efforts and resources, through the provision of Federal assistance to . . . http://oeri2.ed.gov/legislation/ESEA/sec4003.html

PSYETA: Culture of Violence—Slide #1c Slide 1c II. Coping with Violence (106K Image). What are some ways that we have tried to reduce the violence in our society? Traditional measures. http://www.psyeta.org/culture/slide1c.html

D.A.R.E. commitment Hi my name is Jazmen, and this is my commitment to be a drug- and violence-free person. These are my feelings about the D.A.R.E. program; now that I am in D.A.R.E. I feel much safer now that I am warned about how drugs can effect my life. http://www.bir.bham.wednet.edu/DARE/STANDS/Jazmen.htm

About the Program About the Program: In-DEPTH (Innovative Drug Education and Prevention Tools for your Health) is a unique drug education, prevention, and intervention program. http://www.indepthprogram.com/about.html

Drugs and Violence Prevention Community Action Organization of Scioto County Drugs and Violence Prevention Contact: Vernon Clagg, Coordinator The Drugs and Violence Prevention program was developed as a resource center and catalyst to help neighborhoods within the Greater Portsmouth Enterprise Community address the escalating problem of drug usage and its resultant violence. http://www.zoomnet.net/~edwaa2/drug_prev.htm

MAVIA News November 11, 1998 Contact: Mike Seely Mothers Against Violence in America (206) 323-2303 Lieutenant Governor Owen To Speak at November 17 Kickoff of Save/Stars Chapter at Denny Middle School Students Committed to Nonviolent, Drug-Free Lifestyle, Seattle—Lieutenant Governor Brad Owen will speak at successive November 17 assemblies commemorating the formation of a joint SAVE/STARS. http://www.mavia.org/pr_ltgov.htm

About Washington/Baltimore HIDTA About Us The Washington/Baltimore area was designated as a HIDTA in 1994 to address the severe problem of illicit drug distribution. Targeting two major metropolitan areas, including the Nation's capital, and surrounding jurisdictions, this HIDTA region experiences significant problems with drug consumption and violent crime, especially related to heroin deaths and cocaine use. http://www.hidta.org/intro. html

President Clinton Visits Roosevelt School Formulating Solutions President Clinton came to Eleanor Roosevelt School today to speak to students on a personal level about drug use and violence. This was a positive experience for most students. http://erooseveltths.pgcps.org/news/clintonvisit.html

D.A.R.E. commitment Hi, My name is Brendan Smith. This is my commitment to be a drug- and violence-free person. These are my feelings about the D.A.R.E. program. It makes me feel safe because I can use the 8 ways to say no to drugs because I know more too. http://www.bir.bham.wednet.edu/ DARE/STANDS/brendan.htm

HSRC: Evil Bedfellows: Drugs, Alcohol, and Crime HSRC Programs. http:// www.hsrc.ac.za/corporate/InFocus/drugs_f.html

Violence and Depression

Teacher Talk Home Page Teacher Talk is published by the Center for Adolescent Studies at the School of Education, Indiana University, Bloomington, IN. It is a publication for preservice and secondary education teachers that exists as a series of World Wide Web documents. http://education.indiana.edu/cas/ tt/tthmpg.html

ADOL Adolescence Directory On-Line (ADOL) is an electronic guide to information on adolescent issues. It is a service of the Center for Adolescent Studies at Indiana University. http://education.indiana.edu/cas/adol/adol.html

AAMFT—Home Page http://www.aamft.org//

Facts About Women and Depression Women are at higher risk than men for major depression (although some researchers maintain that depression is underdiagnosed in men). One in four women is likely to experience severe depression. Yet of all women who suffer from depression, only about one-fifth will get the treatment they need. http://www.domestic-violence.net/health/ depressi.htm

Violence Against Women—The Statistics How common is violence against women? One in two Canadian women (51 percent) experiences at least one incident of male violence after the age of 16. The highest rate of violence (59

percent) is reported by women in British Columbia. http://www.weq.gov. bc.ca/stv/statistics.html

What You Should Know About Women and Depression Facts on women and depression. http://www.apa.org/pubinfo/depress.html

Depression Relief Depressed? Is someone you love depressed? All natural relief is here. http://www.computerpal.net/healthy/depression.html

The cycle of violence and children What happens to children in violent homes? Will they repeat the cycle? How does domestic violence effect children? Children from violent homes also become victims. http://www. callamerica.net/~wsp/children.htm

MenWeb—Men's Issues: Interview with Terry Real A book review from MenWeb on men and depression. Comprehensive men's issues site: men spirit and soul; mythopoetic, men's movement, psychology, therapy, healing, men's rights, gender justice. Articles, men's stories, book reviews. books, poems, on-line book store, men's resources. Men's Voices magazine. http://www. vix.com/pub/menmag/realivss.htm

Domestic Violence Websites Contact Information Seminar Schedule WWW Resources DOMESTIC VIOLENCE RESOURCES Identification and Management of Battered Women in the Primary Care Setting: Information compiled by K.Snyder, MS4 Oregon Health Sciences University August 1997. http:// cybermed.ucsd.edu/curricular_resources/Primary_Care/dv.html

Journiers Grow as you Go We are a nonprofit organization dedicated to serving all victims of violence. We teach the public about Post Traumatic Stress Disorder and other after effects caused by violence. http://www.journiers. com//

Emotional Intelligence: No Anger, Abuse, Violence, Resentment, Shame Emotional intelligence eliminates anger, alcohol, drug abuse, domestic violence, child abuse, emotional abuse, youth violence, increases self-esteem, parenting, teaching, driving skills, helps adolescents, business, women. http://www.compassionpower.com//

Depression Symptoms One of the most common causes of awakening in the middle of the night, early morning awakening and changes in memory, concentration and appetite is major depression. http://www.hsri.org/cmhs/ deprsx.htm

The Company Therapist The Company Therapist is a literary web drama for adults. Enter a psychiatrist's world as he sees patients from a large computer company. http://www.thetherapist.com//

Men's Violence MEN'S VIOLENCE—ACTION OR REACTION? Author Michael HART, Private Health Researcher. Domestic Violence. A hot topic and 'the crime of the 80's'. All states have now introduced Domestic Violence legislation designed specifically to protect women from emotional and physical abuse. http://www.ozemail.com.au/~irgeo/hart02.htm

Healthtouch—Table of Contents Table of Contents To help you find information more quickly and easily, type the key word/area of interest in the space below, and click on "Search for Match." A list of documents that have the key word in their title will appear on the screen. http://www.healthtouch.com/level1/hi_toc.htm

Family Education Opening Comments Warning Signs Dealing with Prejudice. Safety vs. Creating a Safe Place. Browse our Topics For easy navigation, check out our topics page. http://familyeducation.com/article/0,1120,3-6423,00.html

Cascade Centers, Inc.—EAP and Human Resource Solution Cascade Centers, Inc. is a national mental health firm which provides Employee Assistance Programs (EAP) to both public and private sector employees. http://www.cascadecenter.com//

The Association of Chief Psychologists with Ontario School Boards Home Page for the Association of Chief Psychologists with Ontario School Boards. It describes the services we provide and the issues that we address in our school boards. http://www.acposb.on.ca/index.html

Briefing Sheet on Funding for Violence Against Women Act Programs Briefing Sheet on Funding for Violence Against Women Act Programs. http://www.apa.org/ppo/vawa.html

Quigley House Facts About Domestic Violence Quigley House offers safe emergency shelter and support services for women and their children in Clay County Florida and the surrounding areas. Opened in 1991 Quigley House is the only shelter for battered women and children in Clay County Florida. http://www.casnet.com/nfc/quigley/qfacts.html

Talking DOMESTIC VIOLENCE UPDATE What You Can Do: Talking With a Victim of Domestic Violence There are people who are currently suffering from domestic violence in every community in this country, including your own. http://www.wsu.edu/HRS/EmployeeDevelopment/talking.htm

Subjects—Social/Psychological Feel free to browse around a forum for Women's Health. The SUBJECTS database is subdivided into four categories, each with its own sub-headings. Select the subject area you want to know about, press the button, and we'll take you to our information. http://www.womenshealth.org/subjects/social.htm

Mid-Columbia Medical Center: Mind and Body So just who gets depressed? If you answered anybody, pat yourself on the back. Depression is a major, treatable illness whose dark cloud settles in upon roughly 17 per cent of the population. http://www.mcmc.net/tools/depression.asp

Abuse Recovery Resources Domestic abuse is one of the largest problems in today's society. Whether it's physical, mental, verbal, sexual or if you otherwise feel that you are being abused then you probably are and you need to seek help as soon as possible. http://home.icdc.com/~softkiss/abuse.html

SUICIDAL.COM—About the Web Author /Author's Goals For New Standards . . . Web-author has cured her own severe, chronic suicidal depression by developing unique biochemical, non-drug treatments. She plans to self-publish her first book and has goals for new, better, and faster treatments for suicidal depression. http://suicidal.com/abouttheauthor//

Violence and Suicide

Risk Factors for Teenage Suicide RISK FACTORS FOR TEENAGE SUICIDE (Author Unknown) Previous Attempts. Youths who attempt suicide remain vulnerable for several years, especially for the first three months following an attempt. http://www.bartow.k12.ga.us/psych/crisis/riskfact.htm

SUICIDE AND VIOLENCE The Problem Suicide took the lives of 31,284 Americans in 1995 (11.9 per 100,000 population). More people die from suicide than from homicide in the United States. http://www.cdc.gov/ncipc/dvp/suifacts.htm

Guns and Suicide—Coordinating Committee on Gun Violence—American Bar Association. The New England Journal of Medicine has determined that the presence of a gun in the home increases the risk of suicide fivefold. In 1994, there were over 31,000 suicides in the United States, the majority of which were completed with firearms. http://www.abanet.org/gunviol/suicide.html

Addressing Violence in Oklahoma Addressing Violence in Oklahoma "Protecting the Aspirations and Dreams of Oklahomans through Network Building and Community Action" Addressing Violence in Oklahoma is a collaborative effort of individuals from many disciplines concerned with the growing problem of violence. http://www.health.state.ok.us/PROGRAM/INJURY/violence/

AAP—Information on Suicide Information on Suicide from the American Academy of Pediatrics Preventing Teen Suicide (AAP Child Health Month) Violence Prevention (AAP Child Health Month). http://www.aap.org/visit/suicideinfo.htm

Elders at Risk SECTION I. Selected References to Journal Articles Focused Specifically on the Abuse, Victimization and Suicide of the Elderly Elder Abuse Family/Domestic Violence. http://www.apa.org/books/eldriskt.html

Youth Violence and Suicide Prevention Team Home Page Youth Violence—The threatened or actual physical force or power initiated by an individual that results in, or has a high likelihood of resulting in physical or psychological injury or death. http://www.cdc.gov/ncipc/dvp/yvpt/yvpt.htm

Fact Sheet—Suicide Early in the morning of October 29, Jeffery shocked neighbours, relatives and friends by tying an 18-foot extension cord around his neck and over the branch of a poplar tree. http://www.cfc-efc.ca/docs/00000012.htm

VPC—Where Did You Get That Statistic? Firearms Suicide Suicide Among Children, Adolescents, and Young Adults—United States, 1980-1992, MMWR (Morbidity and Mortality Weekly Report), Vol. 44, No. 15, April 21, 1995, pp. 289–291. http://www.vpc.org/studies/whersuic.htm

Division of Violence Prevention The Centers for Disease Control and Prevention (CDC) has focused on violence prevention since the early 1980s, when efforts included the prevention of youth violence, suicide, and suicide attempts. http://www.cdc.gov/ncipc/dvp/dvp.htm

American Academy of Pediatrics Web Site (AAP) American Academy of Pediatrics Web site: the AAP is an organization of over 55,000 pediatricians. AAP: information on child health, baby, infant, kids, pediatrics, family, teen, SIDS, safety, injury, and much more. http://www.aap.org//

LAPSR—Resources in Firearms and Medicine Resources in Medicine and Firearms Physicians for Social Responsibility, the 1985 Nobel Prize-winning organization, is offering the medical community fact sheets and abstracts on the health effects of gun violence. http://www.labridge.com/PSR/resources.html

VPC—Where Did You Get That Statistic? A Firearms and Firearms Violence Bibliography and Resource Guide for Advocates Working to Reduce Firearms Violence Table of Contents This is the full text of the February 1998 Violence Policy Center study Where Did You Get That Statistic?—A Firearms and Firearms Violence Bibliography and Resource Guide for Advocates Working to Reduce Firearms Violence. http://www.vpc.org/studies/whercont.htm

VPC—Where Did You Get That Statistic? Firearms Suicide Among Older Americans Suicide Among Older Persons—United States, 1980-1992, MMWR (Morbidity and Mortality Weekly Report), Vol. 45, No. 1, January 12, 1996, pp. 3–6. http://www.vpc.org/studies/wherseld.htm

ATA NEWS—Volume 30, Number 6 – Measuring youth crime is not straight-forward Volume 30, Number 6, Publication of The Alberta Teachers' Association October 31, 1995 By Brigitte Desmeules, Department of Justice Canada "Measuring youth crime is not straightforward." http://www.teachers.ab.ca/news/volume_30/number_06/youth.htm

Violence on the Job APA Books, the premier publisher of books in psychology. http://www.apa.org/books/violjob.html

Solutions to Youth Violence and Suicide An Interdisciplinary Approach to Violence Solving the problem of violence requires an interdisciplinary approach. Professionals from sociology, criminology, economics, law, public policy, psychology, anthropology, education and public health must work together to understand the causes and develop the solutions. http://www.cdc.gov/ncipc/dvp/yvpt/solution.htm

PAVE Bibliography: Domestic Violence PAVE is a joint project of the Center for Early Education and Development in the College of Education and Human Development, University of Minnesota, and Minneapolis Technical College. http://www.cyfc.umn.edu/pave/library/domestic.htm

Domestic Violence New Beginnings is a crisis center serving victims of domestic violence and/or sexual assault in Belknap County, NH. http://www.newbeginningsnh.org/html/domestic_violence.html

Suicidal.com—About the Web Author/Author's Goals For New Standards Web-author has cured her own severe, chronic suicidal depression by developing unique biochemical, non-drug treatments. She plans to self-publish her first book and has goals for new, better, and faster treatments for suicidal depression. http://suicidal.com/abouttheauthor//

INDEX